Metaphors
and Action Schemes

Metaphors
and Action Schemes

Some Themes
in Intellectual History

Robert L. Schwarz

Lewisburg
Bucknell University Press
London: Associated University Presses

Associated University Presses
440 Forsgate Drive
Cranbury, N.J. 08512

Associated University Presses
16 Barter Street
London WC1A 2AH, England

Associated University Presses
P.O. Box 338, Port Credit
Mississauga, Ontario
Canada L5G 4L8

The paper used in this publication meets the requirements
of the American National Standard for Permanence of Paper
for Printed Library Materials Z39.48–1984.

Library of Congress Cataloging-in-Publication Data

Schwarz, Robert L., 1937–
    Metaphors and action schemes : some themes in intellectual history
/ Robert L. Schwarz.
        p.   cm.
    Includes bibliographical references and index.
    ISBN 0-8387-5355-8 (alk. paper)
    1. Civilization, Western. 2. Intellectual life—History.
3. Metaphor. I. Title.
CB 245.S325   1997
909'.09812—dc20   96-35861
                                                            CIP

PRINTED IN THE UNITED STATES OF AMERICA

To my sister, Ruth,
my truest companion
through life

Contents

Acknowledgments   9
Introduction   11

1. The Nature of Metaphor   21
2. Metaphor and Intellectual History   43
3. Action Schemes and
     Topological Transformations   65
4. The Ancient World   86
5. The Medieval Period   117
6. The Renaissance   133
7. The Enlightenment to 1900   154
8. The Twentieth Century   181

Glossary of Metaphors and Schemes   216
Notes   229
Bibliography   261
Index   278

Acknowledgments

This book would probably not have seen the light of day without the benefi-cence of Paul Williams, who transcribed hundreds of pages of material to word processor. Although he no longer remembers the task, a near-fatal accident having blotted out his memory of that period, I remember it for both of us and set it down here for whatever posterity these modest words may enjoy.

For her unflagging support and her valuable assistance in proofreading the manuscript in its final stages, my thanks to Laura Price, a lady gifted with words, whose works I soon hope to see in print.

I have also been well served by the editors at Bucknell University Press and Associated University Presses, and especially by Wyatt Benner, who copyedited the book. Their alertness and diligence have made me see all too clearly the errors of my ways.

Introduction

This book had its inception from a reading of Lakoff and Johnson's *Metaphors We Live By*.[1] I was intrigued by the role that they demonstrated metaphor to play in the genesis of everyday ideas and attitudes. It seemed that they barely scratched the surface of the applicability of their insight. One of the essential lessons contained in *Metaphors We Live By* is that we can understand one thing only in terms of another. Anyone who has tried to define a word has experienced the truth of this. So, if we know the primary percept or concept in terms of which we understand an idea, we have that much of a handle on the essence of our understanding. I wondered, therefore, about the metaphors underlying the great ideas of Western civilization. Surely they would reveal something interesting about the foundations of those ideas.

I began to make a running inventory of the metaphors underlying certain key ideas of the major philosophers, scientists, and theologians. I expected to accumulate a vast catalog of metaphors that might show neither rhyme nor reason. For quite some time, I never even inspected the results, because I did not want to predetermine any pattern that would then invade and prejudice my subsequent investigations. Only after I had completed my preliminary survey did I examine the results.

At that juncture, I was surprised to find that all the metaphors naturally fell under a small number of main headings. They varied only in the way in which they were used, what I have come to call their deployment. Skeptical about this all too neat result, I decided to go on and investigate the metaphors underlying Eastern thought. My survey of Eastern thought was less encompassing than that of Western traditions. The only major difference I found between Eastern and Western thought from the standpoint of metaphorical foundations was one in the usage of negation, which is discussed in the main body of the text. Otherwise the same metaphors under study characterize both divisions of the global culture, at least within the limited range of ideas in my survey. This should not be surprising, given that these metaphors arise out of the most elemental human experiences, which tend to hold transculturally.

11

Further to test the legitimacy of the root metaphors, I began tracing the etymologies of words pertaining to the key ideas from which the inventory of metaphors had been derived. If the metaphors were truly fundamental, they should
show up in the etymological roots of these words, which indeed turned out to be
the case. Beyond that, however, the etymological research turned up something
unanticipated: I observed that countless words describing abstract notions were
compounded from concrete roots. Onto these, prepositional prefixes or suffixes
were grafted. By *prepositional* I mean language elements that express spatial, temporal, instrumental, causal, and other relationships.

In short, many abstract ideas are formed by creating geometric or, more generally, topological schemata of nominative or verbal primitives. In fact, as I later
noticed, the course of any argument is plotted in terms of spatial transformations
and motions. Thinking, in the final analysis, seems to revolve around moving, relating, and transforming counters. The counters may be mere symbols or they may
be models of ideas. In any case, discursive thought, whether internalized or exter-
nalized, has a topological structure that can be analyzed; and continuity in this
structure parallels the reasonableness of the thought.

Subsequent to my own research in this area, I found a similar hypothesis in
Mark Johnson's *The Body in the Mind*, in which he announced that "any adequate
account of meaning and rationality must give a central place to embodied and
imaginative structures of understanding by which we grasp our world."[2] He uses
the word *embodied* to mean literally grounded in bodily experience. And later in the
book, he makes the point that "understanding is the way we 'have a world.'"[3] In
other words, bodily experience is the epistemological ground of any worldview. For
Johnson, the body designates not simply the physical person or the body as perceived inwardly but an interactive embodiment in which private body-experience
and experience of the public world form a kind of whole constructed from ongoing
experiential processes. He uses the terms *schema, embodied schema,* and *image schema*
interchangeably to designate what I in certain instances call metaphors and topological schemata or relations.[4] "Image schemata," he writes, "are not propositional,
in that they are not abstract subject-predicate structures (e.g., 'The cat is on the
mat') that express truth conditions or other conditions of satisfaction (e.g., the cat's
being on the mat)." A further caveat is that, "while we may be able to describe
features of their structure propositionally using finitary representations, we thereby
lose our ability to explain their natural operations and transformations."[5]

Now, image schemata are postulational. What is known of their nature can be
deduced only from their observed effects. I say this not to call their existence into
question but to point out their elusiveness. They are rather like the Cheshire cat's
grin. Neurologically, they probably correspond to what Day and Bellezza call "organized generic knowledge structures" based on "relations among objects in the
physical world rather than their mode of representation."[6] Researchers hypoth-
esize that image formation involves *coarse coding*, in which general image properties

are stored diffusely in the cortex and operate downward on incoming sensory data to impart meaning to that data.[7] Such structures, therefore, cannot be experienced per se but are manifest in particularized perception or private image formation. This is something to which I will return in discussing certain of the metaphors with which we will be dealing.

Not surprisingly, Johnson's exposition singled out several of the metaphors and topological relations that had showed up in my own taxonomy, but he did not attempt any systematic, comprehensive presentation of the subject, though he did note the need for one at the close of his book. I hope that this work, though ante-dating his in conception, may go some distance toward supplying the comprehensive treatment for which he calls.

This book is about the role of key metaphors and topological schemata in human thought. It is not a survey of Western intellectual history. It is a study of certain metaphor themes on which that history is partly based. I propose that basic metaphors underlying human conceptualization act in somewhat the same fashion as the rules elemental to cellular automata as displayed in Conway's Game of Life.[8] That is, they are few but nevertheless prove capable of generating an endless variety of concepts in many fields of human activity, just as the simple rules of the Game of Life produce generations of altered constellations. Turned around, the implied lesson is that something of awesome complexity need not be postulated as the substrate of human thought.

I call these metaphors part of a code because they may be used to decipher the genesis of ideas and even what Kuhn would call paradigms—procedures, traditions, protocols, and even attitudes surrounding or ensuing from ideas.[9] From this broad sense of paradigm, it is easy to see that basic metaphors, explored historically, could provide the keys to explicit analyses of the ethos of any given period and culture. Of course, the metaphors I cite throughout this work may more properly be labeled groundwork for a code, since I have followed out only certain major themes in intellectual history predominantly in the Western tradition and much has yet to be done in exploring the metaphorical foundations of other cultures as well as disciplines to which I have given only partial or even no attention. There is also much left to do in mapping folk theory and common modes of conceptions outside the more purely academic domain to which I give my main attention in this work. Doubtlessly the code will be extended, perhaps so much that there will need to be discovered a metacode.[10] At any rate, I use the metaphor of *code* not necessarily literally but only to stimulate further heuristic enterprise. The metaphors could also be described simply as tools, keys, or what have you.

There will be those who quarrel with the precise formulation of the metaphors that I identify throughout this book. Some might choose designations at variance with mine. I am not certain how important this might be. I am inclined to think that the guiding differentiae of the metaphors are correct, in that they seem to fit the historical facts without ad hoc qualifications. How they are labeled, while important, does not strike me as crucial, and I would not rule out improvements on my initial classification. Moreover, there may be room to quarrel over those metaphors I have found to be basic. I have limited my scope to the broad ideas of each major discipline, finding the influence of the corresponding, underlying metaphors to reach down into the narrower and more specialized avenues of thought. I have not witnessed specialized metaphors, such as the spinning wheel for fate or fluid flow for electricity, generalizing systematically beyond their specific applications so as to expand knowledge. Consequently, I have concentrated on those ideas, and their metaphors, which have spanned time and had an integrating effect on broader fields of knowledge.

Metaphors are the primary theme of this book, and topological schemata are the secondary one. These schemata define how thinking moves, so to speak, from point to point, often from premises to conclusion. Deployment of metaphor depends heavily, therefore, on topological schemata and what I choose to call transformations. The term *topological schemata* too much suggests action schemata. A topological transformation is more a mode of thought in which idea counters or models are actually manipulated in mental space. These manipulations may not mimic habitual action routines. They may be quite innovative (especially in mathematics and the arts). Hence, it would be misleading to equate them with action schemes, though through use they may be incorporated as action schemes. This may be seen in the introduction of a new mathematical procedure or a novel dance step or musical turn of phrase as it catches on. I shall be at pains to point out how topological transformations operate in various disciplines, displaying the similarity between abstract thinking and more mechanical behaviors.

It is always a temptation to become carried away by a new approach, making the most extravagant claims for it, and I wish to avoid that here. First, the metaphoric approach is not new. It was suggested by the German school of linguistic analysis that sprang up in the last century. Notable within that school was Fritz Mauthner, who claimed that all thought is metaphorical. Weiler wrote that Mauthner's "thesis that language is merely a means of introducing order into the mass of sense-experience can . . . be interpreted as meaning that the kind of order involved is attained by means of figurative comparison of observed similarities and dissimilarities. Since the faculty involved in making these comparisons is . . . creative selectivity, we are forced to conclude that the order achieved in this way bears our own mark and is not an adequate recording of what we claim to observe."[11] Mauthner took his departure from the sensationalism of Locke and Mach. "Substantives are the result of abstraction or are purely metaphorical," because only qualities are given or primary.[12] However, he never employed his insight to investigate the metaphorical process in any systematic fashion.

Snell employed metaphor in elucidating the evolution of rational thought in ancient Greece;[13] Stephen Pepper and others have suggested that metaphor plays a pivotal rule in the generation of scientific models.[14] Discussions of metaphor in literature are legion,[15] but these have been confined to rather narrow applications.[16] Johnson has provided a brief but classic survey of metaphor in the Western philosophical tradition.[17]

I do not wish to imply that the metaphoric approach alone is sufficient for a complete interpretation of intellectual history. I merely want to stress that it affords the advantage of developing all areas of intellectual history along identical parameters, yielding a type of unification to the subject hitherto unattained. We can witness the same code operating in science and the arts, philosophy and historiography, binding together the contemporaneous developments in all these seemingly disparate arenas of human intellectual endeavor. Speaking analogically, the variegated forms of human thought are spelled from the same sort of code or box of tools, just as the phenotype of any species receives its structure from the amino acid code of genes.

Following out this analogy, just as it would not be good science to consider embryonic morphogenesis in isolation from environmental contexts, it would not be good historiography to ignore the social, economic, physical, and other factors in the ethotic morphogenesis of a culture. At the same time, stress on any of these factors could take precedence over all others, including the metaphoric, depending upon the aims to be served by the given history. The metaphoric approach is central here simply because I wish to explore its consequences.

My aims in this work are modest. I wish to trace out the metaphorical foundations of certain dominant themes in intellectual history, centering on broad ideas like freedom, truth, time, space, and mind, as they have been conceived by the major thinkers of their period and culture. My selection of topics is meant to be representative rather than comprehensive. To minimize the tendency to pursue only what interests me personally, I have tried to encompass the broadest ideas usually singled out for special treatment in standard works on the disciplines to which I give most of my attention: philosophy, science, and theology. These are the ideas that provide the conceptual framework in which many subsidiary ideas are engendered, and so the metaphorical bases of these ideas account for a large part of the intellectual architecture out of which the conceptual ground of many other disciplines is composed. How freedom is conceived, for example, helps to shape many other concepts in law (e.g., rights and duties, terms of contract, and even due process), political philosophy (e.g., apatheia, general will, democracy, and other forms of government and their legitimate functions), and so on. To be sure, there is a dialectic between ideas, so that the supposedly broader idea may not always foster the subsidiary ideas; yet they are usually taken as doing so in most expositions. The point is that the broader ideas must dovetail with the subsidiary ones to give the appearance that the latter follow naturally from the former. Ideas that give rise to intellectual dissonance within their own discipline are doomed to extinction.

Doubtlessly this view of intellectual history as dealing with the so-called blockbuster ideas may be slightly old-fashioned, but something like it has inclined me to

follow traditional selections of those ideas generally thought to be broadest in implication. I am aware that other approaches are open to me, and I am not prepared to defend mine other than by saying that it provides me with consistent and
comfortable guidelines for conducting my explorations. I claim no primacy for it.
It has the advantage of enabling me to confine myself to investigating a manage-
able body of material, yet it is extensive enough to display the fruitful application of
metaphorical methods of analysis to the history of ideas.

Likewise, to keep this project within practical constraints, I have focused on
Western traditions of thought. My forays into Eastern thought are limited mainly
to examining a few principal concepts in religion and philosophy to demonstrate
the transcultural validity of basic metaphors. Taken altogether, this work follows
the transmutations of a small repertoire of metaphors as they have infused certain
prominent ideas mainly in Western culture throughout the centuries. It is a case
study in how metaphors have shaped many of our most cherished notions, laying
bare some of the historical dynamics of conceptual change. Some may find rather
more history than unrelenting discussion of metaphor in the pages that follow, but
my conviction is that the dynamics of metaphor formation and transformation has
been sufficiently examined by other authorities whom I cite and that what is needed
in the present context is a careful placement of metaphor processes within the
larger framework of intellectual history. At the same time, certain historical figures,
otherwise important in general intellectual history, do not find place here, if their
contribution has not seemed to me to be seminal from the standpoint of metaphor
or topological scheme development. Cases in point would be Averroës, Avicenna,
and Duns Scotus; all of them were key figures in medieval thought, but essentially
they revived ideas already clearly established in the classical period.

Certain emphases require comment. Mathematics is given the place of honor
among the sciences for two reasons. First, it has become the preeminent language
of modern science, in which explanation has come more and more to mean elucidation in mathematical terms. Second, it is the discipline in which topological transformations (described later in this text) may most clearly be seen to operate in
conjunction with root metaphors.

My attention to musical developments is intended to offset a deficit. The history of ideas, I feel, has not adequately dealt with this theme. Because music is
conceived largely as an abstract art devoid of specific semantic content, historians
of ideas apparently have felt that it lies comfortably beyond the purview of their
consideration. I do not approach this with any intent to take anyone to task for the
oversight, but, as with mathematics, I believe that applying the method of analysis
by metaphor and topological transformations yields some worthwhile insights into
the ideational basis of musical change not attainable through traditional means of
historiography.

Finally, I should say a word about the bibliography. My purpose in this work is
not to give an encyclopedic coverage of past and recent thought and research on

metaphor. It is rather to pursue the implications of a particular metaphoric approach, inspired by Lakoff and Johnson, to tracing certain themes in intellectual history. My methodology resembles that of Stephen C. Pepper, though I have not consciously followed his lead.[18] I have attempted a fair appraisal of recent trends in metaphor research and speculation but have not far exceeded the reasonable implementation of my limited project. Certain sources consulted but not specifically employed in the text of this book have been included in the bibliography for their possible peripheral interest to the reader. More comprehensive bibliographies are cited for those who wish to perambulate further abroad.

Throughout the text, I indicate underlying metaphors included in the glossary by enclosing them in parentheses preceded by a colon—e.g., (:Container).

Metaphors
and Action Schemes

1

The Nature
of Metaphor

The word *metaphor* derives from the Greek *metaphora*, from *meta*, over, and *pherein*, to carry. Aristotle and the classical rhetoricians used the term (*translatio* in Latin) to mean the transference of the sense of one term to a second term, which is then construed in terms of the first; this definition is echoed by the anonymous *Rhetorica ad herennium* (c. 86 B.C.E.) and on down through the centuries. Cicero observed that a metaphor is a short form of simile.[1] In his *Poetics*, he averred that of all the tropes, metaphor is by far the most important to master.[2] And in *Rhetoric*, he added that ordinary words convey merely what we already know, whereas it is only by metaphor that we can gain new insight.[3] Roman rhetoricians emphasized the use of metaphor to promote a sublime style for the expression of noble thoughts. This ushered in a phase that carried right through to the nineteenth century. Medieval theorists delighted in multiplying the *figurae verborum* with as much pettifoggery as modern academicians. Geoffrey of Vinsauf in his *Poetria Nova* and *De Coloribus Rhetoricis*, for example, discussed sixty-three ornaments, divided into difficult and easy tropes, each variety prescribed for its proper context and effect. Interestingly, he singled out for preference what would now be called personification, feeling that it conveys an especially powerful impact.

Vico returned to the Aristotelian aperçu that metaphor makes possible the formation of new ideas. In metaphor, symbol, and myth, he sought the origin and development of human thought, a theme taken up by J. G. Herder in *Abhandlung über den Ursprung der Sprache* (1772). Every language, he said, has its *Metapherngeist*, and it is through this that the abstract is made concrete. Metaphor thus became once more identified with primitive creativity, facilitating the notion popular among the romantics that poetry, and hence also metaphor, as Shelley said in his *Defence of Poetry*, is connate with the origins of man and is the expression of imagination. Jeremy Bentham recognized metaphorization as the ground of abstract thought, considering the resulting concepts convenient but deplorable *fictions;* he said that metaphor poisons the sense of every instrument it comes near.[4]

The classicists were concerned to mirror the order of nature. They sought to read from the divine book of creation in which everything is subordinate to providential decorum. The romantics, by contrast, searched inward for an idiosyncratic vision, revealing not the verity of an eternal order but the fluctuations and unboundedness of the imagination. In a word, metaphor became the vehicle for unfettered exploration. Again, this was not a new idea but had largely been ignored after the Roman rhetoricians laid such heavy stress on nobility of style as the purpose to be served by figures of speech and all other stylistic devices.

Coleridge made much of the more favorable attitude toward metaphor in the nineteenth century, analyzing imagination with an anatomical sense of structure. At the heart of imagination, the matrix of creativity, is the perception of similitude in dissimilitude, which is none other than metaphor.

> This power, first put into action by the will and understanding, and retained under their irremissive, though gentle and unnoticed control, . . . reveals itself in the balance or reconcilement of opposite or discordant qualities: of sameness, with difference; of the general with the concrete; the idea with the image; the individual with the representative; the sense of novelty and freshness with old and familiar objects; a more than usual state of emotion with more than usual order; judgement ever awake and steady self-possession with enthusiasm and feeling profound or vehement; and while it blends and harmonizes the natural and the artificial, still subordinates art to nature; the manner to the matter; and our admiration of the poet to our sympathy with the poetry.[5]

Of course, the romantic doctrine of imagination is, as Allers[6] says of the Freudian topography of mind, a model only, not a description of reality. Though this may be no more than a reminder that reality is a construct, such a reminder is periodically needed.

Nietzsche, like Bentham, anticipated much in metaphor theory that is now being passed off as new. He saw metaphorization as a construction of reality but, unlike Bentham, hailed this as primary creation, intrinsic to the human will. The creation of metaphors for him was a fundamental instinct in humans. They function properly to orient us among our percepts or to create aesthetic illusion. To think, it is necessary to create pictures, concrete images on which the mind can work. Knowledge is merely the application of favored metaphors to a situation.

> What therefore is truth? A mobile army of metaphors, metonymies, anthropomorphisms: in short a sum of human relations which become poetically and rhetorically intensified, metamorphosed, adorned, and after long usage seem to a nation fixed, canonic and binding; truths are illusions of which one has forgotten that they *are* illusions; worn-out metaphors which have become powerless to affect the senses.[7]

This constructivist viewpoint is not dissimilar in its general epistemology to that suggested by Ernst Cassirer, for whom "there is no factuality . . . as an absolute . . . immutable datum; but what we call a fact is always theoretically oriented in some way, seen in regard to some . . . context and implicitly determined thereby. Theoretical elements do not somehow become added to a 'merely factual,' but they enter into the definition of the factual itself."[8] That every datum is "theoretically oriented" relative to a "context" is further reminiscent of Nietzsche's perspectivism. Elsewhere Cassirer wrote that "humanity really attains its insight into objective reality only through the medium of its own activity and the progressive differentiation of that activity."[9] This is straight out of the Hindu tradition of the self-actuating Brahman or *atman*, the One manifesting itself through *maya* as the Many. So stated, it implies much but says little. It can be saved by treating the knower as a mathematically chaotic dynamism in which actualization occurs through unpredictable bifurcations. The elements of consciousness—self, space, time, entities—then are bifurcated out of the activity of the whole. The whole is an ongoing process in which structures emerge, like eddies in a river, some of which are relatively stable and appear as *entities*.[10]

This picture, of course, is no more ultimate than any other; and it is transparently metaphorical. Metaphor is not to be escaped. There is no use looking for knowledge beyond metaphor, as if it were possible to strip away metaphor to reveal the *Ding-an-sich*. As Nietzsche, Vaihinger, and others have claimed, the issue is not whether a theory gets us closer to the putative truth, but whether it facilitates the functions of life—in pragmatist terms, whether it is useful. Turning their back on the ineluctability of this is, it seems to me, the crucial mistake in the motivation of the deconstructionists. Aside from the fact that their position is self-contradictory, it represents an ill-tempered defeatism. If no absolute and unchanging objective reality is either attainable or even coherently tenable, then they want to destroy the game. They conveniently ignore that humankind has managed to survive, build and destroy civilizations, create art, science, philosophy, religion, and law, and, yes, even communicate with one another in the process. The question is not whether or not that communication bore upon an absolute objective reality but whether or not it facilitated the interaction of the participants in achieving their goals. Judging by the longevity of the human race, so far it has obviously done so. We build reality by metaphor and action schemes, and the critical point is the degree to which these interact harmoniously. The concordance is never complete; but that is not a matter for despair: it is the struggle for cognitive consonance that keeps us evolving.

Nietzsche and Vaihinger both suggested a typology for metaphors. Nietzsche did it in passing, but Vaihinger carried out a taxonomy in terms of fictions, classifying them as legal, mathematical, and so on, according to the areas in which they are used. Blumenberg again issued a call for a typology, taking the constructivist position that metaphors are neither true nor false but themselves constitute truth and falseness.[11] Cassirer, one of the prime constructivists of this century, proffered a typology based on his historical account of symbolic representation, moving from nominalism to the differentiation between symbol and symbolized, and finally to the reification of relations in the sciences (especially mathematics).[12]

Now, it is not my intention to review the various schools of thought on the interpretation of metaphor, as most of them revolve around technical issues that have little or no bearing on my thesis. Only those notions germane to my thesis are attributed. Certainly Max Black and I. A. Richards must be credited with sparking the modern cognitive approach that led to the work of George Lakoff and Mark Johnson. Black introduced a structural analysis of metaphor in which the figure is decomposed into *frame* and *focus*. Thus, in "we waded through mountains of verbiage," *mountains* is the focus, carrying the metaphoric twist, and the rest of the sentence is the frame. Obviously the same focus in a different frame—e.g., "we waded in the pool"—might not be metaphorical.[13] The Group Mu at the University of Liège allowed that the grammatical structure of metaphor often facilitates a transference of meaning in both directions between the root word, or metaphorand (what I. A. Richards called the *vehicle*), and that to which it applies, the *tenor*—in modern parlance, the source domain and the target domain. This interplay can be important in the deployment of the metaphor, the way in which it plays out through some abstract idea over an extended period of time. Kuhn,[14] Pepper,[15] Hesse[16] and Papin[17] have delineated the dynamics of metaphor as the generative basis for scientific theorizing. Their analyses provide valuable insights into the role of metaphor in shaping discursive thought.

In the contemporary literature, there is much debate over just what a metaphor is. Beardsley[18] and Davidson[19] contend that it is in the words, though they differ on exactly how the words function. Searle[20] places it in the *intent* of the speaker or writer. Yoos[21] finds it, as I do, at the level of understanding and experience. Research by Blasko and Connine, finding that ideational rather than lexical cues determine metaphor comprehension, also supports this contention.[22] Looking for it at the level of thought has certain advantages. First of all, it seems that thought must precede words; otherwise how are the words even ordered? And if metaphorization is a modus operandi of thought, it becomes evident that it can be manifested in many different verbal forms: hence the endless and futile wrangling over the proper verbal instantiation of metaphor. Finally, it resolves the rather too delicate question whether metaphor comprehends a unique insight or whether it can be paraphrased in such a way as not to lose any of its import. The answer is yes and no. A metaphor, as I am using the term, is an instance of conceiving A somehow or other in terms of B. Conceiving A in terms of B is a state of affairs — and I am deliberately vague here because there are countless metaphors that could be chosen to characterize this and none would please everyone. It is a state of affairs in which one is free within the constraints of the context to roam over whatever relationships between A and B seem relevant or interesting. A paraphrase could call attention to this, but it could never exhaust its implications, which it is supposed to do. If the paraphrase is to carry exactly the same information implicit in the metaphor, then all the details must be made explicit.

Suppose we have the metaphor, "her face is a rose." We could say perhaps that this means her face is soft, fragrant, dewy, pink, and on and on, but we would never exhaust the possibilities. A trivial case, no doubt, but there are instances in which the missing item in the paraphrase could be crucial. It is especially characteristic of metaphors in science. There are in relativity theory what are known as field equations that establish complex relations between what we call mass and gravity, on one side, and the geometry of a four-dimensional space-time continuum, on the other. They represent a mathematical metaphor that in words says roughly that in some sense "gravity is a mathematical property of spacetime." I paraphrase only to characterize and not to give a putative complete account of the metaphor for those who might not be adequately familiar with these equations. Actually, *mathematical property* is made specific in the equations, but the full implications of these relationships is open to interpretation. Further, it seems probable that some future scientist may see in these equations something that no one so far has discerned, something that will give a key to unifying gravity with the other main physical forces studied in quantum theory. So a full paraphrase is definitely out of the question. Maybe it would be fairest to say that a metaphor holds no *special* insight untranslatable into other words but that the relationships inherent in it are never exhausted. As Wheelwright says: "There is always, in any inquiry, something more than meets the eye, even the inner eye; the permanent possibility of extending one's imaginative awareness has no limits. A person of intellectual sensitivity is plagued by the sense of a perpetual Something More beyond anything that is actually known or conceived."[23]

So, yes, a metaphor can be paraphrased to convey a partial meaning but, no, it cannot be paraphrased in the sense of fully unpacking its potential meaning. But nearly the same may be said of any expression, because words will change meaning and any word or expression has within it infinitely varied import, depending on the semantic and pragmatic context in which it is placed. In the end, then, I can't decide whether this whole question is worth a dime, two nickels or ten pennies. Ballard[24] may indeed have a point: the division between *literal* and *metaphorical* in the end may reflect only what is or is not at a given time taken to be *clear*. Strutterheim[25] throws up his hands, saying that the concept of metaphor is itself a metaphor and that it is simply the sum of all the things various people over the centuries have thought it was.

If we adhere to the position that metaphor is primarily a linguistic construct, rather than a modus operandi of thought instantiable in verbal terms, we fall into the deconstructionist booby trap: we become hopelessly lost in an illusory labyrinth of intertextual reference. However, as a figure of thought, metaphor becomes a mental open door for the free exploration of possibilities. In this sense, metaphors are not merely mental; they are experiential, mechanisms that are partly the means by which reality *is*. To be sure, the relationships implicit in metaphor are shiftable, but the historical evidence suggests that over long periods—centuries and sometimes millennia—the salient features of the metaphorand as explanans remains stable. In this sense and to this extent, Lowenberg[26] is correct in stating that a metaphor has implicit within it a new view of the explanandum to which it applies, suggesting once more an explanans that is expansive.

Contrary to this, Barfield wishes to blur the distinction between literal and metaphorical meaning:

> The concept of born literalness assumes that all words of immaterial import began with an exclusively material reference and subsequently acquired an immaterial tenor as a result of the metaphor-making activity of human minds. Now adherents [of this school of thought] are bound to assume that the immaterial tenor, upon its first appearance among our primitive ancestors, could in the alternative have been expressed literally. But in order to achieve this, those ancestors must already have possessed other words with an immaterial reference. But how did *those* words acquire their immaterial reference? Not by metaphorical activity—unless there had already been still other words available; and so on *ad infinitum*. It follows that, if you believe that whatever can be expressed metaphorically can be expressed literally, you cannot at the same time believe that man's first words had a purely material reference and that an immaterial tenor was subsequently added by way of metaphor.[27]

"What we are trying to imagine now," Barfield continues, "is the first metaphor in a wholly literal world." He cannot imagine metaphor coming into being at a postliteral stage, "because consciousness and symbolization are simultaneous and correlative."[28] Barfield seems caught in the trap of conceiving metaphor as a linguistic construction. Again, if we think of word formation following thought, then clearly the move from word-to-object pairing to noticing other relationships, reifying them, and naming them is perfectly intelligible. Instead, Barfield postulates some kind of intrinsic relation between the vehicle and the tenor, as, to cite his example, between *wind* and *spirit*. But, if such intrinsic relations exist ab initio, we would expect the tenors to be recognized at the inception of speech itself, which is contrary to historical evidence, besides being clearly absurd. Further to elaborate, his example of *spirit*, if examined (which he does not do), demonstrates the converse of what he claims. He claims by implication that, if the idea of *spirit* could have been expressed other than metaphorically by reference to *wind* (more accurately *breath*), "those ancestors must already have possessed other words with an immaterial reference," an erroneous assumption. First of all, he discounts the possibility that the idea or intuition of a life-giving *something* could have preceded having a name for it. Second, to the primitive ancestor who observed and thought about the fact that living animals, when they die, stop breathing, it seems inevitable that she would conclude that the breath *is* the life of the individual, so that *breath* would come to connote, and then to denote, the life-giving agent. To deny such a process would be to disavow the fact of word-meaning shifts, which can be observed well within a normal lifetime. To say, then, of a dead man, "His breath is gone," not only would convey that he is dead but would open the mind to explore possible relations between breath and being alive. Metaphor is not necessarily born in an instant but may evolve, like many insights. Speculation such as that in which Barfield indulges really cannot in all probability prove anything about the origins of metaphor any more than can a rebuttal of that speculation. Speculation can attempt only to establish a more or less internally consistent scenario about such things, formulated so that it may subsequently be tested.

Research findings on the ontogenesis of metaphor comprehension are sketchy. Kintsch argued that metaphor comprehension hinges on long-term semantic memory.[29] Cometa found that the operationalization of intersection at the stage of concrete operations, between the ages of eight and eleven years, is a prerequisite for children to understand metaphor.[30] This roughly paralleled the earlier findings of Smith.[31] While children often produce metaphoric speech when trying to express an idea for which their vocabulary is deficient, their comprehension of metaphor lags behind this early spontaneous linguistic creativity.[32] Children must first be able to maintain stable categories for animate versus inanimate objects before they can form metaphors in terms of their own bodies.[33] Although laconic, these findings taken together definitely support the hypothesis that metaphor is not synchronic with language per se but that it rises out of a premetaphoric stage .

Be that as it may, expansiveness of the metaphor's explanatory capacity is constrained by several factors. First, there is the dead weight of tradition. This accords with the same factors marshaling against paradigm shifts as described by Kuhn.[34] No metaphor exists in isolation; metaphors operate in networks or often hierarchies.[35] Therefore associated metaphors also tend to anchor a cognitive metaphor. Then there are the exigencies of the situation. Never hopelessly arbitrary, they, too, possess long-term stability because human needs do not vary widely over time, certainly not in their primality. In the sciences, contextual demands change, to be sure, but even there the changes are not frequent nor willy-nilly. Breaks away from the established paradigm, which means here primarily the metaphors involved, occur only at revolutionary junctures.

A concrete example will best bring this home. Force, for the Greeks, was conceived as an innate propensity to move, an obvious depersonalization of earlier envisioned anthropomorphic spirits as agents of motion. From Aristotle to Galileo, the same basic picture held: there was a *vis viva*, or living force, innate within a moving body. Celestial motions were seen by the Christian theologians as the result of flying angels guiding the heavenly bodies through space, a throwback to the primitive stage of thought but obviously aligned with the more mechanical refinement. When Galileo began systematically to measure forces, he did so in terms of velocity and acceleration (especially in his studies of falling bodies). Empirical measurement shifted attention from the *vis viva* to a consideration of the *effects* of force, which could be associated with various physical or mathematical variables. Meanwhile, the folk model of force as a pull or a push, disembodied or spiritually motivated, acted as a backdrop against which the physicists could stage their agon. Newton left the question moot but did suggest that the mathematical relationships involved were really his main interest. This was sufficient to make some theoreticians espouse the notion of force, if at all, as a convenient *fiction* by which mathematically to interrelate physical phenomena. How things stood at the end of the nineteenth century may be gleaned from Ernst Mach's rather noncommittal definition of force as "any circumstance that determines motion."[36]

Reconstructing this historical scenario, we have the following phases against the constant folk model of force identified with the common experience of moving bodies by pushing or pulling them:

Phase 1: animism. Force is an anthropomorphic spirit acting on a body.

Phase 2: depersonalized animism. Force is an innate propensity to cause motion, a *vis viva* (:Breath). Here we have the transformation: breath → spirit → (by depersonalization, or the rejection of anthropomorphism) agent of force.

Phase 3: mechanism. Force is the effect of motion in terms of resulting velocity, acceleration or momentum (:Pattern). Mathematical relationships alone define a pattern.

Phase 4: empiricism. Force is a conserved quantity (:Commodity), which can be saved, stored, and spent or used up.

Phase 5: mathematism. Force is an abstract relationship between variables (topological schematization), a fiction. It ceases to be so much a question of pattern, reflected in physical counterparts (viz., moving bodies), as a mere relationship between symbolic variables.

Modern physics is divided between the metaphoric view that force is a fiction (or mathematical relation) and that it is a conserved quantity (:Commodity). Each view has led to a distinctly different picture of reality. Relativity theory most dominantly represents the fictive view, applied specifically to gravitation, which is depicted as a geometric property of space-time. Force, primitively the active bodily sense of being able to move objects, becomes passive geometry. Quantum theory has developed along the Commodity metaphor, construing force actively as either a field or a particle. Also, in the quantum mechanical model, the primitive muscular notion of force is more noticeably preserved. Forces are carried by always moving particles. Significantly, these forces, or their particle equivalents, are subject to *conservation laws*. According to these laws, energy cannot be created ex nihilo or destroyed and, on the particulate level, certain properties of elementary particles (which embody forces) must also be conserved. The Commodity metaphor, therefore, holds explicitly.

Some interesting trends may be remarked here. First, the geometric field approach has so far failed in application beyond gravitation to the other three putative fundamental forces, the weak, the strong, and the electromagnetic. Promising generalizations have usually involved the introduction of six or more extra dimensions. In other words, the underlying metaphor must be purged and replaced by implicit topological schemes mathematically derived. Contrarily, the Commodity metaphor has failed as an explanans of gravitation. Notice, however, that the theoretical and experimental strategies call for the search for a gravitational particle, the graviton, that would reify gravity as an entity potentially conservable. In other words, the salient property of the underlying Commodity metaphor—that it can be bought, stored, and exchanged—dictates theoretical and experimental protocol. Physicists formulate and look for something that will satisfy those criteria.

METAPHOR AND THE SOCIAL CONSTRUCTION OF REALITY

Now, the doctrine of the social construction of reality suggests that the way an experiment is designed has something to do with what it will produce. A commonplace in the social sciences, it may be more difficult to reveal in the physical sciences, but historians of science are beginning to hint at it.[37] A number of diverse observations subtly undermine the credibility of strict objectivity in the sciences, let alone anywhere else. Heisenberg's uncertainty principle not only smears the accuracy of subatomic measurement, but the whole measurement problem becomes one in which the coupling of a measuring instrument to a subatomic phenomenon deranges things at the Planck level[38] in unpredictable and unknowable ways. Here nature can do her skullduggery undetected. Supposedly electrons and other charged particles possess infinite charge (whatever that really means) but appear to have finite charges because they are surrounded by a cloud of virtual particles constantly popping in and out of the polarized vacuum.[39] Obviously, hypothesizing such doings in the Planck interval is contrary to the positivistic, or operational, bias of science, according to which all hypotheses are to be testable. End measurements are the only stringent tests to which these hypotheses are subjected. The details of what actually happens in the Planck interval are by definition unobservable.

Let's be clear about this. Measurements that need explanation are not always predictions. An electron charge is a measured given. The hypothesis that the *naked* electron possesses an infinite charge hidden behind a cloud of virtual particles remains an unobservable fiction. Presumably, alternate hypotheses could also account for the measured charge. Reality, thus, is a matter of construction. And what is theorized to occur in the Planck interval is metaphysical. It need only accord, in the final analysis, with other related measurements via the existing mathematical formalism. In turn, this network of formalism and measurements can be construed into a picture of reality under any metaphor that will make the whole thing appear reasonably coherent. Further, that metaphor which demands the least overall cognitive disruption will be favored; thus does the cultural complex of metaphors tend toward self-conservation.

If we accept the metaphysical hodgepodge assumed to go on in the Planck interval, then the coupling of measuring instruments to physical phenomena presents an interface at which virtually anything might happen, especially since the fundamental physical laws can momentarily be violated. Under these conditions, it hardly seems stretching things to conjecture that the experimental setup may constrain the results, at least within limits, and that these limits cannot precisely be defined. Add to this the play with which explanatory metaphors may be deployed to induce an understanding of experimental results, and the freedom with which reality may be metaphorically defined becomes appreciable.

We may seem to be slipping into the deconstructionist pit. What saves us from total relativism is that "man is the measure of all things," as Protagoras said.[40] That is, there is a limited set of basic metaphors by which we construe reality, because the things we as humans do habitually, and so in terms of which we can understand, is quite finite. Root metaphors, especially those which pertain to high levels of abstraction around which subsidiary ideas form and in terms of which they are conceptually organized, tend to derive from invariants of human experience. Thesauri can be written because what we know and the ways in which we think are limited and can be systematically categorized. Even at the topological level—which will be discussed in detail in the next chapter—the number of distinct spatial transformations is small. Like the painter's palette, the choice for reality making is limited, but by combinatorial skill a wide range of pictures can be created.

However at odds this constructionism may be with folk models of reality, it dovetails with the work of Lakoff and Johnson, in which metaphor finally becomes recognized once more as fundamental to epistemology, not only in scientific theory building but in all walks of life, in the conceptual vocabulary of everyone. By analyzing common expressions, they demonstrated that metaphors are crucial in the social construction of reality. The present work arose from the application and extension of the Lakoff and Johnson approach to the major ideas of Western and Eastern civilization. Of course, quarrel might be made over what constitutes a *major* idea. Rather than enter that fray, I have contented myself with the fundamental ideas as established by general consensus over the years. My selection is uncontroversial. My method being rather transparent, anyone who is so disposed may bring it to bear on any topics I have failed to consider. I readily renounce any claim to comprehensiveness. I have sought only to trace out some major themes, encompassing religion, philosophy, the physical, biological and social sciences, law, and, more limitedly, the arts. Some comment may be in order regarding the latter limitation.

Two Types of Metaphor: Rhetorical and Discursive

Certainly painting and sculpture, literature and drama, opera and ballet, all make wide use of symbolism, and much of that symbolism is metaphoric. Here a distinction must be made between discursive and rhetorical metaphor. A discursive metaphor — with which this work is concerned - has a generalized character such that its literal differentiae may act as heuristic guides in the rational exploration of an abstract idea, whereas those of a rhetorical metaphor provide little in the way of heuristic but rather embellish an idea with associative values that lend a particular aesthetic quality to the idea. From the metaphor of a *babbling brook*, no sane person would set out in search of vocal chords in a brook. Contrarily, under the metaphor of the One and the Many as a general organizing basis of thought, people are always analyzing things with a view to reducing all components to a minimum, ideally one, which is supposed to be the substratum.

By and large, the metaphors of the arts call for treatment different from that proper to the discursive variety. Inevitably, there must be gray areas of question, but this is a problem common to nearly every case of making distinctions. It is not peculiar to metaphors; and quite candidly, these gray areas cannot be resolved to general applause. If ironclad rules could be laid down for the resolution of the gray areas for a given field, that would merely shift the gray areas to the region where the cases governed by the rules and all other cases interface. Pursuit of this would lead to an infinite regression; this is ideal food for idle academic debate but not my cup of tea. In short, I have left such pettifoggery to those who relish it and have confined myself only to cursory comments on the arts.

Methodology: How Root Metaphors May Be Uncovered

Determination of the metaphors underlying a given discourse may be accomplished through the conflation of several methods. The Lakoff-Johnson method, of course, is to examine the expressions used. Usually they fall into groups around readily apparent metaphors. These define themes along which the argument is constructed. The well-known hydraulic and economic metaphors employed by Freud to describe the workings of the unconscious are typical examples. Freud used a model of mental processes in which memories and concerns are kept, like commodities, in the basement of the mind. These stored items carry a force toward release, so that they are under hydraulic-like pressure. Another example is Plato's constant discussion of the ideal world copied in the world of appearance. For Plato, a dominant metaphoric aspect of the relation between the ideal and the phenomenal is copying. Viewed in a larger historical perspective, however, the salient feature that is deployed by later thinkers is a kind of projection or reflection through a glass darkly, so that it seems most aptly subsumed under the metaphor of reflection—what

I call the Mirror metaphor. This encompasses all processes by which one thing becomes replicated, made parallel with, projected, or mapped onto another. In all these processes, the first thing must be held in mind as a standard while the second thing is selected or brought into being. As metaphors of thought are examined and collected, such common features are sorted out, principally on the basis of what aspects of the metaphorand are frequently deployed.

Still another complementary method for tracking metaphors in a discourse is through key terms. In discussions of ethics and certain legal matters, for instance, there usually emerges reference to boundaries or limits not to be transgressed. The boundary marks the interface between that which is inside, proper, or legitimate, and outside, improper, or illegitimate. Most generically this distinction—an inside and outside separated by an interface—defines a container; hence it is described as the Container metaphor, one of the most broadly used of all metaphors. That the Container metaphor is being invoked is indicated by prepositions like *in, into, within, without, out of, out from* or their other language equivalents. When someone asks, "What do you have *in* mind?" one conjures the mind as container; likewise, expressions like "there's nothing *in* it for me," "she can't get *into* it," or "listen to the voice *within*," imply a metaphorical container.

Lakoff and Johnson treat the Container not as a metaphor but as an image schema. I should, therefore, say something in defense of my treatment of it as a metaphor. Johnson stated that image schemata are not propositional. Of the containment schemata, which significantly he variously calls "in-out schemata" and "in-out orientation," he describes five salient characteristics: protectiveness, restriction of force, fixity of location, accessibility or inaccessibility to view from outside observer, and transivity of containment.[41] Much as I hesitate to do so, I must take issue with this assessment. It seems to me that these characteristics are ex post facto deductions from the likely more abstract image schemata embracing the unanalyzed senses of containment: being contained oneself and perceiving objects in containing bodies. This would in all probability correspond to a visual-kinesthetic neuronal set, diffusely coarse coded in the visual and motor regions of the cortex. *As an articulated structure,* operating downward on the lower sensory centers in the form of an image, it assumes the status of a metaphor because, pursuant to Johnson's own criterion, it becomes propositional. Of the *experience of containment,* it cannot be proposed as either full or empty, large or small, deep or shallow, whereas such properties can be assigned to a *container.* The container as metaphor may be defined concretely as a volume marked off by an interface separating an inside from an outside. That there is an image schema, or image schemata, underlying it, I readily concede; but that they are one and the same would fly in the face of Johnson's own criterion of propositionality.

A similar argument would apply to another of my metaphors, Pattern. The core meaning I take to be elements perceived in interrelationship such as to form a configuration the overall structure or shape of which creates a complete gestalt. It has the feel of an image schema, but again, the test of propositionality precludes its being one. We can say the pattern becomes unraveled, it is star-shaped, pointed, simple, complex, coarse, delicate, etc. No such propositions can be made about the image schema of *orderedness*. It might be objected that Pattern is too generic an abstraction to qualify as a metaphor, but it finds embodiment from the earliest times in motifs in ceramics and the plastic arts. There, various designs give concreteness to the sense of orderedness. This accords well with the reported tendency for people to conceive abstractions in terms of prototypical images or fragmentary images.[42] Orderedness thus becomes concretized as pattern through prototypical instantiation. In that way, whereas pattern as metaphor is quite impoverished as a conception, it early acquired instantiation first in natural forms, such as shells and spider webs, and then in imitative man-made designs. It would seem more consistent, then, to distinguish *containment* and *orderedness* as image schemata, and *container* and *pattern* as metaphors.

Crucial here may be the question of prototypes. I have already mentioned patterns in prehistoric ceramic and plastic arts. These demonstrate the natural human proclivity to discernable structure. To what extent these may have served as prototypes for metaphoric conceptualization, we may never know for lack of adequate historical record. There is a larger sense in which human experience and understanding require structure and therefore a metaphoric basis for dealing with structure. This hardly needs special pleading. It explains why there are a number of fundamental metaphors for a variety of structures: Pattern, Hierarchy (which I have not singled out but perhaps should have), Mechanism, and Organism.

It may be argued that the broadest idea of structure, embodied in the Pattern metaphor, is too all-inclusive to be meaningful. Of course, everything has a structure, and so it might appear that all metaphors would be subtypes of Pattern. It seems to me to be a matter of what is to be emphasized in a conceptualization whether the structure or some other attribute of a target domain is to be spotlighted. Only when structure is a fundamental consideration is a subtype of Pattern invoked. However, because structure is pervasive in everything we know and experience, whatever touchstone or prototype is taken to define the character of the source domain will vary from culture to culture and from era to era. Perhaps there is a better way in which to handle this whole question, but, if so, it remains for me elusive.

Returning to questions of methodology, key words may also reveal underlying metaphors through their etymologies and the histories of their usage. Thus, *spirit* derives from Latin *spirare*, to breathe. Cognates are the Greek *psyche* and *pneuma*, Latin *anima*, Old Norse *ond* and *andi*, Lithuanian *dvasia*, Slavic *dusa*, and Sanskrit *atman*, all of which have as roots verbs meaning *to breathe* or nouns meaning *air*. Millennia before the chemical nature of air was recognized, the breath, which could be felt but not seen unless the atmosphere were cold, was conceived as a superfine substance that infuses a creature with life. At death, this agent leaves the body, apparently carrying within it the gift of life. In Egyptian, the hieroglyphic for the spirit-breath was the bird, whose flight was sensed as isomorphic to the breath rising upward, a visible event in the cold air. Greek *psyche* of course has also its root in the verb *to breathe.* Identifying the principle of life with the breath had important consequences. It being natural for humans to think in terms of their own embodied experience, this superfine substance could best be understood through personification, as a being or agent. This mode of explanation can then be generalized: Greek *ousia* and cognate Latin *essentia,* both based on the verb *to be,* come to express that which makes a thing peculiarly what it is, just as the spirit makes a human what he or she peculiarly is—alive, thinking and feeling. Aristotle used the term *entelecheia* (usually rendered *entelechy*) to describe the complete reality of a thing as well as the power that it had to achieve completeness, as when the acorn grows into a tree. Here the word broke up into *en,* in, *telos,* purpose, and *echein,* to have or hold. Again the personified indwelling agent is at work. Explanations based on an original metaphor are gradually generalized. The indwelling agent moves from breath to life to essence to entelechy to disease to mind to charm (the imaginary property ascribed to certain quarks in modern physics). Like an evolving word, the metaphor changes with time but always as dictated by the parameters of the current meaning or differentiae interplaying with the conditions of usage. Obviously a chaotic process, metaphor deployment, like word usage, played off against just the right circumstances, can unexpectedly bifurcate and give rise to something quite unlike the original. Sometimes there is sufficient evidence to reconstruct the transformation, and sometimes not. If it were always easy, it would undoubtedly lose its interest.

Word and image analysis aside, the larger question is how an idea is used. The originator of an idea may never actually define it in so many words. He or she may simply employ it in differing contexts so that a feel for its import is all that is projected. It enters the culture and is interpreted, its meaning expanding, becoming more articulated, or drifting into some variant of the original import. Consequently, the historian of ideas must be as much, or sometimes more, reliant upon secondary sources as upon primary, because only in the secondary may the idea become crystallized and its metaphorical foundation most clearly bared. Most of the ideas with which this work is concerned are of the broad type for which general usage is more important than the exact original formulation (if there is any). Hence, reliance on primary source quotations, usual in scholarly research, will have a lower priority here than might be expected; and particularities of wordings in the original languages of quoted texts will not be addressed unless they are truly germane. Translations will be selected for their aptness, however. My main objective is to uncover the metaphors upon which ideas are based, and to do so, my method will move from close word analysis, mainly etymological, to surveying how any given idea operates within a wide cultural context. As Lakoff and Johnson show over and over, metaphors transmute, just as words do, and these transmutations can be followed only by casting a large net. In general, where the question is simply of origin, I will tend to use word and image analysis, and where it is a question of deployment, I will describe or cite sources that demonstrate metaphor and ideational usage in a broad, cultural sense.

WORKING DEFINITION OF METAPHOR

It is, I think, fairly clear even at this point what a metaphor is. Aristotle's definition given at the beginning of this chapter continues to hold water. Still, the matter needs elaboration. Much of the philosophical debate about metaphor revolves around how one thing may be conceived in terms of another. Herein lies much sucker bait. Most, if not all, of the hairsplitting that goes on over this could be avoided by a simple realization: the ways in which one thing can be conceived in terms of another are limited only by the imagination, which varies over time and culture. Imagination, invention, ingenuity, innovation, call it what you will, is not some fixed mechanism operating with a once-and-for-all inventory of possibilities. It comprises the ability to take apart and reassemble, to mix elements, to recognize similarities and differences, relationships and patterns, and much more, supported by the faculty to manipulate all these variables in an endless variety of ways. Furthermore, the material available to the imagination is constantly growing, opening possibilities and manipulations that could not all be foreseen and therefore described and cataloged in advance.

It is one of the salient properties of imagination that it is never totally predictable and never finished. This is because relationships can be multiplied indefinitely. Given only A, B, and C: $AB, AC, BC, CB, \ldots (AB + BC), (BB + AA + BC), \ldots [(BB + AA + BC) + (ABC + BCA + CBA)] \ldots$ It makes little difference what A, B and C are, whether they are mathematical or symbolic, objects or ideas. A solo is different from a duo is different from a trio is different from a quartet, etc. Discoveries and new information can make things possible that were previously not imaginable, like distillation, electricity, or the substantiation of higher dimensions (making possible, say, the removal of an organ without invading the body at all).[43]

Imagination is a disjunctive concept. It is a grab bag into which we are constantly throwing new gimmicks. It can never be fully defined. The game is never over. We can always think of something else. In the words of Henry Adams, "[A]ll opinion founded on fact must be error, because the facts can never be complete, and their relations must always be infinite."[44] More picturesquely, Bruno Shulz wrote that the "life of the word consists in tensing and stretching itself toward a thousand connections, like the cut-up snake in the legend whose pieces search for each other in the dark."[45] And as Huizinga has pointed out, the element of play has always been an important, though neglected, factor in human history.[46] Metaphor deployment works much like the game described above. How one thing is conceived in terms of another depends upon the person and the circumstance in unpredictable interaction. No hard-and-fast rules can be laid down. All that can be said is how a metaphor has been deployed to this time and on that basis what the salient features currently seem to be. The elements of play, necessity, tradition, discovery, and chance all factor into past, present, and future deployment. Those who would on this account decry the value or even the possibility of history miss the simple fact that everything we know is history; as soon as we know anything, it is in the past. Even the theory that history is impossible is itself history. To deny history is to deny memory or that it is useful. To say that it is not perfect is undoubtedly true, but it is a trivial truism: nothing is perfect. As the Zen Buddhists long ago recognized, thinking about thinking, whereas it might sometimes be fun, can tie the thinker into delusional knots, if the thinking does not at some juncture serve living.

METAPHOR AND PROTOTYPE THEORY: EXTENSIONS OF A DEFINITION

A word or two are in order on the prototype theory of categories.[47] According to recent research, many categories are not conceived in terms of groups of properties; they are represented by prototypes. *Tree*, for example, would be represented in a person's mind by some tree she found typical, such as a maple tree, probably a particular one with which she was familiar. Supposedly this vitiates the classical theory that categories operate as property lists. For my purposes, I believe the distinction is not critical. On the level of cultural analysis, many prototypes will come into play over a population and through historical periods. In deploying a prototype, the individual will, at any event, be comparing data with a prototype and in doing so will be attending to the properties of the latter. In other words, that the individual works with prototypes, rather than with properties in abstraction, does not remove properties from consideration; it simply embodies them in an exemplum. For the study of individuals, this could make a difference, and Johnson[48] has argued that it is crucial in determining moral questions, but I believe it is moot in the present study. It should be noted, too, that it has clearly been shown that providing the learner with concept definitions in terms of defining properties even in the presence of examples facilitates concept learning.[49] And it has been demonstrated that the use of categories entails induction based upon general knowledge that can be brought to bear on the subject matter of the categories, dovetailing with the unpredictable play element in concept and metaphor deployment.[50] Prototype theory, then, is not at variance with the general position of the present study.[51]

Gathering all these strands together, the definition of metaphor just outlined parallels that of Lakoff and Johnson, according to whom the "essence of metaphor is understanding and experiencing one kind of thing in terms of another."[52] What this means is that one domain of experience, presumably exemplified by a prototype, is mapped onto the target domain. In other words, salient features of the prototype (representing the source domain) are projected onto the target domain, which is then actually experienced to evince those features. Again, Lakoff and Johnson exclaim that "no metaphor can ever be comprehended or even adequately represented independently of its experiential basis."[53] Furthermore, the features of any domain form an indefinitely large set, $\{A_1 \ldots A_n\}$. This is because features, in general, subsist in relationships ("Tom is taller than Fred," "rocks are hard [compared to something like mud]," "the sun is 93 million miles from earth"). The number of possible relationships is indefinitely large because there are indefinitely many things to which a given something can be related. Thus Johnson:

> In any metaphorical projection (e.g., THEORIES ARE BUILDINGS) only part of the structure of the source-domain (buildings) is typically projected onto the target-domain (theories). Lakoff and I have called this the "used" portion of the metaphor. In THEORIES ARE BUILDINGS, for instance, the used part consists of the foundation and outer shell, from which the typical projected structures are drawn. Expressions such as "construct," "foundation," and "buttress" belong to this used portion, and they are therefore part of our ordinary literal language about theories. However, it is perfectly acceptable to draw on the unused portion of the metaphor by focusing on neglected aspects of the source-domain such as rooms, staircases, facades, and so forth.[54]

I am stressing that only a subset of the set of features of the source domain is used, leaving a still indefinitely large set of features from which to draw. It is this indefinitely large store that makes possible the slight adjustments necessary to the projection of the source-domain to a wide range of exempla in the target domain. This store also supplies alternative salient features by which the use of the metaphor may shift over time.

Consider as an example the concept of the divine plan of the universe. This was at first conceived in the Judeo-Christian tradition as a kind of prophecy laid out in the Bible. "The Lord has planned and who can annul it?"[55] Thus spake Isaiah, and in many places it is echoed, "God planned it long ago."[56] Or again, "The people did whatever your hand predestined to occur," for "God prepared our good works beforehand."[57] The future course of the universe is a plan in the mind of God, a kind of shopping list of intentions. Plato used the same metaphor in the *Timaeus*, making the Demiurge into a master carpenter who copied ideal forms into the flux of material substance, an image in which the plan takes on a more graphic character, in which the prototype is a builder's schematic. Generally speaking, the early church fathers interpreted the divine plan as pertaining to the economy of grace.[58] St. Augustine thus affirmed it. However, attempts to extend this idea to wider aspects of the universe led to problems: the problem of evil in the world, human freedom, and retribution in the next life. Then, the temptation arose to

play down certain features of the plan or its implementation, giving rise to hetero-
doxies. According to Pelagianism, God does not intervene in history. Manichaeism
claimed divine nonintervention in human freedom. In these, the plan is incomplete. Certain schools of gnosticism saw the plan as doubtful, and so denied the
metaphor. With the rise of science during the Renaissance, the salient features of a
plan, or design as it was sometimes called, were revisited and it was decided that
physical order had to be one of the main goals of the plan. Newton, in the
"General Scholium" added to the third book of his *Principia* in 1713 and revised
thirteen years later, argued that the physical arrangement of the firmament necessitated an intelligent agent to account for its perfection. Galileo, as we shall see,
attempted to unlock the divine plan by deriving the planetary orbits from a nesting
of perfect solids. And so the plan (:Design) shifted from inner intention to graphic
scheme to mathematical formulae, each significantly different by virtue of being
based on different prototypes representing distinct subsets of the indefinitely large
set of features of a plan or design. As this example shows, too, the salient features
that will ultimately be selected depend on unpredictable exigencies of the time. The
earliest church fathers could hardly have been expected to have foreseen an appropriate role for mathematics in the mind of God. The source domain, thus, remains
never fully disclosed or comprehended, and is ever a source for innovation.

THE ROOT METAPHORS CONSIDERED IN THIS STUDY

With this background established, it is time to introduce and explain the root
metaphors underlying the major ideas the evolution of which we will be tracing.
We understand one thing conceptually in terms of another, the unfamiliar in terms
of the familiar. In calling this metaphoric, we do not wish to imply that it is a
conscious process of comparison. In general, it is more subtle. Common referents
in our experience provide properties by implicit correlation with which the main
body of incoming information is processed. Colloquial expressions perhaps give us
the best example of this unconscious processing. When someone says, "He broke
the law," she usually is unaware, or barely aware, that she is implying that the law
is being analogized to a container. This interpretation is buttressed by related expressions such as "operate inside or outside the law," "legal transgression," and
"stay within the law." I mean to go no further toward clarifying the issue of how the
mind models metaphors, as it can be properly explored and decided only through
experimental means.

Primitive humans began to construe their reality in terms of that which they
best knew; and in the course of time, certain universals of experience became sta-
bilized as primary frames of reference by which other experience was cognitively
processed. The basic metaphors we shall be pursuing fall into four subdivisions,
and these are listed below.[59] Some years ago, Friedrich Müller[60] noted that, as he

put it, all words expressing immaterial concepts are derived by metaphor from words expressive of sensible ideas. The gist of his argument was echoed a few years later by Féré.[61] Lakoff, Johnson, and Turner[62] have recently pursued this line of thought, and what is offered here is an extension of it systematically carried out across a broad spectrum of ideas over a long span of time.

Of the root metaphors, those having to do specifically with the structure and functioning of the body are: Breath, Hot/Cold, Fire, Light/Dark, Mirror Image, Right/Left, Sight, Strength/Ability, Taste/Smell, and Word/Speech. Fire is included here for its close association with the proximal sense of warmth as well as the fact that it was primitively conceived to reside in the body as the source of "vital heat," which was taken as a sign of life itself.

Those having to do with family and human relations are: Commodity, Contract, Debt/Payment, Father/Mother (Parent), First Position, Lot/Share.

Those pertaining to elemental states of being: Container, Floor/Ground, Form, Mechanism, Motion/Rest, One/Many, Organism, and Pattern.

Finally, there are five main action schemes: Bind, Count, Cut/Join, Point/Show, and Take/Reject.

It is apparent that certain of the metaphors and action schemes are polar. This is only to say that, given an exemplar, it is natural to process information in terms of it and its opposite. All the more should we expect this in view of the role played by negation in human concept formation.

Slightly less evident are some of the natural relations tying certain of the metaphors and two of the action schemes together into families. It should be sufficient simply to list these families, since, once the members are put side by side, the family resemblance is obvious.

(1) Breath — Word/Speech
(2) Sight — Light/Dark — Fire — Mirror Image
(3) Fire — Hot/Cold
(4) Parent — First Position
(5) Commodity — Contract — Debt/Payment — Lot/Share
(6) Point/Show — Count
(7) One/Many — Form — Pattern — Mechanism — Organism
(8) Container — Floor/Ground

The seventh family, being the largest, deserves comment. Its members are arranged in increasing order of complexity. One/Many represents the most rudimentary discrimination of parts, and Form, the outline shape of the sum of parts, yields, when given an internal organization, Pattern. Two patterns or structures that attain to a function, then, are Mechanism and Organism. It would seem further that Form and Organism are the more holistic metaphors, appealing to right cerebral hemispheric process, whereas their left hemispheric counterparts would be Pattern and Organism. We might look at this family as One/Many elaborations.

These metaphor families are significant in that deployment of any one metaphor often will involve other members of the same family. Problems in epistemology have been formulated largely through the second and seventh families, and those in ethics, understandably, through the fifth. Never entirely exclusive, the metaphors employed in one area tend to spread out to touch those in adjacent areas. Dovetailing of metaphors helps to facilitate general discourse. Where it is missing or incomplete, disagreement is rife, opposing camps aligning themselves with the disparate metaphor complexes.

This work is divided into two sections: theoretical and historical. As our historical survey will show, certain of the root metaphors and action schemes have been pivotal in generating intellectual progress and revolution. I have already remarked that the primary member of the fourth family and the members of the seventh have been relied upon to consolidate the right and left cerebral hemispheric modes of information processing. Aside from these—and they have also played more general roles—and the Family group of metaphors used in ethics and social thought, other metaphors that have stood out above the rest as continuing matrices of thought are Breath, Mirror Image, Floor/Ground, and Container. It is fair to say that the others are secondary in that they played their roles once and once only, in giving birth to concepts that were central but remained unchanged. Also, these secondary metaphors have for the most part been allied with the standard topological transformations in facilitating discursive thinking. This is especially true of Motion/Rest and the Simple Actions group.

Metaphor deployment deserves more careful study. Cursorily we may observe that it is certainly prompted by contemporary events. The dominance of the Mechanism metaphor in the Renaissance was certainly initiated by the invention and spread of the clock, but cases are rarely so clear-cut. For the greater number of instances, the basic metaphors were set down primitively at the dawn of human understanding, and we have simply been playing variations on them ever since. It is with exactly how these variations have evolved, the metaphor deployments, that we need to be concerned, if we are to enhance further our understanding of the structure of human thought.

SUMMARY

Pulling all this together into a summary, the concept of metaphor on which this study is based is a cognitive one. A metaphor, as I choose to use the term, is a mode of thinking, a mode of having reality, in which, quite simply, one thing is conceived in terms of another. As many commentators have noted, everything resembles everything else in one way or another. Consequently, the relations by which the tenor or target domain of a metaphor becomes associated with a particular vehicle or source domain are so diverse, forming a disjunctive class, that it is impossible adequately to subsume them under any descriptive label. The possibilities are endless. Furthermore, once an association between a tenor and a vehicle has been established, any property of the vehicle may, through the sheer element of play amid changing circumstances, be exploited to deploy the metaphor. This makes the relationship open-ended, and it is precisely this open-endedness that makes it impossible to paraphrase a metaphor with finality. Further, a metaphor, as I am using the term, is a way of looking at something, a perspective, and so paraphrasing would be an inappropriate strategy to apply to it. Prototypes usually stand in to represent source domains. In this study, the categorical properties of the metaphorand, or source domain, are still used to delineate it, with the caveat that these properties are generally carried by a prototype in thought processes. It seems doubtful that the prototype is stable across culture or time, and so a qualified classical approach to metaphor is here adopted. From the perspective of this author, it is salient features of the metaphorand that are important, not whether they are attached to a category or a prototype.

As mental operation instantiable in words, a metaphor can be expressed in many different ways, no one of which exhausts the possibilities implicit in the operation. From this angle, the verbal form of the metaphor may be interesting, but never expresses the essential character of the metaphor. Linguistic analysis, then, helps to unlock how the metaphor is being used, rather than revealing the metaphor itself. In other words, behind the written or spoken metaphor is a relation out of which many variant linguistic forms could emerge. I take no position, therefore, on arguments concerning the language of metaphor except insofar as it may give clues to an established relation between a tenor and a vehicle.

Rhetorical metaphors are endless, but basic metaphors acting as explanantia to lend coherence to thought are more limited in number because humans understand things in terms of their own bodies and actions and from the repertory of body functions and actions only a few are suitable as vehicles for rational and heuristic thought. Historical analysis shows that these metaphors and the ways in which they are deployed are remarkably constant through time, which of course would be requisite for social stability. Being derived from elemental body functions and actions, basic metaphors have an intuitive appeal and a meaning that translate across time and culture, revealing a universality that, though not eternal, changes slowly enough to furnish a stable framework for human thought and communication with ambiguity minimized usually below the threshold of social disruption. Thought and communication, however, are complex and go well beyond metaphor, and I am postulating nothing beyond the fact that metaphors in thought may clearly enough be delineated (not exhausted) to form the basis of ideational and historical study. Metaphors, like words, change through time, but certain ones, like basic vocabulary, remain relatively fixed, and it is to those that this study is directed.

Etymological analysis is a primary method by which to establish the historical origins of the metaphorical foundations of ideas. Usage supplements this in showing how the metaphors are deployed. We must examine how metaphors are employed to substantiate what etymology tells us and to pursue the history of ideas and the metaphors behind them.

There have been many theories of metaphor. We have discussed several, concentrating mainly on those from which the present theory borrows. My definition accords with that of Lakoff and Johnson, although I do not stress the importance of prototypes as mediators of metaphorization. This is solely because of the near impossibility of determining prototypes in the context of intellectual history. We looked at the concept of force as an example of how metaphor usage shifts over time in response to social and cultural changes. Finally, the methodology employed in this study was described as revolving around etymological analysis coupled with the examination of how metaphors and ideas are actually used.

One point of possible confusion should be addressed. It may seem that I waver between the comparison theory of metaphor and the more fashionable interactive theory spawned largely by Lakoff and Johnson. According to the comparison theory, a metaphor merely points out preexisting similarities between the source and target domains, whereas in the interactive view, the metaphor may actually *constitute* them. For my money, this is a metaphysical distinction, for the concept of interaction implies two domains that act upon each other. We are to assume that in this interaction similarities may come into being, that the process is holistic rather than dualistic. That may well be, but I do not believe that it is susceptible to empirical verification. Whether one or the other theory is adopted seems to be not a matter of ontological factuality so much as pragmatic expedience. My predilection is for the interactive theory, but I do not balk at using either approach when it serves heuristic or elucidative purposes.

2

Metaphor and
Intellectual History

After having briefly surveyed theories of metaphor and laid out my own definition
and approach to the subject, I wish to place metaphor in a broader context. This is
in preparation for the task of following selected metaphorical and action-sche-
matic themes through history. In this chapter, I will examine the role of metaphor
in thought from the perspective of history, psychology and epistemology. The process of forming metaphors as vehicles for understanding is placed in the larger
framework of how and why mental data become related in the first place. We
might call this the prehistory of metaphor.

Forming metaphors arises out of a more general process called here relatedness, beginning from the simple act of consciously juxtaposing two or more mental
items. Note that we are not yet speaking of metaphorization, but only comparing
two things—noticing, say, that one item is taller than another. Sharper focus of
attention picks out similarities between these items, and when we notice similarities in a series of items, we say that the members of the series form a class. Through
gradual developments not clearly understood, from elementary categorical discrimination arises the ability to conceive of one thing in terms of another. This is
metaphorization.

To appreciate the role of metaphorization in thought, we will have to look at
the dynamics by which conceiving one thing in terms of another progresses. Thus,
we will trace out the history of an idea, universal order, through the metaphors
used at various times and in different cultures to embody it. In so doing, we should
gain more insight into how metaphors are deployed to express changing constructions of fundamental ideas. Moreover, this insight will include a preliminary picture of the interaction between metaphorization and topological schemata. The
role of spatial relationships in discursive thought will then be treated more explicitly in the next chapter.

At this point it is appropriate to reintroduce the working definition of metaphor. A metaphor, as I have been employing the term, establishes a relation of

similarity between something familiar and something less well understood. Usually a key similarity sparks the initial assumption of the metaphor, which is then deployed in a cultural context by exploration of further similarities at first not explicitly noted as well as the implications of all similarities consciously understood. Again, recognition of a similarity and mediation of the comparison or mapping is undoubtedly through a series of prototypes. Prototype selection varies from person to person but must remain within certain limits for a culture at a given time to ensure consensual communication. This deployment is not necessarily witting and methodical but customarily is dictated by contemporaneous developments in the environmental context, physical or cultural. Furthermore, I wish to draw an immediate distinction between the rhetorical and the explanatory, even though it is an artificial distinction and solely heuristic.

A rhetorical metaphor, such as in "this discussion will throw light on the subject," lends color to language by anchoring it in concrete experience. The comparisons may, through similarities and contrasts, associations and even phonics, enliven our sense of what is being described. But the terms of the metaphor, the metaphorand and its differentiae, do not provide guidance for further exploration of the subject. To say that a discussion throws light is to conceive the discussion as an agent—in effect, to personify it—capable of the action of throwing. Light is a metaphorand in terms of which to picture understanding. Clearly, any investigation into the dynamics or physiology of throwing will not help us to unravel the psychology of learning, nor will the physics of light. Yet, part of this metaphor touches one of the basic explanatory metaphors, Light/Darkness, making poetic use of it.

Knowledge and understanding are universally conceived in terms of light. This is because of the general primacy of sight for gathering sensory information. It is distal and has the greatest degree of discrimination among all the senses for humans. Images of distinct visual awareness, therefore, concretize the inner sense of understanding: "it is clear that . . . ," "we are in the dark," "she is enlightened." Analogously, the visual conditions induced by greater light up to practical limits are isomorphic to the conditions sought in matters of knowledge and understanding: increased articulation of detail, making possible definitional distinctness, more synoptic apprehension, and awareness of more potential relationships among parts.

An explanatory metaphor, by contrast to the rhetorical, supplies differentiae in terms of which behavior toward the target domain will be dictated, beyond the taking of an emotional attitude. The differentiae will have heuristic import. Disease conceived as the effects of an evil spirit (:Breath) possessing the body of the sick person led to specific forms of treatment. The spirit might be appeased. It might be frightened away. It might even be drained away in the blood, though bloodletting was more inspired by a humoral theory of disease. The point is that disease as indwelling evil spirit suggested therapeutic strategies.

RELATIONAL KNOWLEDGE: BACKGROUND TO METAPHOR

To understand more fully what is involved here, it is well to place metaphorization in the larger context of relational knowledge. Relational knowledge, which subsumes metaphorization, is simply a further extension of the systemic hierarchy that reaches from the structure of atoms, to molecules, cells, organisms, ecosystems, and onward to galaxies and galactic clusters. Nor is the ability to relate one thing to another within the realm of conscious behavior solely human. Certainly the monkey who puts together two short sticks to form a longer stick and then sees that it can be used to knock down a bunch of bananas demonstrates the ability consciously to relate one thing to another. In fact, it is unnecessary to trace this sort of behavior tediously back through the animal kingdom to every next simpler form of organism. The seemingly purposeful behavior that characterizes living organisms can be conceived as proceeding through the faculties of being able to advance from one step of behavior to another to maintain homeostasis over lifetimes. Much of the basis for this consistent homeostatic progression has been laid down in molecular biology.

Pivotal here is not when this relatedness came into human consciousness. It seems likely that it paralleled the emergence of consciousness. Of more concern here is the import of relatedness to the subsequent development of human knowledge. We wish to know in just what ways this relatedness infused our reality.

In the earliest appearance of conscious relatedness, we are talking most probably about two primary instances: an awareness of purpose and of conjunction. If we are to fasten onto some arbitrary beginning point for taking account of the awareness of purpose, a good candidate would be the inception of tool making. What can be said of tool making in this regard can be projected backward or forward in time with reasonable caution.

Nor do we have to begin with man. We have already cited the experiment involving the monkey with two sticks trying to obtain a bunch of bananas. Surely at his moment of insight, the monkey's consciousness of the newly constructed stick took on a sudden implicative extension that it did not previously have. That is what is meant by an awareness of relatedness, an awareness, in this case, of purpose. The monkey had to have envisioned internally the situation in which he would use the stick to knock the bananas. He had to have perceived the stick as something-with-which-to-knock-down-the-bananas, though of course the notion would have been nonverbal. Likewise, primates who use sticks to dig out bugs from the earth must view these sticks differently from the way the banana-minded monkey did.

But purpose is only one of the two instances of the awareness of relatedness that we cited; the other is conjunction. Things that occur repeatedly together are soon experienced as each participating somehow in the existence of the other. At first, this kind of conjunctive relatedness is perceived as nothing more than an unquestioned togetherness—however we characterize it, in doing so, we make it much more explicit than at first it could have been. It makes no difference whether the togetherness is spatial or temporal. The sense of togetherness, the sense of AB as opposed to A and B separately, is there. And this unarticulated conjunction of things persists long into human history, even to the present, for the earliest layers of cognitive evolution may become overlaid but never really disappear.

We must realize that earlier modes of cognition are always contemporary and operative everywhere. Think of someone who has a favorite recipe which everyone loves. She can't tell anyone else how she does it, because she does it "by guess and by gosh," intuitively, by a "feel" for what she has to do. She could probably be made to observe herself more closely, to write every step down, so we could learn her secret, but then the self-awareness would predictably throw everything out of kilter and the recipe wouldn't work. Think of riding a bike, playing golf, catching a ball. These are all things that various civilized people know how to do very well, but for most people, it is difficult to articulate the processes. Special factors enter into these activities, but even so, there is an intuitiveness hard to articulate, an intuitiveness that may even be destroyed by articulation.

In a very real sense, the awareness of purpose and that of conjunction were differentiated out of an even more primitive monistic awareness. Organisms moving toward goals under preprogrammed constraints, as with birds building a nest, need not have those goals in awareness. They do what they must. Only as they evolve a nervous system sophisticated enough to interact within itself, reacting to aspects of a mental reality, does the distinction arise between purpose and simple conjunction. Even at that point the distinction is much more elusive than it is to us.

RELATIONAL KNOWLEDGE EVOLVED
FROM HEMISPHERIC SPECIALIZATION

Studies involving surgically split brains have shown quite conclusively that this primitive cognition resides in the right hemisphere of the brain.

Each hemisphere can autonomously generate opinions, judgments, attitudes, and emotions. Thus, these experiment support a model of interacting coconscious mental systems that directly study the interaction of cognitive processes which must be coordinated for a final behavioral act and which allow controlled observation of the distinctly human behavior of talking about these acts. The data suggest that a dynamic relation holds between nonverbal information processing systems, which can organize, represent, and retrieve information, and the more apparent verbal system.[1]

A fairly clear picture of the dynamics of interhemispheric function is gradually emerging.

Experiments have shown that after a behavior is produced by the nonspeaking (generally right) hemisphere, the subsequent verbal explanation produced by the speaking (generally left) hemisphere delineates an explicit motivation for such activity in spite of the speaking hemisphere having no real prior knowledge of the behavior. . . . an individual is a series of coconscious mental systems each competing for the limited output mechanisms. Of the multiple mental systems present in human beings, usually only one can talk and interpret events linguistically. The view is that the constant flow of emitted behavior is generally interpreted by the verbal system, and provides one with knowledge, opinion, belief about the environment, about oneself, and about one's behavior. By such acts linguistic behavior provides an organizational framework for the individual.[2]

An interesting facet of these investigations is that each of the lateral systems has a degree of independence so that emotions, attitudes, opinions and interpretations in one need not coincide with those in the other; and when this happens, the overt behavior may become "agitated, aggressive, and restless."[3] We thus have a model for certain types of elusive anxiety. It also comes about that behaviors hitherto regarded as subconscious are interpretable as right-hemisphere processes prompting with unequal success the left hemisphere.

All told, the model of coconscious brain function postulated by Gazzaniga and Volpe accords well with the genesis of lateralization. One hemisphere holds holistic plans while the other decodes them digitally, so to speak, into executable subunits of behavior. When gestalten in the right hemisphere do not admit to verbal or symbolic decoding strategies established in the left hemisphere, we have hunches, intuition, uneasy apprehensions "in the back of the mind"; and this, incidentally, illumines much of the creative process, which is undoubtedly largely a process of right to left hemispheric decoding. While we cannot pursue this potentially fruitful lead here, we shall have occasion to return to it, when exploring the potency of metaphors in the governing of human behavior.

HEMISPHERIC SPECIALIZATION WAS CATALYZED BY TOOL MAKING

By now, it should be clear that in tool making, purpose must begin to differentiate out from the earliest nonsymbolic monistic mode of awareness to stand in contrast with conjunction. It is in tool making that humans first launch upon sequential behavior of a protracted nature, requiring careful decoding from a holistic model or plan to an ordered serial execution. And it is with the arrival of tools and other accessories of primitive life that the initial arsenal appears from which to generate the prototype metaphors. These infused human reality with an articulated inner architecture, an introspective awareness of an explicit structure of reality, public as well as private, though the outer order must have preceded the inner as a conscious construct. This is because awareness arises first as response to the environment and only later achieves the support of a underlying neural substrate complicated enough to make possible interaction among its own parts. In other words, introspection of a private reality suggests that a complex brain must underlie it and that it requires a certain experiential history to bring it into being.

Summary of the Prehistory of Metaphorization

In summary, we have suggested a progression from autonomous serial enactive schemata, an autonomously controlled doing of things, to an awareness that such things are being done. Then the doing is perceived as an atemporal visual scheme, which serves as a model for the direction of sequences of actions requiring a bit-by-bit processing of information. Lateralization of brain function arises to accommodate the holistic and the serial phases of complex actions such as tool making and hunting. As separate phases of various behaviors (including perception) become consciously distinct, one phase is related to another and it is this relatedness—usually one of purpose or simply joint appearance or conjunction—which is the basis of conscious comparing, of metaphorical thought, conceiving one thing somehow in terms of another, the clearest form of which is the strict analogy or simile.

From this point of cognitive evolution on, we enter the vast arena of the history of ideas, where we can hope only to indicate some of the basic principles of development and to sketch, in the briefest and most incomplete fashion, the paleontology of metaphoric thought.

Some Rules of Metaphor Deployment

Turning to the history and dynamics of metaphorical thought, I can state a few general rules of metaphorical transformation. First, once a metaphor is installed, it tends to restrict behavior within the limits that it suggests. If we see argumentation as a form of war, then we shall be inclined to conduct it according to strategies of war. Second, a fundamental metaphor is rarely abandoned even in the face of new experience that does not fall easily within its compass. Instead, the situation is accommodated by secondary metaphors that harmonize with the primary one. And third, the inner architecture of the mind imitates structures of external reality.

As an instance of the second rule, disease was first conceived as a curse from the gods (:Word/Speech), then an entity that one gets (:Commodity), and finally an organismic malfunction (:Organism). At least on the level of popular thought, all three metaphors continue to operate—"Syphilis is the curse of God on the sinner," "You'll catch a cold." Accommodation continues until the original metaphor becomes obscured by the secondary elaborations or the entire system ceases to accord in an emotionally or experientially satisfactory manner with the known facts. When either of these conditions prevails, there is a sudden shift, a revolution in thought, resolved by the establishment of a new primary metaphor or metaphor complex. Thomas Kuhn has outlined this process, utilizing the concept of the paradigm, roughly equivalent but slightly more ambiguous than my concept of metaphor.[4]

There is a corollary to this rule in the arts. Artistic forms and motifs tend to persist even across media changes, probably because they are isomorphic to body states and modes of experiencing. Suffice it now to cite a couple of examples. In ancient Greek architecture, the form of the entablature was preserved in some detail from wood prototypes to the constructions in stone. Late-Renaissance instrumental canzone were modeled on vocal counterparts. Throughout the history of sculpture from ancient Greece to the present, certain poses, such as Praxiteles' curve and *contrapposto*, have been copied into every medium and have even been carried as a topological characteristic into abstract works.

Not only do artistic forms persist; they are invariably elaborated as time goes on. The form of the sonata passed over into the concerto and symphony, where it was subjected to gradual elaboration and transformation. Rib vaulting began as part of the structural innovation of the Gothic style, slowly became an ornamental detail, and then proliferated into the complexities of the flamboyant style. We might even say that in the broadest sense life forms tend naturally to evolve into multiplicity, in opposition to simple mechanical systems, which degenerate into simpler and simpler configurations. It is interesting to speculate that at the level of elementary particles there may be a reversion to proliferation of formal possibilities, especially if resonances (i.e., transitory quark-bond states too short-lived to be considered particles) are taken into account. Be that as it may, historical development of many kinds advance through stages of increasing refinement and complexity. Thus, the stages of the baroque are closely paralleled in Hellenistic art,[5] and governmental organization seems to move through inevitable phases of expanding bureaucratization.

Finally, a third rule of metaphoric evolution is that the organization of mental structures arises from the assimilation of structures in the physical world or, from the more interactional perspective of the metaphor approach, a rapprochement between public structures and private understandings. Piaget has seized upon this rule in explaining the ontogeny of intelligence. All we need do here is to extend this to the phylogeny of the structure of human consciousness. Whether in ontogeny or phylogeny, there is a twofold process involved. First, function is reified into form. Gilbert Ryle has called attention to this in pointing out that "mind" is not a thing but a process; it is something we do, not something we have, or, as he says, "mind is minding."[6] Second, reification in erecting the architecture of mentation usually occurs under the cohesive force of substantial disjunctive conceptualization. Mind is not just minding; it is mindings, a category under which are subsumed many different functions: symbolic thinking, feeling, emoting, picturing, hearing, tasting, smelling, hallucinating, dreaming, etc.

Piaget has brilliantly articulated the process of assimilation by which human consciousness attains its structure. Flavell explains:

> Assimilation . . . refers to the fact that every cognitive encounter with an environmental object necessarily involves some kind of cognitive structuring (or restructuring) of that object in accord with the nature of the organism's existing intellectual organization. As Piaget says; "Assimilation is hence the very functioning of the system of which organization is the structural aspect."
> . . . Every act of intelligence, however rudimentary and concrete, presupposes an interpretation of something in external reality, that is, an assimilation of that something to some kind of meaning system in the subject's cognitive organization. To use a happy phrase of Kelly's . . . , to adapt intellectually to reality is to *construe* that reality, and to construe it in terms of some enduring *construct* within oneself. . . . And it is Piaget's argument that intellectual assimilation is not different in principle from a more primary biological assimilation: in both cases the essential process is that of bending a reality event to the template of one's ongoing structure.[7]

Accommodation through assimilation certainly has its counterpart in configurational transformations of purely mechanical systems under internal and external forces. And this analogy may perhaps go toward clarifying the notion that mentation does not require agency, that is, a central directing entity, such as self or will, any more than a mechanical system does. Rather, the structure-functions that come to be designated as agents of mentation follow not as formally logical necessities but as by-products of the total organization as it evolves. These are parallel to the formation of phase interfaces and other boundaries within time-dependent physical systems. The early Hindus seem to have understood this. In the Vedantic literature the origins of the world of appearance were seen to be in the acausal splitting of the One into the Many.

METAPHORIZATION AND METAPHOR SHIFT: A HISTORICAL EXAMPLE

With these preliminaries aside, as an illustration, consider the concept of the atom (:One), conceived first by Democritus as an impenetrable sphere. The atom for Democritus was the basic constituent of all material substance. It was thus the One from which the Many of appearance arose. This analogy held and was deployed in various ways to explain the behavior of matter until well into the nineteenth century. Only when the electron was discovered and experiments suggested an internal structure for the atom was the spherical analogy discarded in favor of a planetary model (:Pattern). When further refinements in physical experimentation and the success of statistical methods applied to atomic phenomena made this metaphor untenable, it was supplanted by a mathematical model (:Mechanism) not susceptible to complete visualization. It was a mechanism in the sense of comprising variables (analogues to parts), the interactive functioning of which was governed by a set of mathematical equations. "The old picture of an atom as a set of quasi-elastically bound electrons was replaced by one in which it contained a set of 'virtual oscillators' whose frequencies were those of the spectral lines [characteristic of the element]." The "virtual oscillator" was nothing more than a fictive counterpart to spectroscopic wave equations.

> Heisenberg concluded that it was impossible to associate an electron with a point in space within an atom or to determine the period of motion of such an electron. It was, however, possible to associate an electron with the radiation emitted or absorbed by an atom, and the emission of radiation depended on the velocity and acceleration, so that these variables had to occur in the theory and have some sort of representation there.[8]

Matrices of probabilities were ultimately substituted for the classical variables of position and momentum, making the atom a completely mathematical, fictive mechanism.

It should be emphasized that each model held sway and was used to explain the behavior of matter to the satisfaction of the best thinkers until the accumulation of experience brought to light sufficient phenomena to which the characteristics of the model could not be extended. Boyle's Law, relating the pressure to the volume of a gas, could be accommodated by atoms conceived as elastic spheroids, whereas the results of particle-scattering experiments could not. In scattering experiments, subatomic particles are directed against atoms or other subatomic particles and the way in which they scatter reflects something of the structure of the target. Even the rather modern statistical theory of the behavior of gases offered no trouble for the spherical model; so we can see that this model could be deployed to account for a diversity of empirical findings before it outreached its capacity to lend coherence to experience.

In a sense, a metaphor carries with it a certain innate logic of deployment. In the metaphoric relationship, the source domain is designated the metaphorand. The properties of the metaphorand together comprise the restrictions, which in operation dictate the logic, followed in the heuristic application of the metaphor. It is a property of a sphere that it may bounce off other spheres (as in the statistical account of the behavior of gases), but it will not admit to certain patterns of the scattering of smaller spheres directed on larger ones (as in the scattering of photons or electrons directed against atomic nuclei). By the same token, the properties of the metaphorand may inhibit lines of thought that would contravene them. Returning once more to the conceptualization of the atom, we can see that the impenetrable spheroid model would forestall entertaining thoughts of atomic constituents and performing experiments aimed at discovering such constituents. Until they begin to fail us, we do not look for what our conceptualization rules out, and we ordinarily do not question our conceptualizations, at least not within the perimeters of discursive thought. Questioning may occur as part of aesthetic play, but here alternative conceptualizations function to amuse and to fulfill requirements of artistic composition rather than to explain external realities. Satirists may lampoon many established ideas without seriously undermining them.

An important instance of the restrictive influence of root metaphors is in the development of ancient Greek physical science, which lacked altogether any exploration into dynamics, the study of the relationship of force to motion. According to Aristotelian physics, which dominated classical and medieval scientific thought, each object seeks its proper place (:Pattern), when freed of all restrictions. This is what Aristotle called "natural motion." Any motion, such as that of a hurled javelin, that causes an object to depart from its natural motion he termed "violent." Violent motions were seen as deviations from the norm, and the norm was conceived as maintained by the innate disposition of all bodies to move in accordance with the natural order. This poses the most urgent question as "What is the natural order?" rather than "What makes bodies move as they do?" Again, it was assumed unconsciously that the latter question had already been answered by reference to the natural order, so there was no motive for asking it. Additionally, the underlying metaphor of Pattern, as we shall see, was one that dominated classical thought.

A FURTHER EXAMPLE OF THE METAPHORIC ANALYSIS OF INTELLECTUAL HISTORY

It will be well to stay with classical science a little longer to clarify wherein the metaphor approach differs from the usual currents of intellectual historiography, while at the same time extending our preliminary understanding of the logic of metaphor deployment. I. Bernard Cohen succinctly observed that "Aristotelian physics . . . was based on two postulates . . . : One was the immobility of the earth; the other was the distinction between the physics of the earthly four elements and the physics of the fifth celestial element."[9] I shall concentrate here on the first postulate.

Ordinary historiography treats such a tenet as an immobile earth as a deduction from more elemental principles, and lets it go at that. However, the matter really goes deeper. If the earth, our frame of reference as observers, is conceived as moving, then such dynamism renders the sense of orderedness problematic when projected onto the universe. Order, or pattern, primitively requires a static picture of things before it can be generalized to frame a dynamic system. For the universe to be construed through the Pattern metaphor, there needed to be a stationary center, which most naturally would be the earth, for we do not on an everyday level perceive it to be moving. With this is mind, let us look briefly at the Greek concept of *kosmos*.

The etymological roots of the Greek word, *kosmos*, lead back to the concept of imposing order, so that it meant the ordered universe. Within this metaphoric framework, the notion that all bodies, unconstrained, fall to their natural positions required the further assumption of a fixed frame of reference to which absolute positions could be assigned. A universe of variable positions does not constitute a comprehensible order. The notion of dynamic order comes historically much later than a static one, just as a child must learn the conservation of quantity before he or she can advance to concepts based on variable quantities. Dynamic orders are ordinarily conceived as successive static orders.

Having come to see the universe as *kosmos*, ordered, the Greeks had subsequently to define that order, and they bequeathed to Western civilization the continuation of that task. Over the centuries, several solutions have been offered, the most prevalent of which have included the spherical model, the microcosm, and the hierarchy, the latter best known as the Great Chain of Being. These all have in common that they are static structures, subsumable under the metaphor of Pattern, which designates any disposition of elements discernible as a structural whole or gestalt. Usually the metaphor is deployed in terms of simple geometric motifs, such as circles, squares, triangles, and spheres. It differs from the Mechanism metaphor in that the emphasis is on form rather than function.

A pattern is a static or stable arrangement, so the root metaphor of Pattern, applied to the universe, dictated a believed immobility of the earth. This belief ruled out the possibility that the earth might revolve around the sun. Then, the peculiar proclivity of Western man toward symmetry placed even more stringent restraints on the deployment of the Pattern metaphor. Circles and spheres were chosen as the most perfect forms, with the result that celestial orbits were construed as circular. As Aristotle wrote, "[T]he perfect is naturally prior to the imperfect, and the circle is a perfect thing," so "circular motion is necessarily primary" and must be assigned to the fifth element, the substratum of the heavens.[10] Then, of course, "The sphere is among solid figures what the circle is among plane figures."[11] Ptolemy was more empirical in his approach to cosmography but nevertheless echoed Aristotle in part by observing that "since the movement of the heavenly bodies ought to be the least impeded and most facile, the circle among plane figures offers the easiest path of motion, and the sphere among solids; likewise . . . of different figures having equal perimeters those having the more angles are the greater, the circle is the greatest of plane figures and the sphere of solid figures, and the heavens are greater than any other body."[12] Ptolemaic astronomy, based on Aristotelian physics, embraced circular planetary orbits and placed the stars and planets in revolving crystal spheres. The great appeal of the circle and sphere was their infinite degree of symmetry. Circular orbits led astronomers down the path of epicycles. To account for observed planetary motions, circles were drawn on the perimeters of other circles until the whole scheme became unmanageable. Even Kepler wasted much of his life attempting to account for the observed celestial motions in terms of nested Platonic forms. I say that he wasted his time in this enterprise because he never achieved a workable model. The circular-orbit universe, on the other hand, successfully imposed coherence on human experience for nearly two millennia.

It is important to note, however, that the spherical model was an ideal form only roughly suggested by empirical observation. When observations of celestial movements contradicted this model, the spherical plan was not abandoned in favor of a less symmetrical one but was extended through epicycles. The Pattern metaphor was deployed under constraints of considerations for the simplest symmetry. This is characteristic of metaphor deployment in general. Logic is subordinated to adherence to the differentiae of the metaphorand.

Returning to the classical adherence to the root metaphor of Pattern, a further dimension of the situation should be delineated. Within a culture, metaphors act in concert, and the deployment of a metaphor depends partly on the breadth of its application. The more broadly it is found to apply, the more entrenched it becomes and the more people seek to apply it to further phenomena. Also, the more broadly it is applied, the more it becomes entangled with other metaphors. To attack a broadly extended and coupled metaphor, then, becomes tantamount to challenging an entire worldview. In fact, a worldview may be defined as a system of coordinated metaphors characteristically deployed.

Consider once more the classical worldview. The cosmos is an ordered universe. The smallest elements of matter are perfect spheres, while the universe as a whole is a macroscopic sphere, the dynamics of which proceeds along circular orbits. The motion of the celestial spheres produces a music that expresses the harmony of nature. This music is linked to the scale, which itself embodies simple mathematical ratios derived from the division of the string of a monochord. These ratios are further connected to a hierarchical order of geometric shapes, and it is possible to find numerical relations of quantitative similarity between many other objects of nature. Mathematics seems to substantiate the notion of cosmic order almost magically. Certain ratios, vaguely related back to the divisions of the scale and the music of the spheres, are extended to the visual arts to determine proportions in buildings, sculpture and probably painting, too. Finally, all things, animate and inanimate, are linked into a Great Chain of Being. Thus, the overarching Pattern metaphor reached into every corner of ancient Greek thought.

THE GREAT CHAIN OF BEING AND OTHER PATTERNS FOR THE UNIVERSE

It will be instructive to follow further the deployment of the Pattern metaphor in the concept of the Great Chain of Being. This concept emerged from a plexus of intellectual speculations predicated on the Pattern metaphor. Beginning again with the concept of the *kosmos*, universal order, the pre-Socratic philosophers posited various principles to account for what they conceived as the orderliness of nature. Anaximander, by far the most obscure on this point, attributed universal order to what he called the *apeiron*, the boundless, evidently going back to the mythic notion of creation out of chaos. Heraclitus fell back on *logos*, reason, as the ordering principle, and Anaxagoras chose *nous*, mind. All these assume a kind of anentropy, a rising of order out of disorder, implicitly embodying a kind of anthropic intent, which Plato articulated as the soul, identified as the primal mover, the initiator of action. Aristotle, as is well known, objected to his teacher's separation of form from substance, and so he made initiation of motion innate within things. Everything has *entelechy*, purpose, within its essence.[13]

When we look back at the early pictures of cosmic order, we find that the concept of pattern arises through the uneven processing of information. Irregularities drop out so that the resulting economy makes possible memory, on the one hand, and symbolic thought, on the other. The very act of concept formation necessitates abstraction, the leaving out of details. Without it, recognition and thought would be impossible. It can be reckoned that even lower animals must resort to this kind of processing, since they, too, clearly demonstrate the ability to recognize different instances of exemplars from a class. Feeding would otherwise be impossible. Thus, there must be some kind of mapping between certain characteristics of food sources, for example, and the responsorial mechanisms of all organisms. Such must be the most elemental basis for recognition, which with man takes on the added dimension of symbolization.

The physiological apparatus of perception coupled with the mechanisms of information processing and memory thus impose some sense of order on what is known. Symbolic thought then searches out metaphorands that can, so to speak, hold that order and give it a discursive structure—that is, provide it with symbolic parameters, the differentiae of the metaphorand. These parameters channel thinking along lines that can in turn be defined at least roughly in symbolic terms, internalized as idealized perceptual forms, or at least assume a coherent, usually continuous system of topological relations. Without a minimal topology, the notion, whatever it may be, would lack the structure necessary to give thought or action any specific direction. This is not to say that unconscious motivation and simple feeling do not give rise to action and thought. They plainly do. In fact, they are often the basis of inspiration in the creative process.[14]

Centrality of structure is a sine qua non then of perception and subsequently of symbolic thought, so that it is not surprising that it emerged early as a key issue in ancient speculative thought. In fact, the metaphorand for cosmic order is crucial, because all subsidiary notions must somehow fit within the compass of that metaphorand. Eastern and Western cultures offered dramatically different solutions, in the form of metaphor choice and deployment, but for the moment the Western worldview is the focus of concern. We may, therefore, return to the consideration of the Great Chain of Being as one of the main embodiments of the Western sense of universal order.

Concern for natural order, *kosmos*, abounded among the Greek philosophers. In the *Timaeus* Plato expounded a cosmology that projected a hierarchical order onto the universe, and his ontology mandated a similar epistemological ascent to the realm of the Idea. Knowledge for Plato begins with the empirical and works up to the abstract, especially mathematics, and thence to the ideal, which is synoptic. Aristotle looked not at the stars, but at plants and animals, wherein he thought he saw a chain of being:

> Nature proceeds little by little from things lifeless to animal life in such a way that it is impossible to determine the exact line of demarcation, nor on which side thereof an intermediate form should lie. Thus, next after lifeless things in the upward scale comes the plant, and of plants one will differ from another as to the amount of apparent vitality; and, in a word, the whole genus of plants, whilst it is devoid of life as compared with an animal, is endowed with life as compared with other corporeal entities. Indeed, as we just remarked, there is observed in plants a continuous scale of ascent towards the animal.[15]

This "scale of ascent" was echoed down through the ages. Cicero posited a gradual ascension "from the first rudimentary orders of being to the last and most perfect," which is God.[16] Hermes Trismegistus repeated essentially the same idea, and Plotinus took it to its extreme.

> It is again in the *Timaeus* that we must seek the source of . . . the "principle of plenitude": the idea that in passing from the eternal order to the temporal, from the ideal to the sensible, there must be realized a fullness of forms in which every possible form becomes actual. If creativity is essential to the very perfection of the supreme Being, existence cannot be begrudged any manner of things, whatever their grade of perfection. . . .
>
> It follows—and Plotinus draws the consequence in all its import—that the divine self-transcendence, or inexhaustible power of the One, must in its creative necessity reach the limits of the possible. There is a kind of chain of delegated productive powers: every hypostasis in this generative scale is involved in this productive necessity, and its creativity must proceed out of itself to the extreme limit of the possible.[17]

This principle of plenitude passed on a difficult heritage to the Middle Ages, but before turning to that as a lesson in the role of rationalization in metaphor conservation, let us complete this brief look at the metaphorization of cosmic order.

Scholars have traced the Great Chain of Being to several sources. Earliest is the golden cord or chain of Homer. Homer has Jove say: "Hang me a golden chain from heaven, and lay hold of it all of you, gods and goddesses together—tug as you will, you will not drag Jove the supreme counsellor from heaven to earth."[18]

Then Aristotle, in elaborating his argument about the unmoved mover, used the chain metaphor as he did also in the quotation previously cited on the organization of plants and animals. Joined into the Christian tradition, the image was further amalgamated with the ladder that appeared to Jacob in a dream. At Gen. 28:10–15, in a dream Jacob sees a ladder stretching down from heaven with angels descending and ascending upon it. The image is potent and has a long history in the myths of the Middle East and elsewhere. Heaven and earth are pictured as linked by a column or, more often, a tree, the World Tree, associated variously with the Tree of Life and the Tree of Knowledge.

Given the inherent ordering value implicit in the up/down orientation, the tangible link between heaven and earth, taking several forms in mythology, is the embodiment of the unavoidable topological relationship by which the two realms are mutually conceived. Assimilation of Jove's golden chain and Jacob's ladder to this cosmography, therefore, was not a whimsical borrowing of rhetorical figures. Rather, these figures had already been conjured by the poetic mind to concretize a universal conception. Dante set out the universal plan along hierarchical lines, a common medieval conceit, and Milton has his Adam say to the "winged Hierarch" of God:

> Well hast thou taught the way that might direct
> Our knowledge, and the scale of nature set
> From center to circumference, whereon
> In contemplation of created things
> By steps we may ascend to God.[19]

Addison spoke of the "little transitions and deviations from one species to another" merging to form "the chain of Beings."[20] In *Summer* James Thompson rhapsodized:

> The mighty Chain of Beings, lessening down
> From infinite Perfection to the brink
> Of dreary Nothing, desolate Abyss![21]

And likewise Pope in *An Essay on Man*:

> Vast chain of being, which from God began,
> Natures aethereal, human angel, man,
> Beast, bird, fish, insect! what no eye can see,
> No glass can reach! from Infinite to thee,
> From thee to Nothing! . . . [22]

Poets' use of the image of the Chain of Being testifies to both its rhetorical nature and its cultural pervasiveness. Certainly it was the inspiration behind biological taxonomy, from Aristotle through Adanson, Linnaeus, Lamarck, and Cuvier. Darwin, too, assumed the Chain of Being but, departing from the notion of species as fixed and immutable, placed it in the context of geological time, wherein it became subject to continuous evolution. In modern biological thought, species, like so many related concepts, has been reduced to little more than a vague and, like race, often misleading convention.

Neither do I mean to suggest that the image of the Chain of Being was merely a historical accident. Insofar as there is to be speculation about the nature of the universe—and it seems impossible to imagine a culture in which such speculation is totally absent—it will be predicated on some sense of cosmic order, which must be concretized in a metaphor. Whereas the metaphor may be partly accidental, nevertheless the degree of accident must be restricted by the fact that the differentiae of the metaphorand accord with the implicit sense of order. In most instances, the cultural repertoire will offer few potential choices of metaphorand that would be appropriate to the target and not be too obviously rhetorical. In a matriarchal society, necklace might have won out over chain to metaphorize universal order, but in a patriarchal one it would seem too rhetorical, poetic but not explanatory, since it is not so much the discrete separation of the beads as their decorativeness that seems the more primary differentiae. Also, in a chain it is the interlockingness of the links that gives it, as a metaphorand, the requisite structural integrity to represent the interpenetration or interdependence of the elements of nature that is usually intuited.

However that may be, the metaphors of hierarchy and Chain of Being continue to exercise an integrative effect on modern sensibilities. The aesthetic of theoretical physics lies squarely on this embodied sense of order. Hunting for the ultimate particle, physicists are guided by a faith in the hierarchical bias of nature. In effect, it is the paradigm of the family of man, with the patriarchal head, that is being unconsciously projected onto nature at large. And again it must be emphasized that this is an article of faith. There is as much evidence now for the rules underlying nature being nonlinear and chaotic as for their being linear and symmetric. In fact, as already noted, the real substance of nature seems indeed to be chaotic, with the principles of symmetry being more Platonic ideals with limited applicability.[23]

THE EASTERN VIEW OF THE COSMOS: TAOISM

We have examined the typical Western view of cosmic order. That this advocacy of symmetry and predictable order is a culturally bound phenomenon can be seen in contrast with the Eastern view. The Eastern perspective more or less favors asymmetry. Rather than requiring a stable order on which to rely, there are Eastern traditions that find solace in lack of neatly definable structure and of predictability. Consider Taoism as an example. Here the highest principle is the Tao, the ideograph for which originally stands for a path or way. *Tzu-jan*, or being such in itself, is the essence of the Tao. Both the *Tao Tê Ch'ing* and the *Chuang Tzu* agree that this *tzu-jan* evolves through *wu-wei* or nonaction. What this means is spontaneity, freedom from motive, desire, or external force. Kuo Hsiang (d. 312 A.D.) in his commentary on the *Chuang Tzu* ruminated about this:

> What came into existence before there were things? If I say yin and yang came first, then since yin and yang are themselves entities, what came before them? Suppose I say nature came first. But nature is only things being themselves. Suppose I say perfect Tao came first. But perfect Tao is perfect nonbeing. Since it is nonbeing, how can it come before anything else? Then what came before it? There must be another thing, and so on ad infinitum. We must understand that things are what they are spontaneously and not caused by something else.[24]

Or again, as early Taoists argued, "To say that a thing comes from Tao is merely to say that it comes from nowhere or from nothing. In truth, it comes from itself."[25] In the framework of Western thought, this concept seems contradictory, for it reduces to action without a cause or action entirely self-caused. With the current revolution in nonlinear physics, there is now widely recognized a class of functions that, while deterministic, are nonetheless unpredictable; and in terms of these, *wu-wei* becomes more understandable in intellectual terms. Rather than being metaphorized in any single metaphorand, the Tao is likened to any natural process, such as a flowing river or a growing tree, occurring without human intervention and with sufficient irregularity to baffle any complete human understanding. As Lao Tzu put it:

> In this world,
> Compare those of the Way
> To torrents that flow
> Into river and sea.[26]

THE EASTERN VIEW OF THE COSMOS: HINDUISM AND BUDDHISM

In Vedanta (especially advaita-vedanta according to Shankara) everything is *maya*, illusion, arising out of *brahman* or *atman*, the ineffable One. Essentially, this is a deployment of the One/Many metaphor, whereby the One, which is simply put beyond human knowing so that it cannot be characterized in any way, becomes the Many of appearance through deception. The numerology behind the One/Many metaphor is especially pertinent here. Any number larger than one is simply a reiteration of one, one in multiple reflections, as it were, as 3 is simply 1 + 1 + 1. Looked at this way—i.e., in its metaphorical foundation—just as there is nothing to understand in 3 that is not contained in 1, so there is nothing in appearance that is not in the *brahman*.

> The Way begot one,
> And the one, two;
> Then the two begot three
> And three, all else.[27]

Further, since the One is all, it cannot be related to anything else; and since it has no parts, no internal structure, there is nothing in itself to understand. Thus, it is equated with *sunyata*, nothingness.

> The Way is a void,
> Used but never filled:
> An abyss it is,
> Like an ancestor
> From which all things come.[28]

The concept of *sunyata* is ancient and is found even in the *Rig Veda:* " Neither not-being nor being was there at that time [i.e., in the beginning]; there was no air-filled space nor was there the sky which is beyond it."[29] As glossed in the *Lalitavistara*, a biography of Buddha dating from around the beginning of the Christian era, this idea becomes:

> All things conditioned are conditioned by ignorance,
> And on final analysis they do not exist,
> For they and the conditioning ignorance alike are Emptiness
> In their essential nature, without power of action. . . .[30]

The Chinese took up this same train of thought: "Before heaven and earth had taken form all was vague and amorphous. Therefore it was called the Great Beginning. The Great Beginning produced emptiness and the emptiness produced the universe."[31]

Such ruminations were inspired more by Vedanta and Taoism than by Buddhism. Buddha never addressed the origins of *samsara*, the cycle of existence, presumably because he felt it had no substantial bearing on liberation. He was not a theoretician. Rather, like Confucius, he was more interested in practical matters. However, nirvana, although it literally means extinction, referring originally to the extinction of a flame (metaphorand for the soul), really signifies a unification with the One, taken also as nothingness. When a flame is extinguished, its heat does not vanish in the sense of ceasing to exist; rather it becomes one with the heat of the cosmos.

Prior to nirvana, according to Mahayana Buddhism, man knows nothing but illusion:

> The philosophers of the Mahayana liken the universe to a magical display, a mirage, a flash of lightning, or the ripples of waves on the sea. The sea itself, the reality beyond and within the rippling forms, cannot be measured in terms of the ripples. Comparably, the objects in the world are of one reality and in reality therefore one; but this reality is beyond description in terms of phenomenology. This one reality, in its ontological aspect, can be termed only *bhuta-tathata*, "the suchness of beings, the essence of existence."[32]

A more mundane analogy may bring this out more clearly. Suppose you have a battalion of lead soldiers, each different from the others. Although the shapes vary, each soldier is in the final analysis lead. Now, if your universe comprised nothing beyond this battalion, no soldier could be understood in a fundamental, ontological sense other than in terms of lead. At this level, to say that any soldier is lead would be to say all. Lead would be the ultimate substratum. To relate it back to forms it could take would be trivial and would reveal nothing more about lead other than it is, since existence subsumes having form. Thus:

> According to the basic argument of this metaphysical philosophy . . . every dharma [phenomenal manifestation] is *pratitya-samutpanna*, "dependent on others." It cannot be explained by reference either to itself or to something else, or by bringing the two sets of references into a relationship. Every system of notions terminates in inconsistencies and is therefore simply void. And yet, to assert that all is "non-existent" (*abhava*) would not be proper either; for that would only be another act of dialectical reasoning, whereas true wisdom is neither an affirmation nor a negation.[33]

It is perhaps misleading, then, to speak of an Eastern sense of cosmic order, since, as Nakamura observes, "[t]here is a tendency among the Indians, divested in general of the concept of a perceptible objective order, not to differentiate too sharply between the actual and the ideal"[34] and "[s]ince the Japanese people for the most part tend to make little of objects unless they are related to familiar human relations, they do not study things enough in their objective or impersonal relations."[35] Consequently, there is no correlative to *kosmos* in their culture. Their sense of order shifts instead to the conduct of daily life, embodied in the Indian concept of *dharma* and the Confucian notion of *li*, both referring to what is appropriate to the social circumstances according to tradition. In other words, the order by which they orient themselves is social rather than physical. The physical universe is assumed to be what we now, in mathematical terms, would call fractal or chaotic. Suzuki catches the spirit of this, when he says, relative to the concept of *sunyata*:

> To the Western mind, "continuum" may be better than *sunyata*, although it is likely to be misunderstood as "objectively" existing and apprehensible by *vijnana* [private mentation]. In the "continuum" immediately given, however, there is no differentiation of subject and object, of the seer and the seen.[36]

Conceived this way, the physical *Umwelt* is merely an unpredictably changing, though by and large stable, background against which human action can take place. It makes no difference whether it is viewed as nothingness or suchness, or thusness (*tathata*), the fullness of being, since, like the lead in the soldier analogy, it is the substratum, which cannot further be reduced and understood in terms of anything more fundamental.

> Thusness *[tathata]* in its static sense is spaceless, timeless, undifferentiated, without beginning or end, formless, and colorless, because Thusness itself without its manifestations cannot be sensed or described. Thusness in its dynamic sense can assume any form.[37]

What is important to understand in all this is that the deployment of the One/Many metaphor behind Taoism, Vedanta, and Buddhism does not hide from the Western mind any inscrutable idea. The deployment concretizes a feeling toward existence for the Easterner every bit as clearly as the hierarchy and Chain of Being deployments of the Pattern and First Position metaphors do for the Westerner. What makes them difficult for the Westerner to grasp is that she does not share the feeling that the One/Many deployment embodies. She can usually find no correlation in her culturally conditioned experience. In this sense, to understand the Eastern position fully, empathetically, so that it belongs to your own experience, you must go through the time-consuming process of acquiring enough of the other culture to be able experientially to participate in its worldview.

Even within the Eastern cultures, a deep understanding of what lies behind the One/Many deployment I have sketched usually requires years, because it is a viewpoint peculiarly at odds with that which is habitually acquired in the pursuit of normal daily life in any culture. Still, it is closer to the native Easterner, because he or she is surrounded by symbolic manifestations of it in religious texts, literature and the arts.

RATIONALIZATION IS OFTEN USED TO CONSERVE AN IMPORTANT METAPHOR

Consistency plays a vital role in the deployment of metaphors within a culture. We have concentrated here on the ways in which the universe is construed, because it is one of those overarching concepts with which the metaphors of lesser compass must be consonant to ensure cultural cohesiveness. This is in line with Festinger's theory of cognitive dissonance, according to which "in the presence of a dissonance, one will be able to observe the *attempts* to reduce it. If attempts to reduce dissonance fail, one should be able to observe the symptoms of psychological discomfort."[38] There are ongoing debates about details of the theory, but the core idea seems almost self-evident. Certainly dissonant ideas are often entertained with impunity, but only when they are not consciously juxtaposed and forced into scrutiny. In a culture, or even a subculture, when such scrutiny occurs, rationalization will be marshaled to conserve the status quo. We need only backtrack to the Neoplatonic concept of plenitude to study a case in point.

RATIONALIZATION IN THE CONSERVATION OF DOMINANT METAPHORS: A CASE

Curiously this principle of plenitude, passed from the Neoplatonists to early Christianity, bore thorny theological consequences. In a nutshell, medieval theologians had to take away from God any imperative to create, since that would limit his freedom. Saint Thomas Aquinas saved the Lord from such a Neoplatonic fate by stipulating that he need create only that which is consistent with his perfection. The doctrine of consistency also ruled out the divine creation of anything evil. Behind it clearly was the motive to save a preconceived notion—viz., that of the Divinity as the personification of perfection—a modus operandi frequently used in the deployment of metaphors. What must be saved is usually a crucial belief or a more elusive nexus of metaphors through which the current worldview is construed.

In common parlance, this may go under the heading of saving face, protecting vested interests, or even, at the institutional level, covering up mistakes. That facts may be twisted for such purposes is nothing new. It is instructive, nevertheless, to view this from the angle of metaphor deployment. A metaphorand, like the chain or ladder, may be chosen to explain a phenomenon or set of phenomena, but then part of the implication of the metaphor is subverted without calling into question its explicative appropriateness, a case of eating the cake and having it, too.

Let's examine this ploy more closely. The doctrine of the plenitude of forms was entertained well into the last century, but one obvious conclusion was never drawn: that, if the universe is full of forms so that every class shades imperceptibly into adjacent classes, then the ensemble of all things comprises a seamless whole. We have not far to look to discover why this conclusion was not made. First of all, the notion of a hierarchical order clearly embodied a gamut of preconceived values. It is based upon the metaphor of Pattern coupled with that of First Position. The First Position metaphor places the highest value at the apex of the hierarchy, in keeping with the topological up/down pair (up designating the positive or greater and down, the negative or lesser value). The hierarchy *is* the pattern. A pure doctrine of the oneness of being within the framework of other Occidental beliefs and practices would have been more difficult to defend than the Chain of Being; that is, the deployment of the metaphor of One would require more doctoring than the Pattern/Chain of Being complex.

Second, the chain, or ladder, metaphorand with its arrangement of discrete linkages or steps maintained the intervalic notion in the face of the implied continuity of the plenitude of forms. Indeed, form itself suggests discrete entities, which also dovetails with the common observation that the *Umwelt* is made up of things. On the observational level, the oneness of everything is counterintuitive; but this does not make it untenable. Given the different climate of the East, it is often the oneness of things that is assumed, whereas the separate existence of apparent objects is denied or relegated to the status of an illusion. Also, the doctrine of the oneness of being is now receiving serious attention among theoretical physicists in the West on account of Bell's Theorem, discussed later on.

CONCLUSION

Out of this disquisition on the metaphorization of the sense of universal order, it becomes plain that different cultures begin from different perceptual and conceptual vantage points. The reality before them is not the same. Where epistemologically the social construction of reality begins is a deeper question than any being posed here. I would venture to say only that it is a nonlinear process involving the full context of the culture: climate, geography, genetics, past history, social organization, and what have you. If there are effable laws to it, we are a long way from being able even to adumbrate them.

Nevertheless, in beginning with metaphorand choice and following metaphor deployment, a deep understanding of intellectual history can be achieved. Further enhancement of this understanding comes from insight into the dynamics of topological schemata in discursive thought, for therein is much of the deployment of metaphors carried out. It is, therefore, to that subject that I turn in the next chapter.

3

Action Schemes and
Topological Transformations

ACTION SCHEMES, TOPOLOGICAL
TRANSFORMATIONS, AND GESTURES

It is unquestionably true that humans have a "need for establishing our place in the world by means of comparisons, in order to arrive at a tolerable degree of certainty and stability."[1] That is the basis of our reliance on metaphors, but metaphors alone do not constitute thought. We must do something with them. One thing we do is to deploy them, to extend the characteristics of the metaphor to ever increasing varieties of phenomena. As previously noted, we do this through the mediation of selected prototypes. However, since historical prototypes are usually impossible to reconstruct, we are left to deal with the points of similarity, the salient features mapped to the target domain. Once having established analogies, having construed the unknown in terms of the known, we still have to do something with these analogies to produce logical discourse. That something is to place metaphorized notions into concrete contexts of experience and to move and manipulate these notions in a mental or fictive topological space. We do this when we prioritize values in a hierarchy ("I like Grieg better than Telemann, and Brahms better than Grieg"), arrange a story linearly, or compare like things as if they were mutual reflections.

All metaphorizing leads back to firsthand human experience. Perceptions and actions of the body are the framework of human understanding. This is borne out by our use of gesture to accompany speech. Recent research into the role of gesture is relevant here because it demonstrates concretely that action schemata and topological transformations do enter into thought processes. According to David McNeil, "[s]peech and gesture are elements of a single integrated process of utterance formation in which there is a synthesis of opposite modes of thought—global-synthetic and instantaneous imagery with linear-segmented temporally extended verbalization."[2] Gesture is largely iconic or mimetic, often representing a schema of topological relations underpinning the speaker's discourse.

> The hand can represent a character's hand, the character as a whole, a ball, a streetcar, or anything else; the space likewise can be freely designated—a table top, a street, the side of a building, midair. In other words, the gesture is capable of expressing the full range of meanings that arise from the speaker.

Gestures often frame abstract idea by the "forming of homologies between imagery and abstract concepts."[3]

McNeil finds that the verbalization-cum-gesture process begins from what he calls a growth point, "the earliest form of the utterance in deep time, and the opening up of a micro-genetic process that yields the surface utterance as the final stage."[4] Moving from a growth point in "deep time" to a "surface utterance" is reminiscent of transformation from deep to surface structure suggested in generative grammar. McNeil, in his research, established that definite criteria exist by which the growth point can be pinpointed in an utterance or discourse: "[T]he growth point is seen in the gesture stroke [the phase of movement following the raising of the hand(s) from quiescence], together with the linguistic segment with which it co-occurs, plus a word that follows this segment if this word preserves semantic and pragmatic synchrony."[5] Earlier on, he stated that "[p]ragmatic synchrony implies that speakers are limited to one pragmatic reference at a time," meaning that a gesture is unireferential.[6]

I would suggest that immanent in the growth point is a latent content being projected through a topological schema, which gives rise to the homological imagery of which McNeil speaks. The latent content is, so to speak, the pivotal intent from which the final utterance is generated. Varying widely as utterances do, it is impossible to reduce the notion of *latent content* to any simple formula. It may be a central image from a remembered event about to be recounted; an abstract equivalence relation central to a law to be expounded; an itch from an insect bite giving rise to complaint. I am not about to attempt any complete explanation of how the latent content gets translated into grammatical utterances. Suffice it to say, I believe that a central ingredient in the process is the topological schema, which dictates choices of spatial (or, more broadly, prepositional) and motional words that carry forward what McNeil calls the *communicative dynamism* of the utterance. As we are about to see, spatial and motional terms are the key words in any discursive discourse, so this point is of more than passing interest.

In discursive thought, then, there must be a structure derived from percepts and bodily actions that makes experience assimilable. From the way in which gesture combines with speech and from various accounts of the creative process,[7] it may reasonably be postulated that a problem or the germ of a creative act consists initially of a topological schema and a mnemonic image or feeling state (especially in the fields of dance and music). The feeling state in turn has a configuration, depending upon how it is perceived, and may itself be concomitant with some sort of imagery. It may also evolve during the course of creation or simple thought. Thus, there is a beginning dynamics of schemata with fragmentary imagery and background tone, feeling, or body state.[8]

Human thought, like overt behavior, is sequential. There are no spatiotemporal discontinuities in human actions. Experiential discontinuities—e.g., coma, hallucination, and amnesia—are problematic and foil rather than support human understanding. This is fundamentally what makes topological connectedness interesting and what makes mathematicians attempt to reduce all forms of discontinuity to some kind of order which will reintroduce connectedness at a metalevel.

Connectedness in thought or discourse arises as the mind moves from one percept or idea to another. This movement must mimic the possible. That is, models of ideas, or symbolic counters simply standing in for ideas, must undergo only sequences of topological transformations that could be carried out on physical counterparts. If this is not the case, then any violation of continuity will signal a fallacy or breach of reason. Discursive thought takes place in a kind of symbolic or fictive topological space.

Verbs of motion are crucial to discourse. They often supply the scheme of action for an argument. Coupled with prepositions, which designate topological relations, they define the topological space of discourse, as well as the discursive actions within that space. What must be noted here is that we cannot trace the historical development of this mental topology, for it is full-blown by the time that written literature begins. I can only surmise that it arose through assimilation of the intricate actions of toolmaking and the subsequent elaborate motions underlying rudimentary social behaviors of the Paleolithic and Neolithic periods.

Problem-solving strategies of animals make it easy to believe that they, too, indulge in topological manipulation of mental data, but such manipulation is probably not symbolic, and certainly not predominantly so. That bees navigate by the sun indicates simple neural substrates for topological schemata; and these substrates can be traced upward through the animal kingdom through creatures of increasingly complex anatomies. We are not dealing with anything peculiarly human. What is undoubtedly human about the whole thing is the proclivity to isolate elements of the topology, to endow them with a reified existence, and to dwell upon them as such. At the same time, we are largely unconscious of having abstracted them from a holistic fabric of experience. Because experience and understanding are always within the moment, so to speak, we are always dealing with present or remembered fragments. We forget the whole from which they are torn, for the whole is inevitably larger than the compass of any instance of awareness.

Another peculiarly human element in discursive topology is the greater variety of internalized action schemes that reflect the broader spectrum of human movements, especially those involving hand-eye coordination. This would lead to

a richness beyond the experience of other animals and would also further generalize the basic topological notions. A glance through the dictionary at the multitude
of usages for any of the common prepositions will bear out this point. Prepositions
are the most disjunctive words in any language; and this bears witness to the difficulties of reducing the world to terms of human experience. However, it is probably this very disjunctiveness which is crucial for the flexibility of human thought.
Ironically, total semantic precision would undoubtedly signal intellectual stasis.

PREPOSITIONS ENCAPSULATE TOPOLOGICAL RELATIONS

Topological relations such as those I have described often find their shadowy
niche in those most troublesome of all part of speech, the prepositions. Here we are
wont to find relationships so tenuous that words fail us when we try to define them.
What does the "of" mean in "Of taste there is no disputing," or "What do you
think of that?"? If we replace the "of" with "in regard to," we have the same as "in
relation to," which is so generic that only dipping back into experience makes the
words more meaningful. In the same light, consider the prepositions in the following expressions: *on time, at once, to the maximum, king of hearts.*

Early in the formation of languages, directions and positions, which are closely
allied with prepositions, acquired connotations based on body movements, postures and activities in relation to phenomena in the natural environment. Up and
down, for example, are conceptual nexuses where many common elements of experience cross. Up is the sky, the sun and moon and stars, and upward is the gesture of supplication to the sky forces, and the natural stretching of the body in a fit
of joy. Plants and trees usually bear their fruit up at the top, and at the top of the
body is the head with the major senses and the organs of speech. When we wake,
we rise up, and up in the sky birds fly free. So we have *up* infused with connotations
of a positive sort that can be made more explicit only by citing more and more
examples. And these topological schemata chain together: the tree of knowledge
grows upward into the sky, and rising upward is the pole of the universe that holds
up the sky. And the spirit as breath rises up out of the mouth of the dying man. And
the Olympian gods dwell up on Mt. Olympus.

On the other hand, down is the ground, and down in the ground is darkness
and cold. When we feel sad, we droop downward, and when plants and trees die,
they wilt down. At the bottom of the trunk are the organs of excretion. We lie down
to sleep and to die, and we are buried down in the earth. So *down* carries negative
connotations. This topological schema conditions such concepts as Hell being down
in the bowels of the earth and villains having a low voice and dressing in dark
colors. Low pitch and dark colors are isomorphic to spatial lowness. When our
state worsens, we say that it falls; hence, the fallen angel and fallen women. When
things are bad, we are down, we hit the bottom, etc. If we were to follow the connotations of lateral motion, spinning, bowing, kicking, relaxing, standing, lying,

etc., we would find these, too, conditioning concepts and imagery, with the meaning always broad and always tracing back to the body and to the emotions that are attendant upon making those movements. Ultimately we can see things only from our human vantage point.

As we have seen from the up-down dichotomy, these primitive topological schemata have continued into our thinking today, where they are prominent in our figures of speech. Feeling *up* is feeling good, whereas feeling *down* is feeling sad. George Lakoff and Mark Johnson, without regard to the historical aspect of concern here, have analyzed the dynamics of such metaphors in their brilliant work, *Metaphors We Live By.* Those interested in further examples could do no better than to refer to that excellent book.

I wish to underscore that these topological relations have their historical as well as their psychological roots in elemental experiences, such as body movements and activities, and repetitive natural phenomena, such as day and night, seasons, rainfall, and the plethora of animal and plant life. And they act as frameworks in which to orient more specific overt and covert behavior.

To see this orienting influence, consider religious monuments. Temples, cathedrals, and altars are all upward-reaching, with the spire atop Gothic cathedrals being perhaps the pinnacle of such upward orientation. In each case, the response might be to some specific portion of the *up* complex, as the orientation of religious monuments relates to the sky as heaven, a metaphor linking with primitive reactions to the celestial bodies and meteorological phenomena.

We have added to the simple rules of association the orientative influence of topological schemata, which continue as powerful forces in modern thinking. We have *up* and *down* quarks. We graph trends upward and downward. We read about *upbeat* music in *Downbeat* magazine.

Metaphorical Thought Compared to Formal Logic

If these topological expressions and the images to which metaphors give rise seem far-fetched, fanciful and fruitless, it is because we have been nurtured on classical logic and rhetoric. We have lost touch with the fact that metaphorizing, like mythopoeia, does not have as its goal logical explanation; instead it lends emotional coherence to reality by placing its elements into a framework the appeal of which is that it taps the roots of common experience. It makes the abstract and elusive familiar and concrete. Also, as opposed to formal logical analysis, metaphorizing complicates, rather than simplifies, human experience. It complicates, rather than simplifies, but complicates in the sense that it adds flesh to the bones of reality.

It is perhaps a bit misleading to set up an opposition between classical logic and metaphorizing, for logic developed in ancient Greece through analyses of the symbolic-metaphorizing processes in the pleading of legal causes and in the East through hermeneutics. Generically described, the underlying metaphors of deductive logic center on nested containers (*A* is a *B* [i.e., in *B*]; *B* is a *C* [in *C*]; therefore, *A* is [in] a *C*) and linked circles (some *A*'s are *B*'s), both made explicit in Venn diagrams. As Johnson has pointed out, this is based on the containment schema and so has its roots in body experience.[9] The fallacies are cataloged from centuries of debate, and most embody certain proclivities of prelogical thinking (e.g., *argumentum ad hominem*, from associating rather monistically the doer and the deed). At any rate, thinking is rarely a matter of formal logic. It is infused with disjunctive-conjunctive confusions,[10] prototype manipulation, image fragments, and shards of prelogical transformations.

My purpose in contrasting metaphorizing and formal logic is simply to allow each to shed light upon the other and to underline how large a role metaphorizing plays in our lives compared to the small part played by reason. Perhaps we should spend less time deploring this and more time attempting to understand this balance as a fact of evolution. Metaphorizing is a much more primitive mode of human thought than reasoning, which is a relative newcomer to the arena of civilization. Hence, we would expect the older and more pervasive mode to remain more ubiquitous because it is responsive to a broader spectrum of experience than the more specialized and therefore narrower mode of reasoning. Also, without topological schemata and metaphors, reason would have little upon which to operate. In fact, reason, far from being an independent faculty, is little more than a specialization within metaphoric and topological mentation. What counts as *reasoning* is more intuitive than purely logical, taking place as it does not syllogistically but by metaphoric and topological processes outside conscious attention.

THE ROLE OF TOPOLOGICAL TRANSFORMATIONS
IN DISCURSIVE THOUGHT

Actual discursive thought begins when the elements of the argument are placed explicitly or implicitly into geometric configurations, spatially displaced and/or topologically transformed. These spatial operations may be implicit in that they are embedded, as it were, etymologically in the terminology. When we say that something *develops*, for example, we are implying etymologically that it unwraps or unfurls like a flower. This is an implicit topological transformation. On the other hand, when we say that it unfurls, we are making the transformation explicit. Often the original transformative operation that went into the formation of a word becomes lost in semantic shifts over time and ceases to be represented for modern users of the word. Still, when the mind is forced explicitly to deal with these words and the concepts for which they stand, it would seem that some analogous operation must be conjured. This is borne out by the research of McNeil previously cited, which showed how gesture gives an iconic representation of the topological transformations concomitant with verbalized thought. Methods other than those applied here would be required empirically to determine the exact nature of these topological transformation. In the present study, historical origins are the main concern. It is important, however, to keep in mind that historical roots do not necessarily imply present continuity.

THE CONCEPT OF SCHEMA

The internal manipulation of ideas corresponds perfectly with Piaget's explanation of the genesis of thinking in the child through the internalization of action schemes (i.e., habitual action routines) and their geometric results, except that these schemes become hidden under the encrustation of changing denotations and connotations. In other words, as prototypical action schemes are extended to ever wider and more diversified applications, their pristine geometry becomes clouded, sometimes beyond recognition.[11] Nevertheless, the underlying geometry continues to provide the ultimate substratum of meaning. I take this to be the meaning of Johnson's caveats about image schemata:

> [I]n order for us to have meaningful, connected experiences that we can comprehend and reason about, there must be pattern and order to our actions, perceptions, and conceptions. *A schema is a recurrent pattern, shape, and regularity in, or of, these ongoing ordering activities.* These patterns emerge as meaningful structures for us chiefly at the level of our bodily movements through space, our manipulation of objects, and our perceptual interactions.[12]

He relates his notion of schema genealogically to that of Kant,[13] for whom a schema had the meaning of the capacity to construct images or models[14] as well as "a figure or outline in imagination that can be 'filled in' by particular images or percepts."[15] He adopts this latter definition as being closest to his own. Although he states that in Plato "imagination is our way of grasping objects through their images, shadows, and reflections," he adds that knowledge, "in this tradition, would involve grasping the unchangeable essence of a thing, and it would seem that images don't supply such essential knowledge."[16] If phenomenal images are intended, this is true. Johnson is, I believe, thrown off the track by what he calls the Divided Line metaphor used by Plato in book 6 of the *Republic* (509C). The famous analogy of the cave in book 10 conveys more clearly the metaphor behind Platonic Ideal Form *(eidos)*. This will be discussed more fully in chapter 4; the salient features of the *eidos* are those of visual shape. Etymologically, the root is *idein*, to see, whence the Greek word for concept, *idea*, that which can clearly be seen. Platonic *eidos* is the original prototype of schema.

It seems odd that Johnson makes no mention of earlier discussions of schema in the psychological literature. Most notable is his exclusion of Piaget. Even before Piaget, however, Bartlett suggested the schema as an active, organized setting within which new experiences are recognized and interpreted in terms of selected features of previous ones.[17] The term had been introduced in its modern meaning by Head to refer to "postural appreciation" or "dispositional system" of standards "against which all subsequent changes in posture are measured before they appear in consciousness."[18]

It may be felt that Johnson's concept of scheme differs from Piaget's in that the former stressed the plasticity of schemata, whereas the latter assumed that they are innate and somewhat fixed. This would be erroneous. Piaget nowhere gives a precise and complete definition of schema. His remarks are scattered throughout his writings. Flavell, his foremost expositor, defines it as "a cognitive structure which has reference to a class of similar action sequences, these sequences of necessity being strong, bounded totalities in which the constituent behavioral elements are tightly interrelated."[19] Here, "cognitive structure" matches "recurrent pattern, shape, and regularity," while "a class of similar action sequences" parallels "ongoing ordering activities" in Johnson's definition. The general impression that schemata for Piaget are rather fixed and innate stems from the greater discussion he provided for their development out of reflexes in the sensory-motor stage of infancy. In fact, says Flavell, a schema "is a more or less fluid form or plastic organization to which actions and objects are assimilated during cognitive functioning." That they accommodate to things, especially in the operational stage of development, "attests to their dynamic, supple quality."[20]

It might be worthwhile to mention that the concept of schema supported by Piaget and Johnson bears a striking resemblance to the notion of a *primitive* in David Marr's analysis of object construction and recognition in visual processing.[21] Primitives are "place tokens" or surface characteristics used to construct what Marr calls a "primal sketch," a kind of schematic by which a person makes the first step toward recognizing what he or she sees. They comprise edge or boundary segments or points of discontinuity in their orientation, bars or their terminations, and blobs. In the visual cortex, this primal sketch is fleshed out with finer detail, but the primal sketch is the skeleton upon which the recognition process begins. What makes this germane is that, if Marr's analysis is correct, it is a similar instance in which schematic structures based on embodied propensities (viz., innate dispositions of neuron complexes in the visual cortex) explain the dynamics of mental interpretation.

That topological schemes are literally operative in thought processes is indicated by research showing that "the process of mental rotation is an analog one in that intermediate states in the process have a one-to-one correspondence with intermediate stages in the external rotation of an object" and "that the internal representation upon which the rotation operates is holistic in that the representation preserves the essential spatial structure of its corresponding external referent."[22]

BODY IMAGE IS CENTRAL TO TOPOLOGICAL TRANSFORMATIONS AND TO THOUGHT

Rosenfield, analyzing cases of brain-damaged patients with body-image disturbances, finds that "all spoken language, like all mental acts, has self-reference and that the brain mechanisms creating self-reference may, when altered, alter our use of language, just as they may alter our knowledge of our bodies or objects in our surroundings. This is not a mere speculative argument: a careful examination of the neurological evidence makes it . . . unavoidable."[23] In speaking of brain-damaged patients who lose the sense that one or more of their limbs does not belong to them, he says:

> The peculiarity of this paradox is expressed in the patient's sense that the visual space, the place, that the leg occupies has disappeared. This partial loss of the sense of the leg's space . . . shows the centrality of self-reference: we sense space by its relation to something else, and essentially to our bodies. Indeed, the disappearance of the place—the part of space—the leg occupies for the brain-damaged patient suggests that the brain creates our sense of space by reference to the body-image; the sense of self that gives the leg meaning creates meaning for the space it occupies as well.[24]

Rosenfield believes that "consciousness arises from the . . . dynamic interrelations of the past, the present, and the body image."[25] What makes an experience personal, what identifies it as mine, is the constant reference to the proprioception of the body, what Rosenfield calls self-reference; and "[s]ince the frame of reference (the body image) is dynamic, understanding, too, is dynamic."[26] He shows that memory is constructed around the body image and various amnesias are often found associated with body-image distortions. Thus, according to his reckoning, meaning centers around the body image. There is a significant accord between this and the account of hypothesizing given by evolutionary epistemologists:

> The relationship between the unfathomable self and the unfathomable theories which it has somehow produced can . . . hardly be one of expression of the one by the other. Such an account fails to take account either of the nature of the theory, or of the constantly changing flamelike quality of the individual, as expressed in his active cybernetic relationship with his cultural world, including his own cultural products, and the creative, unpredictable character that is intrinsic to that relationship. This relationship is one of give and take between the individual and the work; it depend upon "feedback" amplified by self-criticism.[27]

Accommodation for Rosenfield involves memory, perception, and the anchoring body image, and for the evolutionary epistemologists, it is a dialectic between the "unfathomable self," tantamount to "the sense of self that gives the leg meaning" and "creates meaning for the space it occupies as well," and the ongoing stream of memory and perception that defines objective reality. At any event, the self, which both I and Rosenfield take to be framed by the body image, is central. In imposing schemas on complexes of experience, there is a common framework from which all abstraction must proceed. It may be referred to the human body as a central axis from which the possibilities of posture and action radiate, so to speak. Each posture or motion carries connotations derived from the habitual feelings or experiences most usually associated with it.[28]

AN IMPORTANT DERIVATIVE OF BODY ACTION: NEGATION

Negation begins from simple body actions. It is the verbal equivalent of a gesture of disengagement or opposition used in metaphor deployment to engender a battery of different concepts. Negation is a grammatical construction. Its import originates from a variety of disparate behavioral situations, and it is probably as old as language itself. Most discussions of negation, both ancient and modern, devolve to tautology, revolving around a definition that states it as a denial of an affirmation—whereas the word, *denial*, is nothing more than a negating. The problem is that disengagement and opposition yield a plethora of semantic possibilities.

Our purpose does not include a full elucidation of the problem, but only sufficient clarification so that we can understand the unique role of negation in metaphor deployment. Note that at the animal level, the behavioral complex giving rise to negation includes a measure of avoidance reaction, or an interventional opposition. Negative response to any behavioral performance may run from indifferent withdrawal to preventative intervention, but it is at the more emotive extreme that it has engendered the most articulate and semantically pregnant signification.

Tentatively, I suggest the hypothesis that the action scheme of negating behavior—turning away—has supplied the original core of the meaning of negation. *Non-*, as a negative prefix, means not simply *other than* but conceptually more often *the opposite of.* What I mean is that, when the negative prefix is used to form a new concept, it carries the strong connotation of opposition latent in the behavioral roots of negation. Note that *opposition* is etymologically a placing or standing against. Direction is implicit, and the negative is thus conceived as the result of a 180° rotation away from that which is being negated (going back to the gesture of turning away). This gives us the affirmative-negative pairs: left-right, up-down, rightside up—upside down, normal-inverted, etc. These can be generalized: if A is the affirmative state and B, its negative, then an application of the topological transformation, A-into-B, twice in succession to A (or B) will bring us back to A (or B) once more.

Negation is further generalized to include removal. Though it implies action, it is not strictly topological. The negative of light (or, as we would more usually say, its opposite) is darkness, i.e., that which follows upon the removal of light. Likewise, remove intelligence and you obtain its opposite, stupidity. Philosophical arguments about opposites occur when we try to determine what constitutes the opposite of a particular case, because of the evident disjunctiveness of negation. More problematic is the fact that the negative procedures can be applied uncritically to cases in which they may not logically or clearly operate in a coherent manner.

A case in point would be in the formation of the concept of infinity. Not a modern notion, infinity is met quite early on. Space, right out of cosmogonic myth, was to the ancient Greeks *pneuma apeiron*, literally the unbounded breath of the gods. The usage of *apeiron* shows the typical linguistic genesis of the notion: the negative prefix *a-* is added to the word for *bounded*. *Infinite* itself is formed similarly, in-finite, not having end. The problem here is that every known physical entity has boundaries, so that to negate boundaries is to contemplate that for which experience gives no substantiation. When we do this, we enter the world of the imaginary—which is perfectly legitimate, of course, but we should be aware that that is what we are doing.

Further light may be shed on this case by focusing on one deployment of it, the void. The void is the containing body that is unbounded. The Container metaphor is obvious as the root of the void. But that leaves us with a container that has no boundaries, that is not a container by definition. It has been argued by proponents of such concepts that they represent a different mode of being. While this possibility may not be absolutely discounted, it is difficult to countenance in the light of their motivation and modus operandi. They are given birth through the desire to transcend certain limitations, or perhaps even a curiosity about what happens when the limitations are removed, quite often in the absence of concern for how the transcendence might in fact be accomplished. Hence, there is always potential conflict between transcendentalists (or idealists) and empiricists. Historically, we only wish to note this conflict and pinpoint its causes. It has always been possible for opposite sides to defend their views with sufficient reasonableness to hold a body of adherents.[29] We should not be surprised at this. Since reasoning is topological manipulation, it is thereby always possible to move from any point to any other point. Even the criterion of continuity may be laid aside, if human intellectual security can thereby in some way be served.

TOPOLOGICAL TRANSFORMATIONS IN DISCURSIVE THOUGHT: SOME ANALYSES

Generally speaking, all that is necessary for the analysis of an argument in terms of the fictive spatial operations is an alertness to those operations and a little practice. Therefore, let us move right to some specific examples. I chose these at random. I required only that they display discursive thought rather than simply descriptive background. In the examples I shall italicize only the main terms expressing fictive spatial operations and arrange the examples chronologically, beginning with the opening paragraphs from Aristotle's *Physics*.

> When the *objects* of an inquiry, *in* any department, have principles, conditions, or elements, it is *through* acquaintance *with* these that knowledge that is to say any scientific knowledge, is *attained*. For we do not think that we know a thing until we are acquainted *with* its *primary* conditions or *first* principles, and have *carried* our *analysis* as *far* as its simplest segments. Plainly therefore *in* the science of nature, as *in* other branches of study, our *first* task will be to try to determine what *relates to* its principles.
>
> The natural way of doing this is to *start from* the things which are more knowable and obvious to us and *proceed towards* those which are clearer and more knowable by nature: for the same things are not "knowable *relatively to* us" and "knowable" *without* qualifications. So *in* the present inquiry we must *follow* this method and *advance from* what is more obscure *by* nature, but clearer *to* us, *towards* what is more clear and more knowable by nature.
>
> Now what is *to* us plain and obvious *at first* is rather *confused* masses, the elements and principles of which *become* known later to us by *analysis*. Thus we must *advance from* generalities *to* particulars: for it is as a *whole* that things are best known *to* sense-perception, and a generality is a kind of *whole, comprehending* many things *within* it, like parts.[30]

Overall, the thing to be most noted here is that Aristotle conducts his thought within a kind of vector space in which imaginary lines of advancement move from simplicity and human clarity to complexity and intrinsic clarity. His whole procedure of reasoning moves along these directive lines. "Through acquaintance with the simplest elements" is a notion that creates a kind of cylinder in the space. By moving through this cylinder and emerging from the other end, knowledge is attained like the light at the end of a tunnel. His analysis is carried through such a tunnel. He marks the entrance into the tunnel by continually designating certain moves as being first.

In the second paragraph, he articulates the cylinder variantly as a way, or path, down which we are to proceed vectorially from the humanly clear toward the intrinsically clear. As we follow this way, we advance towards our goal. This advancement is reiterated in the third paragraph, in which Aristotle also introduces confused or mixed-together masses, topological knots to be undone by analysis. This is the only departure from linear relations.

Aristotle makes use of the container metaphor, indicated by *in* and *within*, to deposit subsidiary notions in a vaguely articulated framework. If any of these notions were to be pressed discursively, they would be extracted from their fictive containers and placed into more specific spatial relations with the other elements of the argument. Similarly, the more vague prepositions fade into the background unless the matters that they interconnect need to be brought more to the fore.

From the standpoint of our analysis, Aristotle's argument reduces to a scheme of vector space involving gradients, lines along which certain properties, such as clarity, vary in an orderly fashion. In considering questions regarding these properties, we are to resolve them by moving from point to point along the gradients. At the same time, within the vector space are first, or primary, positions that prioritize considerations of matters associated with those positions. In other words, the vector space serves as an orientative model for further thought. The thought process would extend or otherwise complicate the space, or subsequent action. And such complications would proceed according to the hierarchy of priorities fixed by first position points. As a behavioral model, the spatial priority relations would be translated into temporal sequences, quite in keeping with the structuring of time from spatial experience. Moreover, the spatial model is literally the skeleton of our understanding of Aristotle's argument. Our knowledge of the substance of the argument comprises both the model and the background against which it is sketched in relation to any situation to which we might apply them.

Our next example is the first lemma from the first section of Newton's *Principles*. This lemma does not concern motion. Nevertheless, observe the terms of discourse.

> Quantities, and the ratio of quantities, which in any finite time *converge* continually *to* equality, and *before* the end of that time *approach nearer to* each other than *by* any given difference, become ultimately equal.[31]

As Aristotle had done, so Newton conjures a vector space in which quantities are imbued with motion. They converge: they approach nearer to each other within a temporalized vector space. When they come together, they become equal. Clearly Newton accomplished his thinking here by manipulating quantities as moving entities in a fictive vector space.

Finally, I shall compare an argument from section 2, "Of the Origin of Ideas," from Hume's *Enquiry Concerning Human Understanding*:

> Every one will readily allow, that there is a considerable difference *between* the perceptions of the mind, when a man feels the pain of excessive heat, or the pleasure of moderate warmth, and when he afterwards *recalls to* his memory this sensation, or anticipates it *by* his imagination. These faculties may mimic or copy the perceptions of the senses: but they never can entirely *reach* the force and vivacity of the original sentiment. The utmost we say of them, even when they operate with greatest vigor, is, that they *represent* their object in so lively a manner, that we could almost say we feel or see it: But, except the

mind be *disordered by* disease or madness, they never can *arrive at* such a pitch of vivacity, as to *render* these perceptions *altogether* undistinguishable. All the colors of poetry, however splendid, can never paint natural objects *in* such a manner as to make the description be *taken* for a real landskip. The most lively thought is still *inferior to* the dullest sensation.[32]

And a sample from Freud's eleventh lecture, "The Dream Work," in his *General Introduction to Psycho-Analysis*, wherein he is explaining the phenomenon of condensation:

> Although condensation *renders* the dream obscure, yet it does not *give* the impression of being an effect of the dream-censorship. Rather we should be *inclined to trace* it *to* mechanical or economic factors: nevertheless the censorship's interests are *served by* it.
>
> What condensation can *achieve* is sometimes quite extraordinary: *by* this device it is *at* times possible for two completely different latent *trains* of thought to be *united in* a single manifest dream, so that we *arrive at* an apparently adequate interpretation of a dream and yet overlook a *second* possible meaning.
>
> Moreover, one of the effects of condensation *upon* the *relationship between* the manifest and the latent dream is that the *connection between* the elements of the one and of the other nowhere remains a simple one: for by a kind of *interlacing* a manifest element represents simultaneously several latent ones and, *conversely*, a latent thought may *enter into* several manifest elements. Again when we *come* to interpret dreams, we see that the *associations to* a single manifest element do not commonly make their appearance in *orderly succession*: we often have to wait *until* we have the interpretation of the whole dream.[33]

In both these examples, the space employed is isotropic; and not only the entities of thought but the thinkers themselves move about—come and arrive—in it. It is latent and subdued, a mere canvas on which images are juxtaposed. Hume is most sparing in his geometry. Perceptions reach and arrive, and they are rendered, given back. But mostly he sets one idea next to another, concentrates on the geometry of congruence, the mirror metaphor, comparing perceptual objects with mnemonic ones. Thus, the key verb is "represent," a verb of implicit congruence.

For Freud, too, the space of thought is isotropic, only a medium in which to establish relationships, connections, associations. His "train of thought" leads him to topological schemata in which "manifest elements" and "latent thoughts" enter into one another and interlace, just the sort of interpenetrative equivalence he sought to metaphorize his concept of condensation.

When we analyze an argument in this fashion, we end up with entities moving about, forming various geometries or relationships, sometimes changing as they go, often interacting topologically, all against a descriptive background that breathes life into them, makes them vivid and palpable to the mind. All these operations yield a model against which we then measure our behavior isomorphically. When we apply our knowledge of the argument, we try to map our actions to the features of the model and the way it was manipulated in the argument appropriately to the situation at hand.

Consider once again Newton's lemma. In it, quantities "converge," "approach nearer to each other," until they "become ultimately equal." Now, in reality Newton surely knew that quantities in the abstract do not move. Nor do we in this superficial sense move when computing with these quantities. Rather, the operations of mental computation find a model in Newton's argument. This model then dictates computations that otherwise described would be cumbersome and verbally circuitous: Take two variable quantities. Compute these quantities, taking the independent variables in an orderly sequence of values, which is to say, a sequence that at every next value will make the difference between the two quantities less than between the prior values, and you will eventually have the difference between the quantities as small as you like. Ultimately the difference diminishes to a negligible sum and we say the quantities are then equal. Newton's model implies all this isomorphically. It is a blueprint for carrying out the procedure.

Discursive thought thus is a schematizing of models for subsequent thought or action. If it is acted upon, by isomorphism it suggests the way in which the action should progress. Freud models condensation as one idea interlacing with another, one entering into another like parts of a telescope. *Interlace*, most evidently a figure of speech based on weaving, becomes twisted through the expression of "entering into" in the total context of the discussion of condensation. In other words, where *cross* might be the expected correlative of *interlace*, Freud uses "enter into" and thereby makes a strangely mixed metaphor that might be read in either or both of two ways. In fact, he perhaps anticipates the weaving aspect when he speaks of "*trains* of thought *united in* a single manifest dream." He further indicates that there are multiple connections between ideas in a dream. This yields the picture of entities with multiple extensions interlaced and interpenetrating. As a model for dream analysis, it translates into a procedure whereby a single idea can manifest itself in a myriad of dream contents. His metaphor models the procedure of dream analysis. It is an isomorphic analogue to dream analysis.

Our understanding of an argument, however it might be characterized, certainly involves having a clear impression of the model and knowing how to read the model topologically as a guide to further thought or action. This is not to discount the descriptive background of discursive thought. It gives substance to the scheme of the model. At the moment I am stressing the structural aspect of thought. Actually, the fleshing out of the scheme, the particularity of the metaphor, often supplies a springboard, too, for further elaboration of the thought. Comparison of qualities is accomplished through a network of spatial relationships, so that discursive thought can certainly take its cues from the descriptive background, but the result will still be structural.

Topological Schematizing in Discursive Thought: Summary

In summary, I may make the following tentative generalizations about the role of spatial schematizing in discursive thought:

Prioritizing is a common and distinct way in which the relative importance of things, as well as the ordering of steps in a procedure, is established. This may be done through spatial or temporal serialization: first, second, third, etc.: superior and inferior next: high and low, et al.

Spatial ordering often is isomorphic to temporal sequencing of actions, and vice versa.

Complex topological schemata isomorphose commonly to matters not clearly understood. These schemata—knots, convolutions, labyrinths, interpenetrations—verbally signify configurations of high complexity and incompletely articulated geometry. Hence, they isomorphose to situations in which only the general outlines or character are known or intuited.

Congruences—parallel, similar, like, represents, mirrors imitates, etc.—refer back to the mirror metaphor to suggest a more or less complete analogy between one thing and another. This suggests, when it is used, that the metaphor is to be taken as a descriptive background to be compared to the topic described freely in all manners that can be conceived.

Verbs of linear, and sometimes rotational, motion are widely used to indicate steps or stages in a procedure: begin, proceed, go, arrive, come, become, etc.

The geometry of containment—basically the use of *in* or *within*—is employed liberally as vague markers to hold subsidiary ideas whose roles are not to be further specified at the time.

In discourse about emotions or subjects with emotional connotations, we either characterize our spatial relations with appropriate adjectives and adverbs, or we use human gesture-motions or postures nonverbally to embody our ideas—e.g., *a perilous connection; the idea repulses us* (pushes us away).

Topological Schematizing in Mathematics

Once again it should be pointed out that these observations about spatial schemes in discursive thought simply support Piaget's thesis that thought arises in the individual through the internalization of external action schemes.[34] Whereas Piaget came to his conclusion through experimentation and observation, I have come to a similar conclusion from the analysis of metaphor in linguistic expression. Long ago Hume laid the foundation for the present position, in alluding to the fact that all thought must proceed through accretion of elemental percepts into greater and greater complexities through what he called laws of association. In computer lingo, an information-processing system (e.g., the brain) can put out only compounds of what has been put into it. Furthermore, the compounds can be built up only through rules of combination that take off from operations already experienced.

Thus we have the dialectic of human reality construction. Percepts are presented to the neonate. Initially the only structure they receive is that imposed by the anatomy and physiology of the sensory and neural systems. Discriminations are made. Relations are then conceptualized. They are reified and become subject to symbolic or abstract manipulation, objects of discursive thought, whereupon they become instruments through which reality is subsequently construed. The circle of the dialectic is completed and begins its spiral development. And herein lies the secret of the amazing efficacy of mathematics.

Most discursive thought is encumbered with the burden of descriptive background, as we have witnessed. That is, spatial operations are imposed upon described objects, and most of the time these objects relate rather directly back to percepts. The percept is important to the operations. But in mathematics, the percept is minimized in its sensory properties so that it assumes a broadly inclusive and abstract character. A point, for example, is divested of all sensory properties except location, and a number is divested of all except matchability to percepts and concepts (with further qualification for special classes of numbers). As it has often been said, in mathematics it is the relation, not the things related, that holds the utmost importance. Peculiarly mathematical entities can be created, but they are always the product of some hybridization of relations, classes formed by an amalgamation of previously discriminated and defined reified relations.

As mathematics has progressed, it has done so largely by establishing and exploring new groups of relations. These relations are often called operations, and they are reified as operators. Now, since these operations are created from the same elemental relations evolving within the dialectic of reality construction, it should be no surprise if the most abstract and abstruse mathematical operations ultimately find application to real situations. Newly conceived mathematical operations, classes or entities supply isomorphs we can then use to construe our percepts. They do not *find* happy congruences with reality: they knit together relationships that permit useful interfacing with reality because the componential relations ultimately point back to body-mediated operations.

Non-Euclidean geometry is a case in point. Its applicability to various curved surfaces was discovered through the search for models that could be used to prove its consistency—in other words, physical isomorphs to its rules of relations.

Let us put the matter, perhaps dangerously, in its simplest terms. In any special field of mathematics, whenever a new operation, class, or entity is defined, we are supplied with an intellectual structure having internal relations that suggest new ways in which to structure our experience. This suggests new discriminations— e.g., a straight line or geodesic as the shortest distance between two points on any given surface—and more than likely we shall be able to find an isomorph in our experience, since it is from relations within our experience that the new operation, class, or entity was compounded in the first place. For all its potential abstractness, mathematics does not evolve in a vacuum.

TOPOLOGICAL SCHEMATIZING IN THE ARTS

In fact, fundamentally all human creation proceeds by elemental laws derived from and therefore isomorphic to the elemental operations derived from perceptual experience, that is, from internalized action schemes. This is no less true in the arts than in the sciences.

In the plastic arts, spatial relations form the basis of composition, whether representational or abstract. It is an ethnocentric bias to assume that a single or double vanishing-point perspective is a kind of perfection toward which spatial representation naturally evolves. In the first place, it is not, without certain modifications, accurate to the optical processes of the human eye. And in the second, a strictly optical approach to the problem of spatial representation somewhat naively discounts the conceptual elements in perception. It is foolhardy to ignore the large body of empirical evidence that now exists for the cultural molding of perception .

With these caveats, we can view the history of spatial representation in the plastic arts, not as an inexorable march toward Renaissance opticality, but rather as a record of the diversity of ways in which the people of various cultures have organized the visual field for conceptual as well as perceptual purposes—not that the two purposes can in practice be separated. We should long ago have transcended the notion that one method of organization is in all respects superior to all others, or that when it is the practice of one culture to employ parallel perspective, this means that the members of that culture are unable to see things in vanishing-point perspective. Rather, the choice (by which I do not intend to imply utterly conscious willfulness) to use one method as opposed to all the others is largely an accommodation to the web of metaphors, customs, and other components peculiar to the total culture.

Nor can we arbitrarily assign fixed significances to specific methods of spatial representation, any more than we can to elements in dreams. The significance must be established in each case through a careful examination of the culture in question to determine whatever historical accidents and necessities may have come into play in the adoption and maintenance of the representational conventions. Certainly the compositional disposition of figures along an S-curve functioned differently in Islamic painting, for example, from how it was used in European baroque painting. So, too, multiple vanishing points in Gothic painting, perhaps in part motivated by early optical considerations, had neither the same impetus nor served the same conceptual ends in, say, seventeenth-century Indian painting. Whereas it might be true that multiple vanishing points indicate a natural stage of development toward true optical geometry, they also can arise under other cultural determinants. Be that as it may, I wish to underline here that spatial representation in the plastic arts is neither linear in progression nor univalued in its cultural import. We are dealing, as in styles of the employment of spatial schemes in discursive thought, with styles of visualization, the arrangement of the components of the visual field to certain culturally circumscribed effects.

Topological Schematizing in Music

It has long been recognized, too, that music can convey isomorphically the sense of motion: ascending and descending notes, leaps of several intervals, jumpy forward motion up and down by medial intervalic spans, sliding through glissandos, etc. In his Second Symphony, Beethoven even managed a topological somersault or two. A topological knot may be conjured by polyphonic convergence of several lines through, say, a common tonic, after which the lines may progress along individual but systematic paths. This temporal drawing of spatial relations forms the skeleton around which most musical creation takes place: and all the compositional elements of melody, rhythm, harmony and orchestration contribute the flesh. Musical tensions and sensuality, the emotional quality of the music, arise in the musical space of the composer, a space always culturally determined to a certain extent.

Rules for the Development of Topological Transformations in the Arts

At this juncture, it seems appropriate to bring in a systems rule of development, viz., that spatial development in the arts proceeds from the elemental components to larger organizational wholes. We can see this clearly in the genesis of ornamentation in the visual arts. It is common in designs in the Indian arts of New Mexico. They were based upon textile weaving patterns. It is not difficult to see how one pattern can be generated from another by suitable transformations of rotation combined with displacement.[35]

Abstract motifs in the visual arts give us in their genealogies a clear picture of how symbolic meaning and abstract form may interact. A motif common to many cultures is that of the rosette. When the petals—or in a rose window the mullions—

are drawn thin and arranged just so, they begin to resemble the spokes of a wheel. And the wheel symbol can be made to be much like certain sun symbols. Thus, the rosette, wheel, and sun are interlinked through this interlocking of structural similarities. Even as a more or less abstract embellishment, the motif may be rendered in such and such a manner, depending on the symbolic meaning assigned to it.

Once an ornamental motif in the decorative arts has been chosen and a suitable set of transformations applied, this forms the germinal center around which the total work will be executed, be it a vase, a rug, or whatever. The intrinsic geometry will spread over the decorated surface according to certain developmental laws— linking, repetition, bordering and other conventions established within the culture. Symbolic significance, color schemes, and other considerations also play a part in the execution of the work.

Certainly the multiplicity of determinative factors and the panoply of transformations applicable to any given work make the process of creation anything but mechanical. The play of the idiosyncratic proclivities of the creator make the evolution of a work in some sense unpredictable, whereas the logic of what takes place makes it all explicable ex post facto. Again referring back to topological schemata, or their isomorphisms, in music, we can see how parallel processes operate in musical creation. A motive acquires a rhythm, which may link to an established pattern derived ultimately from a dance form. This dance form, even operative on the subconscious level, suggests possible patterns of motivic development. From the accepted repertory of modulations (defined by the tradition within which the composer works) the composer chooses those which suit his or her immediate purpose and employs them in the topological transformation of the motive. Bridges are inserted that may contrast, amplify, embellish or simply connect thematic sections. And as the material expands to fill the form, there is an almost imperceptible shift from the elemental to the formal systems level. At the formal level, the larger aspect of the work becomes a transformation of some prototype—binary song, fugue, polonaise, sonata. Metaphoric and explicit meanings (e.g., song, opera) play their role in the structural evolution of the piece. But always the work arises from the structural skeleton of the spatiotemporal schemes that are the seeds of musical creation. This is the gist of the analyses suggested by Heinrich Schenker[36] and Rudolph Reti.[37] Neither man was successful in forcing his analysis into a complete explanation of musical creation, because each hewed too narrowly to formal considerations, neglecting metaphoric and other cultural factors.

I have previously cited the similarity of the functioning of metaphor in dance and in music. Choreography expands along culturally bound gestures linked either by narrative or abstract tensions overlying more implicit isomorphic metaphorization. And I have just outlined the role of spatial schemes in discursive thought, which is the bedrock of both prose and poetry. The compositional elements in literature have been adequately delineated in prosody and rhetoric. Literature has the rather unique stricture that form is dictated largely by explicit discursive or narrative content. That aside, we still have the basic elements of metrics, rhyme, alliteration, repetition, etc., which form the germinal motives around which literary creation is excogitated.

These formal observations on the arts and sciences have no pretense to newness. What is new here is the manner in which the formal bases of all the fields of human creativity have been shown to display a unity in a common foundation in the assimilation of spatial action schemes to introspective thought processes. It would be rash to assume this is their only commonality: but it is plainly one important key to a unified theory of human behavior.

4

The Ancient World

The mnemonic substrate of prehistoric art probably formed the procrustean bed for later philosophical and scientific thought. There the foundations of symbolic thought were laid. Symbolization has within it the implicit cognitive formation of relationships, the necessary first step toward metaphorization. These processes arise slowly out of the more diffuse experience of the semantic field. Mental operations familiar from dreaming and perhaps even drug-induced hallucination are carried over into mythopoeia, from whence they become refined and are adopted ultimately into more abstract speculative thought. These strands we are about to adumbrate in greater detail form the historical roots of metaphorization in discursive thought.

PALEOLITHIC BACKGROUNDS

Consider a hunting scene in a Paleolithic cave. There is the main scene of killing, and then off to the side, footprints leading away, a device of pictorial narration still used today in cartoons. Here we may have one of the earliest examples of an implicit linear spatialization of time.[1]

We should remind ourselves how potent the visual image must have been in prehistoric times. Judging by the difficult location of cave paintings, we can be sure that they were reserved for initiates. But that they had a magical significance is perhaps wrongly to project our categories of thought backward in time. Magic implies a transcendence of the natural order, a notion too sophisticated for that period of time.

Paleolithic painting in the Asian subcontinent as well as in Australia is still repainted by the natives to ensure the issuance of the plants and animals depicted. To interpret this as magic is to imply notions of causality that could not have applied. We are dealing here with the phenomena of semantic fields. A semantic field is a domain of significance centered around a single subject. The components of this domain, while distinguished separately, do not have their distinctiveness pushed to the point of becoming conceptually isolated. That is to say, the components of a semantic field are conceived as aspects of the same thing. We do not isolate the components of our perceptual experience unless we have reason for doing so . Did you notice, for example, that the fourth word of the previous sentence had seven letters in it? Yes and no. You noticed it in the sense of being aware of its length at the time, but you did not isolate it for separate consideration.

What transforms consciousness is distinctions; and distinctions are made only in response to intrinsic or extrinsic demands. In the field of consciousness there are thousands of distinctions *in potentia,* but attention focuses on them only when there is a motive to grasp them. If that motive is absent from the environmental and cultural settings, they go by the board.

SEMANTIC FIELDS: THE BIRTH OF COMPARISON

So, with prehistoric art, the created image and what it represents were probably originally poles, as it were, of a semantic field, like the front and back of a coin. Certainly prehistoric man knew the difference between the two—he was aware that he could not eat a painting of a stag—but he had no motive for separating them out completely. In fact, the full continuum of his semantic field for what we would call objects probably ran from mnemonic object to image-depiction-symbol. Even modern man separates out this continuum only to the extent that the occasion demands. How many Catholics, for instance, behave in certain ways toward the icon of the Virgin Mary as if it were she? How many people are not disturbed by having their name profaned or slandered in name calling and the like? How often do we hear someone say that she keeps the (mnemonic) image of another person pure in her mind? All this in a *civilized* world in which nearly everyone could separate out the components of these semantic fields completely for purposes of analysis.

If by *magic,* then, we mean operation within an incompletely differentiated semantic field, Paleolithic art may be assigned to the category of magic. With that much understood, we can move on to the related developments of myth and religion. For the further back we go, the closer the various domains of human thought—artistic, pragmatic, speculative, emotional—become one to another, because the social demands are not sufficiently complex to require that these domains be sorted out.

THE ROLE OF DREAM EXPERIENCE IN
THE RISE OF SPECULATIVE THOUGHT

The fluidity of thought operative within undifferentiated semantic continua is paralleled by that in dreams. Dream life is important in considering the prehistoric

origins of thought because it furnished prototypes for the notion of spirit and paradigms for identity transformations that infused totemism and probably instigated
the type of comparative thought necessary to metaphor formation and deployment. It also provided the scaffolding for mythopoeia, an essential bridge to more
abstract speculation.[2]

Prehistoric humans enjoyed the reality of waking, dreaming, and hallucinating, something that for us must be separated into three isolated modes, but for
them formed a continuum. As Tylor observed, prehistoric man, "beholding the
reflection of his own mind like a child looking at itself in a glass, . . . humbly received the teaching of his second self."[3] Altered states of consciousness were for
these people alternative realities. "It is frequently observed or implied that the
religious beliefs of the lower races are in no small measure based on the evidence of
visions and dreams regarded as actual intercourse with spiritual beings."[4] This
same author noted that among many tribes of American Indians, dreams and fast-
ing visions encountered in ritual contexts often establish expectations of what is to
be in the future life of the individual, regarding marriage, vocation, and the like.
"At manhood the Indian lad, retiring to a solitary place to fast and meditate and
pray, receives visionary impressions which stamp his character for life, and especially he waits till there appears to him in a dream some animal or thing which will
henceforth be his 'medicine,' the fetish representative of his monitor or protecting
genius."[5] R. S. Rattray relates that among the Ashanti, if one dreams of sex with a
woman not one's own, one has to pay an adultery fee.[6] And Gunnar Landtman
says of dreams among the Papuans, "[T]he importance of the part played by dreams
in the life of the natives can hardly be exaggerated. They are one of the principal
factors shaping the beliefs and supernaturalistic practices of the people."[7]

There are a number of features of dreams that found their ways into prehistoric thought. To begin with, the ancients were moved to account for glaring discrepancies between dreaming and waking reality. Symbolization was a major strategy
for the resolution of these discrepancies. Some symbolized dream figures undoubtedly found counterparts in mythical characters, from whence they passed into rhetorical metaphor by acting as prototypes. Themis, or Justitia, blindfolded, holding
a balance in one hand, a sword in the other, emblematized the qualities of justice:
weighing evidence impartially and then dispensing the punishment of the sword to
those found guilty. Plato's demiurge and Aristotle's unmoved mover are
depersonalized remnants of former deities. Alchera, or the dreamtime, of the ab-
original Australians expresses this debt of myth to dream explicitly. Incidents in the
lives of the gods often resemble dream mechanisms rather than real events. Take
the story of Metis and Zeus. Metis was Zeus's first wife. He was forewarned that his
children by Metis would try to usurp his position. His solution, certainly dreamlike,
was to swallow her, and the children were born from his forehead. Such magical
acts abound in all mythology. So, too, do transformations, like that of Philomel into
a nightingale, Arachne into a spider, or Actaeon into a stag. This same kind of para-

logical thinking lay behind such notions as the transmutation of elements in alchemy, Aristotle's theory of embryonic morphogenesis, and the Hippocratic account of digestion as the conversion of food into chyle and then chyle into the four humors.

One particularly interesting way in which dream reality carries over into waking life is the sense of the presence of a person not visually there, or the presence of an identity different from the person who is there. Since the hippocampus unifies mnemonic data to form mnemonic images which then must be interpreted apparently by a higher structure in the cortical hierarchy, this form of dream confusion probably arises from a desynchrony between hippocampal input into the cortex and cortical recognition of a given person in response to memory consolidation normally occurring during REM sleep. At any rate, the result is the sense of a disembodied identity or of an identity misplaced onto another being.[8]

In the case of a disembodied identity, we have the *experiential paradigm for the concept of spirit*. This makes equation of spirit with breath all the more plausible. Since the concept of essence is allied with that of spirit, it is easy to see what important consequences this dream phenomenon has. Essence is a concept ubiquitous even in everyday thought. Attempts to understand anything are often aimed at discovering the essence of it. Essence defines a heuristic strategy in many contexts.

Dreaming, as a parallel reality, establishes certain modes of thought as legitimate at least within limitations. We should not be surprised that prehistoric man was prone to carry the modes of dreaming into the modes of waking, for this propensity operates even today in the most sophisticated arenas of thought. Hans Vaihinger has shown how this "method of unjustified transference" has been used to generalize a host of mathematical concepts.[9] The structure of the reasoning is the same: what is established under one set of conditions is uncritically transferred to an essentially different set. Law abounds in such transferences, for they are the bases for argument by precedent. And that these precedents are often transferred unjustifiably to later circumstances is shown by the number of lower court cases overturned by the higher courts. This is one of the ways in which generalized concepts are reached.

RESTRICTED NATURE OF EARLY THOUGHT

In all activities for which we have suitable historical documentation, early empirical rules related always to restricted cases; they were rules of thumb, rather than generalized principles. As such, they had not broad enough implications to be metaphorized except in a trivial sense, and so did not have to accord with the deployed metaphors of the group or culture. That a stone may flake when struck, a branch break when bent, or water flow when poured are phenomena so simple and immediate in their presentations to the senses that they called only for host spirits to permit and facilitate their occurrences. We call these metaphorizations trivial in the sense that they do not, in the absence of generalized scientific notions, provoke further inquiry. The primary dictates of thought at this level call only for a kind of felt coherence in experience that takes as its model the family and the small social group. The paradigm is the parent permitting or causing a thing to happen. That part of parental behavior which is inscrutable to the child furnishes the experiential base for those things in nature that seem irregular and unpredictable—meteorological changes, sickness, death, natural disasters. The gods can be inscrutable, as can the parent.

This inscrutability must have played a large role in early thought. It mandated the projection of parental behaviors onto the gods. It also motivated the selection of animals as gods, for the behavior of animals is not lucid to human observation. We have here the *tertium comparationis* in that human traits are read into an animal and then read back out, but this is probably too neat an explanation. Even without the primary projection, animal behavior is sufficiently unfathomable to man to serve in and of itself as a model for explaining inscrutable phenomena. Oneiric transformations between men and animals would have further inspired deification of animals for explicative purposes. Animals as emblems entered the folk tradition through fables and their pictorial depictions, where again they provided prototypes for metaphorized abstractions: the fox for cunning, the dove for peace, the pig for gluttony, and so forth. As prototypes in fables, they allowed a working out of notions in a kind of psychodramatic fashion. At least for the broad populace, this was equivalent to the abstract speculation that the intellectually more elite practiced. Exactly where this kind of reasoning ends and purely abstract thinking begins is probably a wrong formulation of the problem. Better to say that both historically and psychologically, the one shades gradually into the other. Certainly the *tertium comparationis* strategy was a necessary forerunner to the metaphorization of abstractions, and it is for this reason that it finds a place here.

Myths as Devices for Solidarity of Minds Prior to Dominant Metaphors

We should not, of course, reduce the motive for mythopoeia to the simple desire for explanation. On the basis of a comparative analysis of myths from many times and places, G. S. Kirk has proposed a typology that divides them into three types—"narrative and entertaining," "operative, iterative, and validatory," and "speculative and explanatory"—noting that these types are not mutually exclusive.[10] What he calls "operative, iterative, and validatory" are myths that are repeated during ritual ceremonies to instill or validate certain cultural traditions. Notwithstanding this typology, all types have in common certain modes of thinking to which we have been alluding.

We err in judging mythical explanation as absurd, because its main function was to make experience feel more coherent, and not to accord with a complex of metaphorical deployments connected by causal and quantitative relations. The appeal that myths have continued to have down to the present day attests to the emotional satisfaction they can provide. Poets and artists continued to use ancient myths because they supplied paradigms of motivational coherence, or coherence in terms of identification with the common human private experience. For people well into the Middle Ages, and in folk traditions beyond that time, myths helped to give a solidarity of mind analogous to that later provided by dominant metaphors such as those supporting notions of cosmic order, of how everything interrelates to form a coherent world.

Mythopoeia proceeds from an amalgamation of waking and dreaming transformative rules or schemes through closer and closer articulation with waking life. Myths become elaborated through restructuring in ritual or simply repeated narration. Storytelling devices are imposed on the raw myths. Character, plot and background are manipulated to achieve the various purposes of narration: to hold interest, maintain suspense, create surprise, and so forth. We know myths mainly in their literary form, and so they come to us much more sophisticated and complex than they must originally have been.

ICONS: VISUAL COUNTERPARTS TO MYTHS

In origin, myths and icons probably flowed from the same wellsprings of imagination. Icons have therefore shared the same kinds of semantic transformation to which myths were subjected, gods and goddesses being continually reinterpreted to meet the demands of changing societies. It is not within our purposes to enter into a detailed discussion of iconography. Suffice it to say, however, that just as there are graphic types,[11] there are also mythic and iconographic types. These types were set down in part during the Paleolithic and Neolithic periods and subsequently were spread throughout Europe and Asia.[12] Their structures followed along lines of facial expression, mimic and dance gesture, regional symbolism, etc. They were transformed in migration according to regional variants of these factors and others such as ethnic somatotypes, costume, and religious ideology. In sum, there remains to be written a history of iconographic types in terms of an underlying metaphoric set; but we suggest that the set will prove isomorphic to that of the metaphors with which it must have evolved side by side.

MUSIC AND THE EVOLUTION OF ACTION SCHEMES

Parallel to the above observations on iconographic types, I should add a few remarks on the early history of music. Formal development in music laid down action schemes and topological transformations tied to those of everyday life. These isomorphisms go far in accounting for the universal emotional responses that music evokes. Musical composition parallels the topological transformations underlying discursive argument and narrative structure. In motival development, variation displays the same play of ideas that goes into any kind of problem solving. It is, therefore, not surprising that so many great thinkers were also amateur musicians. Among twentieth-century examples, Albert Einstein and Richard Feynman come immediately to mind.

A comprehensive account of the isomorphic metaphorization implicit in music is beyond the scope of this book. The details necessary for such an accounting have not yet even been worked out by musicologists, primarily because the subject has not been broached in those terms. For that reason, let us briefly rehearse the fundamental facts. First of all, it is elementary that music evolved from speech and emotive vocalization coupled with the rhythmic structures of dance movements. We might add to this that dance movements would have regional variations due to somatotypes, movement restrictions of costume, local topography influencing the ways people habitually walk and run, diet (affecting energy levels), climate, and so on. "The term 'dance music' usually implies strong pulses and rhythmic patterns that are organized into repeated metric groupings synchronizing exactly with those of the dance. Rhythmic accents and phrase lengths normally coincide with those of dance also, as does the mood of the music. . . . Such elements as form, melody, harmony and texture can perhaps be more independent of the dance. . . ."[13] Form, however, would to some extent have been generated out of the repetition and development of rhythmic patterns in the dance.

Then, too, it is not as if man had invented music. That was left to the birds, which must have inspired imitation in man. Neither am I suggesting this as the sole origin. I only wish to point out that bird songs were a present model to assist in the shaping of vocalization toward melodic ends.

We might remind ourselves of the various models that were copied into the structure of music: dance patterns, communicative and emotive gesture and vocalization, speech patterns, visceral tension and more general physiological patterns (e.g., heart beat, respiration, etc.), visual designs, natural sounds, and so on. Variations of these isomorphisms were essential for sustained attention and caused a gradual drifting of the isomorphic structures. This became particularly important in musical development after music was freed from ritual performance. Vocal inflection dominated as the model for expressive devices in both the vocal and the instrumental performance of early music. Also out of vocal inflection under varying emotional conditions came characteristic uses of tones within the octave that were later categorized as the modes.

Until about 1450, the forms of music were exclusively modeled on regional dances and solo and group vocal practices: plainsong tropes and sequences, clausula, conductus, motet, and monodic song; estampie, danse royale, rota, saltarello, and so forth. Sacred music in particular gained much of its form by isomorphic adherence to the text. As we shall see, it is notable that troubadour practices led to greater dialectic variances in performance practice, signaling the revolution that burst upon the musical scene around 1450—but we are getting ahead of ourselves. We only wished to sketch in the constraints that led to the evolution of existent musical types. A musical type, harking back to the work of Rawson[14] in the visual mode, is a characteristic way of deploying an auditory isomorphism through the temporal scheme of tonal, rhythmic, metrical, harmonic, and textural or timbral variation. The deployment is partly dialectical in that the interaction of the elements of composition or performance is partly responsible for the outcome and takes place within the constraints of a traditional set of performance practices. It is no different, however, than in the other arts. It only seems so—it seems freer—because we lose sight of the isomorphic code as well as the performance scheme.

In the play of musical composition and performance, it is not too much to see part of a dialectic out of which the structures of formal argumentation evolved. Statement of theme, development, and coda define the same formalism of premises, deductive relations and conclusion. I think it not coincidental that modern tonal harmony disengaged from the earlier modal system at the same time that modern mathematics was being born. Further, Schoenberg's experimentations with atonality came just two decades before Gödel's epic paper on the intrinsic incompleteness of logico-mathematical systems. We have barely begun to put the topological transformational and metaphoric aspects of music history into the larger perspective of intellectual history. The preceding remarks offer barely a preamble.[15] We might bear them in mind, when perpending more traditional coverage of metaphorization.

BEGINNINGS OF METAPHORIZATION IN RHETORICAL FIGURES

Bruno Snell has analyzed the nature of simile and metaphor in Homer and other early Greek writers and has adduced evidence that literary comparisons were made strictly to vivify their subjects. "Rosy-fingered dawn" and "fleet-footed Apollo" are epithets that add tone and color to their subjects without arousing an impetus to explore the comparisons for implicit information. On the other hand, when, in *Iliad* 11:284f. Hector is said to have "spurred on" the courage of his men, the metaphorization is *necessary* to embody an abstraction about which, without such metaphorization, we could not speak. As metaphorizations of an abstraction accumulate, they form a body that can be examined for commonalities in terms of which discursive thought on the subject may then be conducted.

Out of literary comparisons, at least in part, comes discursive thought. To generalize this result, the externalization of mnemonic architecture may be seen as a means for testing and perfecting interpretations of the world. There is a constant interplay between the world of private experience and that of public consensus. Metaphorical and topological structures mediate between the two worlds.

GREEK ORIGINS OF WESTERN THOUGHT

If we begin with ancient Greece in our survey of postliterate Western thought, it is largely a matter of historical convenience. Our survey will pursue two major metaphorical lines, one running from the Pattern metaphor and the other from the Breath metaphor. The first is a dominant metaphor, which embodied the Greek sense of the order of things. It is what Stephen Pepper called a world hypothesis. Given such an embracing metaphor, much of the speculation in a culture must proceed outward from that base. Every subtheme of the metaphor behind a world hypothesis must contribute to the broad sense of the world shared by members of the culture. Otherwise, that hypothesis gains no dominance. It either falls by the wayside or becomes subservient to some other metaphor that subsequently becomes dominant.

The second branch of metaphors we will be outlining stems from the Breath metaphor. It was literally vital, defining first the biological and spiritual sense of what life is. From the spark of life, it jumped to encompass the invariable nature of anything. The thought process was one of crude analogy: just as a human being must have within himself or herself an agency that imparts life, so anything must have in it something that makes it uniquely what it is. We will examine the reasoning and the metaphor deployment that made such a perspective possible.

Greek literature gives us our first comprehensive documentation of an ancient worldview, and there is a continuity from the Greek ethos to our own. Furthermore, only in Greece did the mythic order give way to the speculative, at least in such a manner that the transition can be tracked. The trail begins with the Ionian philosophers headquartered at Miletus.

Miletus, a harbor city on the coast of Asia Minor near the mouth of the Meander River, was ideally situated on the doorstep of the East. Many of the great thinkers of the sixth century B.C.E. had the advantage of having traveled or studied in the Near East. Milesian civilization was built upon earlier Minoan and Mycenaean settlements, cementing ties with the Near Eastern countries back to pre-Homeric times. As in Anatolia during the Neolithic and Chalcolithic periods, this admixture of cultures spawned a flowering of innovation. Citizens of Miletus were in a unique position to benefit from this cross-cultural exchange.

The Greeks were organized into poleis, the political character of which ranged from tyranny to democracy. Generally, however, the citizens enjoyed something approaching limited democracy. The polis took roots probably in tribal times, when population was sparse.

Everyone knew everyone by sight; rich and poor, rulers and ruled, stood in direct personal relationships one to another. Kings and nobles were not hemmed in, as at eastern courts, by etiquette and state-ceremony; no formalities of introduction served as a barrier to human intercourse.[16]

Each polis was politically independent, divided from its neighboring poleis only by minor geographical barriers. They shared a common language, but religious views varied locally and were not in most cases maintained, as in Asian nations, by central theocracies. Thus, they were induced to compare viewpoints in an atmosphere of relative intellectual freedom rare in the ancient world. The very size and form of government of the poleis intensified dialectic thinking, for the free male citizens were expected to participate directly in the assembly form of government in which verbal exchange of viewpoint was the central dynamism. They were forced to listen and compare ideas, and comparison, as we have been observing, is the natural mother to abstract speculation.

Intimate acquaintance with the polis and its political functionings, at least by the free citizens, made it an ideal prototype for the metaphor of Pattern deployed to embody the cosmos. Augustine gave explicit evidence of this prototype when he equated heaven with *civitas dei* and the material universe with *civitas terrena*, although he used these terms also to distinguish between the Catholic Church or the body of believers and the Roman state. Plato even looked to the city prototype as a metaphor for inner order, speaking of the city within oneself.[17]

So there were at least two elements in the ethos of Miletus that fostered speculative thinking. First was the juxtaposition of divergent cultures, a situation that always sets off a keener awareness of differences than is common in more insulated societies and is the ideal ground on which to spawn new metaphors and novel metaphor deployments. Second, the absence of theocracy and a prevailingly democratic cast of government enabled a free exchange of ideas that made it possible to explore the ideas that cultural diversity threw into relief. Union of these factors prepared the ideal conditions to promote the development and exercise of natural intellectual curiosity.

Thus, at Miletus, the southernmost city of the Greek colonies of Asia Minor, the conflict of differing cultural views blossomed into the first speculations of Thales, Anaximander, and Anaximenes. Heraclitus was from neighboring Ephesus. Philosophers of this earliest period who were not from the colonies were nevertheless subjected in one way or another to the influence of Asian cultures. The geopolitics of the Greek poleis favored the decline of religious myth as an ordering matrix of experience. The polis was initially small enough not to foster any kind of theocratic bureaucracy, and the relative insularity of each militated against the accretion of any elaborate, official religious dogma. Mystery cults were the closest analogue to the shamanism seen in many central Asian tribes; and they seem to have been founded more on emotional engagement than on intellectual persuasion. Religion had more to do with crops and the safety of the city than with morality and personal perpetuation. Consequently, priests were political appointees who had to learn no *summa totius theologiae*; they had only to be schooled in mainly propitiative ritual, not much more than simple sacrifices. Undoubtedly it was the lack of political power that worked against the establishment of any priestly class; and without such a class there was no motive for theologizing. Instead, speculation revolved around political issues and other secular matters. In the process of comparing ideas, common differentiae of root metaphors (or their prototypes) stand out and form the basis for abstract constructs. Myth is dismantled in this analytic process.

MATHEMATICS: THE PATH AWAY
FROM MYTH TOWARD ABSTRACTION

The advancement of speculative thought is clearly traceable in the development of mathematics.

> Between the workable empiricism of the early land measurers who parceled out the fields of ancient Egypt and the geometry of the Greeks in the sixth century before Christ there is a great chasm. On the remoter side lies what preceded mathematics, on the nearer, mathematics; and the chasm is bridged by deductive reasoning applied consciously and deliberately to the practical inductions of daily life. Without the strictest deductive proof from admitted assumptions, explicitly stated as such, mathematics does not exist.[18]

Although the predecessors of the Greeks may have had passing concern for theoretical issues in mathematics, "[e]xtant papyri and tablets contain specific cases and problems only, with no general formulations, and one may question whether these early civilizations really appreciated the unifying principles that are at the core of mathematics."[19] Morris Kline agrees:

> Let us review the status of mathematics before the Greeks entered the picture. We find in the Babylonian and Egyptian civilizations an arithmetic of integers and fractions, the beginnings of algebra, and some empirical formulas in geometry. There was almost no symbolism, hardly any conscious thought about abstraction, no formulation of general methodology, and no concept of proof or even of plausible arguments that might convince one of the correctness of a procedure or formula. There was, in fact, no conception of any kind of theoretical science.[20]

And Sir Thomas Heath opined that the "Greek genius for mathematics was simply one aspect of their genius for philosophy in general."[21] They were the first people in

Western civilization to articulate the structure of action schemes that previously had developed in particularized situations. This led directly to the axiomatic methods of Euclid, the syllogistic form of Aristotelian logic, and the abstract concept of number.

Number, for Pythagoreans, was reified; and this reification persisted in medieval thought. Aristotle rejected the reification, saying that "it is evident that the objects of mathematics do not exist apart; for if they existed apart their attributes would not have been present in bodies."[22] We have already noted the ancient tendency to regard qualities as indwelling agents, as a depersonalization of deistic accounts of qualities in myths. Number filled the bill, because the Greeks notated their numbers by dots, so that these dots became associated habitually with corresponding geometric forms—e.g., the number three was associated with a triangle, four with the square, and so on.

Furthermore, just as they narrowed down the geometric forms considered basic by limiting them to those which could be drawn with compass and ruler, the Greeks imposed a similar stricture on number. "Greek mathematics included no general concept of number, and consequently, no notion of a continuous algebraic variable."[23] Euclid stated that "a number is a multitude composed of units."[24] And similarly Aristotle: "[N]umber . . . is a plurality of ones and a certain quantity of them"[25] and "[N]umber will not, either as mover or as form, produce a continuum."[26] So, despite his avowal to the contrary, Aristotle maintained a reification of number as "mover." By defining numbers as composites of unity, he made the number one the generator of all other numbers, which form a discrete series of integers.

As we have noted in regard to their numerical notation, the Greeks associated magnitude with geometric forms and dimensions; nonintegral relative proportions were not seen as numbers but as illusions of the ideal brought on by the imperfections of the phenomenal world. The problem of irrational numbers, as in the length of the diagonal of a square the sides of which measure an integral multiple of one, was approached by measuring off, in the cited example, the length of one of the sides against the diagonal. The remainder was a sort of imperfection, a fragment of a whole number. This fragment could not be conceived as a number. The Greeks preferred to think of it simply as a line segment. Similarly, a fraction was construed not as a number but as a ratio or proportion between two numbers, which might have at the most a geometric representation.

Again, we are faced with the typical Greek adherence to the notion of the symmetrical order; and that order quite naturally is initially construed in the simplest and most static terms: geometric forms easy to construct and nothing but whole numbers. "The inability of Greek mathematicians to answer in a clear manner the paradoxes of Zeno made it necessary for them to forgo the attempt to give to the phenomena of motion and variability a quantitative explanation."[27] For, "as long as Aristotle and the Greeks considered motion continuous and number discontinuous, a rigorous mathematical analysis and a satisfactory science of dynamics were difficult of achievement."[28] The closest Aristotle got to treating motion in the modern way was in his notion of potentiality. This he construed as an indwelling agent, just as he did the propensity to move. He said that every body has a propensity to move to its proper place (in the cosmic order), and this propensity is an indwelling property (again the depersonalized mover).

DEPERSONALIZATION OF MYTHIC PROTOTYPES

As we shall see, much of ancient thought devolves from the myths by depersonalization. This is especially true of the fundamental concepts of the physical sciences. The doer of the myths becomes the agency of doing in scientific thought. Force is the personalized god (:Parent) who moves things. Clear vestiges of this are seen in the Aristotelian notion of the unmoved mover. Using the metaphor of a chain, consisting of things that move other things, Aristotle reasoned that there must be a first link, an original imparter of movement, that itself must be unmoved. It cannot be moved, he argued, for then part of it would move the rest and that part would then be the unmoved mover. Further, "if the whole moves itself we may distinguish in it that which imparts the motion and that which is moved,"[29] and we would be back to the same situation.

Aristotle's choice of a chain as exploratory metaphor was not an accident of his personal way of thinking. Rather, it was a natural outgrowth of the fateful turn of thought adopted—or at any rate articulated—by the Milesian philosophers. Beginning from the Eastern notion of the universe arising out of the division of the One into the Many (itself a combination of biological generation of parent to child and the elementary mathematical operation of division), the Milesians imposed on this division the metaphor of Pattern, a true revolution in thought. It was a step away from intuitionism, or the uncritical acceptance of the image schema of orderedness, toward a rational projection of it in terms of metaphorization. The Greek notion of *kosmos,* as we have noted, may have been a projection of the order of the polis, a sense that the political mechanics of the city-state mirrored the physical mechanics of the world at large. All the more plausible is this genesis in light of the ubiquity of the macrocosmos-microcosmos correspondence in much of classical thought. Again we face the geopolitical situations of the Greek poleis as formative factors in molding characteristic ways of thinking, although there is always the natural tendency to reduce everything to human terms.

MACROCOSM-MICROCOSM CORRESPONDENCE

Not truly a metaphor, the macrocosm-microcosm correspondence is a special case of anthropomorphism. Essentially it is seeing a physical and psychic identity between the human being and the universe.[30] Empedocles explained the workings of the universe in terms analogous to yin-yang. His forces were mythological: the gods, Aphrodite and Ares, representing love and strife. In the Platonic division of the populace into appetitive, irascible, and rational in the *Republic*, the same kind of antagonism between prototypical figures is established to account for the dynamism of the social order. Nor was that Plato's only bout with the macrocosmos-microcosmos question. In *Philebus*, he suggested that, just as the universe is made up of four elements, so are humans. Furthermore, human have governing reason through the agency of the soul, and so the universe, too, must have a soul. It must be governed by a rational principle or agent, which Plotinus called *anima mundi*. In fact, Plato duplicates Genesis, saying in *Timaeus* that the cosmos is in the image of the Demiurge. These ideas, of course, became popular in the Middle Ages under the influence of the biblical account of the creation of man and woman in the image of God. They were promulgated by Philo of Alexandria and also in the body of works known as the *Hermetica*, both popular works throughout the medieval period. Augustine paralleled the ages of the world with those of the individual. Godefrey de Saint Victor extended this parallel in his *Microcosmos*. He details correspondences between the ages of a human and the six days of creation. Astrologers imagined the zodiac in the form of a human, a picture still fashionable today. All these correspondences were felicitous within the Pattern and Mirror metaphors. They confirmed the symmetrical order of the universe, doing so by setting up mirror images, or correspondences, between humans and universal elements. How easily such ideas play out is a lesson in the importance of the consonance of subsidiary ideas and metaphors with dominant ones that represent the larger sense of how the whole universe works.

COSMIC ORDER AND THE CLASSICAL IDEA OF BEAUTY

If we are to understand Western thought to display a kind of unity, the key may well be found in the deployment of the original metaphor of Pattern. The Greeks enshrined this sense of order in nearly everything of timeless significance that they left behind them. What comes most immediately to mind in this regard is the typical Greek notion of beauty as "harmony of parts." Thus, Plato wrote that "measure and symmetry are beauty and virtue."[31] And Aristotle, of the unity of drama, noted that the parts must be so disposed "that the transposal or withdrawal of any one of them will disjoin and dislocate the whole."[32] We should note, too, that Plato's word translated as proportion was *symmetron*, literally a measuring together, the obvious etymological root of *symmetry*. That these ideas were shared by all Greeks is testified in their arts. In dramaturgy, framing the action within the span of a day, broken into a beginning, middle and end, was a formula lasting into our century.

Greek sculpture has always represented the epitome of aesthetic balance. And Greek architecture was more often than not built around elaborate schemes of mathematical proportions, not the least of which was the Golden Section (the smaller part is to the larger as the larger is to the whole).

Canons of proportion were known also in Eastern culture but there they remained rules of thumb more than integral parts of an aesthetic.[33] They were used to transpose the plan of a work from paper into the media of the arts and subsequently were solidified as rules for the transmission of relatively static religious traditions. The Greeks, by contrast, saw them as formulae for an ideal beauty in correspondence with the overall order of the cosmos, and it is in these terms that they passed down through the Renaissance and beyond, being literally replicated in the architectural modus of Le Corbusier.

Proportional canons ceased to have real artistic importance as soon as anatomic plates became common property (even though they contain very rigorous proportions). The consultation of such studies was habitually practiced with the object of discovering the presumed meeting point of natural beauty and artistic beauty, which has been a constant aspiration in the West. But at this point artistic beauty becomes identified quite simply with ancient statuary, and proportions as studied in sculpture become stereotyped and of secondary importance in comparison with the rendering of muscles or of the vague and ductile outline of the image.

> Proportion, in other words, becomes a latent element, if not altogether absent. To encounter it, one may turn to anatomic treatises, which demonstrate how traditional the proportional modules remain . . . underneath the scientific objectivity and how their constant application is accentuated, sometimes almost too blatantly.[34]

Adherence to proportion as an aesthetic ideal therefore has become implicit in nearly all Western art until the present century, with obvious antiacademic forerunners who rejected that ideal in the nineteenth century.

In architecture the rule of proportion is more evident to the eye and therefore more easily traced than in any other field. The Greek temple was an exemplification of mathematical ideals. "The height of the capitals in relation to the length of the columns, the distance between the columns themselves . . . and between the columns and the cella wall, the height of the entablature in relation to the length of the columns, the depth of the architrave, frieze and cornice in relation to the height of the entablature, the slight swelling of the columns in the centre (the entasis) and the degree to which they tapered at the top, the slightly concave curvature of the stylobate and the entablature, the angle at which the columns leant inward, the corner-work of the entablature, etc.—all these measurements were minutely calculated according to a particular scale of proportions."[35] Aesthetic variations were based on ideal ratios.

> The number of columns for the standard peristyle would be set at 6 by 14, counting the corner columns twice, but earlier temples [pre-Doric] sometimes had longer flanks. . . . In the sixth century, the height of the shafts measured 4.5 to 5 times the lower diameter; the column was 8 times as high as its capital. The tendency was to make these proportions leaner and more elegant in the course of decades, so that by the fifth century the relation of diameter to shaft was 1:5.5 or even 1:5.75, and the total column stood 11 to 12 times as tall as its capital.[36]

Number as *eidos* dominated aesthetic thought insofar as *symmetria* applied. "The generative ratio of the Doric Order was fixed as 2 to 1 in the earliest times of which we have knowledge."[37] To say that Greek architecture is coldly mathematical, however, would be misleading. Canons of proportion were only sources of inspiration. "There can of course be no doubt of the conscious use of this simplest of all numerical ratios [2:1] as a generative formula in the Doric Order, but it should not be imagined that all the measurements therefore will be found to be mathematically exact. . . . in the ancient Doric temples."[38] Even in classic cases such as the Parthenon, there is always found "the tempering of geometric accuracy by minute deviations in the interest of irregularity," but the "employment of the Greek 'refinements' would be neither useful nor explicable if these did not constitute appreciable departures from clearly recognizable and already familiar norms."[39] And it seems that this skein of concerns leads back to the human being as focus, a concept pronounced by Protagoras and surmised by Snell. "Perhaps inevitably in the light of their self-awareness, the metaphor of the Greek column has to do with the human body. It is as though we were there bearing the load of the superstructure and would know in our own bodies, emphatically, what is too much or too little for the constitution of the columns."[40]

Hardly fanciful, this notion was made explicit even by Vitruvius, who defined proportion in an Aristotelian manner as "a correspondence among the measures of the members of an entire work, and of the whole to a certain part selected as standard . . . as in the case of a well-shaped man."[41] Vitruvius suggests ideal proportions for both man and woman, relating these to different types of columns. These were the basis for Fra Giocondo's well-known drawings showing the ideal proportional relation of the human body to the column and the head to the capital. In the Renaissance, Cennino Cennini took this even further, establishing in his *Libro dell'Arte* proportions for every part of the body, using as modules the lengths of the forehead, nose, and entire face, and the distance from the nose to the chin.

Caskey has demonstrated that ideal proportions, especially those based upon the Golden Section, were also followed in the fabrication of Greek vases.[42]

COSMIC ORDER AND ONTOLOGY

Given an ordered universe, speculation would naturally turn to the question of the principle(s) by which that order becomes manifest from a supposed background of Oneness variously pictured as infinity or chaos. For the Greeks, order was closely associated with form, so that infinity, which they called the *apeiron* or *unbounded*, was simply that which by magnitude is unbounded and thereby formless and chaotic. *Metro* and *symmetron* found their isomorphic equivalents in nonvisual terms in the notions of the proportions and dispositions of parts. From there, it is a small step to the translation of this into numerical terms, which was done by the Pythagoreans in their exploration of the relation between divisions of the monochord and divisions of the scale. These studies certainly must have seemed an irrefutable validation of their sense of cosmic order to the Greeks.

> Pythagoras and his followers developed a series of analogies between musical consonances—derived from proportionate lengths of a stretched string—and natural phenomena. In Plato's *Timaeus*, the creation of the World-Soul, a model for the physical universe, is accomplished through the use of Pythagorean proportions: duple and triple geometric series are filled in with arithmetic and harmonic means, as a result of which one can see the whole universe to be a scale and a number (Aristotle, *Metaphysics*). The musical scale thus produced is that of Pythagorean tuning, and the World-Soul is created through the use of a kind of celestial monochord. . . .
>
> Pythagorean ideas about cosmic harmony continued to be elaborated by neo-Platonists from Carolingian times until the end of the Renaissance. These ideas strongly influenced astronomers and astrologers, physicians, architects, humanist scholars and poets.[43]

Most particularly, Pythagorean doctrines about cosmic harmonies found expression in the numerology that underlay medieval superstition. The literature is too extensive even to review.[44] Suffice it to say that the notion of a numeric cosmic order as embodied in doctrines of correspondences (:Mirror) dictated courses of thought in everything from alchemy and astronomy to music.[45]

COSMIC ORDER AND MATHEMATICS

Returning to the question of the principles underlying the cosmic order, we have seen that one principle construed was that of numeric, or mathematical, relation. This deployment of the Pattern metaphor has guided the evolution of Western science and continues deployment as the purely logical relations established in set theory and category theory now taken to be foundations of mathematical reasoning.

COSMIC ORDER AND THE CONCEPT OF CAUSALITY

A second principle of the cosmic order was construed from early legal proceedings and political debates. As early as the fifth century B.C.E. among the Sophists, and probably earlier, a distinction was made between *physis*, the natural order, and *nomos*, the legal order, the former being absolute and eternal, whereas the latter was arbitrated according to conditions of expedience. Again the geopolitics of the poleis, forcing comparison of differing mores, made this distinction all but inevitable.

In the conduct of legal proceedings involving free citizens of the poleis, it was necessary to establish the *aitia* or responsibility for the prosecuted action. *Aitia*, whence *aetiology*, was taken over from the legal profession as the term for what we call *cause*. However, that it was not equivalent to the present notion of cause—and certainly not to the Humean concept—is testified by Aristotle's postulation of four causes, of which "one is the essence or essential nature of the thing . . . the second is the matter or substratum, the third is the source of motion; and the fourth is the cause which is opposite to this, namely the purpose or 'good'. . . ."[46]

In his analysis of change, Aristotle distinguished two possibilities: motion and transformation. Either case involved a material substrate to which the change occurs. He designated this the material cause. When the change was a transformation, there had to be an alteration of form: the formal cause, what he described as "the essence or essential nature of the thing," alluding simultaneously to Platonic form and to his own notion of entelechy (from *en* + *telos*, end, in the sense of completion). Both allusions carried the denotation of innate potentiality, one of Aristotle's most original ideas, by which he was able to refute the paradoxes of Zeno. If we follow this convolution of reasoning, we see that the formal cause and the final cause are reverse sides of the same thing. The formal cause is to the final as the seed to the acorn tree. Both causes embody the form of a thing. Thus they are deployments of the Pattern metaphor. Again we remark the tendency of the ancients to conceive of qualities or properties as indwelling agencies, harking back to that depersonalization of mythic beings to which we have previously called attention.

COSMIC ORDER AND TIME

Today we would definitely not construe the future end of a thing to be a cause of its reaching that end, for, in the first place, that would entail a reversal of time action (the future influencing the present) and, in the second, a tautology (the end using itself). The Greeks saw it differently. They were averse to all forms of incompleteness, so addicted were they to the need for order. They therefore saw time itself as complete. When Aristotle says that "Time, past, present, and future, forms a continuous whole,"[47] presumably he means not quite what we would mean by the same words. He echoes the same notion that Plato espouses when he describes in the *Timaeus* that the maker "resolved to have a moving image of eternity, and when he set in order the heavens, he made this image eternal but moving according to number, while eternity itself rests in unity; and this image we call time."[48] Certainly here is the metaphorical basis for Aristotle's concept of entelechy and potentiality. Time is eternity, an accomplished whole, moving across the face of the cosmos. The relative motion, so to speak, between the eternity and entelechy create what we perceive as change, yet both are in a sense unitary and complete in themselves. The form of a thing, then, is like the tail end of the completed transformation already present in eternity. No reverse temporal causality is therefore involved in the final cause. Part of the beauty of this metaphorization of time is that the linear spatialization of time, which was clearly conceived by the Greeks, could be neatly accommodated without its becoming dominant. The diminished deployment of the linear time metaphor unquestionably had an effect on Greek science, helping to hold back speculation in the area of dynamics—lack of precision timepieces also played a part. However, we cannot say that this backseat allotment to linear time did not in itself hold back the invention of more precise chronometers. Safer to incline to a dialectic interpretation.

We should be careful to note now, in the perspective just drawn, that Aristotle's analysis of change avoided a completely linear concept of causation, narrowing it down to the efficient cause, "the source of motion." Of his four causes, this is the only one that has persisted into modern scientific thought. Roger Bacon was among the earliest to relegate the other three to the realm of metaphysics.

COSMIC ORDER AND THE CONCEPT OF CHANGE

Closely related to the concept of time is that of change. Clearly we can discern in the Greek view of change tactics of adaptation quite different from our own; and a consideration of it will carry us into a plexus of metaphors that will greatly illuminate our understanding of the deployment of the Pattern metaphor. At the heart of all ancient thought, East and West, is a preoccupation with the flux of things, born from the experience of the day-to-day image of a thing drifting away from the mnemonic image,[49] which is often kept constant. It is a given of all human experience and must be dealt with one way or another, for at the end of it is death.

Eastern cultures have typically disposed of change by relegating it to an illusory world dictated by spontaneous generation. They choose to adopt an organic metaphor: a seed sprouting from its own inexplicable potentialities. In the Vedic Hymns, this is the *hiranyargabha*, the golden germ.[50] They avoid logical inquiry by the ploy of the reflexive or tautological; it cannot be pursued discursively to any further logical principles. Lao Tzu, writing of it as the Tao, said:

> They call it elusive, and say
> That one looks
> But it never appears.

It is "[b]eyond all resolution."[51] Things "undergo change from one form to another," wrote Chuang Tzu. "Their beginning and end are like a circle, no part of which is any more the beginning than any other part."[52]

By contrast, in the West the beginning is the bifurcation of the world into the phenomenal and the ideal, but the overriding need for symmetry leads to the postulation of a correspondence between the two, so that the logic of the one must somehow be translatable into that of the other. This is most clearly articulated in Plato's theory of ideal forms, really the enshrined mnemonic images, of which he claimed that all phenomenal things are but poor copies.

> Now everything that becomes or is created must of necessity be created by some cause, for without a cause nothing can be created. The work of the creator, whenever he looks to the unchangeable and fashions the form and nature of his work after an unchangeable pattern, must necessarily be made fair and perfect; but when he looks to the created only, and uses a created pattern, it is not fair or perfect.[53]

So potent has this notion of ideal forms been in Western philosophy that Richard Rorty contends that the metaphor of the mirror has tricked us into believing in absolutes, when he insists that there are none. He sees the Mirror metaphor as dominating Western thought.[54]

IDEAL FORM EXPLAINED THROUGH THE CLASSICAL THEORY OF PERCEPTION

A clearer picture of the Platonic ideal form emerges from the closely related subject of perception. The early Greeks conceived our mental faculties to reside in three separate organs: the *thymos*, the *noos*, and the *psyche*. The latter we have already examined. In the blood and sinews is the *thymos*, and it is seated at the heart or liver, the organ of emotion. Perception takes place in the *noos* (a word of unknown etymology), which is like a mirror catching the image of everything placed before it. For whatever reasons, the Greeks conceived of perception largely in terms of sight.

Within this context of the Greek prioritizing of vision, we should note that linear outline is what most clearly defines a thing visually; and it is outline which first appears in the art of children and prehistoric cave painting. Outline delineates the mnemonic image. So it was natural that form should come in Platonic thought to delimit the ideal. Compatibility with the Mirror metaphor of perception was also a leading factor in the choice of form. In the *noos*, the image of an object was caught, like the reflection on a mirror. It was often said that "like recognizes like," in other words, that the similitude of an object reflected in the *noos* is sufficient to explain recognition. Epicurus first enunciated this doctrine, claiming that objects radiate minute copies of themselves that are then taken into the eye. Later humoral theories postulated a similar notion that objects exude self-replicas that become mixed into the humors.

Mirror reflection posits an object, which is genuine, and a reflection, which is insubstantial. Plato had it that phenomenal objects themselves are copies (reflections) of ideal objects, thereby taking the mirror metaphor of perception one step back. That he metaphorized them as copies, rather than as reflections, was probably motivated by the fact that the Greek word for matter or substance, *hyle*, had the root meaning of "wood." Hence also the demiurge as master craftsman. We can begin to see how all these metaphors fit together and reinforced one another in their deployment. We begin with the felt sense of order, the action schema of orderedness, which becomes, as earlier noted, articulated into the metaphor of Pattern. For the Greeks, this meant predominantly visual pattern. Form was central to their thinking, forever enshrined by Plato in his notion of *eidos*. That form could be explored in its essence by number was probably suggested partly by the fact that the Greeks, as earlier remarked, notated their numbers with dots arranged in shapes. That the notes of the octave were defined by simple ratios of the length of a sounding string, on top of the already suggestive geometrized numeric notation, convinced the Pythagoreans that numbers and their correspondences with things in the physical world held the key to understanding the natural order. So, a link was forged between *eidos* and number. On the one hand, form was conceived as defining eternal being and truth (as ideal forms and comprehension of them), and on the other, ratios, ideal proportions, were seen as the basis of beauty. Correspondence—first between ideal forms and ideas and physical objects, and second, between numbers representing properties of objects and ideas inherent in the objects (e.g., ratios establishing beauty of form)—was a common link between different domains of thought. *Metron*, measuring physical properties into numbers, and *symmetron*, comparing measurements so as to obtain ideal proportions or symmetry, thus are key concepts by which many ideas were held together for the Greeks. In all these instances, the Mirror metaphor established the common experiential substrate upon which these ideas could evolve with a natural intuitive appeal. Everyone has seen reflections, if only in a mud puddle. Thus, for the Greeks, perception was explained in terms of reflection in the *noos*. Comparing, then, often involves moving back and forth between a mnemonic image (a captured reflection, according to this theory of perception) and an immediately perceived image (a present reflection). Reality is inextricably bound up in this picture with mirror reflections and correspondences, which are conceptual derivations of mirror reflections. We do not suggest that the doctrine of correspondences was in every case born directly from the mirror metaphor, but only that in its deployment it has a similar structure, making it harmonize with notions derived from the mirror metaphor. This is important, because when two notions come so close together in underlying structure, one may tend to be interpreted and deployed in terms of the metaphor of the other.

ORDER, THE MIRROR METAPHOR, AND EPISTEMOLOGY

So far, the concepts we have examined show the Greeks to have been preoccupied with the need for order, especially *symmetron*, proportion or symmetry. Cosmic order is a reflection of ideal order, though it is an imperfect reflection. Knowledge, then, begins with a comparison of data, both Greek and Latin having words for knowing that display root meanings of bringing together. According to the Platonic tradition, the highest knowledge, noesis (from *noos*), is attained through the dialectic, properly a systematic comparison of mnemonic forms (that is, the essential forms of things abstracted from their phenomenal presentations) until all ideal forms come together in a synoptic vision. This same noesis is identified by Plato with the good, but not the good in the social and legal sense of the word. Plato was only interested in the ultimate good, which he put at the pinnacle of the eidetic hierarchy.[55] Before commenting on Platonic epistemology, let us set in contrast to it the typical Eastern attitude toward knowledge and the cosmic order.

In the intellectual traditions of the East, knowledge is not simply a comparing of data; it is a fragmenting of what is intrinsically One (:One/Many), and therefore a violation of existence. Dialectic will get us nowhere but into a further falsification of reality through endless fragmentation. The highest form of knowledge, in these terms, must be a negation of knowledge and of the fragmentation on which it is based. To put it crudely, whereas the Westerner is exhorted to take everything apart so that he can then put it back together, the Easterner is encouraged to turn away from taking things apart and go back to a state in which he was before he started deconstructing.

Although there is insufficient evidence to prove it, we put forth the tentative hypothesis that the difference between the two approaches is one of comparative cerebral hemispheric dominance. In the East, right hemisphere function with ho-listic information processing seems to prevail, contrasted with the West, where the serial processing of the left hemisphere appears to dominate. Consequently, dialec-tic is known to the East but is subsidiary to holistic enlightenment. It is primary in the West as virtually the only legitimate means to synoptic knowledge (outside the tradition of religious mysticism). The latest version of noetic understanding is rep-resented by the sought-after general unified theories of modern physics, revised versions of the unified field theories envisioned by Einstein and his generation.

ORDER AND DISORDER, HEALTH AND DISEASE

Disease is an indwelling agency of disorder that has come down to us and lingered in our linguistic expressions. It was first conceived, like almost everything else, as the doings of a god, but then it switched to possession by an evil spirit, and finally the evil spirit was depersonalized into an agent of disease. The disease agency is finally treated as an entity. "He has a cold." "She came down with the flu." Compare this with the French *Qu'avez-vous?*, which is literally "What do you have?" but has the idiomatic meaning, "What's wrong with you?"

Health and disease accorded with concepts of order. Socrates voiced a wide-spread attitude when he spoke of a sound mind in a sound body. Balance was the key in health as in art. Even in medical thought, this was true. Humoral balance for Hippocrates and his followers determined the health of the body. Disease is thus equated with imbalance, which links it through order and disorder with ugli-ness. Asymmetry in Far Eastern countries, on the other hand, is more apt to be seen as beautiful, acting through the dominant metaphor of the Organism, repre-senting order rising spontaneously through unpredictable patterns of growth. While both the Greco-Romans and the Hindus and Chinese postulated channels in the body, for the former it was the inert four humors that circulated through them in a kind of mechanical balance, but for the latter, the inexplicable agency of the One.

In Greco-Roman medicine, illness was due to an imbalance of the humors; in Indian and Chinese medicine, it was due to obstruction of the *spirit* moving through the chakras or meridians.[56] Yin and yang in Chinese medicine must be in balance as the *ch'i* flows through the meridians, but this balance is dynamic and asymmet-ric, though some therapeutic principles are dyadic. Of ancient vintage, this con-cept of pathology and treatment was set down in the legendary *Huang Ti Nei Ching Su Wen* (Yellow Emperor's classic of internal medicine). Huang Ti supposedly reigned in the twenty-sixth century B.C.E. However, the "text of Huang Ti's classic can be traced only to the Early Han Dynasty, and then only in references made by physi-cians in their own works." The earliest existing version was that compiled in the Tang dynasty by Wang Ping, who "claimed that he had access to Huang Ti's origi-nal manuscript," which seems unlikely, since his edition came out in 762 A.D.[57]

THE MIRROR METAPHOR AND DYADIC STRUCTURES:
A BRIEF SUMMARY

Aesthetics, epistemology, and ontology, then in the cradle of ancient civilization, all were determined by metaphors of a dyadic structure, ultimately founded upon that of mirror reflection, a phenomenon that baffled and fascinated man for thousands of years.[58] We cannot dismiss this as trivial. To see a likeness of oneself upon still water, without the least understanding of light, vision, and optics, must have been something truly magical. Reflection and shadow gives one a double, forever instilling in the mind a mysterious sense of duality. Plato, through whom this idea of the duality of existence was forever installed in Western thought, described this notion clearly in the tenth book of *The Republic*. He takes as his example a common bed. Addressing the difference between appearance and reality, he says that "you may look at a bed from different points of view, obliquely or directly or from any other point of view, and the bed will appear different, but there is no difference in reality. And the same of all things."[59] When a carpenter makes a bed, he copies the ideal bed that resides in heaven. Lest there be any doubt what lay behind Plato's thinking, he likens this imitative creation to that of turning a mirror to various objects and creating images of them.[60] Similarly, Aristotle in his *Poetics* presents literary creation as imitation of the possible. Imitation, he opines, is natural to man.[61] He focuses not on form, as Plato did, but on purpose. He sees nature as purposeful, so that imitation manifests purpose, and when this purpose is intelligently presented, beauty is the result.[62] Shakespeare caught the Aristotelian notion of mimesis, when he had Hamlet say, "The purpose of playing, whose end, both at the first and now, was and is, to hold, as 'twere, the mirror up to nature."[63]

When duality turns up in the relation between numbers, it is an unshakable substantiation that therein must lie a very deep-seated truth. Truth itself rests upon a dyadic relation between word or notion and reality: this is the so-called correspondence theory of truth. For the Greeks, the correspondence was between word, or its semantic import, and *eidos*. Knowledge of the *eidos* was attained through dialectic, a kind of stringent inner inquiry. All subsequent theories of truth have similar dyadic bases. In modern terms, it is impossible to think of any statement as true without envisioning something to which the import of the statement is to be compared. A truth must be *about* something. To be true, a statement must in some sense *reflect* an aspect of that to which it applies. This is a natural way in which to order our sense of the world. An alternative approach is represented by pragmatism in which the Mirror metaphor is supervened.

THE PATTERN METAPHOR AND ORDER: SUMMARY

We have been playing off metaphoric strands in an almost fugal manner, and it is time to restate the theme and give a kind of recapitulation that will bring all the strands together. First, there is the innate tendency of Western man to prefer serial and symmetric order—probably dictated by his left hemisphere brain dominance and initially expressed in the ideas of a patterned cosmos, the organizational elements of which are whole numbers and simple geometric forms—and the dyadic Mirror metaphor. Metaphors with an underlying dyadic structure were unconsciously chosen and deployed to accord with the sense of order embodied in the Pattern metaphor. Deployment was carried out with the rationale that, within a cosmic hierarchy (another deployment of the Pattern metaphor), all elements must interlock to constitute the symmetrically ordered whole. This interlocking is largely through various kinds of correspondence. Obviously this dyadicism has much to do with the bilateral symmetry of the human body, with its two arms, two legs, two eyes, and two ears. Discursive topology, predicated as it is heavily on human action schemes, necessarily reflects bilaterally symmetric physiology and motivates the selection of dyadic metaphors to implement the thought processes.

INDWELLING AGENTS WITHIN THE PATTERN ON THE WAY TO SPIRIT

Outside this constellation of the metaphors woven around the dominant and organizing Pattern metaphor, which characterized the Greek ethos or worldview is the concept of physical properties as indwelling agencies, including the propensity to move or be at rest, mass, dimension, and all the so-called secondary characteristics (color, smell, taste, etc.). Infusing the cosmos with dynamism, these agents were but depersonalized remnants of the gods; yet, ironically these agents would lead to a reconstitution of the spiritual. This abrogation of the mythical order forestalled the approach of considering certain properties to be relations or, alternatively, variables.

> Aristotle's error arose from the fact that, in common with other philosophers before Archimedes, he had no idea of the conception now known as density or specific gravity; he failed to see that it is the weight per unit volume compared with that of the surrounding medium which determines rise or fall, and, following the teaching of Plato, he attributed the motion to an innate instinct leading everything to seek its own natural resting-place.[64]

Archimedes offers a fine example of the constraints imposed by implicit metaphors. "Though he was very much in the tradition of *pure* Greek science, we know from the chance discovery of his work on *method* that he actually used mechanical models *to arrive at* mathematical results, though he discarded them *in the proof.* For the most part his work was not followed up in classical times."[65] Thus, he used empirical methods, which seems natural to us but to the Greeks was not because it is contrary to the metaphorical basis of noesis (which requires a piecing together of ideal forms to achieve a synoptic vision of the cosmic order). Though he arrived at a relativistic notion of the property of density, he was not able to generalize this into terms of a new metaphor nor to discard the old metaphor nor even to apply some topological transformation to it that might have brought to light its inadequacies for imposing a convincing coherence on existing data. Instead:

> He was the founder of *hydrostatics*, the laws of floating bodies, which was to have two important uses. One was for the determination of the densities of bodies by weighing them in water; this, because it could be used for the testing of precious metals, was taken up at once and never lost. The other, the estimation of the burden of a ship, was well enough known by tradition to shipbuilders and was not calculated till the late seventeenth century.[66]

It took nearly two thousand years before the metaphor of the indwelling agency as a physical property lost its hold sufficiently for men to burst its confines, which they did, not so much by substituting a new metaphor as by reducing the agency (acting principle) to an entity in a network of topological relations. That is, the agent became a mere mathematical variable, more and more detached from any picture of reality.

BACK TO THE ELEMENTS

Let us remember that, in their effort to construe a simple order from nature, the Greeks haltingly assembled the four elements: earth, water, fire, and air. These are not to be taken quite literally. Three of the elements—earth, water and air—represented an intuitive grasp of the three phases of matter: solid, liquid, and gaseous. At the same time, each was a distillation from ancient creation myths of what supported first life. We do not have to look far for the motivations here. Seeds were seen to grow from the earth, algae and the like seemed to sprout spontaneously from waters, air and heat infused animal bodies with life—pressure on the eyeballs would even make manifest the fire in the body (in the form of dazzling spots or flashes of light).

Each primal element had its shroud of mystery. Air was obviously a form of matter, but a finer form, easily construed as superior, since it rises upward, eludes clear perception, and is beyond the primary sense of sight. *Pneuma*, as the Greeks called this element, was conceived to circulate through the body via a network of minute tubes, where it doubled as the vehicle by which nourishment is distributed throughout the body and as the medium by which are conducted thought, sensation, and voluntary movement. By the time of Galen, this primitive theory had given rise to one based on humors, itself going back at least to the Hippocratic treatise, *On the Nature of Man* (c. 390 B.C.E.). Under the inspiration of theories of correspondence (microcosm/macrocosm), the theory of the humors evolved in many directions, tangling with branches of numerology, to form a large swath of the intellectual brambles of the Middle Ages.

In Search of the Transcendental Fifth Element

Probably from sun myths, the idea arose very early that the earth and its atmosphere are surrounded by a fiery element, potent with life, separate and distinct from the four elements but conceptually a refined hybrid of fire and air. Aristotle called this the ether, the etymological root of which means to burn, or the fifth element, translated into Latin as the *quinta essentia*, whence the word *quintessence*. *Quinta essentia* was itself a translation of the Greek *pempte ousia*, literally *fifth being*, referring to the ether. *Ousia* was a present participial form of *einai*, to be, and *essentia* was an assumed counterpart in Latin. These connections are not merely of academic importance; they establish linkages between ideas that have absolutely infused every corner of Western thought.

Whenever Aristotle spoke of what has been translated as *substance*, he used the term *ousia*. This makes his duality of form and substance a bit clearer, for he was saying, more strictly, that all things are composites of being and form—in other words, a thing is a form of being. However, he rejected the earlier Ionian notion of creation, so that when the early Christian thinkers took him as a model, they had to superimpose upon his thought the ideas of a sudden creation and a sudden end, leaving everything in the middle as he had described it. Aquinas rationalized the Aristotelian duality of being and form by supposing that to formed being must be imparted by divine decree the property of existence. He did this by calling attention to the fact that nonexistent things, such as unicorns, might have essences, by which he meant that which defines it to be what it is (the central notion in Aristotle's exposition of form and entelechy). Yet they do not have existence in the substantial sense. Existence can come only through divine creation.

It will be instructive to examine Aristotle's rather tortuous argument for the existence of the ether, or fifth element, because from it evolved the notion of essence, which pervades philosophical as well as everyday thinking. We shall abridge his rather lengthy presentation in the second and third chapters of *On the Heavens*. He begins by stating, essentially without proof, that there are two categories of "simple motion," viz., rectilinear and circular. Already we witness the operation of the Greek mind in search of simple symmetric order—Aristotle can almost assume that his readers will agree with him, for they would commonly have been indoctrinated by the same deployment of the Pattern metaphor. He moves on to an extraordinary tautology: "Supposing, then, that there is such a thing as simple motion, and that circular motion is an instance of it, and that both motion of a simple body is simple and simple movement is of a simple body . . . then there must necessarily be some simple body which revolves naturally and in virtue of its own nature with a circular motion."[67] Such an argument could not have issued from the father of the syllogism unless he knew he had tacit assent by virtue of the intellectual ethos of the times.

He continues that, since the earthly four elements move naturally upward (fire and air) or downward (water and earth), which is to say rectilinearly, then the simple body having circular motion as its natural mode must be other than these.

> Further, this circular motion is necessarily primary. For the perfect is naturally prior to the imperfect, and the circle is a perfect thing. This cannot be said of any straight line: not of an infinite line; for, if it were perfect, it would have a limit and an end: nor of any finite line; for in every case there is something beyond it, since any finite line can be extended. And so, since the prior movement belongs to the body which is naturally prior, and circular movement is prior to straight, and movement in a straight line belongs to simple bodies—fire moving straight upward and earth bodies straight downward toward the center—since this is so it follows that circular movement also must be the movement of some simple body. . . . These premises give the conclusion that there is in nature some bodily substance other than the formations which we know, prior to them all and more divine than they.[68]

In the next chapter, Aristotle states, again as a matter beyond dispute, that "everything that comes to be comes into being from its contrary."[69] A correspondence principle, baldly dyadic, this Ionian notion is the basis on which Aristotle argues that all material substances are blends of opposites—dryness and wetness, heaviness and lightness—implicit in the four elements. It is also the rationale for elemental transmutation in alchemy. Now let us put this principle in its original context:

> It is equally reasonable to assume that this body [the ether] will be ungenerated and indestructible and exempt from increase or alteration, since everything that comes to be comes into being from its contrary and in some substrate, and passes away likewise in a substrate by the action of the contrary into the contrary. . . . Now the motions of contraries are contrary. If then this body can have no contrary, because there can be no contrary motion to the circular, nature seems justly to have exempted from contraries the body which was to be ungenerated and indestructible.[70]

Finally, appealing to common observation, he reminds us that the celestial bodies revolve in circular paths and "in the whole range of time past, so far as our inherited records reach, no change appears to have taken place in the whole scheme of the outermost heaven or in any one of its proper parts."[71] All in all, we could not ask for a clearer illustration of how an underlying metaphoric system constrains reason itself to its deployment. Relying implicitly on the Pattern metaphor to construe the cosmos as having a specific order, Aristotelian physics has it that all bodies move geometrically according to their physical nature. A line is imperfect, compared to a circle, because it has a beginning and an end. This was a matter of cultural taste. The Greeks had a mistrust for asymmetry. A circle, being most symmetrical of all two-dimensional figures, was reckoned to be the most perfect. Therefore, imperfect bodies would move rectilinearly and perfect bodies circularly.

Next, Aristotle brings in the Greek predilection for dyadic correspondence (congenial to the Mirror metaphor). Everything arises out of opposites (mirror images of each other). Ionian philosophers had already established that all terrestrial things are mixtures of the four basic elements of fire, air, water, and earth. Further, fire and air, being dry, are opposite to water and earth, which are wet. From his doctrine of opposites, Aristotle reasons that all earthly things are composed of fire or air combined with water or earth. All earthly things, too, are imperfect, so that nothing perfect can be made from the four elements; it must be made from a fifth element.

Now, the celestial bodies move in circular orbits. Circular orbits through symmetry are perfect paths, and only perfect bodies move on perfect paths. Hence, the celestial bodies must be perfect. Being perfect, they must be made from a fifth element, the ether, which is more refined than the four terrestrial elements. Thereby he purportedly proves the existence of the fifth element.

Underlying this argument are the ideas of opposites and symmetry, both conformal to mirror imaging. A symmetrical figure or body is one in which one half is the mirror image of the other half. Opposites can also be visualized as mirror counterparts. He is able to enunciate the principles based on these two ideas without further proof because they are congenial to the Greek way of looking at things in terms of cosmic order (:Pattern) and mirror imaging. Everything has its place and natural motion, given a certain balanced (again, mirror-imaging) order of the universe. This is given and needs no further proof.

FROM FIFTH ELEMENT TO SPIRIT:
THE GRAECO-CHRISTIAN SYNTHESIS

So, we have the primitive breath-spirit, on the one hand, and the *quinta essentia*, on the other. How did the two become merged? Through the intervention of Christian dogma. Aristotle, who was second only to the Bible as an authority for medieval thought, had said that the ether is the divine substance, superior to the four earthly elements. The Bible said that God breathed life into man. What could this breath have been other than the divine element, the *quinta essentia*?

But further than even this, the scholastic philosophers, searching for a way to mend the Aristotelian rejection of creation, latched onto a distinction that Avicenna made between existence and essence. We have already indicated how Aquinas used this distinction to save the day. Now, Aristotle had based his concept of essence partly on Platonic form and partly on the linguistic analyses necessary to the development of his treatise on logic. In the latter case, he had obviously identified *ousia* or being with the "It is . . ." of predication, prompting him to say at one point that *ousia* is that of which nothing can be predicated other than its existence (i.e., "It is"). Essence then became that of which "It is . . ." is the predicator, or that which is predicated of a thing: its defining differentiae.

The defining differentiae of a thing are merely verbal articulations of those properties which make a thing what it is—certainly compatible with the visual metaphor of form suggested by Plato as constituting the ideal prototype of which the earthly counterpart is but a poor simulacrum. On analogy with the divine spirit making man what he is, namely the rational animal, the Scholastics reasoned that the presence of certain amounts of the *quinta essentia* must account for the essence of material but inanimate bodies. Thus, we have the following equations or transformations: breath → spirit → entelechy → form, and breath → spirit → ether → quinta essentia → quintessence → essence. By these equations, we also have essence → form → defining differentiae.

This deployment has vexed thinkers down through the ages by luring them into attempting to define the essence of this and that, whereas most categories of being are highly enough disjunctive that the breath-spirit metaphor fails to impose satisfactory coherence upon them. Nevertheless, the deployment of this metaphor complex is highly instructive, and it is for this reason that we have examined so closely the details of Aristotle's arguments as well as the linguistic transformation of terms. It should be clear from this case that deployment occurs by analogy, permitting categorical linkages antithetical to deductive reasoning. Extremes of this process are found in psychotic thought, first investigated and analyzed by E. von Domarus:

> Von Domarus . . . described the thought of schizophrenics as "paralogical," defining its formal aspects as follows: "Whereas the logician accepts identity only on the basis of identical subjects, the paralogician accepts identity on the basis of identical predicates." As an example, Von Domarus describes a schizophrenic patient who believed that Jesus, cigar boxes, and sex were identical. Investigation revealed that the link connecting these disparate items was the concept of being encircled: Jesus' head is encircled by a halo, cigar boxes by a tax band, and women by the sex glance of a man. Thus, the slightest similarity between items or events becomes a connecting link that makes them identical.[72]

If we turn back to Aristotle, we shall see that the unconscious assumption of metaphors allowed him to make linkages that were based more on similarity of predicates rather than on similarity of subjects. Thus, the extremities of psychotic thought processes are to be found latent in so-called normal reasoning. Paralogic is merely the reductio ad absurdum of logic.

Perfect and complete identity of subjects exists only by definition, mainly in mathematics and logic, where it is tautological. In practice, equivalencies are only approximate, and human thought proceeds by swinging back and forth between the tautological and the paralogical. In deploying the metaphors through which we construe reality, we grope for similarities. These offer patches of the familiar in a forest of the unknown, where anxiety rides high enough to spur us to forge connections. The only justification for them is that they bring together strands of existence, helping to cover a vulnerability to the buffets of insufferable chaos. No price seems too high to pay for this sense of security.

CONCLUSION

For the Greeks, the world had to be made to correspond with the way in which the Western brain processed its inputs, serially and with the greatest of economy of order to facilitate information storage and retrieval; hence, by discrete numbers, *metron* and *symmetron*, neat correspondences, in a space-time scheme where that which is past is the pattern *in potentia* of what is completed in the future. Design spans time. Reason and emotion, thought and feeling, beauty and truth, permanence and change, all were construed in terms of *metron* and *symmetron*, measure in the absolute and measure set against measure. *Ratio* is reason. Spirit is form. Absence of form is chaos, the unthinkable. *Karek noos*, outside the image faculty of mind, was a Greek expression for *in a senseless manner*. What lay outside the formative matrix of vision had no meaning for the Greeks. It was truly a *vision* of the cosmos that they bequeathed to Western civilization.

5

The Medieval Period

To understand intellectual history after the classic Greek apogee, it is necessary to focus on the migrations that both destroyed and rebuilt empires. The first was the overpowering of the Greek empire by the Romans, and the second was the crumbling of the Roman Empire under the battering of the Germanic tribes. Both migrations had at least one thing in common: they overlaid an intellectually more sophisticated culture with an ethos still at the mythic level. Also, both the Romans and the Germans were fresh from nomadism and accustomed to lives of practical work. When they imitated the aristocracy they saw before them, they rose only to ostentation, never to the leisurely cultivation of the arts and speculative thought for their own sake. Although the Romans achieved great things—perfection of the dome, improved bridge construction, articulation of law—none of them represented truly innovative thought; and the early settlers of Europe hardly knew how to write. The tendency away from the traditions of the Greek elite toward a renewed preoccupation with everyday matters meant that the sophisticated appeal of the Pattern metaphor was diminished. Agrarian concerns overshadowed speculation over the cosmos. *Metron* and *symmetron* had no role to play for the harried farmer worried about putting food on the table. Niceties of symmetry, theories of proportion, and consideration of ideal forms had no bearing on the fate of the year's crops. Yet, these were the things that had made the Pattern metaphor so viable for the Greek culture. A dominant metaphor, one that organizes the world, cannot be sustained without the subsidiary metaphors and ideas that draw upon it. Such metaphor complexes are mutually supportive.

Classical civilization was based on slavery, with consequent exultation of aristocratic ideals. Its values were essentially opposite to the those of the slave: disdain for and removal from practical or manual work, refinement of sensorial pleasures, and cultivation of mental abilities. In Greek science purely rational structures, such as geometry and logic, rhetoric and linguistics, were perfected, but speculation and debate ultimately bogged down in sophistic stalemates. Practical science, as attempted by Archimedes and Eudoxus, could not surmount the speculative *Weltanschauung*, and so classical civilization lay trapped in a completely theory-based deployment of certain root metaphors that favored a static sense of structure.

Classical thought did manage to discredit the older mythical order, but it was reinstated first by the Romans and then, after it had again largely come into intellectual disrepute, by the Germanic tribes who brought the Roman Empire to ruin. The personalities of the gods once more entered the common explanation of how things work, displacing more abstract heuristic devices that favored a less anthropomorphic approach to knowledge. With the decay of the Roman Empire and its state religion, the West was opened to the inrush of Eastern mystery cults. It has always been the case that the masses fall behind the intelligentsia in their ability to handle their spiritual needs in the absence of a faith in deity. Indeed, truth to tell, spiritual needs do not easily melt away at the fiery touch of reason, even for the literati. Therefore, it has always been a matter of trading old religions for new, until the old becomes new again and can be resurrected. Early medieval Europe was rife with Eastern cults, among them Christianity. One aspect that these cults usually had in common was that of duality, especially prominent in cults of Persian origin. This duality was predicated on very ancient efforts to solve the problem of change—the discrepancy between the mnemonic and phenomenal images—through the Mirror metaphor.

Out of the cauldron of mysticism brewing on the hearth of the ruined Roman state came the dominant philosophy of the age, Neoplatonism; and its most influential spokesman was Plotinus. Plotinus brought together strands of Platonism, Pythagoreanism, and Persian dualism. It is significant that the passages from Plato and Aristotle on which he drew were among the most ambiguous written by those thinkers—some were even of doubtful authorship. His writings were compatible with the tendencies of the time to seek in obscurantist mysticism a refuge from the world, which was collapsing into rubble and, at the level of the rich few, decadence. The metaphors of Greek culture as deployed by an impractical intellectual elite ceased to impose coherence on the experience of the masses or, indeed, on that of the elite themselves. The universe was not displaying the aspect of static symmetry that had been embodied in the town plans of the classic Greek poleis. The cities were decaying, and marauders were torching them, leaving behind nothing resembling order. No longer able to function as microcosms of the universe, instilling in the citizen a sense of orderedness, the city was toppled physically and as a potent metaphor prototype.

THE PARENT METAPHOR REPLACES THE PATTERN METAPHOR

Reinstated was the more primitive metaphor of the Parent as god, whose guiding principle is not so much order as willed authority, the partially obscure parental intent. From the East came the metaphor of intelligence as enlightenment, literally an identification of knowledge with Light. God, as the supreme principle of intelligence, also was identified with light—a symbolism prevalent in the *Commedia* of

Dante, where, for example, God speaks through the tip of a flame and announces his presence through a nimbic luminosity. The visible symbol of this metaphor was the halo, which originated in Eastern sun worship and made its appearance as a symbol of holiness in Christianity around the fourth century.

In alliance with the mythic Parent metaphor, Plotinus supplanted the Greek *metron* and *symmetron*, the static Design, with the order of hierarchy modeled on the Family, a cascade of relative authority and duty. The switch was neatly achieved because the sense of *order* was not rejected but merely redefined. Responsibility, abducted by the state, was shifted to a higher authority subject neither to full comprehension nor to logical examination. The more untidy aspect of things can always be hidden in the mysterious will of God (isomorphic to that part of the parent that the child cannot fathom). There is comfort in this because it appeals to human experiences that are ontogenically early, hence deep-rooted and largely nonverbal.

PLATONIC FORMS BECOME BENEFACTIONS OF THE PARENT

Platonic Forms in Plotinus are shorn of their geometric roots and redefined as the thoughts of God, an idea first suggested by Albinus and Antiochus of Ascalon. Furthermore, these thoughts emanate from God not in time but through an eternal process of overflowing, making time once more a monolith moving across the formlessness of matter.

> It is precisely because there is nothing within the One that all things are from it: in order that Being may be brought about, the source must be no Being but Being's generator, in what is to be thought of as the primal act of generation. Seeking nothing, possessing nothing, lacking nothing, the One is perfect and, in our metaphor, has overflowed, and its exuberance has produced the new: this product has turned again to its begetter and been filled and has become its contemplator and so an Intellectual-Principle.[1]

Emanation draws upon the Organism metaphor, differing from the expansion of a Design in not having an apparent logic to it, but having motivation in the personalized will of God. "The One is all things and no one of them," Plotinus says cryptically; "the source of all things is not all things; all things are its possession— running back, so to speak, to it—or, more precisely, not yet so, they will be."[2] We are obviously back at the mythic level of mentation, where God, the One, is the inscrutable parent-creator.

Emanation has, in certain places in Plotinus's writings, the Pythagorean meaning of the production of the Many out of the plurality of the One, leading back to Euclid's definition of number. Inevitably, numerology gets mixed up in the whole thing through rather arbitrary doctrines of correspondence. We are not here interested in the muddy details of Plotinus's arguments, but only in their metaphoric bases, which are rather complicated. On one hand, an emanation is based on the One/Many metaphor; on the other, it is a Commodity that the One (:Parent) gives to humankind, the children. Beyond that, it suggests a modification of spirit (:Breath), since emanation indicates a kind of gaseous or liquid effluvium.

> When [the One] takes lot with multiplicity, Being becomes Number by the fact of awakening to manifoldness; before, it was a preparation, so to speak, of the Beings, their fore-promise, a total of henads offering a stay for what was to be based on them.[3]

As may be imagined, the hierarchical order of Plotinus's emanations found surprising parallelism and consequent support in the similarly ordered feudal system, certainly one of the most fortuitous alliances between accident and preconception that history can record. It goes far in explaining the longevity of Neoplatonism throughout the Middle Ages and the early Renaissance. As a metaphor prototype, Plotinus's emanative hierarchy meshed with the network of alliances in feudalism. Personality, motive, and commitment, not structure, most characterized the feudal order. These were all traits congenial to the Parent metaphor and the mythopoeic bent of medieval thought.

PROOF OF THE EXISTENCE OF GOD:
THE PARENT METAPHOR VINDICATED

Against a background of Neoplatonism, two major philosophical questions occupied the thinkers of the Middle Ages: proof of the existence of God and the ontological status of universals. The two problems were interrelated through the simple system of metaphors deployed in Neoplatonism. Universals were easily viewed as Platonic forms or as Neoplatonic emanations (:Breath). Being the thoughts of God, universals were ensured perfection.

Beginning from the opposite side of the argument and trying to derive a proof for the existence of God from an ascribed real status to universals was a simple procedure, as long as universals were granted an existence independent of the human mind.[4] Plato had first assigned a higher reality to Forms than to phenomenal species of being, whereas Aristotle took the modified position that Forms are the defining differentiae of beings. Aristotle reduced Forms to indwelling properties.

Ascribing objective reality to universals, *eidos*, made it in some respects easier for early Christian theologians to claim proof of their doctrines. Universals were conceived to exist as ideas in God's mind and hence as reflected images (:Mirror). Naming consequently seemed to assure the existence of the things named, which was all right as long as the things named were acceptable. Anselm took this one step further and thus argued for the existence of God on the grounds that, since it was impossible to conceive of anything more perfect than God, he must therefore exist. God, as the perfect being, must exist, for otherwise he would not be perfect—not to exist would not be perfect. Kant, of course, rightly pointed out that existence cannot be the object of predication.

GOD, THE PARENT, ONE OR THREE?

At the center of the debate over universals were more serious theological issues. Especially thorny was the dogma of the Trinity, which defined God, the Holy Spirit, and Christ as unitary in substance *(ousia)* but trinitary in person *(hypostasis)*. Rolling the three beings into one was intrinsically paradoxical and there was no logical way to resolve the matter with finality. Only by fiat or by faith—both expected appeals from the Parent metaphor of the Church—could the question be grounded.

At this point, the fate of universals was determined not by reason but by politico-economic factors. Harry Elmer Barnes has remarked aptly,

> One of the leading aspects of European civilization during the Dark Ages was its provincialism and its ignorance of foreign cultures and learning. Intellectually speaking, it was an inbred age, and this accounted in part for its relative stagnation.[5]

And by contrast:

> The most important single factor in the institutional background of the decline of the medieval system was the growth of towns, of trade, and of an urban middle class.[6]

Logic cannot decide the relative ontological status of universals and particulars. Value systems decide this, perhaps by the rules of logic; but the propositions on which the logic operates are dictated by politico-economic power. When abstract reasoning about questions that cannot empirically be decided begins to lose its rhetorical appeal, it withers into inconspicuousness. It takes on the trappings of a game. As urbanization and trade were being reestablished in Europe, praxis took precedence over theory. Ideas had to address practical issues to gain a wide audience, for the practical exigencies of everyday life and commerce rose quickly in ascendancy. With renewed opportunities for material gain at hand, and with some form of local political stability reinstated, people were less intrigued by problems of the hereafter. Theological inquiry, to remain vibrant and influential, had to address secular matters, like the political roles of church and state.

DISPUTATION OVER PARENTAL AUTHORITY:
CHURCH VERSUS STATE

It has been traditional to treat the Church in medieval history as ruling the spiritual realm and the state, the secular; but our approach necessitates further qualification. As we have seen, the scientific and philosophical domains for the Greeks were ruled by metaphors of symmetrical order, *metron* and *symmetron*, suited to mathematical deployment and exactness of definition. Contrasting with these are the mythic metaphors of church dogma centered around Parent and family, embodying fiat as organizing principle and therefore supportive of authority established by social convention, persuasion, and coercion (all parental means for controlling children's behavior). Now let us examine some of the implications of these metaphoric differences.

Metron and *symmetron*, deployments of the metaphor of Pattern, are suited to imposing consistency on those things that are quantifiable and that can be analyzed into parts whose disposition can have a felt structure (e.g., acts of a play, parts of a city plan, or geometric models of the universe). Largely this means the physical objects of everyday life, reflected mainly in the construction of man-made things. Pattern lies within itself, manifest and complete, open to inspection and sensory verification.

Parent and family, on the other hand, pertain to behavioral modes and goals. It is a prescriptive approach that is fostered, as opposed to the descriptive frame of the Pattern metaphor. It is not easily subverted in its own terms, because its intent or extent is never fully disclosed. A measurement can be agreed upon consensually; a parental command may be subjected to differing interpretations. A measurement may be questioned; a parental command may not. In sum, the Pattern metaphor is suited to construe inanimate nature, and the Parent-Family complex, the field of human behavioral interaction. The latter promises rewards and punishments; the former, concrete understanding.

Consider, then, what would have been important in feudal Europe. Literacy was virtually nonexistent. The masses were poor, were sporadically placed on fiefs, and were subject to marauders, save for the protection of the manorial lord and his army. Diets were poor, disease rampant, leisure time sparse, and living conditions difficult except for those at the very top of the social scale. Educational institutions died with the Roman Empire, destroying the continuity of the intellectual and artistic conventions. There was little hope of reward in a world of ceaseless violence, and there was no knowledge of the outside world except that bred by fancy. *Metron* and *symmetron* would have been valueless in such circumstances, when there was not even the knowledge for deploying them. Better to have authorities who could settle all disputes, and a sense of order that could be adjusted daily to fit a topsy-turvy world via fluid interpretations of the Scriptures by those parental authorities (i.e., the church fathers). Parent-Family had the distinct advantage over

Design in imposing coherence on the chaotic world of the Middle Ages. The church *fathers,* like good parents, could tell their *children* how to think and act.

A. C. Flick, in *The Decline of the Medieval Church,* divided the causes of the decline into negative and positive, which Harry Elmer Barnes has paraphrased as follows:

> The negative causes were: (1) The revolt against the temporal pretensions of the pope; (2) the insistence of the pope on the exclusive right of ecclesiastical appointment; (3) the exemption of the clergy from secular courts and laws; (4) the papal determination to exempt church property from taxation; (5) the political application of papal power and papal intrusion into secular politics; (6) the venality and corruption of papal administration; (7) the immorality and degradation of the clergy; (8) the purely formal nature of much of religious ritual; and (9) the failure of the church to keep pace with cultural and intellectual changes.[7]

Among the positive causes, Flick included the rise of skeptical inquiry and intellectual independence, nationalism, the popularity of Roman law and its theory of secular absolutism (a question metaphorically of parental authority), the impact of printing, the rise of towns and trade, the growth of capitalism, the development of the bourgeoisie, the weakening of the manorial system, and the restlessness of the peasants.[8]

We cannot hope to comment in detail on each cause listed. Of the negative, probably nos. 6 to 9 would have been tolerated, had it not been for nos. 1 to 5, which basically amounted to the imposition of the Parent-Family complex and church authority on the rising tide of enlarged economic and technological activity described under the positive causes. Again, behind the positive causes was the enlarged perspective of the world inaugurated by the Crusades, a perspective that centered on the Eastern world as a source and a marketplace for economic gain. To be sure, realization of that gain was made possible by the cessation of large-scale and disruptive migration into the nascent European states, affording the stability necessary for political consolidation.

NATIONALISM FAVORED THE STATE AS PARENTAL AUTHORITY

We should say something about the development of the "theory of secular absolutism" concomitant with "the triumph of nationalism and nationalistic political theory," because they give perfect examples of extraneous causes of metaphoric shifts. Nationalism, whether from the standpoint of the government or the people, is little more than consolidarity of an in-group in opposition to surrounding outgroups. At a certain level of political and economic sufficiency, a people forms a closed group, the in-group, to protect itself from resented incursions upon its property and rights by others, the out-groups. Rationalization of this consolidarity is a natural mode of self-defense and self-justification. All of the original formulators of early nationalist political theory were paid employees of the state or persons seeking the favors of the state.

On the other side was the Church, for whom nationalist trends and the rise of secular power was worrisome. Early Christianity had been without political ambitions, counseling its followers in Matt. 22:21 to "render unto Caesar the things that are Caesar's." The Apostle Paul said quite explicitly in Rom. 13:1–4, 7–8,

> Let every soul be in subjection to the higher powers: for there is no power but of God; and the powers that be are ordained of God. Therefore he that resisteth the power, withstandeth the ordinance of God: and they that withstand shall receive to themselves judgment. For the rulers are not a terror to the good work, but to the evil. And wouldst thou have no fear of the power? do that which is good, and thou shalt have praise from the same: for he is a minister of God to thee for good. . . . For this cause ye pay tribute also. . . . Render to all their due; tribute to whom tribute is due; custom to whom custom; fear to whom fear; honor to whom honor.

Early patristic thought rested comfortably on the division of rule, with the Church ministering to the spirit and the affairs of state left to the secular rulers. An easy cooperation between the two was assumed. On this basis, Gelasius I in his *Letters* set forth a division that Augustine subsequently carved in stone. "There are, then, august Emperor," Gelasius wrote to Anastasius, "two powers by which the world is chiefly ruled, the sacred power of the prelates and the royal power."[9] This precarious balance lasted until the rebirth of towns and commerce, which placed new wealth in the hands of the aristocracy and those of the middle class who succeeded in trade.

A contention between the Church and the secular rulers centered on the appointment of bishops, which had fallen to the state. These appointments gave the state a huge entering wedge into the properties of the Church. Not at all a point of reason, this was purely a power struggle. Nothing was to be clarified by logic. All positions were clear and dogmatic at the onset. On the side of the Church, Egidius Romanus, a papal legalist, summarized the official position in saying that "[a]s in the universe itself corporeal substance is ruled by spiritual . . . so among Christians all temporal lords and all earthly power ought to be governed and ruled by spiritual and ecclesiastical authority, and especially by the pope."[10] John of Paris, speaking for the royalists, declared that "secular power is greater than spiritual power in certain matters, namely, temporal matters; and with respect to this it is not subject to it in anything, because it does not stem from it. Rather, both powers

stem directly from one supreme power, namely divine power."[11] Both used the
Ability metaphor in the form of power, but each had his own topological scheme.
The papal scheme was:

And the royalist:

Power, whether physical or political, is nothing more than a kind of reification of
the ability to do something—in this case, to dictate the behavior of others. Here it was
a question of how that ability was to be delegated. In the papal version, power came
to the political ruler through the intermediary of the pope, whereas in the royalist
version both the pope and the political ruler derived power directly from God.

The stakes were high. The Church stooped to forging documents: first the
Donation of Constantine, in which Constantine supposedly gave the western part of
his kingdom to Pope Sylvester I for having cured him of leprosy, and then the
Pseudo-Isidorean Decretals, which denied secular rulers the right to confiscate the
property of bishops. These documents had little force when introduced, but papal
lawyers were later to manipulate them with considerable skill to make their position seem plausible. When real advantage was at hand for the populace in the
material world, the strength was with those who could marshal the greater politico-economic force.

MARSILIUS OF PADUA:
A CASE STUDY OF PARENT METAPHOR DEPLOYMENT

If we take Marsilius of Padua as an example, we may observe the basics of
change in metaphor deployment in action. St. Augustine had established the duality of sacred and secular power, the church and the state, opting for the Church as
superior on the basis of its divine origin and affiliations. This, too, was an obvious
rationalization of the priority of the papacy in earthly matters. In our perspective,
it is the preconceived ends of the arguer that determine the choice of initial propositions. Had Augustine lived in a primitive society where typically the universe was

construed as an organism, he probably would have followed somewhat the same metaphoric strategy as Plato. The Microcosm-Macrocosm duality would be used to set up a breakdown of faculties in the universal organism. The Church would then be identified with the superior faculty. As it was, he could fall back on an easy duality for which the dyadic structure of classical Greek metaphors was ideally suited.

Marsilius simply tipped Augustine's scales, making the secular power superior to the sacred on the grounds that the Church has proper domain over matters concerning "the other world" and not this one, which is base and imperfect. He could implicitly assume assent to the biblical proclamation of human free will—man is free to sin, or not. Political power, accordingly, rests in the people, hardly a new idea. What was new in Marsilius was the beginnings of the modern trend to reify power, itself an abstraction from physical strength. For him,

> [I]t suffices to show . . . that Christ himself came into this world not to domi-
> nate men, nor to judge them . . . nor to wield temporal rule, but rather to be
> subject as regards the status of the present life; and moreover, that he wanted
> to and did exclude himself, his apostles and disciples, and their successors, the
> bishops or priests, from all such coercive authority or worldly rule, both by his
> example and by his words of counsel and command. . . . and that both Christ
> and the apostles wanted to be and were continuously subject in property and
> in person to the coercive jurisdiction of secular rulers, and that they taught
> and commanded all others, to whom they preached or wrote the law of truth,
> to do likewise, under pain of eternal damnation.[12]

For Marsilius, this was an easy exercise in biblical quotation.[13]

> His heresy was to apply to the secular community the criteria of the *bonum
> commune*, or the common good, which the Avignon canonists claimed were
> exclusively applicable to the Church. Marsilius argued that the state was the
> work of human reason and will; it was men who made the state.[14]

Some political polemicists combined the First Position and the Parent meta-phor to argue for the absolute power of the monarchy. Like the father figure, the monarch was supposed to be in the first position of power. So argued Jean Bodin. Bishop Bossuet, on behalf of Louis XIV, used the argument that the king occupies a position (the First Position) in the state analogous to that of God in the universe. Borrowing from Hobbes, he also claimed that every citizen gains security by sur-rendering individual rights to the sovereign. Such polemics for absolute monarchy arrange political power hierarchically, with the king or queen, as parent figures, at the apex, in first position, and all other offices of power arranged in descending order, family style. But this was essentially a Renaissance development. The first thing to get done was the separation of church and state, with superiority in this world going to the latter. As we have seen, metaphorically it was a simple task involving no revolutions in underlying intellectual foundations. Also, we should note that the switch in deployment, directing attention from sacred to secular activity, upset only the balance of power. The Parent-Family complex was left intact so that the state could easily assume rights of behavioral control. Rationalizations of state power became ever more acute as wealth was more widely distributed among the people. The extreme parental form of the metaphor supporting monarchy in the late-Renaissance and baroque periods attests to that.

The Sciences in the Medieval Period

Aristotle was known during this period through his chief works,[15] although more interest was paid to his thoughts on logic and rhetoric than to his scientific treatises, which were regarded as secondary. This was because of the relevance of the former to polemicizing religious issues, and especially the main concerns for nominalism versus realism in the debate over universals and constructions of proofs of the existence of God. Nevertheless, his scientific works achieved the status of nearly sacred texts when it came to the limited scientific inquiry that did take place. Aristotle is the wellspring of nearly all medieval science, whether empirical or purely superstitious.

From Magic Back to the Fifth Element

"Astrology, alchemy and magic, the legacy of ancient times, played a prominent role in medieval science. The ignorant and the credulous, as well as the learned, upheld their validity."[16] The backbone of these belief systems was the Pythagorean doctrines about number wedded to the Western proclivity toward theories of correspondence. Miraculous results were thought achievable through the exploration of correspondences, quantifiable in alchemical formulations, between the putative elements and other properties of the universe. "Alchemy, the forerunner of modern chemistry, had two principal aims. It was designed to lengthen human life, and to transmute the baser metals into gold. It was hoped that both of these objectives might be realized by the discovery of the mysterious fifth element or the 'philosopher's stone.'"[17] It was a long deployment by which the fifth element, the ether, of the ancient Greeks, got turned into the philosopher's stone, generally thought to be some mixture of sulfur and mercury, and the elixir of life. There are always many tortuous turns in magical thinking determined by flurries of accidental correspondences—instances of paralogical reasoning—and we shall not try to unravel the transformations of ether into sulfur and mercury in complete detail. Suffice it to say, in the most ancient forms of alchemy, deriving from Egypt, China, and India, gold was associated with the sun, the source of life. The celestial bodies, as we have seen, were construed by the ancients to be comprised of a fifth element finer than the four earthly elements. Gold, insofar as it also participated along with mercury in the qualities of the sun and the other celestial bodies, represented the highest state of matter by virtue of having infused within it some measure of the *quinta essentia* (:Breath). If any element had the *quinta essentia* as an indwelling agent, it was easy to slide into equivalencing it, or some chemical mixture thought to contain the *quinta essentia* as a property, to a transmutative, in view of the classical theory of properties as agencies still prevalent in the Middle Ages. Thus the identification was complete, at least by magical, paralogical reasoning. The sun is the source of life; the sun as celestial body is of the *quinta essentia*. Gold, mercury, and sulfur (by virtue of its color, especially in the molten state) partake of the qualities of the sun.

That scientists could return to the idea of the fifth element is a commentary on how magical thought remained within the medieval sciences. Science, as a body of thought directed toward understanding the physical world, has the unique project before it of mediating physical observations and already established metaphors and their deployments. Unlike those in areas of free creation—the arts and those fields of philosophy undeterminable by empirical experimentation—scientists are not unconstrained in their model building. To the extent that medieval scientific speculation touched the matters of magic, they had to find a compromise with the vast and unwieldy body of magical lore that had accumulated since ancient times. Fortunately, being paralogical, magical thought is highly syncretic and can accommodate otherwise unorthodox material. We have a situation parallel with that of sacred texts. Nevertheless, magical notions and the metaphor deployments that supported them served in some measure to divert attention from matters science might under more auspicious circumstances have tackled at earlier dates.

Chemistry offers a good case in point, although here the restrictions were classical in origin but bolstered by magical lore woven around them. First, there was the belief in the four elements and in qualities as indwelling agencies. And second, the whole enterprise of alchemy—itself embedded in a larger context of magical lore—rested on the fifth element present in matter as an indwelling quality. As long as chemical changes could be accounted for in terms of mixtures of the five agencies, often interpreted as Aristotelian forms or essences imposed on a blank substrate, any attempt to discriminate chemically distinct substances and consequently to seek to purify them was tellingly forestalled. The greatest contribution made by the alchemists toward the chemical revolutions of the seventeenth century was the sheer accumulation of data and practical knowledge, which would eventually fuel and support a metaphorical shift and a true intellectual revolution. A five-element model of the material world eventually failed to accommodate the accumulated data and had to be replaced by one of greater diversity. The notion of *element* remained but loosened its attachment to the One/Many metaphor. No longer would the elements seem quite the foundations of physical substance that they had previously. That place would be ceded in turn to the atom, the elementary particles, and finally the quarks, for the further manifestations of the One (i.e., the Many) are from the Many, the less fundamental something becomes.

Chemistry made the greatest strides among the physical sciences during the Middle Ages. Here is Harry Elmer Barnes commenting on the various other medieval sciences:

> Astronomy . . . was primarily astrology. . . . Biology was based only slightly on practical observation. In the early medieval period the bestiaries were used as illustrations to drive home Christian truths. . . . Psychology was nonexistent. . . . The medieval knowledge of geography was very limited. Little was known of Strabo, Ptolemy, and other eminent classical geographers. Until the time of Marco Polo, few traveled widely. . . . Medicine was chiefly a combination of magic and superstition until the coming of Muslim medicine, and the revival of Galen and other Greeks.[18]

In short, there were no metaphorically new ideas, nor any metaphor deployments which proved of profound significance.

MATHEMATICS

Until Arabic numerals were established around 1500, mathematics was encumbered by Roman numerals, which made even advancement in arithmetic all but impossible. Over and above this, the ancient discrete number line hindered the mathematical formulation of continuous processes. Numbers were still conceived as *eidos*, ideal forms. As in classical times, they remained conceived in terms of the One/Many and the Mirror metaphors. They had to be complete within themselves, which means whole (multiples of One) and ideal (:Mirror). Even Galileo experienced initial difficulty in articulating mathematically the phenomenon of accelerated motion. Dynamics, as a branch of mechanics, was all but ruled out. It was not until nearly 1600 that François Viete published his works, which introduced what has become standard algebraic notation, a hundred years after the introduction of algebra from Muslim treatises. Geometry was known only through fragments of Euclid, and trigonometry was largely a dream of the future. Had anyone attempted to transcend the Platonic and Aristotelian legacies of the Greeks, the Church would have quelled them. In any case, there was insufficient empirical data to mount a serious challenge to the medieval *Weltanschauung*. Only in alchemy was broad data produced, and that was neither free from magical taint nor sufficient in quantity to tip the metaphor balance of the period.

Conclusion

Thought in the Middle Ages was ruled by magical correspondences. Mere analogy, rather than metaphor, was the preferred method of analysis. Furthermore, the analogy did not need to be particularly embracing; the most disjunctive similarity was sufficient. In this respect, the thought processes were archaic, just as Von Domarus described for the schizophrenic: "Whereas the logician accepts identity only upon the basis of identical subjects, the paralogician [the schizophrenic] accepts identity on the basis of identical predicates."[19] An instance cited was the "patient who believed that Jesus, cigar boxes, and sex were identical" because "Jesus' head is encircled by a halo, cigar boxes by a tax band, and women by the sex glance of a man."[20] Paralogic falls under what psychiatrists often label as primary psychic process, characterized in part by "the use of allusion, analogy, displacement, condensation, and symbolic representation."[21] Certainly this tallies with the nature of much of the medieval output, from magic and alchemy to fabliaux and bestiaries. Indeed, Isidore of Seville's *Etymologiae*, popular as an encyclopedia throughout the Middle Ages, is the perfect embodiment of primary-process thought, with its fantastical explanations, much of it partly digested Pliny.

It is easy to forget, too, that medieval scholars were virtually without historical perspective. Other than the narrative of the Bible, they knew only the historians Orosius, Fredegarius (the pseudo-Fredegar), and Eusebius. In other words, they knew only a Christian account, dovetailing with the perspective of the *Civitas Dei*.[22] They were acquainted with formal logic but didn't give it serious attention, for the most part, until the rise of Scholasticism. Allegorical interpretation was the preferred method of textual analysis.[23] Profane material could thus be rendered acceptable to the Christian palette. Lack of classical historical perspective undoubtedly made the enterprise all the easier.

Speaking of the critical tradition of the Middle Ages, J. W. H. Atkins claimed that "[a]mong the innovations of the period, none is more significant in its bearing on literary theory than the place that was now assigned to allegory in the sphere of literature, and the unwritten doctrine that in consequence resulted."[24] The drift toward allegory began in the early centuries of the Christian era, and "the idea that all literature contained an allegorical element was slowly forming as a result of the exegetical methods pursued by the Church in its interpretation of sacred literature."[25] In fact, the medieval conception of the cosmos was replete with correspondences, complementary to the Organism metaphor. Explanation by analogy is merely suggestive. There is almost always a vagueness to it. Because the analogy calls attention to parallels, rather than one thing being construed in terms of another, these must be interpreted. In the interpretive act, it is the Divine Mind or plan that must be fathomed, for it is from God that the magic correspondences of the universe derive. Hence, there is the same inscrutability of intent in this brand of analogical thought as in those things construed as organic, for an organism differs from a mechanism in not being subject to full causal disclosure.

It is the lack of specific structure denoted by the Organism metaphorand that made possible the amazing gamut of the medieval imagination. The individual was free to speculate on those things about which the Church held no official opinion. Further impetus in that direction came from the ethnic diversity of the stocks brought in by continuous migrations. Each had its own body of beliefs. And those beliefs were by and large on the mythic level of thought, expressed in personification and symbolism.

> For the study of vernacular literature we are concerned not so much with the actual allegorization or reinterpretation as with the kind of attitude it produced. The cultured reader expected to have to search for different levels of meaning in a sophisticated work. He could enjoy the literal meaning of, say, an Arthurian romance and be excited by the adventures of the knights, the glowing colors of the courts, the sorrows of lovers. But he expected more than this. The characters represented something greater than themselves.[26]

Likewise with symbolism in general. As Chevalier and Gheerbrant observe, "[s]ymbols are always pluri-dimensional. . . . synthesis of contraries, the symbol has a diurnal side and a nocturnal side. Moreover, many of these bipolar couples have analogies between them that are also expressed in symbols."[27] These same authors go on to say that "the primary function of the symbol is exploratory order," which is also one of the main functions of metaphors, rhetorical or explanatory. "It makes it possible in effect to seize in a certain manner a relation that reason cannot define, because one term of it is known and the other unknown."[28]

Interestingly, Chevalier and Gheerbrant believe that behind the dynamism of the symbol lies what they call a "vectoral image or an eidetico-motor scheme."[29] They give no definition, but, since they refer explicitly to Piaget's epistemological psychology, it would seem that they have in mind an internalized action scheme vaguely like the topological scheme I have described. All this serves to clarify the medieval worldview and the metaphor usage peculiar to the period.

Freed of the classical metaphor complex of cosmic order suggesting the possibility of mathematical articulation, set loose in the framework of the serendipitous Organism metaphor, restrained only by the pronouncements of the Church, pocketed in conflicting local belief systems, and encouraged by the allegorical method to see multiple meanings everywhere, the medieval thinkers were in a unique position. Mythical thought was already natural to them. They entered Europe as tribes and retained much of their tribal organization and customs in their settlements. Unsophisticated, they assimilated Christianity and the remnants of classical civilization by finding correlations with their native thought. These correlations did not have to conform to Aristotelian logic and notions of scientific causality. They needed to be nothing beyond paralogical. Paralogic is the manner of thought natural to those for whom myth suffices to impose a sense of order on the universe and a feeling that humankind belongs to that order. It is primary in the sense of coming in ontogeny and in phylogeny before the so-called secondary or logical modes of mental operation. Understandably, it has a deeply emotional appeal, making it tenacious, although malleable. Being pluridimensional, or polysemous, it can extend outward in many different directions with equal ease. Rather than progressing by elimination and moving to alternatives, like the mind it grows by accretion, layering meaning over meaning.

The genius of the Middle Ages, at least from this perspective, lay not in metaphorical innovation but in embellishment. It was, so to speak, a rhetorical age. By falling back on rhetorical metaphors, medieval thinkers and artists fashioned a world of fancy. Such metaphors gave color to thought but did not open any broad avenues of discursive speculation. Rather, they defined a period of imitation. Most philosophy of the period was a rehash of classical sterility; most art was a factory-like fabrication of well-worn icons. All that was interesting in this lay in the details, the ornament. From details, some of the greatest accomplishments of the medieval mind accrued: systems of magic, illuminated manuscripts, and the Gothic cathedral.

6

The Renaissance

As a tendency, the Renaissance was the result of those forces that have been noted as ending the medieval order and initiating the rediscovery of classical culture.[1] However we interpret it, we can see the catalysts coming from the Crusades, even though certain cities, notably Venice, had managed to maintain commercial ties with the East during the Muslim hegemony. Those ties supply another reason for construing the Renaissance as a tendency rather than as a period.

Let us outline the basic ingredients of the Renaissance. Whereas the medieval period was marked by the stagnation that comes from provincialism, Europe after the Crusades was suddenly made newly aware of the lands of the East. Trade, sometimes accompanied by plunder, required trained manpower and brought the wealth to pay for it, creating job opportunities in the cities, where populations began to swell, providing a labor and tax base for urban construction. Shipbuilding, navigation, accounting, commercial law, and other specialties required reconstitution of the educational system. Universities appeared early on in the major cities of trade and banking. Some had been founded for church purposes but gradually assumed more secular curricula. As texts were brought back from Byzantium and beyond, the demand for translators installed greater departments of philosophy in the universities. The rediscovery of classical texts on biology, medicine, mathematics, and the physical sciences went hand-in-hand with this academic movement.

Greater money and leisure for what remained a growing but limited minority created a class that could exploit the reborn classical learning, often for direct economic gain, in the facilitation of trade or the development of potentially profitable new technologies, but often, too, it was pursued for sheer curiosity and intellectual stimulation. For whatever motive it was carried out, this renewed intellectual activity must be placed also in a political context properly to be understood.

By survival of the fittest, regional political barons killed each other off, formed marital alliances, and maneuvered in every way imaginable, emerging into a much reduced league of power brokers able to knit the political patchwork of medieval Europe into consolidated nations. Trade furnished the economic base for this consolidation. The opportunities of the new society made the domain of the hereafter less attractive than the here and now for the major arena in which to seek life's rewards. That, above all, led to the decline of the Church and to the humanist bent that supplanted religious concerns. As a consequence, the ubiquity and efficacity of the Parent metaphor began to wane, giving room for the ascent of a new organizing metaphor for the age.

Transportation in an age of trade, however cumbersome in those days, brought peoples of differing ethnic backgrounds once more into regular contact, creating a situation of ideological exchange and comparison parallel to that which fostered the golden age of Greece. The results were a similar intellectual and artistic fomentation, to the metaphorical bases of which we now turn.

MATHEMATICS IN THE RENAISSANCE

Mathematics underwent several revolutionary changes. First was the adoption of Arabic numerical notation that was based on ten, positional, and employed the zero. Traditionally the invention of such notation is attributed to the Hindus, but there is evidence that it first appeared in Indo-China early in the seventh century, and according to a Syriac source, the notation was found at the monastery of Qinnasrin in 662.[2] Arithmetic calculation was facilitated through the consistency of the decimal notation, and progress in that field was quick to proceed, fostered by demands in accounting, surveying, and navigation (allied with astronomical observations), and later joined by engineering, mechanics and the physical sciences. There was an obvious dialectic of mutual enhancement between mathematics and the pure and applied sciences.

Second, from Islam came the rudiments of algebra, the generalization of the number concept, facilitated by the eventual adoption of Viete's algebraic notation. Instead of solving numerically specific problems, each of which is unique unto itself, it became possible to solve families of problems of a general type. The concept of quantity had been loosened from the One/Many metaphor that dominated classical number theory, one of several steps that moved mathematics away from metaphorical moorings and cast it in a more purely topological mold.

Third, and primarily from Euclid, mathematicians gradually developed axiomatics, the application of definition and deduction to the proof of mathematical propositions. This, along with the development of analytic geometry and algebra, laid further foundation for the shift in emphasis away from quantity and toward relations, a fundamental revolution in mathematics that would be integral to the transformation of scientific thought in the late-nineteenth and the twentieth centuries.

Fourth, harking back to Apollonius of Perga (fl. c. 230 B.C.E.), whose works were newly rediscovered, Descartes and Fermat both latched onto the suggestion that an equation in two unknowns represents a locus, i.e., a configuration of points whose values correspond to those of the unknowns and which are plotted relative to mutually perpendicular axes. Street layouts may well have been models for this idea. Here, an orientational framework by which people had for centuries made their ways through city layouts became a model, a kind of metaphor, for the interrelation between number and shape. It forged a link between quantity and form, algebra and geometry. At first, this made equations more concrete in having a graphic representation. Later, in algebraic topology this alliance between number (or symbol) and shape would be broken, with a renewed abstraction in which topological relations would be all but robbed of their spatial significance.

Fifth, under the new order of Arabic notation and the pressure of dealing with dynamics and other areas of physics requiring the manipulation of analytic functions, the classical notion of number as discrete gave way to the modern notion that it represents a continuum. Certainly the invention of analytic geometry would have mandated the change even without other factors, for there the continuity of loci of equations embodied the corresponding continuity of values assignable to the variables of the equation.

The continuity of number presented a major revolution in mathematical thought. Not only did it make it easier to solve many problems in the physical sciences, but it introduced a series of challenges to the mathematical imagination. These were not fully realized until after the Renaissance, but even during this period mathematicians had to begin to deal with them. Obviously the calculus would have been impossible without this change in the number concept. The concept of limit (a value to which a function approaches without discontinuity at any point between specified values), one of the cornerstones of the calculus, depends on it.

A continuous number or value line resurrects one of the nemeses of Greek mathematical thought: the infinitely small and the infinitely large. Definitions of infinity are achieved by application of negation to the metaphor chosen as a base, usually either a Container or a series (which is a deployment of the Container metaphor). Infinity is a container without boundaries, or a series without beginning or end. In either case, the definition is fictive in that it runs contrary to anything in empirical experience; that is, it cannot be validated experimentally.[3] Formalists can point out that this is nothing new, that Euclid's definitions (e.g., of line, point, and plane, etc.) are equally ideal, and this is true. But infinity and nothingness, both concepts achieved through negation, have domain outside mathematics, where they have been implicatively intertwined with other notions, usually of a mystical nature. In fact, infinity as a concept lay in mystical thought since the classical period and was then reintroduced into mathematical speculation.

INFINITY, NOTHINGNESS, AND OTHER NEGATIONS

Negative concepts like nothingness and infinity have always held a peculiar fascination, because they are derived from seemingly plausible procedures. Yet they do not accord well with the other root metaphors of thought, except the negative ones, all of which (with the possible exception of the latter half of Light/Dark) are themselves negative deployments of positives. We might say that negative concepts define a kind of antiuniverse. Rather than models for reality, they might best be approached as topological transformations of reality models, for, aside from the procedure of grammatical negation, all of the other processes of negation (except removal), we should remember, are topological. One of the major uses of these transformations may well be in modeling discursive thought. Indeed, much of Buddhist and Taoist reasoning follows this very plan.[4]

Negation and reflexiveness (metaphor applied to itself, or other conceptual constructs applied to themselves), as we have had occasion to note elsewhere, are foundations of mystical thought, in which the motive is to get away from the limits of sensory experience. Perhaps the earliest manifestation is in the *netti, netti* doctrine of the *Brihadaranyaka Upanishad*. According to it, ultimate reality is neither this nor that *(netti, netti)*, a tack pursued by Zen and by various schools of Western mysticism. There is obviously an intrinsic ludic interest in all this, and meditative modes of thought correlate with brain wave states that are experienced as rewarding by all who pass through them, leading to the tentative hypothesis that a cerebral biochemical reward system may be involved. If this has evolved as a favorable adaptation, it may be because it encourages the exercise of introspective topological manipulation of a most difficult kind, predisposing to acuity in reasoning. Mystical writings conceived along this line tend to be highly ingenious and hard to follow— good mental exercises.

CHEMISTRY: THE ELEMENTS PROLIFERATE

Analogous to what was happening in mathematics, the medieval legacy was being challenged in the other sciences. Chemistry finally broke the bounds of the four elements, but not without a struggle. Out of the medieval herbals, iatrochemistry was born. Perhaps the most significant point in this course of development, from the standpoint of intellectual history, is that distillation arose as a practice in the preparation of medications. This was the first technical step toward purification, a procedure essential for the discrimination of distinct elements.

One reason chemists did not earlier conclude that substances are analyzable into elements other than the classical four is that most alchemy had to do with metals. In alloys often the properties of the constituents cannot separately be discerned. Nevertheless, iatrochemistry with its many preparations made an invaluable contribution to the isolation and identification of numerous elements and compounds.

To complete the background for the discovery of the elements, we must make a detour into classical physics. Aristotle had advanced the notion that motion under a continuing force would quicken as the medium through with it passed grew thinner. "Let the speed have the same ratio to the speed, then, that air had to water," said Aristotle, choosing those two media for comparison. "Then if air is twice as thin, the body will traverse [the same distance as through water] in twice the time." But then he ran afoul of zero. "Now there is no ratio in which the void is exceeded by body, as there is no ratio of 0 to a number." Consequently, a body moving through a void would move "with a speed beyond any ratio," i.e., at an infinite velocity.[5] From this and other more purely semantic arguments, Aristotle concluded that there can be no void, which is also to say no vacuum.

From the technology of mining came the first telling empirical challenge to Aristotle's theory. Water drainage, always a problem in mining, was resolved quite early by the use of pumps. Practical observation had shown that a column of water could be raised only to a level of between 32 and 33 feet before the column would break and fall back. By the Aristotelian dictum that nature abhors a vacuum, however, there should be no limit to how high water or any other fluid can be lifted by a vacuum pump. The theory was that, as the vacuum in a line is created, it is instantly filled because the vacuum state is an impossibility.

Weak hypotheses were offered, including that the column of water somehow breaks from its own weight and incohesiveness. But these explanations were too lacking in theoretical bases to be convincing. They were all laid to rest by the invention of the vacuum pump by Otto von Guericke in 1650. We should refer to this as a rediscovery, since the Greek engineer, Hero, had constructed such pumps fifteen centuries earlier but then they were used to construct adult toys. Boyle improved on Guericke's design and began experimenting with gases, ultimately discovering that the volume of a gas is inversely proportional to the pressure to which it is subjected (Boyle's Law). This shattered the ancient idea that air, as one of the four elements, is a homogeneous and continuous medium. It was apparent that it is composed of particles separated by empty space—as indeed Hero had concluded. Nature does not abhor a vacuum. The atomic theory was reestablished.

At the heart of this long controversy was the always troublesome problem of negation. Operations with zero must in part be defined in mathematics so that everything works out right. That is, the operations must be defined to work rather than following naturally from analogy with other numerical operations. Division by zero, for instance, is said to be meaningless, whereas multiplication by zero is zero. Now, given a number, X, if you don't multiply it, which is what $0X$ implies, you would think that would leave X as it was and not reduce it to 0. Without this quandary, Aristotle might not have reasoned as he did about the vacuum.

At any rate, the elements took on an altogether different connotation than they had in classical thinking. Working out of the One/Many metaphor, the four elements—earth, fire, air and water—originally were thought to be the primary constituents to which all matter could be reduced. Subsequently, with the proliferation of the elements, the search for the primary, that which comes first (:First Position), shifted to the atom, thence to the putative elementary particles, and finally to the quarks. The search for the first link in the chain seems unquenchable. The firstborn of anything carries with it privileged status.

New metals, such as bismuth and platinum, had been discovered in the New World. Phosphorus was soon isolated, followed by other elements. The atomic theory seemed better suited for accounting for these elements than any theory in which the four elements were deduced philosophically from first principles. In essence, the chemists of the Renaissance established the empirical method, which in turn brought to light a wealth of data that could not *parsimoniously* be explained on the basis of the old theory but could be, on the basis of the atomic theory.

The empirical approach, in contradistinction to the reliance on ancient authority, had a profound effect on chemistry. Along with the discovery and preparation of thousands of new substances there was a revolution in thought. Boyle's experiments, for example, confirmed that two substances could be combined to form a third, the properties of which were totally different from those of the original two. Qualities, therefore, cannot be inherent, as the ancients believed, but must be emergent, again supporting the atomic theory. For the Greeks, substance *(hyle)* took upon itself form and other qualities. *Hyle* originally meant wood, and qualities were imagined to be imposed on it much as a carver imparts shape to a piece of stock. Plato espoused this view. Aristotle inclined more toward regarding qualities as indwelling agents. If qualities were explained in terms of things like atoms in different configurations and states of motion, neither of these metaphors would work. Even the metaphor of One/Many to account for combinations of many different elements could not satisfy the quest for the primary, the First Position in the Great Chain of Being.

As long as alchemists thought within the framework of the classical four elements, their attention was directed to the notation of rather narrowly defined properties. Once the paradigm of the four elements was laid aside, attention became free-floating, as it were, open to whatever properties experimentation revealed. It was released from the Parent metaphor of theological authority to return to the classical metaphor of Design as the guide to cosmic order. Theoretically, transformations of atomic configuration could give way to any kind of emergent properties, so that chemists returned to the primary stage of observational notation. Only as data accumulated were coherent theories of physical chemistry propounded: these were ultimately unified under the full-fledged atomic theory of the late-nineteenth and early-twentieth centuries.

EMERGENT QUALITIES IN AND OUT OF CHEMISTRY

Here we step out of the narrow confines of chemistry, for the emergent theory of qualities is the basis of scientific reductionism. According to the classical theory of qualities as inherent agents (depersonalized indwelling gods or spirits), anything could be explained by hypostatizing the quality as a virtue or faculty. Thus, two magnets were said to be drawn together by innate agencies of sympathy: this was the conventional view of magnetism. But the emergent theory sought to reduce every quality to a few fundamental ones and resulted in the division in philosophy between primary and secondary qualities—dimension and shape versus color and temperature. Spawned thereby was the debate over the ontological status of the primary qualities, with Kant maintaining that they are inborn categories of human experience and the British empiricists arguing that they are deduced from raw sense data. In terms of metaphors, Kant's thinking remained stuck with the ancient notion of qualities as in-dwelling agencies—a thought process similar to that of Jung in postulating engrams to explain archetypes—whereas the British empiricists switched over to the new metaphor of qualities as Patterns (of something more primary).

From Qualities as Pattern to Pattern as Cause

Still more broadly, this switch in metaphors led to a drastic revision in the theories of causation. Virtues, faculties, spirits, and other indwelling agencies could no longer supply satisfying links between contingent phenomena. Fundamentally, causal linkage was reduced to configurational transformation (alteration of Design or Pattern), so that a continuity could be established between phenomena as transitions of state. The state of a substance was conceived as a disposition of atoms in space, an atomic pattern. Changes of state, therefore, were caused by changes of pattern. This would ultimately remove Hume's demand for a "necessary connection" between causally related phenomena. However, the cul-de-sac of the Pattern metaphor is that everything is reduced to terms of certain fundamentals that themselves turn out to be progeny of the indwelling agencies, tracing lineage right back to the mythical gods.

From Patterns to Myths behind the Forces of Nature

The chief case in point is the concept of force. All words denoting force derive from roots designating strength or ableness. Whereas in myth, each unexplained phenomenon was thought to be brought about by a god, the Ionian philosophers depersonalized the doing god into an indwelling agent, then an agency, and Renaissance scientists completed the transformation by ascribing changes to forces. It is true that force can be defined impersonally as any action that alters a body's state of rest or uniform motion, but such a definition is incomplete in that a source of action is implied. In other words, the god has been banished offstage where he cannot be seen, but he continues to manipulate the happenings on stage.

Where causation can be stated in structural terms only, the ancestral god is further obscured. The strong lure of the Parent metaphor makes the mind inquire about what lies behind the structural change, and the shadowy figure of the god as force reappears. The history of the concept of force offers a kind of microcosm of what happened to scientific thought from ancient to modern times.

We have already seen that the ancients saw motion as caused by an indwelling agent. Aristotle built on this primitive notion by ascribing in his *Metaphysics* the motion of the celestial bodies to the prime mover, though elsewhere he subscribes to the older conception of astral souls (which later degenerated into the astrologers equating the stars and planets with deities). These were easily translated by medieval Christian thinkers into God and the angels. God, through his angels, moved the heavens. Christian symbolism was infused with this picture. In Rev. 22:16, Christ is described as the "bright star of dawn"; the Virgin Mary becomes Stella Maris, star of the sea, the literal translation of her Jewish name, Miriam. Mover and moved are fused in mythopoeia.

Aristotle also sowed the seeds of the undoing of this mythologizing of force by discussing the underlying order of it. He could not escape the metaphor of Design that suffused Greek thought about the cosmos. According to his analysis, the velocity v (or alternatively the distance traveled) of a mobile is proportionate to the ratio of the motive force f to the resistance r of the medium through which it moves: $v = f/r$. Obviously then, as already noted, there can be no vacuum, for in that case, $v = f/r = f/0$, which would imply infinite velocity.[6]

An early attempt to deal with the fallacies of Aristotelian mechanics on this point was made by Thomas Bradwardine in his *Tractatus de Proportionibus* (1328). He noticed that, when the force and resistance are equal, the ratio yields 1 rather than 0, which would imply that motion would result even if the force and resistance canceled each other out. He wrote that the "proportion of the proportions of motive to resistive powers is equal to the proportion of their respective speeds of motion, and conversely. This is to be understood in the sense of geometric proportionality."[7] What this comes down to is $v = log (f/r)$. The exact form of his law is not important, however, since it is incorrect. What is important is that thinkers like Bradwardine at the beginning of the Renaissance were scrutinizing classical dynamics with critical eyes and that their observations prepared the ground for Newton.

The past was hard to let go of. Kepler is a perfect example of one who could bestride both worlds, a profound mystic with an indefatigable empirical bent. In his annotations to the second edition of *Mysterium cosmographicum* (1621), he admitted: "Formerly I believed that the cause of the planetary motion is a soul, fascinated as I was by the teachings of J. C. Scaliger on the motor intelligence. But when I realized that these motive causes attenuate with the distance from the sun, I came to the conclusion that this force is something corporeal, if not so properly, at least in a certain sense."[8] Temper his empiricism as he might, intellectual integrity made him accept the verdict of observation and reason.

Galileo recognized that terrestrial gravity is related to the motion of the planets, yet he summarized contemporary notions of force when in the *Dialogue on the Great World Systems* he had Salviati say: "For the cause of circular motion, in more general terms we assign 'vertue impressed' [*virtù impressa*] and call the same an 'intelligence,' either *assisting* or *informing*, and to infinite other motions we ascribe *Nature* for their cause."[9] Nevertheless, he was moving toward a generalization of force that was finally made complete by Newton, who averred in the discussion following Definition 8 in his *Mathematical Principles of Natural Philosophy:*

> I refer the motive force to the body as an endeavor and propensity of the whole towards a centre, arising from the propensities of the several parts taken together . . . and the absolute force to the centre, as endued with some cause, without which those motive forces would not be propagated through the space round about; whether that cause be some central body (such as is the magnet in the centre of the magnetic force, or the earth in the centre of the gravitating force), or anything else that does not yet appear. For I here design only to give a mathematical notion of those forces without considering their physical causes and seats.[10]

This last statement marks a turning point not only in Western science but, more broadly, in epistemology. It did not escape contemporary notice. "With respect to attraction," wrote Berkeley, "it is clear that this was not introduced by Newton as a true physical quality, but only as a mathematical hypothesis."[11] Under this interpretation, the aim of science is to observe regularities and uniformities in nature and to relate them by subsuming them under general rules. Force, declared Maupertuis, is only "a word that serves to hide our ignorance."[12] On this point, Max Jammer comments:

> It is in analogy to the sensation we have when moving an object from its place or arresting the motion of another that we ascribe a similar state of affairs to the phenomena of physical motion. However, says Maupertuis, since we cannot emancipate ourselves completely from the idea that bodies exert mutual influences upon each other, we may continue to use the term "force." But we should always remember that the concept of force is but an invention to satisfy our desire for explanation.[13]

In other words, personification enables us to project ourselves empathetically into a phenomenon, and assimilating it to some inwardly experienced action schema is the act of understanding. Whereas the substrative schema is the understanding in its most abstract essence, if the schema is detached from an acting agent, as in depersonification, it loses much of its explanatory potency. To be explicative in the most vivid sense, the substrative schema most be anchored in a prototypical action.

One must, in other words, be able to imagine performing a prototypical action on which the substrative schema might reasonably be based.

Thomas Reid, a reactionary to David Hume, put the case quite clearly when he wrote: "It is very probable that the very conception or idea of active power, and of efficient causes, is derived from our voluntary exertions in producing effects; and that, if we were not conscious of such exertion, we should have no conception at all of a cause, or of active power, and consequently no conviction of the necessity of a cause of every change which we observe in nature."[14] There is a sense in which what has not been experienced cannot be known and it is to that sense that Reid refers.[15]

> Modern physics recognizes the concept of force . . . as a methodological inter-mediate that in itself carries no explanatory power whatever. It is a construct to which no immediate rule of interpretation or epistemic correlation can be attached; only a long chain of logical relations, leading over the concepts of mass and acceleration, themselves complicated constructs, refers it to the data of sensory experience.[16]

It is usual in the historiography of science to treat this transition from classical to modern explanation as moving from descriptive to predictive modeling. Explicative constructs cease to be invented to offer a picture of reality; instead, they are "intermediates" that facilitate the interpolation of rules to forecast future phenomena. Like the x in an algebraic equation, they drop out, once the desired result is achieved.

In the depersonification of concepts, the metaphorical base is stripped away, leaving behind only the topological form, essentially a system of relations. In the case of *force*, the relations are embodied in Newton's equations of motion, or in subsequent equations defining force in terms of work or energy. For the average person, these are less satisfying than older accounts because they do not explain the phenomena. Not only does purely mathematical explanation give way to prediction; the phenomena are divorced from projectable human experience. All that remains is a regularity of relation.

Myth is often cast aside by those of positivist disposition as childish, which in a sense it is; but there may be a more fruitful way in which to look at it. For early humans as for the child, understanding begins in terms of the knower. Personification imputes to phenomena voluntary action with which the knower can identify. Over the course of time, humans discover that the framework of their own inward voluntary action does not always accord with the behavior of inanimate things around them. Yet there is a regularity to the cosmos, which over time is duly noted, articulated as laws of nature. It is the divorce from the framework of voluntary action that makes these laws abstract (L., *abs-*, away from + *trahere*, to draw). Once the relations (i.e., the observed regularities) are abstracted from concrete actions (usually only imagined), they can be manipulated *in abstraction*, resulting in topological constructs that cannot thereafter necessarily be regrounded in concrete experience. It is precisely there, in the manipulation of relations absent from identifiable action schemes, that a revolution in human understanding takes place. This we have traced out in detail for the concept of force, but the same thing happens when any concept is depersonified.

PHYSICS AND THE UNIVERSAL MACHINE

Physics, on the other hand, underwent a major revolution, part of which—the notion of force—has already been noted. To understand the greatest revolution, however, we must begin by rehearsing the development of the clock. A necessary ingredient of the modern clock, the escapement, was invented by the Chinese engineer I Hing in 725 but did not make its way to the West for several centuries. In fact, the earliest weight-driven clock is ascribed to a pope, Sylvester II, born Gerbert d'Aurillac, toward the end of the tenth century. The Florentine architect Brunelleschi fabricated the first portable clock in 1410, and thereafter private ownership of clocks became widespread.

As the new French historians have pointed out, the clock imposed a rigid time scheme on daily life, which had thitherto flowed with the variable tides of natural phenomena—sunrise and sunset, agricultural seasons, gestation, life spans. Henceforth, life would be regulated by invariant clock time; and the notion of time itself would change. From being a variable cycle, that is a cycle with variable periods or phases (e.g., long winter and short spring), it became a framework of fixed sequence, a linear progression of invariant instants (:One/Many). Psychologically, this is a crucial transition, for in the earlier notion of time, the variance of spans rises out of the circumstances and the subjective judgment of the individual, but under the new clock regime the order of time is *externally imposed*. From being of experience, it becomes something outside experience—outside in the sense that we go to the clock to find out for sure where in time we are. From Plato's time as the moving image of eternity (the One passing across the Many of phenomenal reality) the medieval mind had moved to Plotinus's assignment of time to the feeling of living change. But the Judeo-Christian notion of time moving linearly from the Creation to the Day of Judgment prepared the way for the acceptance of linear clock time. The metaphor changed from the One/Many of Plato to the scheme of motion in the soul (Plotinus) and finally to the scheme of moving along a Path or simply to time as the Path along which all things move in change.[17]

To understand this final twist to time, we must remember that the clock was the first complex mechanism to become an integral part of public and private life.

It became a sentinel in the tower of some main municipal building in nearly every town throughout Europe. People knew it as a fact of life, and it regulated the activities of the town. We might say that its mechanicity was a novelty of public proportions. Little wonder, then, that it captured the imagination of scientists of the day.

Let us bear in mind that up until the Renaissance, the universe had been conceived as an organism. Plato used the metaphor of Microcosm/Macrocosm to argue for a correspondence between aspects of the cosmos and parts of the body. It was a common mythical theme, since many creation myths had the universe being born literally from the body of the creator. This was little modified by Christian thinkers who worked from the premise of animism, that all that moves does so because it is infused with spirit or spirits of divine origin.

It was a leap of inestimable magnitude, therefore, when, contemplating the writing of his *Astronomica Nova*, Kepler wrote to Herhart von Hohenburg, 10 February 1605: "I am much occupied with the investigation of physical causes. My aim in this is to show that the celestial machine is to be likened not to a divine organism but rather to a clockwork."[18] As Holton comments, "In one brilliant image, Kepler saw the three basic themes or cosmological models superimposed: the universe as physical machine, the universe as mathematical harmony, and the universe as central theological order."[19]

Kepler was a neo-Pythagorean. Renewing the metaphor of One/Many in mathematics, he treated number once again as multiples of One. Out of the One comes the Many, and the integral ratios of numbers expressed the magic efficacy in the One. He believed in a literal harmony of the universe, a music of the spheres that he hoped to notate.[20] This meant that the parts of the universe—for him, notably the planets—must be related by fixed ratios. "What may be constructed in geometry," he said, "is consonant in music."[21] Probably it was that stricture which made him turn away from the Organism metaphor to embrace the machine, in which the parts are fixed in size and configuration. It is surely ironical that this basically medieval thinker should have been a key figure in the overturning of what was a mainstay metaphor of medieval thought.

Of course, Organism and Mechanism are both variants of the more general metaphor, Pattern, but each contains inherently different possibilities. Whether the world or universe, as target domain, is seen as organism or mechanism is a matter of cultural proclivity. Initially, the universe is simply seen as having order, supported by an action schema of orderedness, which is then usually ascribed to the intentions of a divine creator: it is a Design. In Genesis, for example, the earth is first without form, and God brings it into order with the waters below and the firmament above, much like the classical creation myths, from Hesiod to Ovid, in which order is brought out of chaos. An earlier parallel is found in the Babylonian creation myth, *Enuma Elish*, in which chaos is personified in the goddess Tiamat.[22] Various architectural structures, such as mounds and ziggurats, become symbolic analogues of the cosmos. Even more elaborated, the cosmic order is mirrored in a plethora of mandalas. When speculation runs to how this pattern of things functions, about the only thing known that displays purposeful action is a living creature—aside from spirits, which are already anthropomorphized beings. Organism therefore becomes the natural metaphor in terms of which to understand the physical and the social order.

An organism is dictated by an inscrutable will or spirit, perfectly subject to the whim of the parent/god; therefore it is suited to myriad ad hoc explanations. The Mechanism, on the other hand, is fully defined in the interrelations of its parts. The workings of the machine are, in principle, clear and open to view, fixed and quantifiable, precluding mysticism. The fixed interrelationship of parts implies that all explanations of the parts and their operation must be as internally and rigidly self-consistent as the parts themselves. Unlike the Organism metaphor, the Mechanism is consonant with determinism, reductionism, and quantification or mathematicization, as well as with atomism and the configurational theory of causation. It was the perfect metaphor in terms of which to impose coherence on the trends emerging from the physical sciences. Indeed, one name applied to this new brand of scientific thought is mechanism. Seeing the universe as a vast, self-perpetuating machine, rather than a deistic puppet world, was the greatest revolution in science in this millennium. Shifting from the Parent and Organism metaphors to the Mechanism metaphor made modern science possible.

Mechanism Invades the Biological Sciences

Biosciences fared poorly during the Renaissance. They were the last bastion of vitalist thinking, controlled by the ancient intellectual paraphernalia of indwelling spirits, faculties, humors, and the like. Much observational groundwork was laid, such as the work of Harvey on the circulation of the blood. New metaphors from within the bioscience domain were not forthcoming. However, it did not take long for mechanism, the doctrine of reductionism, to seep through to the biological sciences. Of course, Democritus had already suggested an atomistic theory of life, but his doctrines ran counter to the prevailing metaphors and failed to take hold. Marin Mersenne (1588–1648) was one of the earliest Renaissance thinkers to conceive the work of God altogether as proceeding by mechanistic principles on the grounds that such principles are the epitome of reason and God must essentialize reason supreme. Descartes went even further by suggesting that man is nothing but a machine; and he could do this only because he made an absolute separation between mind and body. The body is the machine that the soul uses to express itself in the material world. The final step in this line of reasoning was taken by Julien de LaMettrie in the baroque era; in his *L'Homme-Machine* he reduced both mind and body to mechanical principles.

We should note that there was really nothing remarkable in the application of mechanism to biology. Living organisms are infinitely more complex than machines, or rather, than any other physical systems; and it is natural to proceed in analysis from the simple to the complex. (Even the so-called top-down approach borrowed from computer science presupposes a knowledge of the simpler principles, and so is not a real subversion of the natural procedure.) Consequently, the metaphors of the biological sciences are inevitably derived from the intellectual foundations of the physical sciences. Nevertheless, the deployment of these metaphors with respect to explanation of phenomena of life has broad implications in terms of value systems and emotional responses to public issues variously touching on the sanctity of life.

THE FINAL TRIUMPH OF MECHANISM

It would simplify the task of the intellectual historian, if when new metaphors supplanted old, the old would completely die out; but such is not the case. The old metaphors are usually built into the language through etymological continuity and colloquial expression, not to mention formal idioms. They often live on, too, in spheres of thought different from the one in which they have been supplanted. In the case of the Organism metaphor, for example, it continued in the biological sciences, principally because the data did not permit full explanation in mechanistic terms. Reductionism remains as a hope, rather than a fait accompli in the biosciences. And, of course, the Organism metaphor is almost a necessity for institutions of political control, so it continues to be sanctioned by church and state. The people form a *body* possessing a *will*. If society were likened to a machine, there would be no room for political persuasion. Control would have to be through brute force. The problem this poses is the reconciliation between competing social institutions—government and church versus science, which can never be entirely satisfactory because the two metaphors of Organism and Mechanism have mutually exclusive internal logics. Correspondences proposed to gloss over these contradictions have so far been unsatisfactory, being clearly makeshift rather than being securely anchored in another root metaphor.

It can be said immediately that the Mechanism metaphor became the dominant one of the age, lasting until the present century. Through it, the preponderance of disparate lines of thought across all the disciplines were drawn together. Much of the impetus of the Enlightenment came from the optimistic deployment of this metaphor as the myth of explication, according to which reason was to unlock the deepest secrets of the universe and resolve the most recalcitrant social problems. The explosion of that myth in turn precipitated the romantic reaction and the uncomfortable partial return to the Organism metaphor in the nineteenth century. This closer contention between the Organism and the Mechanism metaphors underlay much of the Sturm und Drang of the romantic movement.

The reinstitution of *metron* in the form of empiricism led not to the complementary *symmetron* but merely to a means by which to standardize procedures to facilitate practical results. Initially, people like Kepler and even Newton looked to mathematical theories of physics as revelations of the Divine Plan, but rapidly, as these theories multiplied and bore fruits of both practical and heuristic value, they were increasingly pursued for themselves—and in that manner, the mathematicization of the sciences rose to become the language of explanation. We term this a crucial transition because it meant the gradual demise of explanation as reality modeling, to be supplanted by explanation as prediction. In simple terms, this means that philosophy and science turned away from trying to build a coherent picture of reality, and instead became content with predicting outcomes. Carried to its extreme, as in quantum physics, a consequence of this turnabout is that one may be able to predict exactly that a physical system will move from state A to state B without being able to say anything about what happens in between. Measurement alone, or the reliance on mathematics, is not a sufficient cause for this trend, as demonstrated in Greek culture; rather, social factors are necessary to tip the balance away from the pursuit of *symmetron* or ideal knowledge and toward blind prediction.

As an example of the different manner in which things were explained, let us take the case of heat. Since classical times, heat had been understood as an indwelling agency, a property of physical bodies, such as could enter a body or be driven out (:Breath). Proponents of atomism, of course, revived the discarded notion of Democritus that heat is a form of particulate motion. The particulate theory won out only after data accumulated in the form of mathematical relations between thermometric observables (e.g., specific heats of various substances, and adiabatic phase changes) to vitiate the Breath metaphor as an explicative model. Carried forward, these mathematical relations ultimately spun out the almost purely mathematical construct of entropy in the mid-nineteenth century to supplant the more intuitive notion of heat.

How the extremum principle evolved is another example of the radical mathematicization of physics. It was generalized from the observation in optics that light always travels the shortest path between two points. This observation had been made in antiquity, but it was Pierre Fermat who formulated it in mathematical terms. Pierre Maupertuis a century later subjected the principle to greater generalization, substituting for time in Fermat's formulation the purely mathematical notion of action (the product of mass by velocity by path length). Euler, Lagrange, and Hamilton brought ever greater mathematical sophistication to the principle so that ultimately the quantity, which is minimal in a dynamic process, became almost purely mathematical—in fact, it was ultimately stated in terms of generalized coordinates (i.e., any coordinates that might be chosen) in multidimensional phase space (i.e., a system of mathematical variables that are interrelated in the same way as the x, y, z variables defining spatial properties in a Cartesian coordinate system).

The arsenal of the new science included a configurational theory of causation, a transforming of faculties, spirits, essences, and the like into forces, empirical methods aimed at the establishment of mathematical relations among data, all taking place within the strictures of a Mechanism metaphor of the universe.

THE REFORMATION

The Reformation, from the standpoint of intellectual history, had nothing to offer in the way of metaphor innovation but rather was a pronounced revolt of the Northern countries against the hegemony of the Southern papacy, motivated by ethnicity and politico-economic interests.[23] Even the ominous Calvinist concept of predestination was nothing but a reductio ad absurdum of the mythical notion of the Fates and the woven design of things to come. In the main, the schism between Protestant and Catholic revolved around excuses for separation, nothing more.

This is not to say that the Reformation has no importance in intellectual history. Quite the contrary, but as Barnes quips, "by all odds, the outstanding contribution to intellectual progress that can be ascribed to Protestantism was an indirect one, namely, its aid in increasing the difficulty of carrying out ecclesiastical repression of intellectual freedom."[24] By making biblical interpretation a personal and private matter, Luther robbed the Church of its main rationale for authority in every corner of daily life. He also made religion relativistic and therefore more vulnerable to the encroachment of science, which was at any rate inevitable.

An interesting and terrible consequence of the general weakening of popular faith in religious dogma as presented by the institutionalized churches was the rash of defensive reactions that it set off. People were caught between religion, an order under attack, and science, an order aborning but not complete enough to support popular values and human needs for security and a sense of overall meaning in life. The authority of the Church was being undermined from all sides. Economic interests were overriding spiritual concerns. Nationalism clashed with the centralism of papal authority. And the rapid progress of science was throwing biblical creationism into doubt. Nevertheless, religion had the deeper and older roots, so allegiance fell to it in a distortedly radical form: occultism and the witchcraft persecutions of the sixteenth century. Sheer emotionalism lay behind these trends. Disguised in the persecutions was a displaced counterattack on science, which itself was protected behind the mantle of logic and demonstrable results. The masses floundered adrift from the values, at times however questionable, on which they had for centuries built their lives—we may say duplicitously, but the duplicity nevertheless required an intellectual foundation.

RISE OF THE SOCIAL CONTRACT AND THE RULE OF LAW

Meanwhile, interesting currents were rising in the economic and political spheres. While they contained nothing new in the way of metaphor shifts, they brought deployments of old metaphors that ultimately transformed social existence to its deepest foundations. World trade brought the workers to the fore as the middle class, a new nexus of economic and therefore political power. When the rising monarchs of feudal Europe had had to face the opposition of the popes, they met the challenge by appealing to the so-called divine right of kings, a deployment of the very Parent metaphor used by the Church. And when the populace, speaking through the bourgeoisie, had to collide with the monarch, they fell back upon an old metaphor underlying much in the field of ethics: the Contract. Social-contract theory envisions an imaginary bond between the people and the government, even conjuring a myth of the original state of society—a dog-eat-dog chaos—to legitimize the metaphorical fiction. When we examine Renaissance political theory from the metaphoristic standpoint, these are the only conceptual innovations that we find.

The economic changes in the Renaissance spawned by expanding trade brought with them a shift in emphasis in law away from property rights toward matters of contract—certainly another reason that the Contract metaphor made such a mark in political theory. It is inextricably associated with the schemes of Cut/Join, Bind, and Debt/Payment. In a contract, parties are *joined* and *bound* by an agreement involving the fulfillment of an obligation (= the payment of a debt).

We have already noted the slow conversion of wealth from property, mainly land, to credit; however, capital was vested also in goods and in the assets of business enterprise. Properties had economic value to the degree to which they could be kept in active use. Trade is a highly competitive enterprise, not least among nations. It is a continuum of transactions, and it is with the details of such transactions that commercial law must be concerned. The individual becomes a mere agent in the transactions. Indeed, often the original contracting parties can sell their roles in contracts to secondary parties. It is the transaction that is paramount. Here were sewn the seeds of modern bureaucratic order that subjugated the individual to a lower rank than the relations forming the network of the corporate system. The corporation itself assumed the legal status of a person. Erich Kahler has provided a classic study of the dehumanization consequent upon the rise of corporate organization in post-Renaissance society in *The Tower and the Abyss*, to which the reader is referred for further details.[25] There is an interesting parallel here between the bureacratization of the politico-economic order and the mathematicization of the physical sciences. In both cases, the underlying metaphors are stretched beyond their capacities to lend coherence to the relevant information and nothing remains but the abstract framework of topological schemes: mathematical relationships for the sciences and legalistic rules for the social bureaucracy.

MUSIC: FURTHER TRIUMPH OF
TOPOLOGICAL SCHEMES OVER METAPHORS

While all this was happening, music underwent a major revolution around 1450, one to which historians of music have given insufficient attention, though authorities duly note, for example, that the "emancipation of instrumental from vocal music is one of the most important developments in the history of music between 1400 and 1600."[26] Historians typically treat this development in terms of the appearance of new forms, such as the ricercare, toccata, and fantasia, without delving deeply into their intellectual roots.[27] What is not discussed is that music became more intimately associated with action schemes, making it peculiarly parallel with what was happening in the mathematicization of physics. Prior to this date, nearly all serious music—and probably even the popular music that has perished—had its roots in vocalization, but "during the second half of the [fifteenth] century a distinction between vocal and instrumental music began to be made."[28] Suddenly there appeared purely instrumental forms that placed a premium on the resources of instrumental improvisation.

> Deprived of the powerful aid of words, instrumental music is compelled to offer an abstract and ideal musical substance, in an idiom and form created by itself. Being the art of pure fantasy, instrumental music must act without the intermediary of other elements. Such a course is not possible through the adoption of the means employed by vocal music, whose very nature is different and whose form and character are more or less dependent on the text. The intrinsic features of instrumental music will emerge, consequently, in the measure in which it eludes the influence of vocal music and pursues its own path.[29]

In the broadest terms, it was the rise of the bourgeoisie that broke the monopoly of the Church and hence of vocal music in the sphere of musical patronage: it was a new audience, in other words, listening in a variety of secular settings. But this is only half the story. New instruments and a novel use for an old instrument account for the other half.

Evidence is insufficient to establish precisely the chronology of ecclesiastical organ music. Although the organ was admitted into the Church as early as perhaps the ninth century, apparently it languished as an embellishment of the building, rather like the bells, and was not integrated into the service until the fifteenth century. Partly this was due to clerical attitudes in rejecting from the service anything worldly, and partly it was due to the inadequacies of the small medieval organs to fill the church acoustically.[30] Once this and other technical matters were rectified, the organ entered into the liturgy. It is recorded that people were astonished at the bravura instrumental effects achievable on the organ; and of course organists were only too happy to exploit this attention. In its earliest form, the organ toccata evidently was a fanfare, imitating the earlier trumpet variety used to announce the beginning or an important stage of the service. Growing in length and stature, no doubt under the impetus of influential organists, it assumed a freely developmental form with emphasis on counterpoint and fugal sections.

Whereas the organ had been around in one form or another since antiquity, the lute was one of the many new instruments entering Europe from the East, either by way of Moorish Spain or via the Crusades; and it became by far the most popular. Being portable, it was ideal for the intimate gatherings fostered by the middle class and the nouveaux riches rising from it. Descended from the oud, it initially was wedded to vocal forms, but again the virtuosi of the instrument quickly exploited the popular adulation that bravura playing inspired.

Listeners to the new instrumental music were, by contemporary accounts, most intrigued by those aspects that were the least derivative from vocal models: passages too intricate and rapid for vocal imitation and motival development largely alien to liturgical vocal repertory. Generally speaking, vocal music follows the sinuous line of speech, a line of small intervals and extended enough to cover a complete verbal sentence or phrase—the text motivates the line. Thomas Morley, the seventeenth-century English composer and theoretician, characterized the departure from vocal models in his description of the fantasia:

> [A] musician taketh a point [i.e., theme] at his pleasure, and wresteth and turneth it as he list, making either much or little of it as shall seeme best in his own conceit [i.e., imagination]. In this may more art be showne than in any other musicke, because the composer is tide to nothing but that he may adde, diminish, and alter at his pleasure. . . . this kind of musick is with them who practice instruments of parts in greatest use, but for voices it is but seldome used.

Thus, Morley was quite aware that a new form of musical invention was at hand. He called it a "kind of musicke which is made without a dittie," a dittie being a tune set to a text.[31]

What is involved here is a transition from *vocal isomorphs* to those based on *manual action schemes*. Modes and modulations reflected vocal emotive states: tones of voice and tonal changes associated with emotional expression. These, plus the phrasing of the text, supplied the basic framework for ancient and medieval musical invention. This was gradually enlivened by the rhythmic patterns of the dance, which found their way into the musical settings of miracle and morality plays. The *Play of Daniel* is an excellent example of this, alternating as it does between the declamatory demands of the text and the rhythmic exuberance of dance interludes.

Dance rhythms and patterns supplied the bases for the first purely instrumental forms—other forms being transcriptions of vocal prototypes. From slow modulations of extended textual-vocal lines, music quickly moved to shorter and often more spaciously intervalic motives that could be executed with a rapidity that would dazzle the audience. Such motives were also easier to manipulate under conditions of improvisation, since the brain can process shorter and more sharply defined melodic units when short-term memory must be accessed quickly and continually. Interest can be maintained with such material only if it is varied in all aspects; hence the genesis of thematically developmental forms, with all appropriate topological schemes being drawn upon to furnish the means of development. Essentially these schemes—juxtaposition, inversion, retrogression, augmentation, diminution, etc.—are identical with those underlying discursive thought.

By no means do I wish to imply that medieval vocal music was not developmental or devoid of variation, but generally speaking development was slower, line variation was more gradual and of a lesser scalar degree, and other action schemes were applied more sparingly, with everything subjugated to the declamatory structure of the text. There was therefore a continuity of structure underlying the instrumental revolution, but likewise it cannot be denied that instruments can do things that a voice cannot replicate, and it is these things that brought about the revolution that gave birth to the modern era in music.

As Victor Rangel-Ribeiro observes, the "roots of baroque ornamentation can be found in the vocal music of the Renaissance."[32] We are well reminded that instrumental music did not suddenly leave vocal music behind, but found nourishment always in the more ancient tradition. However, action schemes were brought to the fore that instigated radical transformations from the execution of an individual note to the larger matters of form. Only by reference to these action schemes can we account coherently for the evolution of the sonata form, the backbone of baroque and romantic composition, and the kind of motival development that underlies the sonata and most other smaller instrumental forms. Ultimately, in the twentieth century, the action schemes of instrumental music—manual schemes predominantly—were veritably separated from their vocal counterpart to produce music inconceivable under vocal schemes.

THE VISUAL ARTS

Strictly speaking, the visual arts fall within our province, but the scope of the metaphorical analysis of iconography or the reduction of creative procedures to action schemes deserves a study unto itself. Determinants of style, too, are monstrously diverse, so much so that they have completely escaped all art historians to date. Rawson's concept of graphic types offers a pregnant principle of unification for any beginning at studying the question, but even that is little more than a heuristic device. An allied approach, followed by Herbert Read,[33] Ortega y Gasset,[34] and in literary history by Auerbach[35] and Kahler,[36] is to view the arts as literal constructions of reality subject to stages of increasingly sophisticated analysis as measured by such criteria as optical detail, anatomical correctness, subtlety of relations, psychological penetration, etc. We can get just an inkling of the inexhaustible richness of the field by considering, say, Kenneth Clark's remarks on the *contrapposto* pose in his classic study, *The Nude*, where it is possible to see that even a gesture can become frozen into the ever-changing ingredients of artistic style.[37] Musical ornamentations suggest themselves as more purely topological counterparts. With the sad remark that nearly everything is left to be done in the intellectual foundations of art history, I am forced to refer the curious reader to Ursala Hadje's *The Styles of European Art* for an entering wedge into the subject.[38]

CONCLUSION

Within the narrow focus of this study, the trend away from root metaphors that lend a worldview to the spectrum of human knowledge and toward reliance on topological schemes alone is the most important theme carried from the Renaissance into the later centuries. As we will see, the rise of topological schemes operative over and above any concrete forms, isolated almost from the usual directive metaphors, proved in the twentieth century to define a decisive reorientation of human thought. The Mechanism metaphor was the vehicle for this radical transformation. By focusing attention on function, it encouraged greater and greater reliance on the discovery, invention, and codification of rules that made the function of physical and social entities predictable and therefore subject to human control. Contract involves the proliferation of rules of law to sustain it; so, in this legalistic aspect, it harmonizes well with the nomothetic proclivities of the scientific orientation around the Mechanism metaphor.

7

The Enlightenment
to 1900

During the Enlightenment, the primary metaphor continued to be that of the Mechanism. Newton immortalized the poetic notion of the universal clockwork. His celestial mechanics reduced the operations of this clockwork to a mathematical simplicity that galvanized the eighteenth-century mind. The equations of motion that he deduced possessed an aesthetic elegance which seemed to do justice to the divine will behind creation. Neither before nor since has the work of a scientist left such a personal mark on an age. In a real sense, the prose style of Newton, with its eloquent precision, became the prototype of the neoclassical literary style in poetry as well as prose.

It was the promise, and not just the reality, of Newton's achievement that unified the typical eighteenth-century enterprise of reducing everything with finality to principles of reason. Never had a metaphor seemed to work so completely to unlock the secrets of nature as did the clockwork metaphor. Reductionism seemed assured. The first door of the celestial mansion had been swung open, and Kepler's dream of notating the music of the spheres appeared within reach. Clockwork order in the celestial mansion seduced artists and poets to succumb to variants of Kepler's dream. "The transition from the seventeenth-century confidence in science as proof of order in nature to the nineteenth-century hostility to science can be found in the profuse number of poems in the eighteenth century that lent a new rhetoric to science in an overwhelming desire to show the wisdom of God in nature."[1]

Poets were inspired by the Newtonian prospect of order thrust before them. In his long poem, *Solomon on the Vanity of the World*, Matthew Prior rhapsodized on the scientific miracle of divine providence:

> From nature's constant or eccentric laws,
> The thoughtful soul this general influence draws,
> That an effect must presuppose a cause:
> And while she does her upward flight sustain,

> Touching each link of the continued chain,
> At length she is oblig's [*sic*] and forc'd to see
> A first, a source, a life, a deity:
> What has forever been, and must forever be.[2]

Prior alludes to the Chain of Being metaphor and poeticizes what is essentially the Aristotelian argument for the Prime Mover. There was no doubt from whom the modern revelation of the cosmic order came; it was, in the words of Moses Browne, "Newton! vast mind! whose piercing pow'rs apply'd / The secret cause of motion first descry'd."[3] Samuel Bowden, in his now rare *Poetical Essays on Several Occasions* (volume 1, 1733; volume 2, 1735), usurped Prior's conception wholesale in *Poem Sacred to the Memory of Sir Isaac Newton,* writing of Newton:

> He sees the chain from heav'n to earth descend,
> And on their latent cause effects depend,
> That unseen Cause which agitates each sphere,
> Pervades the mass, and rules the circling year.[4]

Eulogies to the new god, Newton, proliferated. In the anonymous poem, *The Vanity of Philosophic Systems: a Poem Addressed to the Royal Society* (1761), we read that:

> Sagacious Newton lost with pond'ring thought,
> To mathematick rules a system brought;
> God as an Eastern monarch, left for show:
> His Viceroy, Gravity, the God below.[5]

In 1733, the same year in which the first volume of Samuel Bowden's poems appeared, Queen Caroline established a grotto at the Royal Hermitage where busts of Locke, Boyle, Wollasten, Samuel Clarke, and, of course, Newton were enshrined in a kind of science hall of fame. As part of the public attention given to the shrine, the *Gentleman's Magazine* of April of that year sponsored a contest for poetry written for the occasion. The winning entries show an uncommon popular knowledge of the sciences among the general population.[6]

Mathematics: The Language of the Clockwork Universe

Much of the advancement of science was underpinned by the mushroom growth of mathematics. It was the elegance of his mathematics, after all, that made Newton so convincing in his presentation of a clockwork universe. Great creative strides were made in many branches of mathematics, not to mention the more practical aspects of science, with which we are not concerned in this survey. Of course, the mathematicization of the sciences continued, but over and above this there was a great surge of creativity within the field of pure mathematics. Analytic geometry, calculus, analysis, and probability theory all rose out of the genius of the period. We have already commented on analytic geometry. In the calculus, Newton and Leibniz exhumed Archimedes' method of exhaustion, essentially breaking up an area or volume into many small cross sections, judging the area or volume of each, then summing them to obtain the whole. Archimedes used the method for estimating the volume of barrels and other irregularly shaped bodies. It is more a technique than a concept, a true topological manipulation. As a whole, mathematics turned into a huge body of topological manipulations defined in the shorthand of symbols. Looked at from this perspective, it is plain why it became so obscure to all but a few. Laying bare such procedures, they look rather like: walk five paces forward, turn left four paces, reverse right and left and flop upside down, move six paces up and turn everything inside out, reversing up and down, etc.; now where are you and what is your orientation? No one step is unfathomable, but the density of variegated operations without reference back to physical models—a reference now not always even possible—can baffle normal minds not specially gifted in suspending such procedures over extended periods. Nevertheless, the whole thing boils down to topology, and strictly speaking, mathematicians have come to this realization in the twentieth century implicitly by adopting topological models to mirror the structure of mathematics itself. Gauss saw this clearly in 1831, when he wrote that "mathematics is concerned only with the enumeration and comparison of relations."[7] Whether these relations are in the objective world or simply fictions of the mind facilitating human actions depends on the metaphors chosen for the epistemology of the inquirer. Mathematicians are divided even now on this point, hardly realizing the metaphoric foundation of their schism.

Essentially, the structure of mathematics is hierarchical. As Bell puts it: "[T]he content of a mathematical theory is the structure of the system of postulates from which the theory is developed by the rules of mathematical logic, and from which are derived its various interpretations."[8] Bell also acknowledges that mathematical logic itself is a structure susceptible to variation in accordance with changing intellectual aims and proclivities, not to mention practical considerations. Hierarchy is grounded mainly in the Family metaphor, strong during the Renaissance, a perfect bridge between the Parent and Organism metaphors of medieval culture and the Mechanism metaphor of the succeeding modern age, because it embodied both the parental concept and the notion of order or mechanical structure. During the seventeenth and eighteenth centuries, the sense of hierarchical order that prevailed in mathematics was part and parcel of the age. This can be seen in a parallel with baroque art. According to Harries, ornamentation in the churches of the time fulfilled a symbolic function, placing things in a hierarchical order.[9] Now, in the

Mechanism metaphor order is based on equality of parts; hence, too, its sustaining the egalitarian social movements of the late-eighteenth century.

At bottom, since, as Bell says, "mathematical theory is the structure of the system of postulates from which the theory is developed by the rules of mathematical logic," it quickly became apparent that logic in the formal sense is at the foundation of mathematics. In fact, formal logic made enormous strides during the last century, alongside of efforts to bring rigor to the mass of mathematical advancement made in the prior two hundred years. These efforts led mathematicians to realize more and more that Gauss had been right in stating that mathematics is concerned only with the enumeration and comparison of relations. This means that mathematicians ceased to be as interested in the representational value or designata of what they were manipulating and developed interest in manipulation itself. Concretely this presents itself as concern for mathematical structure. From this perspective, Galois, Jordan, Klein, and others who contributed to what eventually emerged as group theory made one of the most significant advancements in mathematical thought. It brought together both the rationalist stand and the *metron* and *symmetron* classical predilection, crystallizing the sense of structure or Pattern with emphasis on symmetry transformations or invariants. That is, what often is most significant within a group is a configuration of elements that remains invariant even after certain transformative procedures have been applied to the group (e.g., rotation of a geometric representation of the group, or permutations of the elements in the group). Since it is the relationship among the elements of the group, and not physically what the group represents, that determines a conservation law, it is easy to see that it is a topological scheme, and not so much an underlying metaphor, that determines the whole procedure. To the extent that there is an underlying metaphor, it must be Pattern, manifest through concern for symmetry.[10]

In physics, the discovery of the conservation of energy had the same metaphoric foundations as group theory, and the extension of conservation laws to elementary particle physics has been largely by way of group theory.

> The principle of the conservation of energy . . . was confirmed between 1840 and 1850, the decade in which Joule's experiments [in which he proved the mechanical equivalence of heat] were carried on. In 1842, J. R. von Mayer suggested the possibility that heat might be converted into work, or work into heat, something that was proved to be true by Joule's experiments. In 1842, also, W. R. Grove defended the idea of the interrelation of physical forces, a doctrine which he elaborated in a book four years later. This conception had been anticipated in part by a French scientist, Sadi Carnot (1796–1832), approximately twenty years earlier. It remained, however, for the most encyclopedic physicist of the nineteenth century, Professor Hermann von Helmholtz (1821–1894) of Berlin, to set forth a systematic presentation of the principle

of the conservation of energy based upon his own independent experiments as well as those of his contemporaries.[11]

The essence of the principle of the conservation of energy is that energy cannot be destroyed; it can only be changed from one form to another—e.g., mechanical to heat, as in friction. This principle is related to group theory because energy is treated as an invariant under various kinds of transformations, each of which has a proper mathematical representation. Subsequently and down into the twentieth century, other conservation laws have been framed. For instance, based upon $E = mc^2$, the principle of energy conservation has been revised as a principle of mass-energy conservation, wherein mass is treated, so to speak, as a form of energy. "In the theory of special relativity, momentum and energy form a four-vector so that the *conservation of the energy-momentum four-vector* defines one covariant law."[12] As the symmetrical bases of such laws became recognized, the principles could be extended systematically: all that is required is to search for important quantities that remain invariant under prescribed circumstances or transformations. That the character of these laws has emerged in the way described is indicated by the fact that they are now more often treated under the rubric of "symmetry laws." They have revolutionized modern physics, making possible much of the progression of quantum theory and more recently the various unified theories attempting to synthesize quantum theory with relativity to explain all physical phenomena in terms of one parsimonious set of postulates.

> A conservation law equates the value of a physical quantity in the initial state to its subsequent values, in particular to its value in the final state, for some process. The great importance of conservation laws is that they provide significant constraints on complicated processes for which a detailed mathematical description may be practically impossible.[13]

Such constraints are especially valuable in elementary particle physics, where the phenomena are exceedingly complex and must be studied only indirectly by their effects.

> All reactions and decays of elementary particles and hadrons are described by a set of laws called conservation laws. Here the term conservation means that some quantity remains unchanged (that is, conserved) in a reaction. The simplest example of a conserved quantity is the total energy.[14]

Referring back to the principle of energy conservation, and connecting it with the substance of group theory, we can perhaps begin to gain a sense of the naked topological transformations underlying the fundamental mathematical processes and may be able to extend them by imagination to the entire field of mathematicized science. Subject variables to certain coherent and systematic transformations (internalized and abstracted manipulations) and see what happens. If the result is "interesting," it may constitute a law (which may be simply a statement of what happens under the transformation, with particular emphasis on any invariants that might occur).

Baring the machinery of this law-making process made it the subject of inquisitive scrutiny; and contingent developments prepared a fertile climate for such investigations. Axiomatics had arisen as a necessary antidote for (or, at any rate, palliative to) the rampant proliferation of mathematical ideas in the previous two centuries. Moving largely in response to urgent applicative needs, seventeenth- and eighteenth-century mathematicians had not observed always the usual amenities of careful proofs for their propositions and procedures. Nineteenth-century mathematicians, as a consequence, were faced with a tangle of uncertainties that could be resolved only by recourse to careful proofs and clarifications.

A crisis in the whole issue was precipitated by the rise of a new methodology described by E. T. Bell as "generalization by suppression of certain postulates defining a given system. The system defined by the curtailed set of postulates is then developed. Linear algebra is obtainable in this way from the algebra of a field. Vector algebras . . . received their initial impulse from Hamilton's suppression of the postulate that multiplication is commutative in common algebra."[15] Hamilton suppressed the commutative rule in the development of quaternions, expressions which were forerunners of vector algebra, in which the product ab is different from ba. Here began the realization that topological manipulations are not always commutative, i.e., it may matter to the outcome in what order the manipulations are performed. We can illustrate this with the simple figure:

$$A\ B$$
$$C\ D$$

If we first give this a quarter turn, thus displacing the elements clockwise by one position each, we have

$$C\ A$$
$$D\ B$$

An exchange of right to left, gives:

$$A\ C$$
$$B\ D$$

But if we make the right-to-left exchange first, getting:

B A
D C

then follow it with the quarter turn, we have:

D B
C A

which is altogether different. Such noncommutative operations have been used now in many fields of mathematics and have numerous practical applications. Often the defining operation of a group is noncommutative, in which case the group is called non-Abelian.

Undoubtedly the most epoch-making systems derived from the new methodology of suppressed postulates were the non-Euclidean geometries. There the postulate suppressed, of course, was the parallel postulate: that if p and L are a point and a line such that p is not on L, there exists one line and only one line that passes through p and does not intersect L (assuming the plane to be infinite). More intuitively, it states that parallel lines never meet, no matter how far they may be extended. The postulate was a good candidate for suppression because it has never received satisfactory proof within plane geometry. At first, geometries evolved from suppression of the parallel postulate were considered merely interesting freaks of mathematical ingenuity, but it was disturbing to mathematicians to find that coherent geometries could be erected with postulates stating either that no lines could be drawn through p or that an infinite number could be drawn through p and not intersect L. The belief that the consistency of such geometries challenged was that all self-consistent mathematical structures have a correspondence with the objective physical world, and of course that world was assumed to be Euclidean.

Subsequently it was determined that the non-Euclidean geometries in two dimensions could be realized on the surfaces generated from the conic sections: the circle, ellipse, parabola, and hyperbola. However, when it was also shown that self-consistent algebras could be created through the willful and arbitrary redefinition of fundamental operations, the two discoveries rendered obsolete the Mirror metaphor for interpreting the relation between mathematics and physical reality. Or rather, the Mirror metaphor was deployed through making it reflexive (self-correspondence). One set of axioms was validated by correspondence with a set of meta-axioms, but both sets were within the province of mathematics proper. Mathematical structure was freed to generate whatever imagination could contrive, given certain rules that could themselves be flexibly contrived. In simple terms, the mathematician was free to invent, without having to worry about the practical value (i.e., physical applicability) of his inventions.

Mechanism and Order in the Arts

Hierarchical order and clarity, so ubiquitous in mathematics, found expression in the arts and other aspects of the era of the Enlightenment. We have already remarked about such elements in baroque and especially rococo architecture. Surely there is also a counterpart to the hierarchical ornamentation of rococo architecture in the ornamental development of baroque music and the growth of that music along lines of theme and variation, on the microlevel of form, and on the next higher level the typical forms based on linking but contrasting movements with underlying forward impetus to a kind of rhetorical denouement. Clear and logical development, like an axiomatic system, was the objective. Rhetorical structure stood as a common nexus between instrumental and vocal music. A very conscious nexus, it was enunciated in the doctrine of affections, which was based on the analogy between music and rhetoric noted by the ancients.

> The innovation of the recitative especially gave theorists ample occasion to observe the parallelism between music and speech, and theorists of the monody, especially Doni, began to evolve concrete musical figures for such "figures of speech" as question, affirmation, emphatic repetition, and others. Toward the middle of the [eighteenth] century Bernhard could already state that "because of the multitude of figures music nowadays has risen to such height that it may well be likened to a *rhetoric*." Mattheson also held forth that music was a form of "sound speech." According to him the two outstanding *loci topici* [sources of rhetorical expression] were the *locus notationis* [notational source] and the *locus descriptionis* [imitative or descriptive source], designated respectively as "the richest" and "the most essential" vehicles of invention and composition.[16]

The *locus notationis* comprised such musical figures as imitation, inversion, repetition, retroversion and other means of formal organization, whereas the *locus descriptionis* designated "metaphorical and allegorical figures." These were meant to supply musical enhancement to a text, as in the leap of a sixth at a textual exclamation or a sudden dissonance for emotional intensity, or imitations of extramusical sounds, such as the popular cuckoo motif or the distinct introduction of the trumpet in Handel's *Messiah* at the text, "The trumpet shall sound."

The doctrine of affections, of course, reaches back into the seventeenth century, to the *musica poetica* of Joachim Burmeister; and it was during that century that the theories of rhetorical-musical interrelationships were perfected. Unearthing classical manuals on rhetoric placed that subject squarely into the university curricula, and this had a profound impact on the musical approach of composers to textually based composition. In fact, "nearly all the elements of music that can be considered typically Baroque . . . are tied, either directly or indirectly, to rhetorical concepts."[17] Though never entirely codified, the doctrine of musical figures, analogous to figures of speech, formed part of the technical means of musical invention. And the larger organization of compositions was also influenced by rhetorical considerations. Formal analogues to rhetorical figures at once moved music away from extramusical metaphorical bases even while it was enhancing them, for attention was shifting away from textual to purely instrumental considerations with emphasis on manual action schemes that had emerged with the virtuoso instrumentalists of the Renaissance.

Obviously the effects of rhetoric as a reinstituted academic discipline had its effects on the literary currents of the day. And these effects were refined by examples set by the national academies and societies of science that had been springing up throughout Europe. The first to appear were in Italy during the sixteenth and seventeenth centuries, and some of the greatest scientists, including Galileo, contributed to them. These organizations dissolved under the pressure of the Church, but they were followed by the Royal Society in London (1645), the French Academy of Science (1666), the Berlin Academy of Science (1700), and others. These organizations promoted ideals of clarity that were instrumental in shaping the neoclassical style of writing that dominated the eighteenth century, especially in English and French literature.

Again, the meshing of clarity and conciseness in literature with the articulation of the Mechanism metaphor should not be taken as suggesting that the latter caused the former. Rather, the dominance of the metaphor and its general deployment throughout the culture of the period created an intellectual climate propitious to the spread of scientific ideals of precision and parsimony. What we are trying to show again and again is that every age is possessed of a certain favored constellation of metaphors set within a social context that demands or constrains extraneous influences to be consistent with it. This is not to say that there are no inconsistencies within an age, even within the prevailing metaphors. However, to the extent that these consistencies prevail, it seems likely that the age will show commensurate consistencies of style in all areas of human endeavor. Consistency is never perfect, but there was a strong current of it in the intellectual capitals of Europe during most of the eighteenth century, and it can most concisely be defined as neoclassical, characterized by clarity, distinct articulation of parts, analysis, wit, and a certain dryness, all consonant with the Mechanism metaphor.

THE HUMAN MACHINE:
DOMINANCE OF THE MECHANISM METAPHOR

Even within the social sciences, the delirium over the Mechanism metaphor took over. Social thinkers did not flinch at applying it to human beings themselves, to the soul. For La Mettrie, humans were but machines:

Qu'on m'accorde seulement que la matière organisée est douée d'un principe
moteur, qui seul la différencie de celle qui ne l'est pas (eh! peut-on rien refuser
à l'observation la plus incontestable?) et que tout dépend dans les animaux de
la diversité de cette organisation, comme je l'ai assez prouvé: c'en est assez
pour deviner l'énigme des substances et celle de l'homme.

[Grant only that organized matter is endowed with a principle of motion,
which alone differentiates it from the inorganic (and can one deny this in the
face of the most incontestable observations?) and that among animals, as I
have sufficiently proved, everything depends upon the diversity of this organization: these admissions suffice for guessing the riddle of substances and of
man.][18]

Whereas for La Mettrie, this was an abstract philosophical principle, for his dis-
ciple, the Marquis de Sade, it was a prescription for living. To the suggestion that
regicide is a crime, his character, Juliette, responds:

Imaginaire . . . mon ami: il y a autant à tuer un savetier qu'un roi, et pas plus
à massacrer l'un ou l'autre, qu'une mouche ou qu'un papillon, également
l'ouvrage de la nature. Crois bien affirmativement, Léopold, que la façon de
ton individu n'a pas plus coûté que celle d'un singe, à notre mère commune,
et qu'elle n'a pas plus de prédilection pour l'un ou pour l'autre.

[Imaginary . . . my friend: there is no more in killing a cobbler than a king,
nor more in wiping out a fly or a butterfly, both equally the work of nature.
Believe it affirmatively, Leopold, the making of your individual person cost
our common mother no more than that for a monkey, and she is more disposed neither to the one nor to the other.][19]

In one of his many philosophical interpolations, Sade wrote of free will:

La faculté de comparer les différentes manières d'agir et de se déterminer
pour celle qui nous paraît la meilleure, est ce qu'on appelle *liberté*. Or, l'homme
a-t-il, oui ou non, cette faculté de se déterminer? J'ose affirmer qu'il ne l'a
pas, et qu'il est impossible qu'il puisse l'avoir. Toutes nos idées doivent leur
origine à des causes physiques et matérielles qui nous entraînent malgré nous,
parce que ces causes tiennent à notre organisation et aux objets extérieurs qui
nous remuent; les motifs sont le résultat de ces causes, et, par conséquent,
notre volonté n'est pas libre. Combattus par différents motifs, nous balançons,
mais l'instant où nous nous déterminons ne nous appartient pas; il est con-
straint, il est nécessité par les différentes dispositions de nos organes; nous
sommes toujours entraîns par eux, et jamais il n'a dépendu de nous d'avoir
pris plutôt un parti que l'autre; toujours mus par la nécessité, toujours esclaves

de la nécessité, l'instant même où nous croyons avoir le mieux prouvé notre liberté est celui où nous sommes plus invinciblement entraînés.

[The faculty of comparing different ways of acting and determining the one that appears best to us is what we call *freedom*. Now, does man have this faculty of self-determination? Yes or no? I dare affirm that he does not and that it is impossible that he might be able to have it. All our ideas have their origin in physical and material causes that carry us along despite ourselves, because these causes hold sway over our organization [physiology] and over external objects that move us; our motives are the result of these causes, and, consequently, our will is not free. Embattled by conflicting motives, we rest in the balance, but the instant that determines us does not belong to us; it is constrained, it is necessitated by the differing dispositions of our organs; we are always carried along by them, and it never depends on us to have taken one course rather than another; always moved by necessity, always the slaves of necessity, the very instant in which we believe that we have best proved our freedom is that in which we are most invincibly constrained.][20]

At an even greater extremity, after sexually enjoying burning several people to death by setting their house ablaze, Juliette, the quintessential Sadean villain-heroine, asks:

Et voilà donc ce que c'est que le meurtre: un peu de matière désorganisée, quelques changements dans les combinaisons, quelques molécules rompues et replongées dans le creuset de la nature, qui les rendra dans quelques jours sous une autre forme à la terre; et où donc est le mal à cela? Si j'ôte la vie à l'un, je la donne à l'autre: où est donc l'offense que je lui fais?

[And so that's what murder is: a little matter disorganized, a few changes in combination, some molecules split and plunged back into the crucible of nature, which will in several days send them back to earth in another form. Where then is the evil in that? If I take away the life of one, I give it to another: wherein then is the offense I have committed?][21]

"A little matter disorganized" in Sade has its counterpart in La Mettrie's statement that "organized matter is endowed with a principle of motion." Organized matter endowed with motion defines, albeit rather skeletally, a machine, *l'homme-machine*. It is this Mechanism metaphor that allows Sade to propose that "[a]ll our ideas have their origin in physical and material causes that carry us along despite ourselves" and that murder amounts to no more than scrapping a machine. This line of thought led Laplace to his famous claim that the "present state of the system of nature is evidently a consequence of what it was in the preceding moment, and if we conceive of an intelligence which at a given instant comprehends all the relations of the entities of the universe, it could state the respective position, motions, and general affects of all these entities at any time in the past or future."[22] It is this essence of materialism to reduce all phenomena to a system of entities (parts) whose interactions are fully predictable that most clearly bares its foundation on the Mechanism metaphor. That essence precisely defines a mechanism.

Sade affords an instructive example of the dilemma of mechanism, because his arguments, as well as the algolagnia he wished to portray, depend upon the ineluctable limits of applying the Mechanism metaphor to human actions. And the obvious inappropriateness of transferring that metaphor from the realm of the physical sciences to that of the social sciences is precisely what is eroding it as the dominant organizing metaphor of the twentieth century—that, and the breakdown of causality in quantum theory, which will be considered later. Although the question of free will versus determinism is a well-worn issue in philosophy, it will nevertheless be worthwhile to examine it once more, but this time purely from the angle of metaphor deployment.

Recall that the Mechanism metaphor designates a body of parts so interrelated that their actions can clearly be traced from one part to another, making it the perfect model for causality. The first thing to notice, when this metaphor is applied to the human being and thence to social phenomena, is that the human being, while composed of parts like every other material being, does not even come close to displaying the transparency of componential interaction requisite to a machine. Even when used to model a complex electrical circuit, such as the CPU of a computer, the Mechanism metaphor may founder. Unless a program is imposed on the circuit, at a certain level of complexity, the circuit loses its transparency. Oscillations couple and the circuit may become chaotic and unpredictable. A machine, in this instance, ceases to be a homologue; so, as the metaphor is pushed, it gradually loses its explicative efficacy.

This is brought out clearly in the mechanistic argument against free will. First of all, the necessity inherent in a logical argument is not mechanistic in the sense that some confluence of prior physical events constrains the conclusion. Rather, the conclusion is constrained by class relationships among the terms of the argument; otherwise it is not, strictly speaking, logical. If, in other words, an argument from premises $A \ldots F$ did not come to a conclusion from the class relations among $A \ldots F$ but from the physical states of the persons engaged in the argument, the conclusion would be a mere event devoid of logical validity, no more denoting a logical conclusion than the final resting place of a stone rolling down a hill.

In his argument against free will, Sade quotes Fénelon as saying that, when he wishes not to do something, he is master of his will in not wishing to do it, meaning that he could will to do it. No, retorts Sade, at the moment he feels that he decides not to act, the physical predeterminants of his action have sealed his fate, and he could not will any differently than he felt he did. The dilemma is that Sade's argument, by his own terms, is not *logical* but merely physically contingent on the entire constellation of all that physically preceded and accompanied it. Finally, the persuasiveness of either side of the debate depends not on the meaning of anything said or thought but only on the course of physical events. *Meaning* entails something other than the physical necessity of event following event, something we may call *intent*, which in turn requires free choice.

If this were merely an academic debate, we could perhaps pass over it with a certain smile of appreciation. But it has practical consequences, which is why the Mechanism metaphor is under constant siege in the social sphere. Without a belief in free choice, the notion of social responsibility collapses and with it the fabric of social order. It makes no sense to punish certain forms of behavior if they are inevitable. To argue further that the punishment is as inevitable as the misconduct only plunges us into a feedback loop of infinite regression.[23] Explicative metaphors and the models built upon them should not precipitate such confusion. The problem clearly seems to be the inappropriate extension of the Mechanism metaphor.

MECHANISM VERSUS FREE WILL

So far, I have discussed only one side of the issue. The notion of *uncaused* action is no less problematic. Again, the arguments to save free will lead to no less chasing one's tail. Somehow we are supposed to be able to direct our actions from causes within ourselves. Metaphorically, this drops the problem into the opaque Container of the mind, which becomes a black box. No philosopher nor psychologist has ever spelled out a viable modus operandi. I venture to say that none ever will, as things stand, because what is happening is a kind of sleight of hand with the root metaphor, a maneuver that undoes itself.

FREE WILL VERSUS CAUSALITY

On the one hand, adherents of the notion of free will deny that human beings are mechanisms; then they proceed to postulate a *mechanism* of internal causation, which they find, of course, they can't describe. In short, they want to put aside the Mechanism metaphor and simultaneously to deploy it as an explicative device to make free will intelligible, which is rather like doing away with the Cheshire cat while trying to retain its grin. Causality is one of our primary explicative tools and it is only natural to fall back on it. It must be recognized, however, that most, if not all, reasoning about causality in any circumstance rests one way or another on the Mechanism metaphor coupled with the Bind scheme. Causal analysis devolves to discovering how one event is continuously connected, or bound, to a successive one. That events must be bound follows from the putative fact that all material things work like a machine.

KANTIAN MANEUVER TO SAVE THE WORLD FROM CAUSALITY BY HIDING IT

Rationalism and mechanism pushed Hume and others to these seemingly reasonable but ultimately futile conclusions. Nor did this go unnoticed. In response to the rationalist dismantling of empirical reality, Kant imagined the secrets of existence to be buried in the *Ding-an-sich*, forever unknowable. "What objects may be in themselves," he wrote, "and apart from all this receptivity of our sensibility, remains completely unknown to us."[24] Using the Mirror metaphor, he declared that "permanence can never be proved of the concept of a substance as a thing in itself, but for the purposes of experience only" and so "synthetical *a priori* propositions can never be proved in themselves, but only in reference to things as objects of possible experience."[25] Or again, "I have . . . no knowledge of myself as I am, but merely as I appear to myself."[26] Kant set up a duality analogous to Plato's real and ideal, the apparent object being a reflection of the *Ding-an-sich* upon sentience.

MECHANISTIC REASON IS SOFTENED BY ORGANISMIC WILL

German philosophy accomplished the inherently self-contradictory feat of shrouding reason itself in mysticism: Hegel identified it with Divine Reason, equated it with *Weltgeist* or World Spirit and made it the mystical emissary of God's will in working out dialectically by thesis, antithesis, and synthesis the destiny of the world. Similarly, through convoluted reasoning, Schopenhauer suggested that the world is a projection of cosmic will.

> The lowest grades of the objectification of will are to be found in those most universal forces of nature which partly appear in all matter without exception, as gravity and impenetrability, and partly have shared the given matter among themselves, so that certain of them reign in one species of matter and others in another species, constituting its specific difference, as rigidity, fluidity, elasticity, electricity, magnetism, chemical properties and qualities of every kind. They are in themselves immediate manifestations of will, just as much as human actions; and as such they are groundless, like human character.[27]

Metaphorically *will* for Schopenhauer is identical to the Hegelian *Geist*, an indwelling agency that directs the course of things.

Eschewing the larger questions of ontology and epistemology, Nietzsche dwelled on the social order as ruled by the will to power. Life he saw as characterized by an innate propensity to grow, spread, seize, and predominate, which he called the will to power, again metaphorically an indwelling directive agency (:Breath). His remarks on the will to power are scattered throughout various of his works, and nowhere does he offer a precise definition of the term. "Philosophers are accustomed to speak of the will," he charged, "as though it were the best-known thing in the world," whereas "[w]illing—seems to me to be above all something *complicated*." He goes on to speak of the "sensation of the condition '*away from which* we go,' the sensation of the condition '*towards which* we go,' the sensation of this '*from*' and '*towards*' itself, and . . . an accompanying muscular sensation." Then there is the "ruling thought," which cannot be isolated as separate from willing per se. To this brew, he adds "the emotion of the command."[28] Seemingly casting this rather careful analysis aside, he later declares that the will to power "will endeavor to grow, to gain ground, attract to itself and acquire ascendency—not owing to any morality or immorality, but because it lives, and because life is precisely Will to Power."[29] It is this version of the concept that has entered more dominantly into the sphere of Nietzschean influence. Weighing the different versions of the concept suggested in Nietzsche's writings, one commentator suggests that the "will to power thus expresses the absolute character of immanent change," that it therefore is "Becoming considered as endowed with its own principle of fertility."[30] Again we have a disembodied or depersonalized agent characterized only by the propensity for certain actions, a metaphorical descendent of spirit (:Breath).

Finally, metaphorically very similar to will is the *élan vital* postulated by Bergson as the vital force of the biosphere: "Life . . . transcends finality, if we understand by finality the realization of an idea conceived or conceivable in advance. The category of finality is therefore too narrow for life in its entirety." The *élan vital* is inherently unpredictable. Bergson grants that "reality is *ordered* exactly in the degree that it satisfies our thought," but this order is only "the mind finding itself in things."[31] Just as the will to power for Nietzsche could be conceived as the proclivity of life to dominate and spread, so for Bergson the *élan vital* is that agency in living things that propels them to transcend the limits of the moment. It represents the same depersonalized spirit as agent. More crudely but perhaps more clearly, if one begins with an indwelling spirit, a sort of homunculus directing things, and allows the physical features of the being to drop away through the gradual disavowal of anthropomorphism, what one is left with is a depersonalized agent of action.

Thus, many prominent nineteenth-century philosophers took refuge in deployments of the Breath metaphor—spirit, will, *élan vital*—which permitted escape from the rigors of clarity fostered in the rationalist or neoclassical tradition. Often the Breath metaphor deployments were allied with overtones of the Parent metaphor emanating from implicit allusions to God, as in the case of Hegel. Either way, spirit or the mythic parent cannot, like the machine, be further reduced by analysis and so bars, at least internally, the encroachment of rationalist critique.

LIMITATIONS OF THE MECHANISM METAPHOR APPLIED TO HUMAN BEINGS

To see the inappropriateness of the Mechanism metaphor to human beings demands a bit of stealth, an attainment to be approached by degrees. As a preliminary step, let me repeat that empirically what is known about humans, or even more simply, about human physiology does not suggest homology to a mechanism, defined as an organization of parts the inner workings of which are transparent so that we may easily see how every part operates with every other part. Nothing near such homology exists even for a single organ. The possibility of homology was even more remote in earlier centuries when the analogy first suggested itself, for then the knowledge of physiology was far less detailed than at present. Therefore, then as now, the hypothesis of mechanism applied to humans was a pure act of faith; nothing more.

Within the past two decades, research has shown that anything approaching the complexity of a living organism is necessarily a chaotic system. Retrogressive tracing of part-to-part interaction is by definition impossible. Now, any system of three or more parts has introduced into it a certain amount of chaos, but at the level of a common machine, the degree of chaos is negligible. The parts are physically constrained; the chaos is hidden, so to speak, in the form of vibration and heat, which ordinarily does not disrupt normal functioning. But in the case of an organism, the chaos is endemic to normal functioning, as evidenced in the biorhythmicity of most, if not all, organismic processes. Biorhythms are never perfectly regular but rather fluctuate within certain ranges, as if constrained by an attractor. Indeed, perfect regularity would define a rigidity that would not allow the organism to survive by adapting to environmental changes.[32]

Advancing to the mental aspect of humankind, there is further mounting evidence that the Mechanism metaphor is incongruous with much that has been established about the mind. Reductionism of mind to machine is, first of all, based upon another article of faith: that there is a perfect correlation between physiology and putative mental processes and introspective experience. To be sure, there is support for this belief in psychopharmacology, cases of brain damage, and other neurological phenomena. However, there is also contravention in near-death experience, where brain function ceases but revived patients are subsequently able to report sensory observations during the period of brain-death. Whatever the ultimate explanation of such experiences, correlation to brain function seems clearly out of the question.[33]

Finally, consider the following *Gedankenexperiment*. We have established complete reductionist maps of everyone, and these have been patched into a complete deterministic mapping of the universe. Every outcome down to the tiniest detail can be known to each person via a pocket computer unit. What does a person do when she knows already what she will do and what the consequences are? Obviously the answer hinges upon the effect of her knowing that; but this effect is already predetermined and known. Why go to look to find out the source of a noise when you can call it up on your computer? Why even do that when you already looked ahead yesterday? In a nutshell, foreknowledge must be already in the future and also knowledge of the foreknowledge, and foreknowledge of knowledge of foreknowledge, and so on ad infinitum. Under this scenario, the future convulses to the complete chaos of an endless feedback loop, a sure sign that our hypothesis and the root metaphor on which it rests are inapposite.

So we may say that the Mechanism metaphor falters on several counts when applied either to human beings or to the human mind. Not only must it fail to do justice to the chaos innate within the human organism, or many other multicellular organisms, because it operates linearly,[34] but it also is inimical to normal social processes. It vitiates any really credible sense of an individual being responsible for his or her actions. Rationalism has inclined toward the Mechanism metaphor because of its clarity and simplicity, but this inclination has spawned as many problems as it has quelled.

Similarly, extension into human behavior on the social level has created another set of problems. Rationalism and the Mechanism metaphor, operative in English philosophy and rampant in mathematics, invaded the social sciences in the last half of the nineteenth century. Quantitative measurement was taken over from the physical scientists as one of the sine qua nons of the empirical method. One of the dilemmas subsequently faced by social scientists has been the Organism-metaphoric basis of most of the conceptual paraphernalia of their discipline apposed to the Mechanism-metaphoric basis of quantification, though the dilemma has naturally not heretofore been expressed quite in those terms. It has been framed rather in terms of the possible inapplicability of reductionist methods to social phenomena. Metaphoric analysis of the situation is not in opposition to this latter treatment, but merely approaches the same thing at a different level.

BIOLOGY AND EVOLUTION: BACK TO THE ORGANISM METAPHOR

There was precipitous advancement of the biological sciences following eighteenth-century successes in the preliminary but necessary stage of animal and plant classification. Prepared by rapid progress in chemistry and microscopy, logical study of life was enhanced by revolutionary discoveries: tissue structures were discerned, then the cell as the basic building block of living organisms. The birth of cytology was a momentous intellectual event, for to suggest that life may properly be said to reside in a single cell vitiates the spiritual foundations of vitalism and renders the Breath metaphor useless as a model for the phenomenon of life. In so doing, it creates a dilemma: the Breath metaphor of vitalism becomes inappropriate, unwieldy at best, and the Mechanism metaphor, seemingly the only alternative, doesn't seem to work, either. However, failure of the latter could be blamed on inadequate information. Many biological scientists still work on the assumption that the Mechanism metaphor will work, once we know enough about living organisms. Then there remain those who cling to vitalism in one form or another. The creationists are the most glaring example.

In the nineteenth century, creationism was fatally attacked (though it persists at the folk level, even from there challenging science in the courts and school systems). The biological sciences were thrust into the foreground of popular awareness by the controversies stirred by Darwin and the theory of evolution. Evolution, as a pure idea, has a long history reaching back to antiquity. Aristotle conceived organic life in an ascending scale from simple to complex in the Great Chain of Being. Albertus Magnus revived the Aristotelian view in the Middle Ages in his capacity as one of the early translators and systematizers of Aristotle's works. Francis Bacon and Leibniz broke with biblical tradition, which taught that God created immutable types; they believed that species were subject to variation. Kant believed that variant species might be traced back to a common ancestor. This idea seemed even more plausible after Linnaeus introduced the first systematic scheme for the classification of life forms, although he himself hewed to the notion of immutable species. Finally, Buffon had a fairly clear understanding of the environmental influence on species change.

> The concept of adaptation to environment was developed more thoroughly by Erasmus Darwin (1731–1802), the grandfather of Charles Darwin. Malthus' law of population emphasized the importance of the struggle for existence. The poet-philosopher, Wolfgang von Goethe (1749–1832), anticipated many of the basic conceptions of organic evolution, such as adaptation to environment, vital force, vestigial organs. Sir Charles Lyell brought together in his *Principles of Geology* (1830–1833) rich geological evidence supporting the evolutionary rather than the creation hypothesis. Finally, Jean Lamarck (1744–1829) enunciated a definite doctrine of organic evolution in which the theory of mutability was based on the inheritance of acquired characteristics. . . . Most of these early contributions to the biological theory of evolution were brought together in an excellent and popular book by a layman, Robert Chambers, *Vestiges of the Natural History of Creation* (1844).[35]

What Charles Darwin did was to lend currency to the technical aspects of evolutionary theory by bringing all of them together in a persuasive unified theory to which he brought a mass of supporting evidence from firsthand observation. He was the successful salesman of the idea, much as Freud was for psychoanalysis.[36]

Neither was an original thinker in the sense of creating new metaphors or radically new deployments. This statement may be jarring, but it must be kept in mind that this is not a general intellectual history but a study of metaphor themes. As the above quotation indicates, the structures for the concepts of natural selection and evolution had been established long before Darwin, gaining status even in the popular press. Darwin put all the pieces together, adding supportive detail to create a coherent theory. As Wightman puts it, he established the theory of evolution but did not originate it.[37] Singer says that it "is the great achievement of Charles Darwin . . . that he persuaded the scientific world, once and for all, that many diverse organic forms are of common descent, that species are inconstant and in some cases impossible of definition, and that some mechanism must be sought to explain their evolution."[38] Certainly he gave new meaning to the folk metaphor for life as a struggle or form of warfare.

Explosive advancements in the biological sciences came at just the right time to consolidate them with many other characteristics of the romantic reaction, often hinging on the Organism metaphor. One way to view this is a shift away from the stark certainty embodied in the Mechanism complex toward the more tentative stance of an uncertain age in which the tenets of authority were rejected and more individualized answers were being sought and accepted. Deployment of the Organism metaphor accommodated the need for obscurity, behind which there would be room to maneuver for better strategic positions. It mitigated the effects of the rationalist Mechanism metaphor.

THE ANTIRATIONALIST REACTION: INTEREST IN THE IRRATIONAL

Late-eighteenth-century thinkers reacted against the tide of reason that was sweeping over them, preparing the way for the romantic movement. As Kahler has observed, it began with an intellectual malaise, which was depicted in Choderlos de Laclos's *Les Liaisons Dangereuses* (1782), an assemblage of "artful badinage and scheming" with the characters "scheming just for the sake of showing their frivolous skill and without the slightest regard for their victims."[39] It moved through self-reflection, typified in the *Nouvelle Heloïse* and *Confessions* of Jean-Jacques Rousseau, to the renunciation of reason and often the glorification of irrationality by the romanticists. Again Kahler calls attention to the ennui of the eighteenth-century *salonistes*, which the Marquise du Deffand described as "la privation du sentiment avec la douleur de ne pouvoir s'en passer [loss of sentiment with the painful feeling not to be able to do without it]," and which he says "stimulates psychological analysis and self-scrutiny."[40]

Self-analysis was largely responsible for the rise of the psychological novel. A natural progression led from the novel of mores that, in the eighteenth century, scrutinized the social interaction of the characters to the novel of the following century that moved gradually into their minds and onward finally to Proust, Dorothy Richardson, James, and Joyce. Internalization focused not on ratiocination but on emotion, especially extremes and perversities. "Le Poète," averred Rimbaud, "se fait voyant par un long, immense et raisonné dérèglement de tous les sens. Toutes les formes d'amour, de souffrance, de folie; il cherche lui-même, il épuise en lui tous les poisons, pour n'en garder que les quintessences" [The Poet makes himself a seer through a long, immense and rationalized derangement of all his senses. All the forms of love, of suffering, of madness; he seeks within himself and extracts from himself all the poisons so as to retain only the quintessences].[41] Not only *mal d'esprit* but all aspects of the irrational were the subject matter of the romantics: a complete turning away from the Mechanism metaphor and all for which it stood. Intellect, the machine of logic, gave way to imagination, the mysterious seat of creation, as a representation of the mind for the romantics. Originally the faculty of the mind to image previously perceived objects, the *decaying senses* of Hobbes, imagination became amalgamated with *fancy*. William Taylor, a British lexicographer, made this distinction in his *British Synonyms Discriminated* (1815):

> A man has imagination in proportion as he can distinctly copy in idea the impressions of sense: it is the faculty that *images* within the mind the phenomena of sensation. A man has fancy in proportion as he can call up, connect, or associate, at pleasure, those internal images . . . so as to complete ideal representations of absent objects. Imagination is the power of depicting, and fancy of evoking and combining.[42]

Coleridge made imagination "the living power and prime Agent of all human Perception, and . . . a repetition in the finite mind of the eternal act of creation in the infinite I AM."[43] Hence, it is the creator as agent; that is, it is the creator god depersonalized to an agent. However, even as agent, it has the magical powers invested in the deities, the power to bring forth images out of the "infinite I AM." In this concept is a peculiar melding of the ancient *noos* as mirror of the mind with creative spirit (:Breath) reduced to agent. Such a hybrid concept had little chance of permanently displacing the Mechanism and Container metaphors of mind, even though it presented a challenge for half a century and more. The romantic concept of creative mind still has its appeal.

THE IRRATIONAL MIND AND MENTAL DISORDER

Romantic interest in the irrational mind often turned toward depiction of insanity and aberrant behavior.[44] Interest in the pathological was not confined to the sphere of the arts but belonged to the overall counterrevolution against rationalism and the Mechanism metaphor. In some cases, the consequences were salubrious, never more so than in the growing concern for those locked in insane asylums. Nowhere can we see the humanitarian concerns of the age more clearly in the fore as in the mental-health movement, which marked a decisive turn away from earlier view of mental aberration:

> The literary and artistic representation of insanity was closer, of course, to the popular beliefs regarding mental illness. On the surface the Renaissance presented a mixed attitude of fear, abuse, and disregard for the mentally ill, coupled with the traditional attribution of insanity to unbalanced humors, which needed evacuation from the body through cathartics, emetics, and bloodletting. But, at a deeper level . . . the mentally ill were considered as the expression of the animality of lower beings—not unlike the lepers of the Middle Ages—whose purpose was to bring testimony of divine intervention into human affairs, manifested through the tempting role of the devil. Hence, the most varied and contrasting approaches to mental illness—from exorcism to punishment, from seclusion to abandonment—found justification at the time.[45]

Blatant disregard of human suffering could intellectually be sustained on the basis of the Cartesian duality of mind and body that made the body the instrument (:Mechanism) of the mind (spirit). Juliette, heroine of de Sade, could within the age rightly declare murder to be a mere rearrangement of chemical elements. And physiologists went in search of the *sensorium commune*, the hypothetical organ marking the point at which mind and body connected. Descartes thought it was the pineal gland, but Renaissance thinkers were no longer prone to capitulate to authority and the matter was one of long controversy. At any rate, there was a shift away from treating the mind, or spirit, under the Breath metaphor in favor of the Mechanism metaphor, to which therapists, as scientists, owed obeisance, if they were to search for natural causes in matters of the mind.

Rationalism had at least changed approaches to insanity, directing attention to natural causes. Their efforts were premature. Nosology had not developed sufficiently to delineate syndromes the etiologies of which might be explored scientifically. And this, in turn, waited upon a more humane treatment of patients that would make them worthy subjects of study.

Under pressures of human rights evolving out of social movements already cited, humane treatment of the mentally ill slowly emerged in the last half of the eighteenth century. Vicenzo Chiarugi, Phillipe Pinel, and others laid the foundations for modern classifications of mental disorders.

Mechanism Metaphor Extended and Challenged in the Economic Sphere

Meanwhile, in the sphere of politico-economic thought, deployment of the Mechanism metaphor further guaranteed its ultimate overthrow. Against nationalistic mercantilism, economic thinkers raised the doctrine of laissez-faire based on the notion of a world divinely ordered in a mechanistic way so that the operation of competition on the private level ought not to be interfered with on the governmental level. This physiocratic argument laid the intellectual groundwork for Social Darwinism. Early advocates of laissez-faire had intended only a harmonious cooperation between private business and the state, but such philosophers as Spencer in the following century were to ally it with the doctrines of evolution and reinterpret economic competition as combat.

God became the supreme lawgiver, with the state, almost his terrestrial counterpart, the rational regulator of the social machine. Law itself, in both the legal and the scientific senses, changed from authoritarian mandates to formulations of divine-natural order. Under rational analysis, the concept of the social contract, which had its ideological roots probably in the Old Testament *covenant* (one of the original terms of ambiguous meaning, variously translated)[46] was seen to be fictitious. Sovereignty was wrested from the monarchs and placed in the hands of various representational bodies, even when the monarch remained enthroned. Also, demographic shifts were moving legal interests from obligations of the individual owed to the state to the question of individual rights. The Debt/Payment metaphor behind moral and legal duties did not fall away but was augmented by the Lot/Share metaphor. That is, with the ascension of the bourgeoisie, the question of realpolitik was how the politico-economic pie should be cut and who should get which piece. This was not so much an intellectual development as a social one. People asked not so much what their duties were to the state (:Debt/Payment), but what was owed them as legal citizens (:Lot/Share). This was the beginning of modern human rights. Socially, the law of first priority became "the greatest good for the greatest number," the dictum of the utilitarians, but it left open any practical definitions of "good," a prescription that the rationalists were unable to fill. It was the heart of the rationalist challenge, and failure to meet it ultimately paved the way for a new complex underlying a worldview that would define the romantic movement. Governments did not ultimately deliver the increasingly powerful bourgeoisie into a social utopia in which reason solved all problems.

DECLINE OF MECHANISM

Actually, the failure of eighteenth-century thinkers to fulfill the rationalist promise stemmed from an inability to extend the Mechanism metaphor to the social sphere, and also from deployments that ran squarely into other established metaphors. A case in point would be Hume's attack on causality and his analysis of experience. Hume took a very mechanistic approach to causality, defining it as a "necessary connection" between two temporally contingent events. Certainly we cannot help remarking that this is a distillation of the atomistic notion of causality as configurational. If we analyze a configurational transformation into two stages, it is a small step to imagine a connecting link between them. Hume did this and could find no concrete link. In effect, he imagined it was there, convinced others of the same, and then of course was unable to find it in the stream of empirical events. He was overextending the Bind scheme.

With this analysis of experience, he adhered to the ancient metaphor of the mind as a Container. Then he showed that the wall of the container forms an interface that keeps us hermetically sealed off from the outside world, which we can know only as it is transmitted across the interface. We are made prisoners of our own mind. Any metaphor of mind that makes it separate and distinct from the world faces similar problems, in that objective reality can be known only through its effects on the sensate mind. No amount of logic will resolve the problem, since in reasoning we are only subjecting the constituents and their defining boundaries to topological manipulations. Thus, Bertrand Russell wrote of Hume: "To refute him has been, ever since he wrote, a favourite pastime among metaphysicians. For my part, I find none of their refutations convincing."[47] The only solution would seem to be to weld together the two elements, the private inner and the public outer, in which case we probably move to an alternative metaphor.

As a generality, it seems fair to say that during the eighteenth century many of the metaphors bequeathed by the classical mentality were explored systematically and to their limits, both by deploying them—that is, by applying their differentiae as broadly as possible to the *facts*—and by subjecting them to fictive topological transformations and manipulations. Such a procedure is bound to discredit the established metaphor complex because no metaphor can fit a cross section of data if that cross section is made large enough—which is a clumsy way of saying that no two things are exactly alike, especially if one of the two things is greatly more diverse or complex than the other. That is why the Enlightenment spawned an essentially critical philosophy, we might even say a destructive one. In the Mechanism metaphor, parts must be cleanly articulated and their operation defined with utmost clarity. In that way, juxtaposed against, say, the Parent metaphor as pivot of an epochal metaphor complex, the intrinsic obscurities of the latter—e.g., the unfathomed motives, the whims—became painfully manifest. Eighteenth-century thinkers, therefore, were in the perfect position to discredit the bulk of medieval thought against which they rebelled. If they could directly demonstrate the laws of nature and validate them through prediction, they could contravene the authority of the Church (as authority and hence exemplum of the Parent metaphor) and prove the correctness of the Mechanism metaphor.

Nevertheless, intellectually the rationalism of the eighteenth century was readied to topple by the overdeployment of the Mechanism metaphor constellation by the empiricists (notably Hume) and in the attempted explanation of social and psychological phenomena as well as the formulation of human values. Weaknesses in the rationalist approach to social problems were made more glaring by the expansion of the middle class and by the rise of an anti-industrial sentiment that sparked the

Arts and Crafts movement as well as the decline of formal gardens in favor of more natural settings, a resurgence of medievalism, and ultimately labor movements and social reforms. The middle class, in fact, posed many of the social problems unsuccessfully addressed by rationalists, and members of the middle class were more sympathetic than the aristocrats to the plight of the poor. In general, the economic enhancement of the base of the economic pyramid made demands for reform increasingly difficult for the ruling class to ignore. Church sentiment also turned to the lower classes, whose masses swelled memberships, serving as a source of power in the never-ending struggle against encroachments by the state.

The power of the bourgeoisie even commanded new means of expression, which in turn could encourage innovative metaphor deployments. A good example is the novel. A seventeenth century form catering to the leisure time and interests of the bourgeoisie, the novel initially placed in analysis the fabric of ordinary human relations, as opposed to the mythic or aristocratic character studies of earlier poetic and dramatic forms. This became inevitably a causal analysis conducted in the mechanistic terms of the Enlightenment.

Actually, human relations prior to the seventeenth century must have been conceived along lines of traits evolving under their own proclivities according to patterns of destiny (:Pattern)—essentially the dramaturgical doctrine of hybris generalized. This is how they are depicted in early literature. It is this unseen destiny that is hierarchical, involving a hierarchy of emotions, Grace, a teleology of Divine Plan, etc. All this is tied together and taken for granted, forming a number of strands of the deployment of the metaphors of Pattern, Parent, and Family. Typical plots involved fate (:Pattern) or a deity (:Parent) decreeing that certain events would befall the characters in the story. Plot development would generally be in terms of the metaphors grouped under Family or human relations. This was true of classical epic, drama, and the putative classical novel, and it remained so through the fabliaux.

With the rationalist analysis of human behavior linked with the sudden scientific examination of mental pathology, human behavior and social interaction took on more complex dimensions. Significantly, they defied logical analysis; motivation became laminar or labyrinthine. Writers began to deal with the complexity of human motivation, moving inexorably from the analysis of interactions in terms of established conventions (e.g., Richardson, Austen) or *manners* to ever closer inspection of the psyches involved, culminating eventually in the psychological novel and stream-of-consciousness approach, moving away from the Mechanism metaphor and gropingly toward the Organism metaphor.[48] A predilection for it was sewn in the foundations of romanticism, with the return to landscape painting, natural gardens, and the organic motifs of medieval art.

Stendhal, one of the founders of the realist school of writing, had "no preconceived rationalistic system concerning the general factors which determine social life, nor any pattern-concept of how the ideal society ought to look"; rather, his representation of events was based on "*analyse du coeur humain*, not upon the discovery or premonitions of historical forces."[49] If this signaled a turning away from the Mechanism metaphor, with Balzac there is a decisive adoption of the Organism metaphor:

> He has a great fondness for biological comparisons; he speaks of physiology or zoology in connection with social phenomena, or the *anatomie du coeur humain*; [in one place] he compares the effect of a social milieu to the exhalations which produce typhoid, and in another passage from *Père Goriot* he says of Rastignac that he had given himself up to the lessons and the temptations of luxury "with the ardor that seizes the calyx of a female date-palm for the fecundating dusts of its nuptials." [50]

Ortega y Gasset suggested the analogy of zoom photography in conceptualizing this gradual refinement of observation, applying it to the development of painting. Such concentrated scrutiny may have resulted in greater realism, but it did not necessarily yield understanding like that gained from analyzing a machine. Hence, the Organism metaphor better served to explain the intricacies of character interaction and the private world of the mind. In this move toward psychological analysis, it was natural that artists and writers should be most taken by that in human behavior which could not rationally be explained—for the open-endedness of such things invited the creative utilization of imagination. Thus, we have a flowering of the perverse: the anticlerical writers of late-eighteenth-century France, the Gothic novelists, that heterogeneous flock of writers treated by Mario Praz under the apt rubric, *The Romantic Agony*, and their counterparts in painting, Fuseli, Friedrich, Goya, and a host of lesser-knowns.

These antirationalist trends also coincided with an influx of philosophical material translated mainly by German scholars from Indian and Chinese sources. Comparative philology had advanced so that the frontiers of translation had just reached the Far East, cultures which even then remained largely unknown and mysterious. Buddhist-Taoist concepts of a kind of unfathomable impetus within nature were transformed into the *Zeitgeist* and the *Weltgeist*, reaching through Hegel into Marx. Living with nature by *wu-wei*, nonaction or natural spontaneity, paralleled anti-industrial sentiments calling for a return to nature and the simple life— and here we must recall the "noble savage" of J.-J. Rousseau, the revival of interest in landscape gardening and its naturalist developments in England under such men as William Kent and Lancelot Brown, the popularity of the country estate, etc. All these things pointed toward the organic, the mysteries of life and growth, and the motif of the Organism metaphor.

Even in music, the clarity of neoclassicism so congenial to mechanism gave ground. Rhetorical phrasing in the neoclassical music of the Viennese school gradually lost its hold as a model. Melodic lines were extended and lost their mechanical clarity, partly through more frequent modulation and less frequent use of partial cadences within the musical period. Sonata form, the crystallization of rationalist musical thought, began to gather encrustations and excrescences organically, moving toward rhapsodic freedom—compare any late Mozart symphony with Liszt's Dante Symphony. Orchestrational practices reached toward ever more enriched timbral effects in which texture often became more primary than line. Likewise, the fate of architectural form was to collapse into undistinguished provincialism. And we need hardly catalog examples to show that similar developments took root in literature: it is only necessary to read a poem of Pope or Dryden next to one of Keats, Byron, or Baudelaire.

In the visual arts, too, we see the dissolution of those properties of neoclassicism that derived from or were sustained by the Mechanism metaphor. In painting, linear draughtsmanship gave way to painterly effects. The predictability and consensual values of mythical and historical subjects were supplanted by idiosyncratic views of the mundane. The dry and glossy surface yielded to texture; analysis was traded for affect. Conventional symbolism made way for personal symbolism; and the naked clarity of mechanical articulation, in general, disappeared in favor of all that is individualistic—and here we must also call attention to the trend in fashion called dandyism.

Now, it is true that the romantic reaction does not accurately account for the whole of nineteenth-century intellectual history. That is because old metaphor systems don't die; they just become subsidiary. The symmetry deployment of the Pattern metaphor so dear to the Greeks survives to this day not only in the arts and aesthetics but also in the foundations of science, notably in a sense of balance in mathematical procedures.

The Mechanism metaphor likewise continues to be active in the generation of ideas. While the 19th century German thinkers were turning the tide toward an Organism metaphor complex, the English bowed to the same rationalist path pursued by Locke, Berkeley, and Hume. Bentham and Mill both contributed heavily to the Mechanism fund. Bentham's utilitarianism was essentially an attempt to mathematicize pleasure and pain. As for Mill, he was a rationalist and an empiricist, who opined:

> The notion that truths external to the human mind may be known by intuition or consciousness, independently of observation and experience, is, I am persuaded, in these times, the greatest intellectual support of false doctrines and bad institutions. By the aid of this theory, every inveterate belief and every intense feeling, of which the origin is not remembered, is enabled to dispense with the obligation of justifying itself by reason, and is erected into its own self-sufficient voucher and justification.[51]

There could hardly be stated more neatly the conflict between the rationalist and the romantic worldviews, a clash alive throughout the nineteenth century.

CONCLUSION

The romantic reaction, a turning to the Organism metaphor with its Parental overtones (the unpredictability of certain of the total processes considered in any situation), resulted in a breakdown of the clarity and articulation intrinsic to the former neoclassical deployment of the Mechanism metaphor. At the same time, the Mechanism metaphor persisted, often joined with the symmetry deployment of the Pattern metaphor derived from classical Greece, as the guiding principle of scientific thought, eventually invading even the social sciences. Much of the tension and emotional pitch of the romantic movement derived from the innate conflict between these disparate metaphor complexes. There were attitudinal as well as ideological conflicts: the two are rarely separated. Underlying these disaccords were social conflicts, political and economic, the dislocations of a changing social order. Part of the rejection of the Mechanism metaphor as a matrix for creative expression in the arts came with the dismissal of the former aristocratic order which had allied itself with the progressive rationalist and neoclassical tendencies of the previous two centuries. Italy and Germany underwent the throes of political consolidation into nationhood. Population soared, more than doubling in Europe between 1800 and 1900. The Industrial Revolution took hold, soon to be augmented by an energy revolution. These pressures brought social problems to the fore, making the human mind the new frontier of intellectual advancement in the twentieth century, a phenomenon presaged by many of the artists and writers of the romantic era. So agitated became the unrest of Europe that it erupted into an intellectual crisis that shattered many of the norms of Western culture, ruptured the elasticity of many of the time-worn metaphors, and left them void and desiccated, ghostly husks of human thought unable to contain the vision of a new dawn that broke without a sun to illuminate the dark corners of a sustained night.

8

The Twentieth Century

There are always many plausible ways in which to characterize an age. Rather than settling on one simplistic approach, I shall point to three dominant forces in twentieth-century civilization: energy, communication, and psychological analysis. Between 1850 and 1920, world energy production increased tenfold, tapping into petroleum and electricity. This democratized technology, introducing the industrial revolution, its demands and its fruits, into every home. At the same time, this put everyone in contact with everyone else through electronic communication and petroleum-driven transportation. Transportation speeds increased a hundredfold from the average 5 mph for the horse and carriage to the 500 mph of the jet passenger plane. Growth of knowledge equaled and surpassed in fifty years knowledge accumulated since the dawn of civilization. And this rate is still accelerating.

What is most immediately apparent about the rates at which things are changing in this century is that they baffle the deployment of either the Organism or the Mechanism metaphor. That this is so is clearly signaled by the expression most often used to describe the pace at which all of twentieth-century life is changing: an explosion. This poetic image is apt, for it connects energy with disorder, two major issues of modern thought. Moreover, science and technology have moved away from what can directly be perceived; they deal with invisible entities and forces the existence of which is vouchsafed only by the accordance between hypotheses and validating measurements and the mathematical formalism underpinning them.

Even technology that has always been associated with the practical has become more and more preoccupied with the unseen: electricity, magnetism, radio waves, cosmic rays, X-rays, molecular and atomic structure and forces, subatomic particles, gravitation, microwaves, ultrasonics, neutron beams, and so on. Outcomes are what counts, and the nexus between procedures and outcomes is mathematical formulation. Equations enable us to predict, even when they fail to elucidate conventional explanation. The guiding principle is *metron* and *symmetron*, and in that sense there is still impetus to define the universal plan (:Pattern); but the desired end is no longer explanation as a visual mirroring of reality. The desired end is successful prediction, outcomes, in technology the practical payoff. Social

181

revolutions of the previous two centuries, as we have already remarked, turned the tide by putting a premium on solving problems of pressing immediacy. Doing battle with the unseen completed the epistemological revolution, turning man from understanding to prediction.

Now, disorder occurs quite naturally as we move from one level of observation to another, chiefly from the macroscopic to the microscopic. Magnification, like analysis, tends to break down the categories and terms of familiarity. It could be argued that each level of observation has its own peculiar order—but this is little more than a weak and wish-fulfilling statement of faith. We are captives of the anthropinistic, things seen at the human scale. Our sense of order is anthropocentric and anthropinistic. Our metaphors of thought, the internalized action schemes of our discursive thinking, the elements of our perceptual world, all that we know, immediately originates at the anthroposcopic level. We may be able to accommodate things that are contrary to this level, but we cannot identify with them and easily graft them onto the larger heritage of our thought without their remaining alien, of an essentially different character, stepchildren in the most prejudicial sense.

In surveying the conceptually more innovative aspects of twentieth-century science, we have implicitly drawn together the three dominant forces overshadowing the past four generations: energy, communication, and psychological analysis. Penetrating the mysteries of energy has been perhaps the chief goal of modern physical science, and from this quest sprang both relativity and quantum theory. Communication has revolutionized thought in maintaining a constant juxtaposition of disparate ideas on a worldwide basis. Ideological concurrence has always been the main spark of innovation, as we have noted, for instance, in the case of many of the Greek colonies—think of the Ionian philosophers. Telecommunication has accelerated this matrical process. And finally, psychological analysis has turned inward upon itself, so that the act of observation itself is scrutinized, reason in its strictest form is subjected to logical analysis, and ultimately the mind is required to disassemble itself. Communication is more a process than a conceptual construct. It falls in the domain of the history of ideas mostly as a catalyst. We shall, therefore, concentrate on energy and the mind. Relativity and quantum theory present the greatest innovations in the way we construe the physical universe. These two theories are built of mathematical brick and mortar. Mathematics has become the skeleton key to science in this century. It is impossible properly to understand the twentieth-century worldview without also understanding modern mathematics. On the physical side, then, we look at relativity, quantum theory, and mathematics.

In apposition to this revolution in physics is the equally radical reappraisal of the mind that has come about in this century. As we learn more and more about how we construct our reality, the problem of mind and consciousness moves to center stage. Physics and psychology meet on the field of artificial intelligence and in their mutual concern with what the mind is and how it works. Mind, therefore, is the third member of the trio that will play out this final chapter.

Theory of Relativity

Lewis S. Feuer has presented a compelling argument to view relativity and quantum theory, the two primary cornerstones of modern physical thought, as arising from the matrix of late-nineteenth-century European social disintegration. Dadaism and relativity were born at the same time in the same city of Zurich.[1] Vienna during the Secession produced a phenomenal welter of revolutionaries, from Freud to Mahler, Klimt to Schoenberg, and later on the famous Vienna Circle of philosophers. The founders of quantum theory, each for his own reasons, flaunted the scientific traditions of the previous generation whom they blamed for the political decay of their homelands. Just as centuries before, Galileo had deliberately set out to overturn the Aristotelian order because he was frustrated at its failings, men like Einstein, Bohr, Heisenberg, and de Broglie, all of whom were involved in the social upheavals of their day, were unconsciously rebelling against the ancien regime.

"Every great physicist approaches the world of physical phenomena with guiding philosophical analogies that express his innermost emotions and longings."[2] For Einstein, the guiding philosophical analogies congealed around a profound distrust of the absolutistic space-time framework of Newtonian mechanics. His distrust was bolstered by two sources: Maxwell's electrodynamics theories and the epistemological skepticism of Ernst Mach. Mach, in his *History of Mechanics*, which Einstein avows had a deep effect on him as a student, criticized the absolutist notions of space and time and treated the concepts of mechanics as heuristic devices and nothing more. Scientific theories are not visual constructs of reality (:Mirror), he said; they are simply devices that enable us to mediate more successfully among our sensations (which, like Hume, he took to be the only *givens*). "Determinations of time," he proclaimed, "are merely abbreviated statements of the dependence of one event upon another, and nothing more."[3]

At the time that young Einstein was reading these Machian heresies, the academic world in which he lived was all agog over the recent success of James Clerk Maxwell in bringing the essential behavior of electromagnetic phenomena under the control of a concise set of field equations. Traditional physicists had expected all physical phenomena to be explained within the framework of Newtonian mechanics—largely because of the seemingly universal scope of the Newtonian principles and the aesthetically pleasing features of their mathematical expression. Newton, therefore, was a perfect target for turn-of-the-century iconoclasts. Mechanics, of course, is an explanation of the evolution of physical systems under effects of force; it therefore requires as substratum physical bodies, not potential fields. Indeed, the concept of field is inimical to mechanical explanation. Iconoclasts consequently were overjoyed at what others took as the perplexing success of the Maxwell field equations in accounting for electromagnetic phenomena that had eluded explanation in conventional mechanics.

Einstein took special notice of Maxwell because, since the age of sixteen, he had been fascinated and disturbed by a thought experiment that centered on what might happen if one were to catch up to a beam of light. Would it look like a frozen or stationary wave? Such a result was unacceptable to Einstein on a priori grounds. This would radically change the observed nature of light as well as other phenomena related directly or indirectly to electromagnetic radiation. Einstein could not conceive that fundamental laws of nature would change merely because of the way we move. He chose rather to make a radical assumption: that the velocity of light is a universal constant independent of the motion of the observer. Light—or, more specifically, electromagnetic radiation—is the only thing we can't catch up to.

Special Relativity Theory followed from this simple assumption. Simultaneity must be an illusion, because light is the communicator of distant events—the speed of sound is variable, depending on the characteristic of the transmitting medium—and two observers cannot rely on any sense of absolute motion to determine their respective distances and states of motion relative to any two distant events, because there is no absolute and motionless framework with reference to which absolute motion can be established and measured. That the velocity of light remains constant for every observer requires that measuring rods, and everything else, contract in the direction of motion by an amount stipulated by the so-called Lorentz-Fitzgerald contraction, the square root of $(1 - v^2/c^2)$, where c is the velocity of light and v that of the observer, both in centimeters per second. To maintain certain necessary invariants, it was further required that mass increase and time dilate with observer velocity as the reciprocal of the spatial contraction. These contractions and dilatations formed a trio of simple equations that could be construed as transformations from one frame of reference to another, one to be taken as moving relative to the other. If a law of nature were intrinsic as opposed to being an effect of relative motion, it had to be invariant under the Lorentz transformations. For example, when spatial length along the axis of motion, mass increment and time dilation are substituted into the mathematical formulations of the law, the overall numerical results had to be unaffected; otherwise absolute motion would be detectable. Length, mass, and time change exactly in proportion to relative motion so that the speed of light is measured always to be the same whether the observer is moving toward it or away from it. Applying this stricture to the law of the conservation of energy, Einstein found to his amazement that the law could be saved only if he substituted into it $e = mc^2$, indicating that mass and energy are interchangeable forms. The atomic age was born.

Special Relativity left space and time relative and interdependent, forming a four-dimensional continuum—there is no point in specifying the location of something unless you say at what time the location is valid. But Einstein was not content. His theory saved universal laws only from the perplexities of absolute and constant motion in a straight line. What about accelerated motion or rotation? Can these be absolute? Supposedly centrifugal force and inertia tip us off that we are accelerating or rotating. Einstein again could not envisage such caprice in nature that uniform rectilinear motion would be relative but that as soon as we departed from it, our motion would suddenly become absolute. Besides, he had long been entertaining another of his famous thought experiments which ultimately gave him the key he needed to generalize the results of Special Relativity.

Einstein was thinking about a man standing in an elevator in free fall somewhere out in empty space. He imagined the elevator to be accelerating upward, say at 32 feet per second per second (that is, it would pick up another 32 feet per second of speed with every second that passed). The man takes a penny out of his pocket and lets go of it. We see the floor rise to meet it, but he sees it fall to the floor just as it would normally here on earth. In fact, the vertical component of gravity would be exactly simulated in the elevator. With this, Einstein had established a remarkable relationship: free fall in empty space simulates the effects of gravitation, which is to say that bodies behave the same way under both circumstances. Now suppose there were a hole in the side of the elevator, and a flashlight attached outside so that a beam of light traversed the elevator. Let's take out the man so he doesn't get squashed, and speed the acceleration of the elevator to near the velocity of light. What happens? The floor of the elevator is rising so fast that, quick as the light beam is, it veers toward the floor, describing a parabolic path.

But, thought Einstein, if the accelerated elevator in empty space is equivalent (in the vertical component) to a frame of reference in a gravitational field—the Equivalence Principle—then light must bend if the field is sufficiently strong. Of course, it would bend in a weaker field, too, but we would never notice it for its slight degree. However, it had long ago been rather firmly established that light rays travel the shortest distance between two points, which, in Euclidean geometry, is a straight line. And everyone knew that space is Euclidean, flat in every direction. Einstein was willing to bet that it isn't flat; it is curved, and the curvature is due to the presence of matter, which brings with it gravitation. Ergo, gravitation is spatial curvature (technically, space-time curvature).

Inertia, the tip-off in acceleration and rotation (where it appears as centrifugal force), then arises not out of the *particleness* of a body but out of the field equations by which a mass-point may be determined. That is to say, inertia is an effect of the relationship between an observer and the mass-energy-gravitational field; and it may be transformed away by the proper choice of reference frames. Imagine that Einstein's elevator is in free fall in a gravitational field: the effects of gravity within the elevator vanish. Inertia vanishes under a transformation to an accelerated reference frame. It is not an invariant.

Let us recapitulate all this from a metaphor standpoint. Space and time cease to be solely containers of experience and become more like relative contingencies of experience itself. The metaphorical vessel is shattered; all that is left are flexible strings that tie experiences together. Mach's conception was fully realized. Yet there was another side to the coin. The space-time continuum was disengaged from the ancient concept of the void and assumed the character of a medium to replace the ether—the ultimate refinement of the Breath metaphor. Ether, the ancient concept of an ultrafine air, was finally stripped of all physical characteristics; yet, like a spirit, it still exercised an influence over material bodies. Unlike spirit, however, it was bereft of personhood. As space-time continuum, it had only mathematical character.

Mass-energy is equivalent to a kind of knot in space. We could say that space-time is a variable medium, the geometry of which defines material existence itself. Technically it is a field, a concept that arose from late-nineteenth-century physics, especially the electrodynamics of Maxwell. Metaphorically it is a deployment of Pattern in which some quantifiable substance or property is conceived to be distributed such that a kind of density measurement can be assigned to every point. A common example would be air temperature in a room, wherein theoretically we could conceive of a temperature measurement taken at every point or, at any rate, a temperature distribution specifiable at any given point.

Matter, substance,[4] traditionally understood through the deployment of the Floor/Ground metaphor, the substratum underlying and sustaining properties much as a mannequin supports clothes, becomes an extension of the breath of space. It is equated with energy, which is in classical physics already an extension of essence (motion first conceived as due to a spirit, then indwelling agent or *vis viva*). The dream was to reduce everything to a field, but this has yet to be achieved. Einstein himself has characterized the way in which we are to evaluate these metaphorical revisions by describing the disparate functions of the scientist:

> [H]e appears as *realist* insofar as he seeks to describe a world independent of the acts of perception; as *idealist* insofar as he looks upon the concepts and theories as free inventions of the human spirit (not logically derivable from what is empirically given); as *positivist* insofar as he considers his concepts and theories justified *only* to the extent to which they furnish a logical representation of relations among other sensory experiences. He may even appear as *Platonist* or *Pythagorean* insofar as he considers the viewpoint of logical simplicity as an indispensable and effective tool of his research."[5]

If we put all these roles together, we see that, even in his later years, Einstein did not markedly depart from his Machian allegiances. He saw his theory as a model for the coordination of actions with sense impressions; it was indeed in those terms that he redefined space and time.

In a real sense, any metaphor for space or for substance in relativity theory is pawned away for predictiveness. They disappear in the equations, replaced by topological transformations too hidden behind the mathematical formalism clearly to be discerned. To be sure, Einstein was looking to *explain* physical phenomena, but the transference from forces to fields effectively cut the tie to primitive action schemes. Essentially the same transference was what upset scientists about Maxwell's explanation of electromagnetism in terms of fields rather than forces, even though at bottom both were equally invisible. No primitive metaphor will accommodate the formalism of relativistic field equations (the equivalent in relativity theory to space, gravitation energy, and mass). The same may be said of quantum theory, as well as of most other theories of modern physics.

QUANTUM THEORY

Even more radical than relativity were the revisions instituted in quantum theory. Here the history is so complex and the issues are so technical that for our present purposes we shall not attempt any detailed reconstruction. Rather, we shall restrict ourselves to a brief outline, with emphasis on results.

We may say that it all began with black-body radiation. A black body is one that absorbs all radiation falling upon it. Such a body can in fact be constructed or, at any rate, something very near the ideal. When saturated, so to speak, it will return the radiation, and that is where the problems of subatomic physics began. The frequency distribution of the reemitted radiation did not accord with the predictions of classical radiation law, the so-called Wien laws.[6] It was Max Planck who first saw that the only way to get the right results from classical wave equations (which had been amply substantiated in other areas) was to assume that atoms absorb and emit energy only in discrete amounts, which he called quanta. Or rather Planck worked out most of the mathematics, and Einstein saw the implications and drew the conclusion that the results could be correct only if the involved energy existed in discrete quanta.[7] Niels Bohr then worked out a model of the atom in which electrons assume only certain discrete orbits around the nuclear center; and the absorption or emission of energy quanta are associated with "jumps" in electron orbits. What was disturbing about this model was that the electrons cannot exist between orbits—as a man climbing or descending a stepladder might be said not to exist as he passes from rung to rung. This restriction was required because any charged body emits radiation when accelerating or decelerating, and the emission of electrons, and other charged subatomic particles, is always discrete, never totally continuous over the spectrum of possible wavelengths or frequencies.

Because the concepts of energy and mass, space and time, are so inextricably bound together in the equations of physics, a discontinuity in one implicates discontinuity in all. Planck effectively broke physical reality into discrete bands. The absurdity of it is that accordingly things are forever blinking in and out of existence. And then there is the matter of the dimensions of the ultrasmall. Werner Heisenberg showed that there is a limit to the certainty with which we can know the details of subatomic reality. On a commonsense level, we might say that there is the problem that we have nothing small enough to probe the smallest details of the subatomic world without significantly disturbing them. Trying to locate an elementary particle with some ultra-high-frequency electromagnetic probe is like trying to spot a billiard ball with another billiard ball. If you find out where it is, you knock it out of position by doing so. There is an ineluctable uncertainty in your knowledge.

Heisenberg arrived at his Uncertainty Principle not by the kind of commonsense reasoning we just displayed, but by mathematical deduction from the equations of subatomic physics. It therefore has a weightiness that mere common sense could not bring to it. By the so-called Copenhagen interpretation (an official version of quantum theory reached by a convention of its founders held in Copenhagen), the Uncertainty Principle is not a mere methodological limitation on human knowledge; it reflects a kind of breakdown of causal order roughly at the subatomic level, growing steadily worse as we approach the level of Planck's constant (6.626×10^{-34}), the ratio of the energy of a photon (light particle) to its frequency. This would seem to be a *universal constant*, in that no smaller energy quantum is known—the photon is the neutral charge equivalent of the electron. Von Neumann tried to prove that the uncertainty suggested by Heisenberg is intrinsic to nature by showing that it follows rigorously from the mathematics of the quantum theory. The mathematics had been substantiated by voluminous empirical data. There is still a debate over the success of von Neuman's enterprise.[8] Classical quantum mechanics assumed that the trio of electron, positron (the antiparticle sister to the electron), and photon is truly elemental, but this idea might itself be subject to revision. Indeed, the quark theory now suggests such a revision, as does the tripartite nature of the Dirac wave equation for this midget trio of particles.[9]

At any rate, the breakdown of causal order at the Planck level gives way to a statistical order. To understand this a little more fully, we must take note of another idea introduced into quantum theory. Louis de Broglie showed that every particle—in fact, every bit of matter—has associated with it a wave, which can be made manifest under certain experimental conditions. His thesis was first supported by particle diffraction. You shoot a beam of particles at a diffraction grating (a plate scored with closely spaced lines or, at a smaller level, a molecular lattice as found in a translucent crystal), and it comes back to you, registered on a photographic plate as a series of waves forming an interference pattern, like the expanding waves from several pebbles tossed into a pond all at the same time. Subsequently Erwin Schrödinger worked out the general equation for matter waves.

The statistical interpretation of the Schrödinger wave equation is that it defines the probability distribution for the position, momentum, or some other property of a particle confined to a certain volume of possibility,[10] thus effectively nullifying any metaphorical notion of waves as pictures of physical reality. If we are considering position or momentum, the volume is literal, but if we are considering properties not strictly spatial, the volume is simply the limits of measurement prescribed within the problem. A Schrödinger wave, if graphed, looks like a modified bell curve or sine wave. In fact, solutions to the Schrödinger wave equation in their mathematical form involve the superimposition of sine waves. The point is that exactitude in measurement gives way to statistical probability. Suppose we confine an electron within a volume and break the volume into, say, eight octants. If position were what we were after, the Schrödinger wave for the electron under whatever conditions may prevail tells us what chance we might have of finding the electron in each of the octants. We might get something like the following breakdown for octants 1 to 8: 5 percent, 20 percent, 30 percent, 2 percent, 17 percent, 1percent, 16 percent, and 9 percent, all adding up to 100 percent.

These probabilities do not measure simply our chances of finding the electron in any of the octants. Somehow the electron *is* in all of the octants at once. We can say it is smeared out throughout the volume, or that it is 5% here and 20% there. None of this makes any physical sense, no matter how we picture it, because, according to the statistical interpretation, the intrinsic order of existence at this level is radically different from the anthroposcopic level. Probability represents simply the way in which the anthropinistic and the subatomic levels couple or interact. Causality, conceived configurationally as described earlier, is not the ordering principle at these ultrafine dimensions. This is why it is difficult to picture or to represent metaphorically what occurs at the quantum level, for any metaphorand drawn from physical experience would necessarily behave causally.

Further to paint in the details of the ultrafine, let us zoom in on the Planck time gap, as we may call it, and see what goes on there according to the latest physics. First of all, space-time has a visible structure at this magnification. It looks like a froth of bubbles. Obviously it isn't empty then. No, even a vacuum is full of potential energy, which appears and disappears out of the invisible bubble machine. Surrounding any particle is this cosmic suds. When particles get together, they attract or repel each other by pulling particles out of the vacuum and passing them back and forth. Often as not, these messenger particles, or *vector bosons* to give them their proper name, weigh much more than their host particles. Never mind. This Planck gap is out of the range of mortal intruders, so anything goes here. Nature can play havoc with the rules she has assigned to us, and we'll never be the wiser. The only limitation is that the coupling between the observed and the unobserved must stay within the boundary conditions surrounding the Schrödinger wave equation, to put the matter loosely.

If this sounds like fairy tale stuff, we should keep in mind that it has all met the test of successful prediction with hair-splitting accuracy. And it is all capped off by the Principle of Complementarity, the brainchild of Niels Bohr, according to which something can be a particle and a wave at the same time. In other words, a non-Aristotelian logic prevails in nature's secret garden: a thing can be A and not-A simultaneously except, of course, relativity permits no simultaneity, so perhaps logic is saved. Ironically, man seems to have passed through stages of mythopoeia to science and through science back to mythopoeia. Certainly quantum reality resembles the world of myth more than it does the dreary domain of everyday experience.

The only difference is that the magical transformations of mythopoeic thought have been mathematicized.

QUANTUM THEORY: INTERIM SUMMARY

Recapitulating, major radical ideas introduced in quantum theory are: discontinuity in nature, acausality, negation for the vacuum, non-Aristotelian identity laws, probability modes of existence, and an abiding faith in *metron* and *symmetron* to save it all from the grips of fantasy. This latter trait has come to the fore in the proliferation of unified theories recently suggested to bring the results of relativity and quantum theory into harmonious accord. All these unified theories revolve around searching for symmetries that can be derived from representing various properties of elementary particles in the form of mathematical groups, discussed earlier. Bereft of the technicalities, the properties are arranged in a kind of tabular form to see if there are any evident patterns.

QUANTUM THEORY: MATHEMATICIZATION OF REALITY

It is significant that few of the novelties of quantum theory were arrived at conceptually. Most were the result of mathematical manipulations. Take the initial notion of energy quanta introduced by Planck. He was faced with the following problem: Wien's radiation law fit the data for black body radiation at low frequencies, but it was grossly incorrect for high frequencies and temperatures, whereas another law, known as Rayleigh's radiation law, worked well at high frequencies but not at low. What was needed, then, was a revision that would pass from Wien's law at low frequencies and temperatures to Rayleigh's law at higher frequencies and temperatures. Planck had been intrigued, as many young physicists were at the time, with the statistical methods that had been introduced into mechanics by Maxwell, Gibbs, and Boltzman, and so he followed in that direction. He decided to treat the black body as an aggregate of oscillators, tiny elements that absorbed and emitted energy by oscillating, the degree of oscillation depending on the frequency of the radiation in question. Then he could deal with the aggregate statistically. Here he had quite an established body of mathematics upon which to draw. Probabilities can be expressed through particular binomial expansions that are related, as it happens, to the power series by which the trigonometric functions are computed. Thus, the graph that shows the distribution of probabilities—the best known being the bell curve—is usually a composite sine wave. The role of the parameters in expressing the mathematical formula for a given probability distribution were well known; certain ones were associated with centrality of distribution, skewness, standard deviation, and so on.

Planck thus had many clues by which to proceed, and they were mainly mathematical. It was a mathematical insight that led him to introduce his famous constant, which ultimately measured the discontinuity in nature.[11] In the paper in which he announced his results, he clearly stated that the constant was merely a mathematical device for obtaining a solution that would fit the empirical data. It was Einstein who first saw that the constant had revolutionary physical implications. And it was only the first of many essentially mathematical developments the full physical import of which had to be worked out largely in mathematical terms, so that the metaphorical shifts involved were ex post facto rather than being determinative. The pioneers of quantum theory were guided almost wholly by mathematical formalism. They had to make certain equations jibe with experimental measurements. By contrast, relativity proceeded from certain preliminary physical insights that had definite metaphorical bases. These insights were greatly amplified after solutions to crucial equations had been achieved, especially the Schwarzchild solutions,[12] which led to the astrophysics of black holes. Here we have another instance of the scientific worldview becoming more mathematically abstract, at once depending on numerical prediction and topological transformations (as the underlying structure of mathematics is reflected in topology).

MATHEMATICS: THE LANGUAGE OF SCIENCE

We may say then that mathematics has become increasingly crucial to the deployment of root metaphors in construing the nature of the physical universe. At the same time, mathematics has turned inward upon itself in an attempt to unravel its own anatomy. We have already mentioned the beginnings of this in the nineteenth century, when there was an upsurge of demand for greater rigor in providing proofs for the many theorems and procedures advanced in the previous two centuries. So momentous was this task that mathematicians were moved to examine the very nature of mathematical proofs, thereby delving intimately into the philosophical foundations of mathematics itself. Here we have the start of a revolution still in the making, with consequences of particular interest to our thesis.

Abstract algebra, set theory, category theory, fiber bundles, operator theory, and topology are among the modern developments in mathematics that center on structure as opposed to quantitative relations. To illustrate what is happening, we shall concentrate on topology, which has become for many the summum bonum of mathematics. Some preliminary remarks will be required on set theory.

First of all, a set is a collection of objects such that, given any object, it is always possible to determine whether or not it is a member of the set. In this respect, conceptually a set has much in common with a logical class, and operations with sets are similar to operations with classes. Set theory sprang from considerations of infinity in the latter half of the nineteenth century, chiefly by Bernhard Bolzano and Georg Cantor. These men clarified countability in sets, pioneering the notion of matching, out of which historically counting evolved. In a nutshell, the contention is that two sets have the same size, if their members can be matched together one-on-one with no members left over in either set. The close alliance between set theory and logic makes it a natural avenue by which to explore axiomatics and the logical foundations of mathematics.

We shall be most concerned with point sets, a notion introduced by Cantor, developed by several other mathematicians, and finally generalized for application to topology by Maurice Frechet. As the name implies, a point set is a collection of points. However, to be of any use, certain properties must be introduced into the definition of the set so that the points have a kind of geometry. Most particularly, we have the notions of open and closed sets and subsets, and of distance between points.

Open and closed sets are distinguished by the absence or presence of boundary points, an idea half algebraic and half geometric. It is best to approach these notions through a few examples. Beginning with a crude intuitive instance, consider an orange. If we take the peel to define the boundary of the orange, then with the peel the points defining the whole orange form a closed set, whereas, if the peel is removed, the interior points are an open set. True, after the peel is removed, it would seem that the exterior exposed surface of the inner fruit is still a boundary, but mathematically, once the boundary is defined, its removal leaves an unbounded point set. We can see more precisely how this works by looking at a numerical example. Open sets are often identified with convergent sequences, called Cauchy sequences, in which the elements of the series become closer and closer together. $1/2, 1/4, 1/8, \ldots 1/2^n$ is such a sequence, converging to, but never quite arriving at, the value of 0. 0 is the boundary point of the series, but it is not contained in the series. The series is, therefore, open, at least at one end. Likewise, if we take the sequence, $2, 1\text{-}1/2, 1\text{-}1/4 \ldots 1$, defining the 1 and 2 as boundary points, we have a closed set, whereas by removing the 1 and 2 we are left with an open set *by definition*.

As with classes in logic, the union of two sets is the set containing the combined elements of both sets (not including repeated elements): *[a, b, c]* + *[b, c, d]* = *[a, b, c, d]*. The intersection of two sets is the set having as elements those which the two share in common. So, *[a, b, c]* intersected with *[b, c, d]* = *[b, c]*. Finally, a subset is simply a set formed from elements of a larger set. The quantity *[a]* is a subset of *[a, b, c]*, as are *[b, c]*, *[a, c]*, *[a, b]*, *[b]* and *[c]*. Any of these sets may be *defined* as open or closed, as the case may require.

TOPOLOGY: SKELETON KEY TO MATHEMATICS

We are now in a position to look at the central concept in topology, a topological space. We should begin by pointing out that this is not in any sense a real space.

Mathematically it is a space analogue. That is, the properties ascribed to topological spaces are extensions or generalizations of those used to describe spatial relations. With that caveat, we cite a formal definition of a topological space: A topological space is a set containing minimally itself and the null set (i.e., the set consisting solely of zero), which are defined to be open; all subsets of the set are open; all unions of the subsets are open; and the intersection of any two subsets is open.

With the open sets of a topological space there are usually Cauchy sequences associated. In effect, this ensures that the points of the space are as close together as desired, because there is a point paired with each element of the sequence, and the elements, as noted, get closer together the farther out they appear in the sequence. This ensures continuity throughout the space, because there are no gaps left; everywhere the elements of the Cauchy sequences are converging. Further tests for continuity are frequently imposed, but we need not bother here with the technicalities. The importance of continuity will be seen shortly.

There are numerous subspecies of topological space gained by adding further properties to those contained in the definition cited. Among these subspecies, perhaps the most widely applied are the metric spaces. A metric space has numbers associated with the points and a formula supplied for determining the distance between two points. This distance formula is the metric of the space. If the points of the space are taken to define the end points of vectors and there are imposed certain rules of arithmetic operations identical to those used for vectors, we then have a vector space. A vector space widely used in physics is called Hilbert space. It has a Euclidean metric—essentially the Pythagorean formula in n-dimensions—and a special vector product operation defined (i.e., there is a procedure defined for multiplying one vector by another).

It should be apparent that the notion of a topological space is a flexible one, admitting to numerous variations. In each subspecies, we have a slightly different set of properties. Unlike real space, topological space cannot be assumed to display properties revealed by empirical observation. It is a defined entity and has only those properties ascribed in its definition. From these properties alone further properties can be derived by strict logical rules, just as we can determine whether or not a chess piece can get from one square to another only by deductions from the moves prescribed for it. I have chosen to discuss topological spaces in detail because it is generally acknowledged that they hold the key to mathematics itself. What this means is that any mathematical operation can be modeled on a topological space. Then it can be dissected and studied in detail because the properties of a topological space are few, precisely stated, and subject to the laws of set theory, which in turn is a rigorous version of deductive logic. Before we back away from this and put it in a broader perspective, let us complete our presentation on topology by sketching briefly its application in the practical sciences.

APPLIED TOPOLOGY

Physical processes, too, can be modeled on topological spaces. Usually this is done by modeling the differential or integral equations that describe the processes. Differentiation and integration both require continuity in the functions to which they are applied. Discontinuities occur when there is a point or value at which a function is undefined. In a graph of such a function, where there is a discontinuity a gap appears, the graph line is broken. Assuming the topological space to be two-dimensional or higher, the gap would be tantamount to a hole in the space—the equivalent would be a plane, or sheet, with a hole cut in it.

Modeling a physical system in a topological space can simplify finding solutions to the equations describing the system. In effect, it establishes additional boundary conditions—i.e., conditions with which any solution must accord—which can narrow the possibilities for the solutions. Often the equations are otherwise too general to yield specific results, or they may lead to a family of results among which the correct solution for the given circumstances must be found. Narrowing the possibilities may be achieved through a kind of structural analysis, using special inequalities (statements that one parameter is greater than, less than, or equal to some value or some other parameter, given certain boundary conditions) and other mathematical tools.

TOPOLOGICAL TRANSFORMATIONS AND INTERNALIZED ACTION SCHEMES

To place this all in the perspective of metaphoric historiography, we shall have to restate certain facts in suitable terms. From our point of view, a topological space is a set of elements subject to prescribed configurations and rules of transformation. The configurations establish the topology of the space—whether it is smooth, has holes, inner boundaries, and so on. How the elements of the space are interrelated other than configurationally, especially in terms of distance, how they may be paired, moved around, combined, and otherwise subjected to operations is specified in the rules of transformation—the algebra of Hilbert space, for example.

A topological space is nothing more than elements in configurations subject to various kinds of manipulation. That any part of mathematics can be modeled on a topological space shows that mathematics is pure discourse, that it is the application of assimilated action schemes to abstract elements.[13] Of course, this is a restatement of what has long been implicitly known, but by articulating it in the present terms we bring it more fully into line with the broader themes that we have been pursuing. It brings us to a definition of mathematics as comprising sets of action schemes applied to defined abstract elements that may or may not be taken to model physical systems and processes. Most critical perhaps is that the action schemes of mathematics are, *at the most elemental level,* no different from those underlying all other discursive thought. It suggests that mathematics might well be developed pedagogically by explicating the underlying action schemes not at the abstract mathematical level only but preliminarily at the more primitive scale of common action.

Recently, Hilary Putnam has called into question the validity of set theory as a model for the transcendental truth of mathematics.[14] He shows that there can exist no definition of a set that would preclude multiple interpretations. Many mathematical structures thus are possible. Mathematics is pluripotential. It does not pertain to a unique transcendental order underlying the physical universe. It is part of the social construction of reality, a flexible extension of abstracted human action schemes. Topological transformations, in the sense used throughout this work, may be extended in any way that assists humans in coping with phenomenal reality.

Action Schemes in Interpreting Mathematicized Reality

There is no reason we should not apply this approach to gain a deeper understanding of what is occurring with modern physics. We have already indicated that much of the theoretical framework, both from the direction of relativity and from that of quantum theory, has evolved along purely mathematical avenues. Equations have been teased out from what have been considered basic assumptions and empirical data, and subsequently been transformed, usually by a whole battery of convoluted action schemes, producing at times hybrid results that baffled physical interpretations. Nevertheless, insofar as these developments were tied to predicting physical phenomena, there had always to be a nexus between the end equations and physical procedures, usually of measurement. What many scientists have ceased to be concerned with is the fact that, after explanation has been supplanted by prediction as the preferred outcome of science, the mathematical system for prediction does not necessarily mirror or model physical reality in any step-by-step way.

At the same time, by working only with action schemes, leaving out of account any physical representation they might reflect, mathematics has advanced without the special limitations of metaphorical construction, or perhaps it would be fairer to say with special limitations different from those of the other areas of intellectual endeavor. All mathematics is fundamentally positional transformation, crudely speaking, movement from place to place such that, analogically, points are carried into other points or, what amounts to the same, into other positions. This is brought out in the fact that it can all be mapped into topological transformations (taken in the strict mathematical sense). In view of the fact that discursive thought is nothing more than action schemes applied to abstract and representational elements in a fictive topological space (in my sense), mathematics has a legitimate claim to being the purest form of discursive thought.

All this being so, it is little wonder that the book on *proofs* has to be written anew. But before we give our version of this, let's rehearse the recent history. We can be brief. The axiomatic revolution began in the late-nineteenth century in an effort to supply a more rigorous foundation for the brilliant efflorescence of the Enlightenment. It quite naturally culminated in a program of examining the very mechanics of proof employed to validate mathematical statements. This was precipitated partly by the appearance of seemingly pure forms of mathematics devoid of rapport with the physical world: non-Euclidean geometries, and noncommutative and nonassociative algebras.

To make a long story short, believers in the absolute truth of mathematics were dealt a severe, indeed fatal, blow by the announcement in 1931 of Kurt Gödel's Incompleteness Theorem. Using the most impeccable logico-mathematical procedures, Gödel showed that in any mathematical or logical system there will always be a first principle that remains unprovable, and there will always be statements that can be made within the system but are not therein provable or disprovable.

Our version of this should now be easily grasped. A mathematical proof comes down to this: you have a state of elements or a relation between states at which you have arrived from some prior state through a series of manipulations (action schemes abstracted to *operations*); and it is required to supply some alternative group of manipulations to arrive at the same state. The alternative group of manipulations, hopefully having proved its worth under previous circumstances, literally *is* the proof. Proof, then, is a matter of alternative congruence, a second sequence of manipulations to achieve the identical end configuration. Validation of proof itself, then, must involve infinite regression, because there is no escape from the tautological circle. Permutations of manipulations carried on endlessly can only spin fancier topological displays. There must be a starting point that is simply accepted, and there must be the realization that discursive thought is manipulation, which can be valuable but cannot go beyond what it is: manipulation, action sequences.

THE UNREASONABLE EFFECTIVENESS OF MATHEMATICS

If mathematics comes down to this, why has it succeeded so well first in helping to elucidate the physical world and then in facilitating the prediction of physical phenomena? In attempting to answer this question, R. W. Hamming has made trenchant observations on the foundations of mathematics without, however, coming to a definitive answer. He has suggested that "we see what we look for" and, having found it, "we select the kind of mathematics to use," by which he means that we construe the world selectively (as we have been arguing) and then, in applying mathematics to it, if the "given version" doesn't work, we alter the rules. And finally, he notes that "science in fact answers few questions," and ultimately "the logical side of the nature of the universe requires further explanation."[15] Observations like these are refreshing, coming from a professional mathematician; but the core of the solution that eluded Hamming seems now apparent within the framework of this discussion.

Internalized action schemes are the nexus between external behavior and internal thought. Quite simply, they are the primary means we have for exploring, imagining and changing our world. Metaphors may delimit construing, but, regardless of the construction placed on something, nothing happens with that construction unless action intervenes. And actions internalized for discursive manipulation comprise a relatively small group. Among those which seem to form the mainstay of reasoning are: translation, rotation, inversion, right-left exchange (or half turn, or reflection), turning inside out or outside in, cutting, separation, joining, jumping, folding, and unfolding. A moment of reflection will show that they could all be treated as point transformations. Furthermore, the more specialized or qualified a movement is, the less discursive value it has. Compare *advance* with *creep*, and the matter should be clear. Qualified movements, such as *saunter*, *wag*, or *snuggle*, tend to give rhetorical flavor to discourse rather than to define the skeleton of rational process. These are matters of degree, and of course there are motions that both establish and characterize frames of thought, as when one thing is said to be in conflict with another. (The etymological root here is *fligere*, to strike.)

THE DOMAIN OF THE MIND: THE PSYCHOANALYTIC TRADITION

In the psychological sciences, no less than in mathematics, the twentieth century brought fundamental metaphor changes. Psychology as a science (using that term in its broadest sense) had its roots in epistemology and autobiography—the *Confessions* of St. Augustine was perhaps the earliest example in this genre. The mental-health movement of the late-eighteenth century brought the interest in the mind within systematic focus, and the romantic reaction placed all the idiosyncrasies of the individual, not the least the mental ones, squarely in the spotlight. The novel of manners gave way to the character study and then the psychological novel, which was carried so far by Joyce as to attempt to record verbatim the inner monologue of thought even at its most fragile coherence, just before sleep. Erich Kahler, in *Man the Measure: A New Approach to History*, has probably put this in the most correct perspective, remarking that humans observe first that which is most distant from them and then move inward toward themselves in the course of history, so that astronomy becomes the science earliest to receive systematic observational codification and psychology is the newest science. Ortega y Gasset's analogy of the zoom lens, cited earlier, also lends support to Kahler's thesis.

The concept of mind has almost always been a deployment of the Container metaphor, and this has seldom been abandoned even in the twentieth century. George Herbert Mead, followed by Gilbert Ryle, has suggested that mind be treated not as an entity but as a process, with the catchy phrase, "mind is minding," but this has run so counter to traditional thought that it has failed to become anchored in the folk model of reality. An interesting case, it shows how difficult it is to deploy a new metaphor within a culture the intellectual vocabulary of which contains insufficient collateral deployments of the new metaphor and of others that might sustain it. A similar fate awaited Wittgenstein's interpretation of mind as a chimera of our language games.[16]

Freud has, for better or worse, bequeathed us a topography of the mind that has the indelible stamp of a modern mythology. Literally it taps the roots of Greek mythology, giving new names to Platonic prototypes: the id is the appetitive element of mind; the ego, the *thymos*; and the superego, reason. Freud acknowledged his source in Plato. He then went on with his mythologizing, introducing Eros and Thanatos, along with the Oedipus and the Elektra complexes. From the English associationists was developed the concept of the unconscious, fully articulated by Karl Eduard von Hartmann in *Philosophie des Unbewussten* (Philosophy of the unconscious), published in 1869.[17] Some authorities trace the concept back to Plato and his notion of eliciting forgotten material from the mind (principally in the *Meno*). Be that as it may, the concept was topical in the nineteenth century when Freud assimilated it to his psychomythology. He further imposed a hydraulic metaphor on the modus operandi of the mind, whereby the contents of the unconscious are repressed and only occasionally break through into the conscious.[18] He rounded out the picture with an economic metaphor of the libido, the energy of the mind that can be *spent* only once. Being almost wholly of mythical origin, his model had the appeal of primitive notions coupled with a nonquantifiable nature so that it could not be tested. This is scientific rhetoric at its most persuasive, lending new bottles to old panaceas under a patent that has yet to expire.

The legacy of Freud is to have entrenched the psychologism of the twentieth century in a metaphor framework so traditional even in its deployment that revolution was all but ruled out. Just as the history of philosophy has been described as a series of footnotes to Plato, the history of psychology in this century could fairly be characterized as footnotes to Freud, himself a footnote to Plato (in terms of underlying conceptual metaphors). Even those who disagreed with him took off from his main metaphor framework, imparting only different meanings to the forms that he had dictated. Indeed, much neo-Freudian revisionism had to do with the Victorian sexual veneer of traditional psychoanalysis and never brought into question the psychomythology of the Master. Freudianism, paradoxically, was ancient and medieval, yet responded to the modern tendency toward self-analysis. We are still exorcising the demons from the mind, whether it be through psychoanalytic transference, psychodrama, or the primal scream. Something is haywire *in* the mind, and it must be taken *out*. The Container metaphor prevails here.

PSYCHOLOGICAL FIELD THEORY

An interesting development in psychology that was not a footnote to Freud is the field theory of Kurt Lewin, an attempt to ally psychology with the conceptual framework of modern physics. Lewin tried to reject the conventional metaphors of Freudianism and not be hooked into reacting against them. He adopted certain concepts from mathematics, envisioning mind as a locus in a field. Vector spaces served as his model. This is an ingenious mental topography that unfortunately, outside its application in social psychology, has not spawned the wealth of new orientations potential within it. Yet again, we may be dealing with the utter entrenchment of Freudian psychology, which baffles alternative programs of thought. Another part to the puzzle is undoubtedly that field theory, the mathematical counterpart, has not engendered collateral deployments sufficient to integrate the psychological version into an intellectual vocabulary and metaphoric underpinning extending farther enough into a more general intellectual tradition in which such a psychology might become culturally relevant or meaningful. Or finally, as noted previously, not all the metaphors and methods of the physical sciences may be appropriate for the social and biological sciences.

MIND: EAST AND WEST

One of the most interesting aspects of all of this, from the standpoint of metaphor deployment, is simply that mind itself has come under such scrutiny. Because of great strides in neuroscience, cognitive science, computer science, and artificial intelligence, questions of mind and consciousness have come to the fore in the last quarter of this century. From the perspective of these disciplines, specialists have looked both to the past Western tradition as well as to the Eastern philosophies in search of answers to key questions in epistemology and the psychology of consciousness. Thus, this has in the West become an age of introspection. Within a less-serial processing tradition of dealing with information, the peoples of the Eastern world came to this juncture early in their history, but with similar paradoxical consequences. The Mirror metaphor has dominated the outcome in both traditions. We can most quickly conceive the paradoxical aspect of the situation by imagining what happens when a mirror is placed before another mirror: infinite regression of reflected images. In Western thought, emphasis has been placed on recursion, represented in mathematics by fractals, which seem to be good for everything from soup to nuts. Western thinkers are caught up in the metaphorically determined notion that self-analysis must bog down in some form of infinite regression, falling back on the ancient metaphor of the perceiving mind as a Mirror upon which sensory images are reflected. Easterners, although giving a certain acknowledgment to that line of thought, seem less restricted by the notion of reflexivity, the doer doing to himself.

Indian psychology is based . . . on such techniques as introspection and observation, and much less on experimentation. Although mind has been considered equivalent to soul, there is ample evidence to suggest that it was referred
to as a psychological instrument and one of the organs of the senses. In ancient Indian writings, the mind was given the status of the sixth sense organ.[19]

The ancient Indian view as known in medical practice, then, was not so much
different from that of the Greco-Roman world. In *Nyaya-Vaisesika*, for example,
"the mind is an inner instrument of perception."[20] Bhela, one of the ancient Indian
medical thinkers, conceived the mind to be divided into the *manas, citta,* and *buddhi,*
corresponding roughly to the Greek division into *noos, thymos,* and *psyche.* "The kind
of mind that the Confucians attributed to man . . . had to be 'like' the qualities that
they assigned to nature."[21] Again, this parallels the Greek concept of perception as
a kind of infusion of essences (:Breath) into the perceiving mind so that the inner
percept is a simulacrum of the objective datum. These notions are not far removed
from current folk models of the mind, although they may be better articulated.

Eastern Psychology: Metaphysical Background

However, these notions applied primarily at the folk level and within the purely
medical sphere. Beyond that, "Indian psychology is based on metaphysics; the psychological accounts of some problems, e.g., perception of the self, perception of the
universe, etc., are unintelligible without consideration of metaphysical foundations."[22] Metaphysically, the boundedness of the individual mind or self is illusory.
Liberated from the ego boundaries, "in pure cognitive *mukti* [liberation] . . . the
question of the individual's relation to other individuals loses all meaning, the discovery of the self = the Absolute being the sole end."[23] It is generally agreed among
Indian scholars that the *atman* is not simply the individual self but "also the Self
hidden behind the competing individual souls . . . the Absolute Self shared by
every individual soul."[24] In other words, the individual selves are manifestations of
the atman, conforming to the metaphor of One/Many.[25]

Insofar as the Chinese diverged from the folk doctrine of the Confucians, it
was to embrace the Indian concept of the *atman.* A typical example is the *Ch'eng
Wei-shih Lun* or *Completion of the Doctrine of Mere Ideation,* according to which the ego
and objective reality have "only a false basis and lack any real nature of their own."
They are both "mental representations dependent upon the evolution of consciousness."[26] Various versions of this abound in Far Eastern philosophy. In the Japanese
book called *Six Essays by Shoshitsu,* it is said that the "Buddha is your Mind."[27] Hui-
neng put it that "[n]ature reflects itself in itself, which is self-illumination not to be
expressed in words."[28] Lu Hsiang-shan (1139–92) was more direct: "The universe
is my mind, and my mind is the universe."[29] Behind these ideas lies the metaphor

of One/Many, the many of *maya* arising out of the ground, *atman, nyat,* or whatever term may be used for the Absolute One.

On the doctrine of *nyat,* Ta-chu Hui-hai wrote:

> When a mind, thoroughly understanding the emptiness of all things, faces forms, it at once realizes their emptiness. With it emptiness is there all the time, whether it faces forms or not, whether it discourses or not, whether it discriminates or not. This applies to everything that belongs to our sight, hearing, memory, and consciousness generally. Why is it so? Because all things in their self-nature are empty; and wherever we go we find this emptiness.[30]

Suzuki aptly says, in a manner reminiscent of Lewis Carroll: "Emptiness is thus unattainable. 'Unattainable' means to be beyond perception, beyond grasping, for emptiness is on the other side of being and non-being." Yet contrarily:

> Emptiness constantly falls within our reach; it is always with us and in us, and conditions all our knowledge, all our deeds, and is our life itself. It is only when we attempt to pick it up and hold it forth as something before our eyes that it eludes us, frustrates all our efforts, and vanishes like vapour.[31]

Inscrutable or mystical as all this talk of emptiness might seem, it becomes quite clear when examined from the angle of metaphor deployment.

First, to see things separately and categorically is like drawing mental lines around them, like slipping a stencil over the scene. Erase the lines, slide the stencil away, and the scene is an undifferentiated whole; in other words, it is all One. The difficulty of grasping this is not conceptual so much as experiential. We cannot easily match it to any familiar experience; yet most people do now and again pass through such a state: in meditation, or total absorption in something we are doing, momentarily the distinctions vanish and there is just the intense presence of something. Distinctions are reestablished only seconds later when we exit the trance. Whether a given person may identify with this or not, the metaphoric basis of seeing classificatory distinctions as the imposition of outlines should be clear enough, so that erasing them should also make perfect sense, at least at the level of metaphor. These, as well as the metaphors used in various traditions, are rhetorical devices used to deploy the underlying One/Many metaphor. Eastern thinkers use rhetorical metaphors to hint at a state of mind in which all categorical distinctions vanish. These metaphors are meant to be persuasive, rather than heuristic. Thus, the Ch'an Buddhist, Lin-chi I-hsüan (d. 866), said that "[a]nything you may find through seeking will be only a wild fox spirit."[32] Nothing of the One is conveyed, but the metaphor of the fox spirit is meant to assist in approaching it.

Arriving at the notion of the undifferentiated whole (the Absolute One), there remains the problem of the categorization of One. Going back to the outline analogy, the problem is to remove the mental outline around the whole so that it will be, as Suzuki says, "on the other side of being and non-being." Here the object is to arrive at something that, at least by definition, transcends human knowing. So, the One is equated with *nothingness* or *emptiness*. This is an intellectual ploy. By definition, nothingness has no characteristics. There is nothing, analogically, around which to draw an outline, although in fact the mind tries through negation, through mathematical equivalence to zero, and so on, exactly as in framing the concept of space. Examine the process:

> Mathematical space is a something that is a nothing and a nothing that is a something. . . . A vacuum would be something contiguous and separated where we find nothing contiguous and nothing separated. If space is the relation of co-existence of real objects, then, in the absence of these, it must be nothing and would disappear with them. . . .
>
> Pure mathematical space is a fiction. Its concept has the marks of a fiction: the idea of an extension without anything extended, of separation without things that are to be separated, is something unthinkable, absurd and impossible.[33]

In a nutshell, space, or nothingness, is a reification of relationships. *Things* related are concrete and belong to experience. Relations belong to experience only in so far as they are concurrent with the *things* on which they depend. To speak of the relation between *A* and *B* when *A* and *B* are absent (negation) is, as Vaihinger says, absurd. Yet this is how the mind frames the concept. It is useful nonetheless because it makes possible the transference of real relationships (i.e., between existing *things*) from one context to another by preserving an abstract scheme—which I shall not more precisely characterize because no one yet knows how the mind processes such schemes.

We may see how this applies to the mind. To Eastern thinkers, any recursiveness arising from self-analysis is illusory. Recursiveness is sidestepped by negating conceptualization itself, by denying the possibility of the mind conceptualizing itself, just as it would be denied that a hand could grasp itself. Equating the mind to the Absolute One, then further equating that to nothingness is all about denying the possibility of conceptualizing the mind. The seeing eye cannot see itself. The mind cannot ultimately reduce itself to terms of itself. That this remains one of the great mysteries may lie not so much in any intrinsic difficulty of the subject as in the impossibility of finding a root metaphor upon which to build an understanding. Metaphorands are elements of experience, whereas the mind itself is the ground, so to speak, of all experience and so, odd as it may sound, is beyond all experience. At least, this is the train of thought pursued not only in Eastern philosophy but among many Western thinkers who reject mechanism. Overall, the problem seems to be that there are none among the root metaphors that correspond appropriately to the experience of mind. In the field of artificial intelligence, new approaches, which probably means metaphors not previously established as basic, are being sought but so far no fully satisfactory model of the mind has been found.[34]

From the standpoint of metaphor and the analysis of thought, perhaps the most confounding perspective on epistemology is that of Zen Buddhism. Many mistakenly believe that the Zen perspective is somehow noncategorical, thus demonstrating a way of knowing that transcends or dispenses with metaphor. While misleading, this assessment has within it a grain of truth. Satori, or enlightenment, leads to a kind of reinterpretation of categorical thought that is best described as ontic. D. T. Suzuki writes:

> Satori may be defined as an intuitive looking into the nature of things in contradistinction to the analytical or logical understanding of it. Practically, it means the unfolding of a new world hitherto unperceived in the confusion of a dualistically-trained mind. Or we may say that with satori our surroundings are viewed from quite an unexpected angle of perception.[35]

It is, he says, "the simplest possible experience perhaps because it is the very foundation of all experience."[36] Hui-neng put it that "[a]s long as there is a dualistic way of looking at things there is no emancipation."[37] In other words, satori is placing all, including intellectualization, on the same level of experience. Soshi said that "[p]eople all over the world try to know what they do not know, instead of trying to know what they already know."[38] Zen Buddhists, after satori, do not withdraw and become mute. They go on living, just like anyone else. The critical difference is that to them ideas, categories, metaphors, and such have the same ontic status as all other *things*. They don't point to other things really, except as a matter of convenience. Or, the referential nature of words, metaphors, and the like is just more *things*. We say a shovel is for digging. They say a shovel *is*. They can still dig with it. They are not intellectually attached to thinking. It does not solve any problems because problems are just the froth on thinking, so to speak. So, their experience is still metaphor-imbued, but they have a different attitude toward it.

There is a famous saying by Ch'ing-yüan that puts all this neatly into perspective:

> Before I had studied Zen for thirty years, I saw mountains as mountains, and waters as waters. When I arrived at a more intimate knowledge, I came to the point where I saw that mountains are not mountains, and waters are not waters. But now that I have got its very substance I am at rest. For it's just that I see mountains once again as mountains, and waters once again as waters.[39]

At the first stage, normal categorical perception and conception reigns. At the second stage, everything is questioned and in doubt. Finally, the mental gymnastics of the second stage are seen as nothing more than the mind creating mental things, which have no privileged status. Categories are human artifacts; nothing more.

Treat them like rocks and rain. Then everything is once more as it is, with the difference that intellectualizations are relegated to the unprivileged status of mental baggage. Thinking is just like playing a game: the moves mean nothing outside of the rules of the game.

Sokei-an Sasaki, a modern Zen master, once wrote:

> One day I wiped all the notions from my mind. I gave up all desire. I discarded all the words with which I thought and stayed in quietude. I felt a little queer as if I were being carried into something, or as if I were touching some power unknown to me. . . . and Ztt! I entered. I lost the boundary of my physical body. I had my skin, of course, but I felt I was standing in the center of the cosmos. I spoke, but my words had lost their meaning. I saw people coming toward me, but all were the same man. All were myself! I had never known this world. I had believed that I was created, but now I must change my opinion: I was never created; I was the cosmos; no individual Mr. Sasaki existed.[40]

If there are any doubts about the categorical thoughts of enlightened Ch'an or Zen Buddhists, this should allay them. *Satori* is not, strictly speaking, a continuous state of being. It is an experience, sometimes sudden and sometimes not, that alters perspective. Sasaki thinks about his *satori*, and as he does, he uses categories and metaphors to show how, in their status as somehow modeling the world of our experience, they are empty in the sense that a move in chess or a tree is empty, that is, not signifying other than within the word game, as Wittgenstein would say. In fact, there are many Zen doctrines, such as that of no-mind and nonaction, predicated on metaphors, as there are in all of Eastern thought. They do seem, however, to form a constellation around a few dominant metaphors and action schemes— negation, maya (:Mirror), One/Many—that invade all avenues of thought outside the purely pragmatic.

So, Zen is not a noncategorical mode of thought. It simply relegates intellectualization to the ontic status of a *thing*. Another way to say this is that the Ch'an Buddhist becomes detached from categorical thinking. Intellectual questions have no hold. They are just mind games. Some are useful for living, just as sticks, water, and glue are; but they tell us nothing about reality. Like everything else, they just *are.*

The Ultimate Paradox of Mind

In view of the antiquity of the Eastern tradition, it is hazardous to venture past the background to suggest reasons for the stalemate about understanding what the mind is or possibilities for its resolution, but the metaphor approach does point to egress from paradox. Paradox is almost always the result of attempting to deploy a metaphor in contravention of its own properties. Past efforts have been directed to resolving paradoxes logically, which seems misguided. Patchwork rationalization, like that found in Bertrand Russell's theory of types, has been the inevitable result. A more radical solution is to discover the metaphor and wittingly discard it. But in the present case, the problem may even go beyond normal metaphor revolution.

Protagoras warned that humankind is the measure of all things, and although scholars may haggle over what he meant, certainly it is true that we are captives of the human perspective. Evidently the brain processes information only in entity form. Processes and actions are reified for mental manipulation. Without pretense to being able to get into the minds of animals, it nevertheless seems probable on comparative physiological bases that all animal brains similarly deal with mental *things*.[41] This is a severe epistemological barrier, and even the dichotomy of things versus action or process is a limitation of how organisms are.

Making mind a thing, therefore, sets us up for paradox when we direct it upon itself (our very manner of stating the problem is bound by the shackles we are attempting to remove). Mind as minding, the process approach of Mead and Ryle, disappointingly fails to circumvent the central paradox: What is minding minding? We are trapped in habits of thought. An action cannot act upon itself. Only things can be the objects of actions. Like waves, actions can interact with one another, but neither is the object of the other. Waves that interact with themselves simply become altered waves—this might happen when a wave is reflected back upon itself.

I am not suggesting this as a truth, but as a tentative alternative, which of course will have its own limitations and, if we would press them, probably their own paradoxes. However, with its acknowledged limitations (which apply to any intellectual construction), the wave as process analogy seems accurately to represent certain psychological phenomena that in a more conventional perspective prove extremely troublesome. A self-interacting wave is simply a wave that modifies itself. Similarly, the mind appears to have that protean quality whereby it sheds layers like an onion, when subjected to analysis or self-analysis. Put otherwise, the more we look at the mind, the more we find, and what we find is largely determined by the metaphoric presuppositions we bring to the analysis.

Modern Western concepts of the mind, in essence, hardly differ from those of the ancients.[42] In Homer there was already the division of the mind into the perceptual, *noos;* the emotional, *thymos;* and rational, *psyche.* Thinkers from Plato onward were compelled to postulate an unconscious to account for certain aspects of memory, selective perception, or intuition. Recall how Socrates in the *Meno* elicits mathematical knowledge from an illiterate boy, demonstrating the existence of out-of-conscious mind. And in the opening of the ninth book of the *Republic,* Plato as much as attributes an unconscious layer to the mind from which incestuous desire breaks out in dreams. Evocations of the unconscious followed through Aquinas to Rousseau and Herder, and it became topical half a century before von Hartmann spelled it out. By and large, these were all divisions of the mind viewed as a Container.

MIND AND MENTAL ILLNESS

Whether it was an evil spirit or a *disease entity*, the cause of mental illness has always been viewed through the Container metaphor as something wrong *in* the mind. Therapy has consisted of various techniques for getting the causative agent *out*. One of the more colorful methods was that of Hermann Boerhaave (1668–1738), who favored various kinds of shock treatment. Following a humoral theory of psychopathy, aside from the purgatives and bloodletting usual to his time, he strapped his patients in a special chair in which he could spin them around until they fainted.[43] Presumably this reestablished a proper humoral equilibrium. Modern psychoanalytic methods are based on some version of catharsis in which the inner cathected complex is worked *out*, so that the psychic energy invested in the complex is released. Psychodrama is a variant of this. Gestalt therapy attempts to reintegrate parts of the self that have somehow become alienated or dissociated. Drug therapies address abnormalities *in* brain chemistry; through mechanism the mind is equated with the brain.

In the many newer therapies that have arisen in the last several decades, emphasis has finally shifted away from the mind and the Container metaphor to consideration of social interaction. The Pattern metaphor is deployed in the definition of maladaptive behaviors, which are fundamentally ways of reacting with other people. Fluid in focusing on process rather than entity (e.g., evil spirit, humoral imbalance, or biochemical aberration), these new approaches nevertheless conceptualize characteristic patterns of interaction forming the diagnostic nosology. Other, more radical, therapies dispense with diagnostic classifications and treat each case as sui generis. In either instance, the characteristic maladaptation of the patient is a *pattern* to be changed.[44]

Mind as container posits an interface between the knowing self and the outside world. This dichotomy of private versus public experience is the basis of Western epistemology. Rorty suggests forgoing metaphors and reducing philosophy to something approaching aesthetic dialogue.[45] For philosophers, being reduced to *salonistes* might not be welcomed as an acceptable occupational stratagem, but over and above this departmental objection, the abandonment of the metaphoric basis of understanding abstract issues like the mind would be impossible for practical reasons. Research into mental processes requires an implicit model of the mind. The mind has always been the subject of keenest inquiry, but after the romantic movement it has become somewhat of an obsession.

SOME CONCLUSIONS

The dissolution of mind under minute examination is emblematic of this century. Whether it be laid, as Kahler suggests, to the natural stage of historical development or to the fortuities of humankind's brief moment in eternity, certainly the political and social decay of Europe at the threshold of the twentieth century acted as a catalyst for the analysis that came to dominate the age. Positivists attempted a purge of metaphysics in a paroxysm of self-congratulation not unlike that which the rationalists bestowed upon themselves two centuries earlier. Here, the results were even more devastating. Analytic philosophers took up where Berkeley, Locke, and Hume left off. Rationality was plunged into self-destruction. We catalog the impact.

First, the laws of the simple arithmetic operations were contravened, followed by the overthrow of geometry. This threw mathematicians back on the bedrock of logic itself, which was blasted by Gödel's Incompleteness Theorem. Simultaneously an assault was carried out on the mind itself, the matrix of logic, and it has evaporated into wish fulfillments, obliging the researcher to find whatever he or she sought. Subsequent to all this, Alan Turing demonstrated that all computations could be carried out by a simple universal program, but, more amazing, legitimate problems in computation can be formulated that intrinsically can never be solved, not because we don't know how to do them but because they literally have no solutions. Along the way, physicists relativized space, time, matter, energy, motion, causality, and just about every other conceptual measure of the physical universe.

We mustn't neglect the arts. Analysis of visual space by the cubists led to the identification of the elements by which dimensionality is conveyed to the eye. Some painters exploited these elements, albeit in nonrepresentational ways. Others expunged even the hint of space from their work. Artists and writers alike, at first searching for a new manner in which to deal with the growing complexities of their time, plunged into a world of personalized expression. The initial divisory schools—expressionism, fauvism, surrealism—yielded to hermetic communication, the voice of the artist addressing only himself. Interpreters rose dauntlessly to explicate the works of the avant-garde, becoming for the public essential intermediaries in the aesthetic act. Again, what occurred with *explication du texte* was the same as had beset mathematics, physics, and philosophy: the explicators turned their craft upon themselves and decided that communication refers not to things, ideas, feelings, and the matters of everyday experience but to other acts of communication. Words, in simplistic terms, refer only to other words. Infinite regression. The medium is the message. Communication is an illusion: that is the news that the hermeneutic and semiotic critics bring us.

Meanwhile, in music the chromatic experiments of the romantics, culminating, some feel, in the "Tristan" chord, extended quite logically into atonality, ending an experiment that began in the early baroque. Eclecticism was the only road open for further development in this direction, which involves synthesis rather than innovation, to employ Ezra Pound's useful distinction between types of creativity. At the extremity of the inevitable compulsion to innovate is the dissolution of the rhetorical structure of music, embodied in *musique concrète*, and those genres of electronic music that dispense with melodic, harmonic, rhythmic, and even patterned structures. Irving Babbit, for example, refers to the deliberate eradication of any vestige of pattern in certain of his compositions. Analysis, once again, has led to complete annihilation of the subject. Communication becomes obsolete:

> And so I dare suggest that the composer would do himself and his music an immediate and eventual service by total, resolute and voluntary withdrawal from the public world to one of private performance and electronic media, with its very real possibility of complete elimination of the public and social aspects of composition. By so doing, the separation between the domains would be defined beyond any possibility of confusion of categories, and the composer would be free to pursue a private life of professional achievement, as opposed to a public life of unprofessional compromise and exhibitionism.[46]

We seem to be faced with one of two alternatives: either a profound metaphoric revolution, or the development of that which has previously been construed as paradoxical. Metaphoric revolutions will certainly continue to appear, but, if the suppositions upon which this short study is based are valid, the likelihood is that such revolutions will not save us from our dilemma. Having pushed the deployment of our preferred metaphors to the limits of their useful application, we have refined a technique for finding these limits almost at once. We project the metaphor onto a set of data, observe the behavior of the data so construed, and then retroject the construct of the data back upon the source of the metaphor. It is a way of turning the metaphor back upon itself, creating a pseudorelationship.

Painting represents reality through graphic types. Graphic types are part of reality, so we aim to represent those, leading to their componential breakdown and the implicit realization that underlying each type is total abstraction. We might call this metarepresentation. It leads from cubism to abstract expressionism.

Music evolves as extended vocalization, including imitation of extramusical sounds and the creation of compositions isomorphic to psychological states. Composers concern themselves with the means of composition and performance as ends in themselves. Form is dictated by abstract principles in which melody and harmony are secondary considerations, if they are considered at all. Final result: preformed sound, noise, expressed as *musique concrète* and aleatory composition.

Mathematicians employ axiomatic systems—symbols, rules for their manipulation, and rules for correspondences with physical reality. They articulate the latter rules and seek their analogues in relating one axiomatic system to another. Underlying these metarules is the fabricating matrix of the mind: we must begin somewhere (arbitrary decision), leaving all that precedes the starting point unprovable. Everything is procedure. Metaphors have been left behind in favor of topological transformations (in both the mental and the mathematical sense).

In short, no matter the metaphor change, this technique will swiftly exhaust it and leave us floating without firm conceptual moorings. It would be naive to characterize this as folly. There is a logic to it, the kind of consistency that orients human behavior; so we cannot simply desist. Also, in a sense, this is an insight, carrying us to a new level. And there may be much to explore here.

THE PRESENT METAPHOR CRISIS

Humans have always oriented themselves by symmetry. Even in the East, where asymmetry has been more fully appreciated, balance and regularity have nevertheless been guiding intellectual principles. There has been, for instance, no truly non-Aristotelian logic developed anywhere in the world. Fuzzy logic may prove the exception that injects new life into an old subject. As yet, authorities differ on what fuzzy logic actually is, in the philosophical sense. It does, at any rate, attenuate the either/or dichotomy of Aristotelian logical analysis, opening the possibility for flexible new modes of reasoning.[47] Strict either/or logic seems not to reflect how the mind works but is a simplification consonant with the environmental and social circumstances that have so far prevailed. It is a testament to the power and longevity of the Mirror metaphor, which favors dichotomies, polarities, and other bipartite conceptual structures.

But until recently, the root metaphors that allow us to comprehend the world of our experience in terms most immediate to us—that is, in terms of our own embodied movements or actions and perceptions—have been the substratum of knowledge. In trading this mode of comprehension for nonexplicative prediction, we have precipitated a crisis.

> There [has been] a tendency away from the quest for a single "truth" toward a pluralistic acceptance of the possibility of many kinds and apprehensions of truths. Attention [has been] focused on process, on "becoming," rather than on origins, ends or changeless forms on events in a space-time continuum.[48]

In the words of Gaston Bachelard, "scientific reality . . . consists in a noumenal context suitable for defining axes of experimentation."[49] Science proceeds via a dialectic with "mathematics projecting a structure of entities to be looked for, experiment exhibiting these entities as found through phenomeno-technology. The dialectic then tunes the instrument to the mathematical theory and adjusts the mathematical theory to what can be exhibited successfully with the instrument."[50] This attitude bleeds over into philosophy and the humanities, where determinate meaning gives way to intertextuality, indefinite deferment, because the "search for truth, if there is no truth, has come to be hopeless."[51]

Under such an impetus, value systems tend to crumble. Relativism provides a kind of calculus of changing from one framework to another, but no framework has a privileged status. Change, again topological transformation, prevails. Belief withers because it is no longer anchored in the soil of immediate experience. Critics of contemporary culture bemoan this lack of values and the societal anomie in which it is expressed but usually with the implied caveat that the cure lies in returning to previous beliefs. On the level of their analysis, this undoubtedly makes sense. But, viewed from the deeper level of the metaphorical foundations of human thought, it can be seen to be impossible. The old metaphors simply will not accommodate the new *Weltanschauung*, which leaves metaphorization completely out of account. Out of the plethora of topological schemes that are coming to dominate the current intellectual scene, in time certain patterns will undoubtedly emerge. From those patterns, it will gradually become possible to reestablish a plexus of metaphors to weld the pieces back into a more or less whole worldview. Of course, this is an article of faith, but it is based on centuries of history that seem to support the belief that there is an underlying continuity to human nature. And human nature has everywhere and at all times required a metaphoric construction of reality. Meanwhile, we can but bear witness to the crumbling of the old metaphoric order under the onslaught of technological exploration and all that attends it.

Consider that the lever, telescope, and microscope, instruments that enlarged our domain of action and perception, were extensions of physical faculties of the human body. These and other apparatuses for manipulating the environment formed the arsenal of science, the basis for our understanding of the world, until the end of the nineteenth century. Data from the application of these apparatuses were translatable, for the most part, directly into terms of sensation and action. With the mathematicization of the sciences, especially after the invention of calculus in the eighteenth century, it became possible to isolate and symbolize generalized properties that could furthermore be subjected to manipulations only faintly relatable back to concrete action schemes. These manipulations, of course, were mathematical. And as already noted, these mathematical procedures have tended more and more to reflect pure relationships (e.g., congruity and symmetry) rather than actions (e.g., arithmetic operations and geometric bisection).

Category theory is a perfect case in point. Here we begin with *mathematical objects*, essentially any entities that can mathematically be represented, already a high-order abstraction. Within a family of such objects, definable by some common property, we take pairs. How each element of each pair is related to the other element—technically, how it can be mapped to it—is called a *morphism*. Finally, how these morphisms combine is called their *composition*. A *category* then is the whole system of the family of objects, the morphisms and their composition. The *objects* in question are usually something like groups or sets, which already comprise a good deal of abstract structure. So, to study the relations between categories is to study relations (of categories) involving relations (of compositions) of relations (of morphisms) of relations (of elements comprising something like groups or sets).[52] The practicality of this is that it makes it possible to determine structural similarities that might otherwise escape attention.

In an interesting way, this tendency for mathematics to turn around more abstract procedures and the establishment of relationships parallels the methods of cubism. In cubism, an object or the elements of a scene are broken apart according to relationships the painter finds significant and the parts are rearranged into a new visual order. Cubist painters, however, did not lose all semblance of perceptual reality. Their new visual order was always recognizable as a variant of the normal world. Not always so the new orders of the mathematicians, who carry the dissection much further to the point where the elements are mere microscopic chips of real-world data that can be rearranged at such a minute level that the resulting construction is no longer traceable to forms or processes recognizable from the world of direct experience. This is what makes modern mathematics at once so difficult and so undercutting of any metaphor-based understanding. It works beautifully but sometimes explains nothing.

Analysis turned upon life itself has also made the vitalistic metaphor, Breath as spirit, obsolescent. As the microscope extended observation to smaller and smaller life forms, the gray area was reached. There, at the level of viruses, the question whether or not these forms are living becomes ultimately unanswerable. The essential disjunctiveness of the category, *life*, comes into play. Viruses have some, but not all, of the defining characteristics of life. Sponsors of artificial life introduce similar problems in raising the issue of whether hypothetical robots might be said to be living or conscious. By stretching the notion of spirit, the underlying Breath metaphor grows increasingly inappropriate. With faith waning in the idea of spirit, the concomitant belief in the sanctity of life is called into question, and the ethical and social consequences are profound.

Unmooring understanding from the safe harbor of metaphor has had the final effect of exposing the worldview projected by science as fictitious. Previously scientists saw themselves as discovering the principles of a reality existing independent of themselves.

> The modern scientist saw this as too simple and too impersonal a view of knowledge. He presumed that the laws of nature did have an existence in themselves but that their character was more delicate, more elaborate and immensely more varied than anything that men were able to trace. Therefore the order that the scientist could find in nature was surely only one of many which might be found. And the particular order found by the scientist was thus in part created and imposed by his own imagination.[53]

The scientific worldview, thus, is *fictive* in the sense in which Hans Vaihinger used the term: unable to validate it in absolutely objective terms, we simply act *as if* it were true, as a matter of necessary expedience. The Newtonian picture of the universe was based on force; in the Einsteinian view, force is replaced by space-time geometry. Yet, to a close approximation, both yield the same results. Only near the speed of light and over astronomical distances do significant divergences appear. Relativity and quantum theory, the cornerstones of twentieth-century physics, differ fundamentally in the assumptions they make about the nature of putative objective reality. Forces in relativity are warps in space-time; in quantum theory, they have a dual nature as particulate and probabilistic fields. Events in relativity are causally linked; in quantum theory, they are probabilistic and causality is non-existent, and so forth.

> The laws of nature, as the twentieth century saw them, might thus be conceived in forms which philosophically are widely different and which may yet give almost the same predictions. The choice which a theoretical scientist may make among possible forms of law is therefore by no means inevitable. The particular order which he finds in nature is in some ways a projection of his mind.[54]

In this scenario, the order of the world, that elusive concept suggested in the ancient Greek image of the *kosmos*, is best interpreted, I suggest, as a manifestation of the way in which humans couple or interface with their experience. I use the term *experience* rather than *world* because experience is what we know most immediately, whereas the world is something we construe from experience. Furthermore, I will bypass the argument that experience itself is never *given* sui generis but is always interpreted, by opting for a concept of mind that is self-constructing. While I do not fully subscribe to his complete theory, Minsky[55] has suggested a practical mechanism by which such a thing is possible, though it is not a stated point of his position. He denies that there is a kind of central point at which the conscious field comes into focus. Instead, he postulates that the mind is comprised of many specialized faculties that interact and battle, so to speak, for central attention. Again, there need not be a localized arbiter that decides the winner. The winner may be determined in a Darwinian fashion by teaming with other faculties to reach some sort of threshold, for example. It would not require much stretch of the imagination to suppose, further, that this whole process follows a course determined by underlying chaotic functions. At any rate, the picture of the mind Minsky presents is one of independent agents struggling for supremacy, the metaphor being that of warfare. However, it is not clear just how any agent wins or how a given content enters awareness.

Operating under chaotic functions, the mind would be deterministic but unpredictable, paralleling the feeling (and, in a way, the reality) of free will. It would support free will as a viable fiction without creating a paradox under deterministic analysis. It would also go far toward explaining why the mind, or consciousness, is so difficult to define: if it is self-structuring, it appears to itself however it is at that time construed. It accommodates experientially whatever metaphoric or topological framework is imposed in the analysis; in this sense it is protean. The only caveat is that whatever metaphors or topological schemes are used to characterize the mind, they must be somewhat consonant with the larger system of metaphors and topological schemes underlying the worldview of the analyst.[56] Nothing of this resolves the problem of consciousness, but the metaphoric approach to intellectual history does suggest why the problem has not been solved: viz., there is so far nothing in experience recognized as sufficiently like consciousness to supply an implicit metaphor deployment that could offer the basis for a fully satisfactory definition of consciousness.

It might be felt that this viewpoint diminishes the creative potential of the human mind because it is deterministic. Such a feeling arises from a failure to appreciate the distinction between simple determinism of the Laplacean ilk and the new determinism based on the theory of chaos. If predictability is extracted from determinism, it meets the requirements of free will and spontaneity without stubbornly ignoring the biophysical substrate of mind. While chaotic determinism may not provide the last word on the mind and I doubt that there can be a last word—I believe that it is a step in the right direction.

Toward the Future

These issues have been taken up here not because I wish to indulge in idle speculation but because the mind is perhaps the ultimate frontier being challenged in the twentieth century. It seems appropriate therefore to show how this whole issue fits into the larger canvas of intellectual history that this book has explored. The difficulties of analyzing mind and consciousness have been discussed endlessly by philosophers, psychologists and those in the field of artificial intelligence. The only excuse for giving it attention here is with the hope that viewing it from the level of metaphor may bring a fresh perspective to the debate.

It is largely due to the confluence of quantum theory and psychology that historians and sociologists have come to the opinion that science is an imaginative enterprise, not removed from purely aesthetic considerations. Quantum theory teaches that observer and observed form a larger whole; and taking their cue from this, psychologists have come to realize that all observation is colored by the context in which it takes place. More broadly, Berger and Luckman argue that all actions and attitudes are constructed among individuals through negotiations.[57] Historians and sociologists of science then go on to show that scientific theories arise from a social matrix of protocols, economic interests, paradigm stabilities and shifts, ego dynamics, peer pressures, and so on. Whatever sense of order rides upon the froth of this cauldron is a byproduct, the road map by which people orient themselves at a particular time and place.

However, order is begot . . . I want to say out of disorder, but instead let us say out of proto-order, that which is neither order nor, therefore preceding it, disorder. And disorder is similarly begot by order, or one is the figure and the other, the ground, or however we may wish to construe it. In any case, there is more irregularity than regularity in all that we know as the world, but conceptually we choose to ignore it or explain it away as a perturbation of order. We may hazard a prophetic guess that the next intellectual era may have as its frontier the assimilation of proto-order to human orientation. This does not mean a new mysticism, nor, indeed, anything like what we already know. Most likely it means, discursively, ascending to a qualitatively different level of construction by means of complexing established schemata of actions to produce a second-order discourse, and metaphorically, recognizing entities in the new complex that can serve as bases in terms of which to construe other data. Paradoxical as it may sound, this means finding regularities in randomness and chaos.[58] If this is anywhere near being correct, it will mark the dawn of a new age, literally a new world, a newly construed reality.

Here and there are already signs of a coming revolution, one of the most suggestive being the discovery of the so-called chaotic functions.[59] These are mathematical abstractions that arise in the study of nonlinear dynamics. A simple example, at least from an intuitive standpoint, is a Henon-Heiles system, consisting of two degenerate harmonic oscillators the interaction of which is describable by cubic polynomials (i.e., polynomials containing variables with exponents no higher than 3). In the Henon-Heiles system, the degeneracy of the oscillators merely means that they both oscillate with the same frequency. We may visualize their interaction as being crudely analogous to acoustical feedback. Instead of producing *regular* waves, the Henon-Heiles system passes through catastrophes, critical points at which the behavior of the oscillations and of course the function describing them goes crazy, breaks away from any set pattern, and becomes random (even as represented in a suitable topological space). So far, no adequate explanation in mathematical terms has been given for such phenomena, and things get more chaotic as the systems become more complex.[60] Fractals also promise possible bridges between proto-order and order. I mention these examples because it would seem that mathematics is the perfect medium through which we might pass into a knowledge of proto-order.[61]

These prognostications may seem rash, so it would be well to offer some rationalization for them. I believe that there can be no question now that metaphors underpin human thought. Those which have proved fundamental over time are associated with irreducible universals of human experience. They operate to generate discursive thought through assimilated action schemes that represent those transformations which can occur in a humanly construed world. Further, this insight will inevitably flower. When this happens, humankind will inevitably bend its efforts toward transcending this recognized limitation and it will succeed. To pronounce any limitation as final is to be a fool in the brief moment of human history that finds us still in the first day of conception wherein our beginnings surely know nothing of our ends.

Glossary of
Metaphors and Schemes

Following is an alphabetical glossary of the chief metaphors and schemata referred to in this work and a few that are not separately discussed but that turned up in the original research on which this work is based. Some of this material will repeat what is in the main text, but there is additional information, as well. Entries serve to consolidate the pertinent details of the metaphors and schemata for quick review.

Each entry is described in terms of determinative characteristics, historical placement, and deployment. *Determinative characteristics* refers to the differentiae by which the metaphor or schema has been deployed; and they give an idea of the inner logic implicit in deployment. Historical placement, where relevant, designates whether the metaphor or schema is *primitive*, meaning that it was early established and retained a stable deployment to the present, or it has been subject to revisions in deployment. *Deployment* covers the concepts that have been based on the metaphor or schema and, in a more general sense, also takes into account particular versions of these concepts. In the entries, the deployments appear in small caps.

Other items noted in the glossary include associated metaphors and schemata, etymological affiliations, and connections with the topology of discursive thought. *Associated metaphors* include schemata and are those with which the main metaphor or schema often operates in deployment. Thus, the Word/Speech metaphor operates with the Parent to yield the concept of disease as a curse, the parent figure being the cursing god and the word, the vehicle for the curse. *Etymological affiliations* comprise word roots that demonstrate the incorporation of the metaphor or schema into language and, thereby, articulated thought. Often we are unaware of these affiliations, but they are still important in shaping thought because figures of speech, frequently of early origin, were built around root meanings and continue to carry those meanings into everyday discourse. The presence of such affiliations indicates the role of a metaphor or schema in the historical origins of an idea, though there is no guarantee that this original affiliation remains operative through meaning shifts. The presence of a certain metaphor must be attested to by evidences of current practice over and above etymological roots. *Connections with the topology of discursive thought* indicate how the metaphor squares with the fictive spatial transformations underlying reasoning, and this is often through etymological affiliations.

Abbreviations

Assoc.:   Associated metaphor(s) and schema(ta)
Etym.:   Etymological affiliations
Prim.:   Primitive (not subject to periodic revision)
Top.:   Connections with the topology of discursive thought

Glossary

BIND: The leading characteristic of this act is to bring one thing permanently in proximity with another and to fix the relationship with a knotted cord. There are two notions
here: proximity and tying together.
Deployments:
CAUSALITY, as formulated by Hume, as a "necessary connection" between events, was
abstracted from a more archaic concept of POWER as efficient cause in bringing a second
event out of a first. This idea of POWER was derived from a confluence of the Parent as doer
and Breath as spirit or active agent.
RELIGION is a binding of man to god (re- + *ligare*, to bind). In ethics, duty or, more
precisely, OBLIGATION is an implicit Debt or Contract that binds one to do something (ob- +
ligare).
Assoc.: Parent, Strength/Ability (POWER), Breath.
Top.: In topological transformations, Binding is often associated with joining together
in the sense of making the juncture permanent. Key words designating this are: tie, connection, bond, alliance, agreement, contract, link, chain, bridge, relation(ship), etc. Cf. Cut/
Join.
Etym.: From Latin *ligare*, we have, ligament, ligature, lien, league, obligation, religion,
alliance, reliance, and delegate. From Latin *nectere*, nexus, connection, annex, and ultimately
knot (French, *noeud*). Thus, by negation, untying the knot is solving the problem, wherein the
knot binds the solution within itself. Secondarily, FREEDOM has been conceived as negation
or absence of bonds. In mythology, this was represented by the Gordian knot; in the *Upanishads*
by the knot of the heart, the undoing of which releases one from the round of reincarnation;
and in the knotted rope tying earth to heaven in Chinese as well as American Indian belief.
Worldwide, in folklore, a problem is depicted as a knot, as is marriage.

BREATH: Characteristics: A refined substance, felt but not seen, residing in another
material body, imbuing it with special qualities—life, in the case of organisms, essence, in
the case of inanimate objects. Originally it was perceived that death occurs as the breath
leaves the body; so, it was personified as life-giving agency. Because life was the most valued
quality of humankind, in generalizing the life-giving agency, people made it the indwelling
agency defining that which an object most is (i.e., the differentiae most important to humans). Deployment of this metaphor demands, then, a definition of the most salient differentiae of a genus, which is then reified into an agent.
Deployments:
SPIRIT
ESSENCE (indwelling agency [= spirit = breath] that makes a thing what it is)
ENTELECHY (indwelling agency [= spirit = breath] that makes a thing become what it
should be)
FINAL CAUSE (what a thing shall become, teleologically determining it)

CHANGE (conceived as with final cause)
DISEASE (an indwelling evil spirit; later, the disease entity [:Commodity])
POWER (indwelling agent causing something to happen)
ENERGY (refinement of power, more depersonalized)
ETHER (the refined substance filling space; the medium of light transmission)
WELTGEIST (Hegel)
ZEITGEIST
VITALISM
ÉLAN VITAL (Bergson)

Etym.: From Latin *spirare*, expire, inspire, and transpire. From Greek, *psyche*, all the psycho- compounds. From Latin, *animus*, soul or mind, with hypothetical verbal root meaning *to breathe*: animate, animal, animosity, equanimity, magnanimity, pusillanimity, and unanimity. In mythology the symbolism of the *breath of life*, as depicted in the Biblical account of the creation of Adam in Genesis, is universal. Yin and yang are sometimes interpreted as inspiration and expiration, and in Han dynasty Taoism the creation was associated with nine breaths from which the world coalesced.

Assoc.: Parent (often depersonalized in some aspect into an abstract agent), Fire (reduced to the agent of life), and First Position (personified as agent: principle and element).

COMMODITY: Characteristics: Something that can be bought through money, effort, or some other medium of exchange, and saved up and stored. In deployment, the questions raised have to do with how the commodity-construed thing can be obtained, kept, and maintained.

Deployment:
TIME ("save time")
FREEDOM ("win your freedom")
LOVE ("give him her love")
POWER ("you have to have power to do that")
ENERGY ("carbohydrates give you energy")
DISEASE (the "disease entity" that one can 'get')

There is a mode of thought in which some quality or action (often an emotion) is reified and then treated as if it had the properties of a commodity. Expressions like *win respect, gain gratitude,* and *earn scorn* exemplify this mode of thought. A notable instance of commodity construction is Freud's concept of the libido as psychic energy that can be conserved, channeled, and so forth. It echoes certain primitive beliefs in a life energy that can be stored up, as in the Tantric practice of orgasmless sex, or cannibalism, in which the vital force of another person is assimilated by ingestion.

Assoc.: It is often difficult to distinguish Commodity concepts from Breath ones in which something is personified, then depersonalized into an agent. Whether or not it is a Commodity concept depends upon whether or not it can be purchased and stored up.

CONTAINER: Characteristics: It is a partially or completely closed configuration the boundaries of which hold that which is within them apart from the exterior space. Most problems generated from this metaphor revolve around the relation of interior to exterior across the interface of the boundary.

Deployments:
MIND ("What do you have *in* mind?")
MEMORY ("Her memory is full of pictures of the past")

DEDUCTION (relating classes within or not within other classes)

INFINITY (by negation of boundaries)

SIN (defined by boundaries transgressed)

GOOD/EVIL (defined as lying "within" or "outside" moral boundaries)

FREEDOM (as absence of certain restrictions)

Assoc.: Floor/Ground construed as foundation of Container, and Form attributed to the Container concept, as in topographies of the mind.

Top.: The inside-outside relationship is obviously topological and is invoked whenever we use prepositions like *in, inside, within*, etc. Setting up a fictive interface between interior and exterior spatializes our thinking in a well defined way which then tailors the course of reasoning.

Etym.: Many words hide their inside-outside topology in prefixes such as: em-, en-, in-, im-, il-, ir-, for *in*, and ab-, ap-, apo-, de-, dis-, e-, ec-, ex-, and out- for *out*. Then we have ento-, eso-, indi-, int-, intro-, intra-, for *within*, and ecto-, ep-, epi-, ex-, exo-, exter- and extra- for *outside*. Quite evidently our vocabulary is replete with this topological reference.

CONTRACT: Characteristics: A written or verbal agreement, or tacit understanding, between two parties stipulating that the first party shall perform certain actions for the second party. Deployment involves determining how the contract was established, the motives it serves, its terms, its form, and the redress for breaking it.

Deployments:

LAW (implicit public agreement to obey contract of the law)

DUTY (that which one agrees to do by implicit contract)

SOCIAL CONTRACT (Rousseau)

SOCIETY (a network of implicit contracts)

SIN (breaking the consensual contract of moral law)

Assoc.: Debt/Payment and Lot/Share, in deployment of both of which a contract may be implied. A sin, construed as incurring a debt to God, assumes a covenant between man and God. More loosely, contract concepts may involve a binding or bond that can be Cut to negate it.

Top.: As noted above, thinking in terms of Contract may entail conjuring connections, which may be imagined liable to being Cut and Separated. For instance, many theologians have argued that man separates himself from his God when he breaks the holy covenants.

CUT/JOIN: Characteristics: Prim. To separate into parts as by a sharp knife, or to bring together that which is separated.

Deployments:

CONSCIOUSNESS (etymologically, a separating out)

KNOWLEDGE (early on, conceived as an analysis into parts)

SIN (a cutting off of a man from his God by breaking a covenant)

REASONING (etymologically, a cutting apart and comparing of parts)

SYMBOL (etymologically, that which joins [mental image and reality])

LANGUAGE (a system of symbols conceived as joining [mental image and reality])

Knowledge gained through reasoning implies analysis, which etymologically is a dissolving, hence breaking down into parts, whence *rationalize*, from Latin *ratio*, meaning *to compare*. Conversely, for Plato, the highest form of knowledge was synoptic, seeing how everything—all the parts—fits together into a whole, at which point the universal Pattern emerges. This is also formulated as the Many of appearance coming together in the absolute One.

Most systems of knowledge, whether religious, mystical, scientific, or philosophical, follow one of these two paradigms. It is significant in this respect that consciousness, reasoning, knowing, symbolizing, and using language all have the same underlying metaphor, for that makes them prone to be discussed together and the terms of the discourse are seductively compatible.

Assoc.: Pattern may be construed as arising from cutting into parts such that the parts articulate a structure. To the Greeks, as well as many Eastern cultures, the highest form of knowledge, INTUITION, is a seeing of the whole from the parts.

Etym.: The idea of joining has been widely used to intensify the meaning of a root word by tacking on a *with* prefix such as co-, com- or con-. In the vernacular, not to *know* what is going on is not to be *with* it.

Top.: Separating items for analysis and bringing them together for completion or comparison are common operations of thought, verbally indicated by *with* and synonymous expressions.

DEBT/PAYMENT: Characteristics: Prim. (See Etym.) A debt is something owed to someone to fulfill an agreement, a contract, an exchange, or a retribution; and satisfaction of the debt is payment. Usually both sides of the debt/payment transaction are considered in deployment. It is necessary to prescribe why the debt/payment concept is owed, to whom or to what, and what the consequences are of not paying.

Assoc.: Contract (by which a debt may be incurred) and Lot/Share (which may also entail a debt).

Etym.: Words denoting duty, obligation, and necessity, such as *should* and *ought* have root meanings of debt in both Germanic and Romance languages. These are archaic expressions.

FIRE: Characteristics: Heat and light, identified with the sun as a source of life. Worship of the sun established the divine character of fire.

Because of the identification with the sun god, fire assumed rich symbolic value, differing from place to place and time to time, but divinity usually played a role in the symbolism.

Deployments:

LIFE FORCE (from warmth of living being vs. coldness of corpse)

DIVINITY (halos, the Burning Bush, stars, sun)

KNOWLEDGE/ENLIGHTENMENT (source of light to dispel darkness, enabling one to see)

FIRST POSITION: Characteristics: First in order and therefore having earliest claims. In deployment, it is frequently necessary to establish the primacy of one thing over another, especially in a historical or evolutionary sequence (including causal arguments). Possibly one of the earliest examples of this is the privileged status of the firstborn.

Deployments:

ELEMENT (primary constituents of matter)

PRINCIPLE (first rule by which a thing operates)

VALUE (often stated in terms of primacy—e.g., A-1, topnotch)

Systematic thought in any discipline requires that the elements of discourse be ordered, usually involving either serial or hierarchical disposition. In either case, the first or top and last or bottom positions have special significance. Value or importance moves from first to last, top to bottom, probably reflecting that the sense organs are mainly located in the head and the hands and arms at the upper pat of the body, making it natural to work from the top down. Linearly, of course, the beginning point of any procedure also has ipso facto a privileged status.

Assoc.: Parent (as in the primary status of a Parental agent), and One/Many (first in series more important than those which follow). The symbolic value of First Position is established in all competitions.

Etym.: Many prefixes denoting *first* or *before* carry connotations of primacy in importance to the root to which they may be affixed: pre-, praeter-, pro-, proto-, prin-, ante-, arch-, and fore-. Additionally, the highest value is often designated by such expressions as *first class, top dog, firstest with the mostest,* etc.

Top.: First in sequence has a primacy of value or significance even in a topological construction; importance may be graded by spatial or temporal order.

FLOOR/GROUND: Characteristics: That upon which everything else rests. It shares certain similarities with First Position, in that it denotes a primacy in holding things in place. We appeal to the Floor/Ground or substratum to establish a point of departure in explanation. And we attribute special meaning to this starting point. Witness the importance attributed to origins.

Deployments:

BEING (that of which something may be predicated; the ground of qualities)

SUBSTANCE (that which stands under—i.e., supports—qualities)

ELEMENTS (chemical)

ELEMENTARY PARTICLES

QUARKS

Notice that these major concepts, moving from the most general (Being) to the most particular (Quarks), all have to do with the ultimate ontological status of things. Deployment of this metaphor reflects concern with tracing things to their origin or that which supports them: *base, basis, foundation, ground, substratum, fundament.*

Assoc.: First Position and Container (in efforts to get to the *bottom* of a Container concept). In this sense, *basic* is more or less synonymous with *primary, foundation* with *first principle.*

Top.: As noted above, the bottom or base of a construction is assigned special value, as when we want to get to the *bottom* of something.

FORM: Characteristics: We take the form of something to mean essentially the visual outline, or the configuration of the boundary. Thus it is synonymous with *shape.* The metaphoric problem is to define its parameters.

Deployments:

PLATONIC IDEALS

FINAL CAUSE (Aristotelian notion that future form is a cause)

EVIL (conceived as that which is misshapen—e.g. *crooked*)

PERFECTION (derivative from Platonic ideals)

In mythology, evil is often represented by a miscreant. The devil is known to have abnormalities in various of his body parts, and in any case to have a monstrous aspect. In folk legends, "he has expressed his bitter resentment at the ugly form given him in Christian iconography." Rudwin wonders "why the Devil was always represented in so repugnant a form." But the answer is clear enough: evil is the opposite of good, and since good is founded on the metaphor of Form deployed as perfect, evil, being the opposite, must be conceived through Form as imperfect. This is not an iconographic peculiarity of Christianity but is worldwide. Thus:

The fact is that the form given the Devil in Christian iconography has an historical foundation. It has been derived from the fabled gods of antiquity. The medieval monster is an amalgamation of all the heathen divinities, from whom he derived, especially of those gods or demons which, already in pagan days, were inimical to the benevolently ruling deities.[1]

So numerous and well known are the examples of evil characters depicted with ugly or terrifying aspect in myth, folklore and literature, not to mention the visual arts, that it hardly seems necessary to catalog them.

Assoc.: Mirror Image (in Platonic ideals).

Top.: Rudolf Arnheim[2] has suggested from experiments that he has conducted that most people associate a concrete image with abstract ideas. It is tempting to suggest that at least sometimes these images become surrogate forms that are topologically manipulated in discursive thought.

HOT/COLD: Immediate sensations that need no characterization. They play mainly symbolic roles, and have primitive deployment solely in delineating life and death. In association with Fire, they played a role in conceptualizing a life force.

Active in ancient speculation about life, where heat, for example, was thought essential to conception, the metaphor has become largely rhetorical, especially in delineating emotions and personality. Whether or not it should be considered basic seems a moot question.

LIGHT/DARK: Characteristics: Used metaphorically, light and dark carry emotional connotations harking back to the primitive state wherein darkness hid the enemies of man and light dispelled that threat.

Deployments:

DIVINITY (earliest in association with the worship of the sun)

KNOWLEDGE (light enables us to *see*)

SIN (darkness hides what should not be seen)

EVIL (as above, harking to the notion that evildoers work by night)

Assoc.: Fire and Sight, Form and Pattern, all working usually with Light.

Etym.: Many words relating to knowledge directly or indirectly invoke Light: *enlightenment, illumination, throw light upon, to see* (meaning to understand), etc.

LOT/SHARE: Characteristics: That which befalls one as a result of drawing a lot, divine intervention, destiny, heritage, effort, agreement, etc.

Deployments:

DISEASE

FATE

RIGHT (legal)

Fate and disease, calamities and fortunes, are often construed as one's lot as determined by birth, prior actions, or divine providence. Used for both social catastrophe and triumph, this metaphor has always been common to historiography. It is apt to be invoked, too, whenever the Pattern metaphor is used to explain broad issues, for every outstanding event must be made to accord with the overall *plan* of things.

Etym.: Through such expressions as *one's lot, share, fate, destiny, luck, cross to bear*, etc., the metaphor is planted firmly in common thought. Rather gratuitous, it explains little but brings a certain resolution to issues by resting them on the firm foundation of a consensual metaphor complex (i.e., Lot/Share coupled with Pattern in its deployment as divine plan).

Fate itself comes from Latin *fari*, to speak, designating that which is spoken or decreed by the gods. A decreed destiny likewise may depend on secular authority.

MECHANISM: Characteristics: A system of parts that interact to perform a certain function. Each part is clearly discernible and in principle the interaction of the parts can fully be elucidated. Deployed to cover functional entities that are believed to be explainable to the last detail.

Deployments:

BEAUTY (Greek notion of beauty as just proportion and function of parts)

PREDETERMINISM (universe as machine)

REDUCTIONISM

Since the Renaissance, this has been in Western civilization the metaphor most favored for the analysis of any situation or problem. Causality, under the Mechanism metaphor, must be traceable through successive configurations in which every displacement of elements is not only continuous but forced to occur because of the way all elements are mechanically fit together into an integral machine. An analysis is complete and satisfactory to the extent that it can set out all elements and displacements in this manner.

Hand-eye coordination is the cybernetic pivot of human action, making the Mechanism metaphor the natural successor to the Pattern metaphor, which in its turn fit well into the primitive picture of the world as controlled by divinities. God as *maker* was the perfect mythical image to facilitate an easy transfer from Pattern to Mechanism in cosmological explanation, whence it was an easy passage to more narrow issues.

Top.: In much discursive reasoning, the elements of the subject are arranged into a functional entity. Each link of the argument ideally depends upon the preceding one and determines the following one. This may be seen statically as Pattern or dynamically as Mechanism.

MIRROR IMAGE: Characteristics: Given an entity, a second entity is a mirror image of the first if it is isomorphic, that is, sufficiently similar in structure so that it would pass as a likeness. Early experience with reflected images must certainly have had a profound effect on man. Primitive people still attribute magical potency to effigies and other likenesses.

In deployment, the Mirror Image has had a deep and lasting influence on human thought both Eastern and Western. Most particularly it has engendered the ubiquitous mode of thinking in terms of *correspondence*, which is a generalization from isomorphism. Correspondence became ingrained in human thought in the matching phase predating counting in the evolution of number systems; and possibly even earlier.

Deployments:

IDEAL FORM (Platonic inversion wherein the real reflects the ideal)

THOUGHT (mental images reflect real objects)

PERCEPTION (formation of mental likeness to an objective correlate)

KNOWLEDGE (intellectual schemes isomorphic to aspects of reality)

TRUTH (correspondence theory of truth)

We could also mention principles of astrology, numerology, and other superstitious forms of divination that seek correspondences between select data and future events. As a mode of thought, correspondence is at the heart of most explanation: statements that mirror actual states of affairs, equations that mirror empirical measurements of phenomena, myths that present personified schemes of causation, etc.

Assoc.: Sight, Light/Dark, Form, Mechanism, Pattern, Organism, Bind (causality as connection), One/Many (KNOWLEDGE as a perception of how parts form a whole corresponding to an actual state of affairs).

Top.: Congruence is a major rational test for identity, similarity, explanatory relationship, and other conditions determined by isomorphism.

Etym.: *Like* and *as*, particles of speech that introduce comparisons, are at the very foundations of metaphoric thought. Consequently, the Mirror Image is implicit and ubiquitous in rational discourse.

MOTION/REST: Characteristics: Prim. Displacement, or lack of it, relative to any chosen fixed point, axis, or plane. This is a basic of perception.

Deployments:

TIME (spatialized as a moving along a time line)

CHANGE (spatial displacement or motion along a rectilinear or circular time line)

FREEDOM (defined in terms of unrestricted ability to act [move])

REASONING (conceived as a moving from thought to thought)

All processes are usually pictured as occurring along a time line, so that narration, life, history, and argumentation are delineated in terms of motion or rest.

Top.: As pointed out, all reason operates by topological manipulation of mental elements, which incorporates various kinds of motion.

Etym.: As per the above, nearly all generic verbs of motion are employed in the scheme of reasoning. The more general the verb, the more widely it is applied, whereas verbs of more qualified motions (e.g., creep, gyrate, waddle) have less application, less implication for rational thought. This is because thought is largely the internalization of topological transformations, which have little to do with the manner in which state 1 passes into state 2 except in the sense of the minimal motion necessary for the transformation.

ONE/MANY: Characteristics: Conditioned by the primitive attachment to initial mental images, most early thought has change as a moving away from an initial state. Perfection is attributed to the initial state, the true nature of a thing, which becomes identified with wholeness. Aging is perceived as a kind of falling apart. Thus, time fragments the One, the perfect whole, into the Many. The thought is stated in numerous ancient sources from the Upanishads onward. Creation myths often relate how the universe was formed from various parts of the Creator. In deployment, there is a two-way relation between the One as perfect to the imperfect Many in the sense that explanation may move either from the One to the Many or vice versa; in the latter case it is a *moving back* to perfection.

Deployments:

PERFECTION/IMPERFECTION (the whole versus the broken)

KNOWLEDGE (seeing how the parts fit together to form the whole, noesis)

SOPHIA or WISDOM (conceived by the Greeks as intuiting wholes)

CHANGE (Plotinus: degradation of the divine One into the Many)

DIALECTIC (thesis and antithesis form a higher whole, synthesis)

Assoc.: Form, Pattern, Mechanism, Organism, Cut/Join.

Top.: Reason often proceeds by breaking a subject into parts, the root meaning of *analysis*. The parts can then be topologically manipulated. Also note the importance in most areas of thought given to *unification*. Such a concept of knowledge has dominated religion, philosophy, science, and just about every other discipline.

ORGANISM: Characteristics: A system of parts interacting to perform certain functions. It differs from a Mechanism in that not all the parts are clearly discernible, nor is their exact mode of interaction fully explicable. Moreover, there is the assumption either that the whole is greater than the sum of its parts, or that the system is imbued with a vital principle usually invisible except through its consequences, which are to lend the system properties not duplicated in any known Mechanism. In deployment, explanation is always incomplete, obviously, since the Organism cannot be fully explained and is possessed of a vital principle or its equivalent that transcends human reason.

Deployments:

LIFE

SOCIETY

HISTORY (the unfolding of a *Weltgeist* or its equivalent)

BEING (conceived in various philosophies as unknowable)

ÉLAN VITAL (Bergson)

VITALISM

The metaphor has been applied to everything from works of art to jokes, literally anything for which it is believed that no satisfactory rational explanation can be given.

Assoc.: Breath and One/Many.

Etym.: *Spiritual, vital,* and the more current *holistic* are terms often conjured when dealing with subjects predicated on Organism.

PARENT: Characteristics: Assuming the familial structure as a defining basis, the parent is the figure of unquestioned authority. Later doubting of the parent (in the natural life sequence) is construed in deployment as reprehensible. From infantile roots, there is a side of the Parent not fathomable, that side whose motives the child cannot understand. The Parent is the doer, the creator, the disciplinarian, the teacher, in short, all roles in one. In deployment, the Parent can be narrowed to any one of the original roles, and can be depersonalized to varying degrees.

Deployments:

GOD

CAUSALITY (depersonalized doer)

FATE (that which dictates the course of our lives)

LAW (Parent formulated into behavioral strictures, also law as court)

NATURE (Mother Nature)

Assoc.: First Position, Strength/Ability, and One/Many (in form of parent and children).

PATTERN: Characteristics: Elements perceived in interrelationship such as to form a configuration the overall structure or shape of which forms a complete mental image. In deployment, there is usually a quest to discern the laws, or regularities, which are construed to determine the way the pattern forms. This metaphor largely answers to the explicit need for order, and so is one of the most widely deployed.

Deployments:

DIVINE PLAN

CUSTOM (conceived as a system of rituals, behaviors, etc.)
LAW (a system of rules analogous to the DIVINE PLAN)
BEAUTY (symmetrical form or form as it should be)
GOOD/EVIL (behavior conforming to or acting against the DIVINE PLAN, etc.)
GREAT CHAIN OF BEING (and other hierarchical orders)
DUTY (assigned by DIVINE PLAN, CUSTOM, or LAW)
VALUE (again relative to DIVINE PLAN, etc.)
FATE (conceived as an inscrutable plan)
HISTORY (as having a design)
NATURE (believed to be *orderly*)
PROPHECY (seeing the DIVINE PLAN for something)
Assoc.: Form.
Top.: See Mechanism.

POINT/SHOW: Characteristics: Rudimentary actions historically predating language, intended to call attention to that which is indicated. In deployment, the metaphoric basis is ignored, and there is always the question of how the metaphorized subject singles out the related data.
Deployments:
SIGN
SYMBOL
LANGUAGE
AUGURY (reading *signs* of future events)
SIN (as displaying *signs* of a person's fall from grace)
Assoc.: Bind.
Top.: Akin to vector concept, incorporating direction into magnitude. In discursive reasoning, one thing may *lead to* another, or other verbal and nonverbal modes may introduce *direction* into an argument such as to move from point A to point B.
Etym.: All expressions denoting motion *toward*: *lead to, advance* or *move toward, turn from* A *to* B, etc.

RIGHT/LEFT: Characteristics: Most people are right-handed, so they form the *in* group, whereas left-handers comprise the *out* group in any society. Left-handedness therefore becomes suspect and is identified with negative values. Like Light/Dark, Right/Left forms a polarity for valuative conceptualization.
Deployments:
GOOD/EVIL (see Etym.)
RIGHT/WRONG
Assoc.: Light/Dark.
Etym.: *Sinister* derives from the Latin word for *left*. The word, *right*, also denotes *straight*. The *right* (proper or correct) path is the straight path. A good person is *upright*. An inappropriate compliment is *left-handed*. A dishonest person is *crooked* (not straight). "Not right in the head" labels the insane. Examples could be multiplied.

SIGHT: Characteristics: Humans are predominantly visual in orientation, so that Sight is the clearest mode of perception. This is literally true inasmuch as the visual field of the eye has the largest number of sensory cells per area of all the senses. Resolution is the finest. In deployment, various modes of mentation are metaphorized as *sights*.

Deployments:

PERCEPTION ("I see this is lighter than that")

KNOWLEDGE ("I see well enough that Einstein was a genius")

PROPHECY ("He foresees disaster")

PRUDENCE (etymologically from *providere*, to foresee)

Assoc.: Light/Dark, Form, and Pattern.

Etym.: The use of visual terminology to describe various aspects or forms of mentation is too vast to catalog here. I list only a few suggestive examples: *intuit* (etym. *to look into*), *foresee*, *scrutinize*, *illuminate* (so that it may be seen), *spotlight*, *highlight*, *cast an eye on*, etc.

STRENGTH/ABILITY: Characteristics: Behind both concepts is the capacity to perform certain acts. This capacity is abstracted and reified, in myths personified, then subsequently depersonalized into properties, agencies, and the like. With this origin through reification, the metaphorized concepts tend to be problematic in being in themselves not explanatory and yet so primitive in origin that they are irreducible to more elemental terms.

Deployments:

CAUSALITY (as the capacity one thing to cause another)

CHANGE or BECOMING (conceived as something making itself)

ENERGY

FORCE

POWER

WORK (physics)

VALUE (cognate with Latin *valor*, strength or ability to do a certain thing)

Assoc.: Breath (often the agency of ability is a spirit or essence).

Top.: Often a *force* (in various guises) is employed as a ghost to move something from place to place in real or fictive space.

TAKE/REJECT: Characteristics: Primitively, to grasp and draw toward one or cast away from one. Generically the idea becomes one of acquiring as one's own or ridding oneself of.

Deployments:

PERCEPTION (as taking sense data in)

KNOWLEDGE (assimilation of information)

Etym.: Merely the usage of *take* exemplifies the diversity of deployment here. "I take it you disagree." "He's taking it very hard." "Take it easy." "They can't take it much longer." "What took you to do that?" And in the negative: "She threw away her last chance." "He cast me aside." "You cast a glance at it." "We all suffer rejection."

TASTE/SMELL: Characteristics: These are proximal senses that bring the thing sensed into the personal space of the perceiver. Thus they connote a special immediacy and subjectivity almost opposite to that connoted by the distal sense of Sight. Deployment is for concepts that are less articulated than those based on Sight, more intuitive as opposed to analytical or rational.

Deployments:

ESSENCE (as flavor)

RASA (Indian equivalent of ESSENCE, root meaning also *flavor*)

In a more connotative sense, the metaphor is used to describe poles of bipolar evaluations, such as GOOD/EVIL, BEAUTY/UGLINESS and on to vaguer and more poetic deployments as noble/ignoble.

Etym.: Expressions denoting good or bad smells or tastes are universally used to express positive versus negative evaluations.

WORD/SPEECH: Characteristics: Harking back to the stage of nominal realism in which word and referent formed aspects of a single whole, speech or words retain a magical efficacy, as even now in the curse.

Deployments:

DISEASE (as result of a curse)

FATE (as the fiat of god[s])

Notes

INTRODUCTION.

1. George Lakoff and Mark Johnson, *Metaphors We Live By* (Chicago: University of Chicago Press, 1980).

2. Mark Johnson, *The Body in the Mind: The Bodily Basis of Meaning, Imagination, and Reason* (Chicago: University of Chicago Press, 1987), xiii. Original italicized.

3. Ibid., 102. Original italicized.

4. In certain cases, such as my use of Container and Pattern as metaphors, my classification differs from that of Lakoff and Johnson. What they call an image scheme, I may call a metaphor. In the grey area where the two notions meet, it may be a matter of what each of us wishes to emphasize, whether we use the one or the other classification. At this point in metaphor research, it seems to me that we lack breadth of understanding to resolve these issues with finality. How, for example, we decide the degree to which a metaphor is fundamental or not strictly conceptual is a matter of tentative opinion. These differences of opinion should spark further necessary deliberation. It is in that spirit that I contend certain issues.

5. Lakoff and Johnson, *Metaphors We Live By*, 23.

6. J. C. Day and F. S. Belleza, "The Relation between Visual Image Mediators and Recall," *Mem. Cognition* 11 (May 1983): 256–57.

7. For further discussion, see Stephen M. Kosslyn and Amy L. Sussman, "Roles of Imagery in Perception: Or, There Is No Such Thing as Immaculate Perception," in *The Cognitive Neurosciences*, ed. Michael S. Gazzaniga (Cambridge: MIT Press, 1995), 1035–42.

8. John L. Casti, *Alternate Realities: Mathematical Models of Nature and Man* (New York: John Wiley & Sons, 1989), chap. 2.

9. Thomas Kuhn, *The Structure of Scientific Revolutions*, 2d ed. (Berkeley and Los Angeles: University of California Press, 1970).

10. The complexity of human conceptualization, I am convinced, is predicated on a relatively simple substructure. Although there are many actions in which we may participate, for example, the underlying topology is rather finite (see chap. 3, n. 28). Likewise, many things may be employed as source domains in metaphorization, but they will be interrelated through a simple system of classification. This is because we choose our

source domains generally because they are *primitives*, that is, components of fundamental experience. Primitives fall within a narrow range of experiences. Lexicographically such a narrow range makes it possible to establish semantic systems for compiling thesauruses.

When we see words of action listed in a thesaurus, we realize that they are as finite as humanly meaningful spatial orientations and topological transformations. They are, after all, spun out of the same geometries and topologies. Similarly, all the *things* that likely would serve as source domains hearken back to fundamental experiences and are similarly limited.

To be sure, through discovery and invention, new things are being introduced into our lives continually and any of them might serve as source domains. By and large, however, all these new things, in terms of their properties, are extensions of the known. They ultimately run back to primitives.

My point is not that all explanatory metaphors define a universal and static code, but that there is an underlying code that is relatively stable and that it is always the point of departure in conceptual innovation. What would it look like, if we could define it? I think it would have two components, one superimposed upon the other. The first component would be a skeleton of topological schemes. Over this would fit a cluster of central experiential primitives that give value and emotive character to our ideas. Such, at any rate, is my hypothesis in a perhaps overly simplified form.

11. Gershom Weiler, *Mauthner's Critique of Language* (Cambridge: Cambridge University Press, 1970), 162.

12. Ibid., 151.

13. Bruno Snell, *The Discovery of the Mind: The Greek Origins of European Thought* (Cambridge: Harvard University Press, 1953).

14. See for example: Stephen C. Pepper, *World Hypotheses: A Study in Evidence* (Berkeley and Los Angeles: University of California Press, 1942); Mary B. Hesse, *Models and Analogies in Science* (Notre Dame, Ind.: Notre Dame University Press, 1966); idem, *Forces and Fields* (Westport, Conn.: Greenwood Press, 1962).

15. See René Wellek and Robert Penn Warren, *Theory of Literature*, 3d ed. (New York: Harcourt, Brace & World, 1962), 186–211, for detailed discussion and bibliography; J. P. van Noppen, S. de Knop, and R. Jongen, eds. *Metaphor: A Bibliography of Post-1970 Publications*. (Amsterdam and Philadelphia: John Benjamins, 1985).

16. Useful bibliographies are Warren A. Shibles, *Metaphor: An Annotated Bibliography and History* (Whitewater, Wisc.: Language Press, 1971); Noppen, de Knop, and Jongen, *Metaphor*.

17. Mark Johnson, "Metaphor in the Philosophical Tradition," in *Philosophical Perspectives on Metaphor*, ed. Mark Johnson (Minneapolis: University of Minnesota Press, 1981), 3–47.

18. Pepper had as his goal to account for all-encompassing philosophies of the universe, which he called world hypotheses. To this end, he employed what he called the "root metaphor method," which he described thus: "The method in principle seems to be this: A man desiring to understand the world looks about for a clue to its comprehension. He pitches upon some area of common-sense fact and tries if he cannot understand other areas in terms of this one. This original area becomes then his basic analogy or root metaphor. He describes as best he can the characteristics of this area, or, if you will, discriminates its structure. A list of its structural characteristics becomes his basic concepts of explanation and description. We call them a set of categories. In terms of these categories he proceeds to study all other areas of fact. . . ." (*World Hypotheses*, 91).

My methodology, though paralleling his, was not consciously derived from him, but I certainly must have unconsciously absorbed much from having read his book.

CHAPTER 1. THE NATURE OF METAPHOR

1. *De oratore* 3.38.155–60.

2. *Poetics,* chap. 22.

3. *Rhetoric* 3.1410b.

4. Ogden, C. K., and I. A. Richards, *Bentham's Theory of Fictions* (Totowa, N.J.: Littlefield, Adams, 1959).

5. Samuel Taylor Coleridge, *Literaria Biographica,* in *Selected Poetry and Prose,* ed. Donald Stauffer (New York: Random House, 1951), 269.

6. Rudolf von Allers, "Vom Nutzen und den Gefahren de Metapher in der Psychologie," *Jahrbuch für Psychologie und Psychtherapie* 3 (1955): 3–15. See also C. C. Anderson, "The Latest Metaphor in Psychology," *Dalhousie Review* 38 (summer 1958):176–87.

7. Frederick Nietzsche, "On Truth and Falsity in their Ultramoral Sense," in *The Complete Works of Frederick Nietzsche,* ed. Oscar Levy, trans. Maximilian A. Magge (New York: Gordon Press, 1974), 180. Original italics.

8. Ernst Cassirer, *Philosophie der Symbolischen Formen,* Buch 3: *Phänomenologie der Erkenntnis* Berlin: Bruno Cassirer, 1929), 475, quoted in Carl H. Hamburg, "Cassirer's Conception of Philosophy," in *The Philosophy of Ernst Cassirer,* ed. Paul Arthur Schilpp (Evanston, Ill.: Library of Living Philosophers, 1949), 79. Translation by Hamburg.

9. Ernst Cassirer, *Language and Myth,* trans. Susanne K. Langer (reprint, New York, 1946), 37.

10. This interpretation accords with that of Philip Wheelwright, *Metaphor and Reality* (Bloomington: Indiana University Press, 1962).

11. Hans Blumenberg, "Paradigmen zu einer Metaphorologie," *Archiv für Begriffsgeschichte* 6 (1960): 5–142, 301–5.

12. Cassirer, *Philosophy of Symbolic Forms.; idem, An Essay on Man* (New Haven: Yale University Press, 1944); idem, *Language and Myth.*

13. I am here ignoring the complication that on a certain level all language may be said to be metaphorical. Black is talking about constructed metaphors, not those etymologically implicit in a language.

14. Thomas Kuhn, *The Structure of Scientific Revolutions,* 2d ed. (Berkeley and Los Angeles: University of California Press, 1970).

15. Stephen C. Pepper, *World Hypotheses: A Study in Evidence* (Berkeley and Los Angeles: University of California Press, 1942).

16. Mary B. Hesse, *Forces and Fields* (Westport, Conn.: Greenwood Press, 1962); idem, *Models and Analogies in Science* (Notre Dame, Ind.: University of Notre Dame Press, 1966).

17. Liliane Papin, "This Is not a Universe: Metaphor, Language, and Representation," *PMLA* 107, no. 5 (October 1992): 1253–65.

18. Monroe C. Beardsley, "The Metaphorical Twist," *Philosophy and Phenomenological Research* 22, no. 3 (1962): 293–307.

19. Donald Davidson, "What Metaphors Mean," *Critical Inquiry* 5, no. 1 (1978): 31–47.

20. John R. Searle, "Metaphor," in *Expression and Meaning* (Cambridge: Cambridge University Press, 1979), 76–116.

21. George Yoos, "A Phenomenological Look at Metaphor," *Philosophy and Phenomenological Research* 32, no. 1 (1971): 78–88.

22. Dawn G. Blasko and Cynthia M.Connine, "Effects of Familiarity and Aptness on Metaphor Processing," *Journal of Experimental Psychology: Learning, Memory, and Cognition* 19, no. 2 (March 1993): 295–308.

23. Wheelwright, *Metaphor and Reality*, 172.

24. Edward G. Ballard, "Metaphysics and Metaphor," *Journal of Philosophy* 45 (8 April 1948): 208–14; see also David E. Rumelhart, "Some Problems with the Notion of Literal Meanings," in *Metaphor and Thought*, ed. Andrew Ortony, 2nd ed. (Cambridge: Cambridge University Press, 1993), 71–82.

25. Cornelius F. P. Strutterheim, *Het Begrip Metaphoor* (Amsterdam: H. J. Paris, 1941).

26. Ina Lowenberg, "Creativity and Correspondence in Fiction and in Metaphor," *Journal of Aesthetics and Art Criticism* 36, no. 3 (1978): 341–50.

27. Owen Barfield, "The Meaning of the Word 'Literal'," in *Metaphor and Symbol*, ed. L. C. Knights and Basil Cottle (London: Butterworths Scientific Publications, 1960), 54.

28. Ibid., 54–55.

29. Walter Kintsch, "Notes on the Structure of Semantic Memory," in *The Organization of Memory*, ed. Endel Tulving and Wayne Donaldson (New York: Academic Press, 1972), 249–309.

30. M. S. Cometa and M. E. Eson, "Logical Operations and Metaphor Interpretation: A Piagetian Model," *Child Development* 49, no. 3 (1978): 649–59.

31. J. W. Smith, "Children's Comprehension of Metaphor: A Piagetian Interpretation," *Language and Speech* 19, no. 3 (1976): 236–43.

32. H. Gardner and E. Winner, "The Child is Father to the Metaphor," *Psychology Today* 12, no. 12 (1979): 81.

33. B. A. Schecter, "Animism and the Development of Metaphoric Thinking in Children" (Ph.D. diss., Columbia University, 1980).

34. Kuhn, *Structure of Scientific Revolutions*.

35. Vonessen makes a similar point. He says that no metaphor can be understood by itself but only as embedded in a *Sprachbild*, a speech-picture or metaphor-complex. Franz Vonessen, "Die Ontologische Struktur der Metapher," *Zeitschrift für Philosophische Forschung* 13 (1959): 397–419.

36. Ernst Mach, *The Science of Mechanics: A Critical and Historical Account of Its Development*, trans. Thomas J. McCormack, 6th ed. (New York, 1960), 96.

37. See Hesse, *Models and Analogies in Science;* idem, *Science and the Human Imagination* (London: SMC Press, 1966.); E. H. Hutten, "The Rôle of Models in Physics," *British Journal for the Philosophy of Science* 4 (1953): 284–301; Theodore Sarbin, "Anxiety: Reification of a Metaphor," *Archives of General Psychiatry* 10 (1964): 630–38. Judith Schlanger, "Metaphor and Invention," trans. Yvonne Burne, *Diogenes* 69 (spring 1970): 12–27; Colin Murray Turbayne, *The Myth of Metaphor* (New Haven: Yale University Press, 1962).

38. Without being too technical, the Planck level refers to an interval in which the uncertainties of measurement dominate so that what is happening in there or at any smaller interval is unknowable and chaotic. Roughly this is at 1.616×10^{-35} meter. There is an analogous Planck time and Planck mass. Various parts of quantum theory postulate that wild fluctuations can occur here. Otherwise ironclad rules of nature can be egregiously violated as long as the violation takes place beyond this level, at which they could be detected.

39. The notion of empty space has been replaced in modern physics by the notion that the vacuum actually comprises a source of indefinitely extensive energy. A charged particle is said to *polarize* the vacuum, from whence *virtual* particles of opposite charge are pulled like fish from the sea. They surround the charged particle, thus masking its infinite charge. Virtual particles are so called because they must appear and vanish within the space and time of a Planck interval.

Uncertainty in measurements, of course, arises not just at what I am calling the Planck level but to varying degrees at the atomic and subatomic levels in general. For a fuller discussion, see *McGraw-Hill Encyclopedia of Physics*, 2d ed., s.v. "Supercritical Fields."

For a more technical and historical review, see Abraham Pais, *Inward Bound: Of Matter and Forces in the Physical World* (Oxford: Clarendon Press; New York: Oxford University Press, 1986), 382–85.

40. This, of course, employs patriarchal shorthand for *man and woman*.

41. Mark Johnson, *The Body in the Mind*, 22.

42. Rudolf Arnheim, *Visual Thinking* (Berkeley: University of California Press, 1969)., esp. chap. 6.

43. Just as you can pluck an object from inside a circle without invasion through the perimeter by coming through the third dimension, you might be able to remove an organ via the fifth or some higher dimension without even breaking the skin. Originally, dimension referred to spatial extension, but it has been extended to designate any mathematical analogue to space the exact nature of which is open to empirical exploration. Modern theoretical physicists work with upward of twenty dimensions in certain versions of superstring theory. Topologists have long dealt with n-dimensional manifolds. These putative higher dimensions are postulated as extensions of the mathematical frameworks used to deal with common Euclidean space or relativistic space-time. All these cases of higher dimensions are excellent examples of how we extend topological schemes and operations beyond immediate experience.

See Rudy Rucker, *The Fourth Dimension: Toward a Geometry of Higher Reality* (Boston: Houghton Mifflin, 1984).

44. Quoted in H. E. Cater, *Henry Adams and His Friends* (Boston: Houghton Mifflin, 1947), 677.

45. Bruno Shulz, "The Mythologizing of Reality," in *Letters and Drawings of Bruno Shulz*, ed. Jerzy Ficowski (New York: Harper & Row, 1988), 115.

46. Johan Huizinga, *Homo Ludens: A Study of the Play Element in Culture* (London: Routledge and Kegan Paul, 1950). See also Mihai I. Spariosu, *Dionysus Reborn: Play and the Aesthetic Dimension in Modern Philosophical and Scientific Discourse* (Ithaca: Cornell University Press, 1989). Jacques Ehrmann, ed., *Game, Play, Literature* (New Haven: Yale University Press, 1968; reprint, Boston: Beacon Press, 1971).

47. Eleanor Rosch, "Natural Categories," *Cognitive Psychology* 4 (1973): 328–50; idem, "Human Categorization," in *Studies in Cross-Cultural Psychology*, ed. Neil Warren (London: Academic Press, 1977); Eleanor Rosch and B. B. Lloyd, eds., *Cognition and Categorization* (Hillsdale, N.J.: Lawrence Erlbaum, 1978).

48. Mark Johnson, *Moral Imagination: Implications of Cognitive Science for Ethics* (Chicago: University of Chicago Press, 1993).

49. J. E. Carey and A. E. Goss, "The Role of Mediating Verbal Responses in the Conceptual Sorting Behavior of Children," *Journal of Genetic Psychology* 90 (1957): 69–74; D. A. Dietze, "The Facilitating Effect of Words on Discrimination and Generalization," *Journal of Experimental Psychology* 50 (1955): 255–60; A. E. Goss and M. C. Moylan, "Conceptual Block-Sorting as a Function of Type and Degree of Mastery of Discriminatory Verbal Responses," *Journal of Genetic Psychology* 93 (1958): 191–98; J. B. Carroll, "Words, Meanings, and Concepts," *Harvard Educational Review* 34 (1964): 178–202; M. D. Merrill and R. D. Tennyson, "Conceptual Classification and Classification Errors as a Function of the Relationship between Examples and Nonexamples," *Improving Human Performance: A Research Quarterly* 7 (1978): 351–64.

50. A. J. Rips, "Inductive Judgements about Natural Categories," *Journal of Verbal Learning and Verbal Behavior* 14 (1975): 665–81; Stella Vosniadou and A. Ortony, eds., *Similarity and Analogical Reasoning* (Cambridge: Cambridge University Press, 1989).

51. For a good discussion of these issues, see Edward E. Smith, "Concepts and Induction," in *Foundations of Cognitive Science*, ed. Michael I. Posner (Cambridge: MIT Press, 1989), 501–26; George Lakoff, *Women, Fire, and Dangerous Things: What Categories Reveal about the Mind* (Chicago: University of Chicago Press, 1987).

52. George Lakoff and Mark Johnson, *Metaphors We Live By* (Chicago: University of Chicago Press, 1980), 5. Original italics.

53. Ibid., 19. Original italics.

54. Johnson, *Body in the Mind*, 106.

55. Isa. 14:27.

56. 2 Kings 19:25; Isa. 22:11, 25:1, 37:26.

57. Acts 4:28 and Eph. 2:10.

58. *Encyclopedia of the Early Church*, s.v. "Predestination."

59. See the glossary at the end of this book for a full list and description of the basic metaphors and action schemes.

60. Friedrich Max Müller, *Lectures on the Science of Language*, 2 vols. (New York: Charles Scribner, 1871).

61. Charles Féré, "La Physiologie dans les Métaphores," *Revue Philosophique* 40 (1895): 352–59.

62. Mark Turner, *Death is the Mother of Beauty: Mind, Metaphor, Criticism* (Chicago: University of Chicago Press, 1987).

CHAPTER 2. METAPHOR AND INTELLECTUAL HISTORY

1. Michael S. Gazzaniga, and Bruce T. Volpe, "Split-Brain Studies: Implications for Psychiatry," in *Advances and New Directions*, ed. Silvano Arieti and H. Keith H. Brodie, . American Handbook of Psychiatry, 2d ed. (New York: Basic Books, 1981), 7:41.

2. Ibid., 26.

3. Ibid., 35.

4. Thomas Kuhn, *The Structure of Scientific Revolutions*, 2d ed. (Berkeley and Los Angeles: University of California Press, 1970). Kuhn's paradigm comprehends, in addition to a metaphoric core, methodological and sociological factors.

5. Jean Charbonneaux, Roland Martin, and François Villard, *Hellenistic Art* (New York: George Braziller, 1973).

6. Gilbert Ryle, *The Concept of Mind* (New York: Barnes and Noble, 1949).

7. John H. Flavell, *The Developmental Psychology of Jean Piaget* (Princeton, N.J.: Van Nostrand, 1963), 48. Original italics.

8. Philip Stehle, *Order, Chaos, Order: The Transition from Classical to Quantum Physics* (New York: Oxford University Press, 1994), 285, 299.

9. I. Bernard Cohen, *The Birth of a New Physics* (New York: W. W. Norton, 1985), 78.

10. Aristotle, *On the Heavens* 1.2.269.20f. and 19, trans. J. L. Stock, in *Works* (Chicago: Encyclopaedia Britannica, 1952), 1:360.

11. Ibid. 2.4.286.26f., in *Works*, 378.

12. Ptolemy, *The Almagest* 1.3, trans. R. Catesby Taliaferro (Chicago: Encyclopaedia Britannica, 1952), 8.

13. Saint Thomas Aquinas provides an interesting case of rather perverse metaphor deployment. He combined and distorted the Platonic and Aristotelian notions of the ordering principle to fashion his argument from design for the existence of God. "We see that things which lack knowledge, such as natural bodies, act for an end, and this is evident from their acting always, or nearly always, in the same way, so as to obtain the best result. Hence it is plain that they achieve their end, not fortuitously, but designedly. Now whatever lacks knowledge cannot move towards an end, unless it be directed by some being endowed with knowledge and intelligence; as the arrow is directed by the archer. Therefore some intelligent being exists by whom all natural things are directed to their end: and this being we call God (*Summa Theologica*, Q. 2, Art. 3).

As Frederick Ferré points out, Saint Thomas's argument displays several interesting flaws. "First, it is taken as obvious that there are end-directed activities within nature." By contrast, Plato had cited mainly the order of the heavens to substantiate his more limited notion of universal order. "Second, we see that Saint Thomas has adopted Aristotle's remark about the presence of 'purpose' in nature without accepting his conclusion that such observable regularities may be accounted for by appeal to an immanent teleology." Further, Saint Thomas goes on to postulate "some intelligent being" behind this teleology, whereas Plato contemplated many possible "souls," and Saint Thomas ends by equating this "intelligent being" with the Christian God, a conclusion that cannot follow strictly from his premises.

From all this, it is not hard to see that what Saint Thomas is doing is deploying the Pattern metaphor to give coherence, and hence credibility, to the existence of God. His conclusion is not reached through his premises; rather, his premises are chosen to lead to his conclusion. They do so only against a presumed theology and under the rhetorical persuasion of the selected metaphor.

Going to the top of Saint Thomas' argument, he says that "[w]e see that things which lack knowledge . . . act for an end." He makes no demonstration of this. Rather, he falls back on the by then well established classical tradition. Anaximander, Heraclitus, Anaxagoras, and Aristotle, to name only the classical authorities cited, all fell victim to a similar ploy: selective inattention. Nature has both order and disorder, the latter outweighing by far the former. Nearly all organic forms are irregular; their symmetry is only approximate, therefore ideal. Clouds are irregular, as are geological formations, the weather, and in fact the whole natural environment. The only things that are regular are those that are man-made, and even those, in fine, are always imperfect. Regularity is only approximate; symmetry, strictly ideal. Plato, of course, recognized this, which is why he contended that absolute knowledge can be reached only through abstract contemplation.

(The quotations from Aquinas and the other citations are from *Dictionary of the History of Ideas*, s.v. "Design Argument.")

14. A short digression into the creative process will bear this out, while also serving to illuminate further the modus operandi of metaphorand choice. Einstein, for example, in describing how he evolved his hypotheses, wrote:

> The words or language, as they are written or spoken, do not seem to play any role in my mechanism of thought. The psychical entities which seem to serve as elements in thought are certain signs and more or less clear images which can be "voluntarily" reproduced and combined.
>
> The above mentioned elements are, in my case, of visual and some of muscular type. Conventional words or other signs have to be sought for laboriously only in a secondary stage, when the mentioned associative play is sufficiently established and

can be reproduced at will. (Quoted in J. Hadamard, *The Psychology of Invention in the Mathematical Field* [Princeton: Princeton University Press, 1945; reprint, New York: Dover Publications, 1954], 142, 143)

Rosamond E. M. Harding, in her wonderful study, *An Anatomy of Inspiration*, observed that "Einstein when faced with a problem has a 'definite vision of its possible solution,'" in other words he feels . . . that the solution will be 'so and so' and he acts accordingly. What is this feeling? Sir Joshua Reynolds describes it as 'the result of the accumulated experience of our whole life' and he cautions . . . against 'an unfounded distrust of the imagination and feeling, in favor of narrow, partial, confined, argumentative theories.'" After considerable review of various accounts of the creative process in the arts and sciences, Harding summarizes:

> The origin of the nucleus of a work of art is a very difficult problem. Alphonse Daudet's views appear, however, to shed some light on the matter. His son Léon tells us that the "problem of the beginning of a work and of the earliest spark of suggestion" occupied them very often. His father, he says, believed "that in the case of all creators there are accumulations of sentient force made without their knowledge. Their nerves, in a state of high excitation, register visions, colors, forms, and odors in those half-realized reservoirs which are the treasuries of poets. All of a sudden, through some influence or emotion, through some accident of thought, these impressions meet each other with the suddenness of a chemical combination."

Harding goes on to refer to "ideas bearing on interests acquiring a certain tone which binds them together," hypothesizing that this "tone appears to act as a sieve preventing incongruous and irrelevant ideas from disturbing the mind" in the creative process. (*An Anatomy of Inspiration* [Cambridge: W. Heffer and Son, 1943], 32, 106, 108.)

Bearing in mind the likely relevance of tone to the creative process, consider these further ruminations of Einstein:

> What, precisely, is "thinking"? When, at the reception of sense-impressions, memory-pictures [*Erinnerungsbilder*] emerge, this is not yet "thinking." And when such pictures form series, each member of which calls forth another, this too is not yet "thinking." When, however, a certain picture turns up in many such series, then—precisely through such return—it becomes an ordering element for such series, in that it connects series which in themselves are unconnected. Such an element becomes an instrument, a concept. I think that the transition from free association or "dreaming" to thinking is characterized by the more or less dominating rôle which the "concept" plays in it. It is by no means necessary that a concept must be connected with a sensorially cognizable and reproducible sign (word); but when this is the case thinking becomes by means of that fact communicable. (Albert Einstein, "Autobiographical Notes," in *Albert Einstein: Philosopher-Scientist*, ed. Paul Arthur Shilpp [Evanston, Ill.: Library of Living Philosophers, 1949], 7)

If we translate *Bilder* as image, rather than picture, and generalize from the visual to all the sensory modalities, we then have an experiential given that is for all practical purposes inseparable from tone. This is especially so when the image is kinaesthetic, the kind that Einstein said often characterized his creative thought processes. But then, what is tone?

Tone and feeling are more or less synonymous. They both refer to the surrounding context of a percept, or that part which is not conceptual. Suppose that you have a feeling of tightness in your stomach. This may be bracketed, or analytically separated out for discrete consideration. A simple focusing of attention accomplishes this. But accompanying this kinesthetic image must be an awareness, relatively central or peripheral, of what might be called the total body state. Broken down into recognizable categories, this presents a hodgepodge: awareness of body surfaces and orientation, internal tensions, hormonal blood levels, brain chemical status, social context, and how this all interfaces with the conscious field to create a context of feeling. Roughly speaking, this is the overall mood or feeling against the background of which objects or events are perceived (actually or in memory). Useless to argue over whether this aura of sentience is given or mediated through interpretation—one of the seminal disputes in theories of emotion—for interpretation itself can easily be assimilated to the total body state. Put another way, interpretation may be regarded as simply another link in the plexus of feedback loops that constitute the experienced moment. In this view, the experienced moment is a shifting focus of sentience that, if analyzed in a reductionist fashion, is, mathematically speaking, chaotic.

The formative image arises out of the confluence of mnemonic associations often, if not always, at the prompting of some body state with which it probably shares some experiential invariant or morphism. Here we arrive at the crux of the matter, where the metaphorand mediates from body state or moment of sentience (two sides of the same coin) to symbolic representation, feeling to idea or communicable image. We can now begin to understand how this happens.

The body state has, somewhere within it, a potential focus of attention, a configuration that can be fit to certain metaphorands or discursive structures on the basis of structural similarity—what mathematicians would call a homeomorphism. It is indeed most clearly conceived as a relationship wherein the body-state configuration is perceived as mappable onto some metaphorand or topological schema. I shall return to this in the next chapter. For each individual, the type of configuration typically bracketed from the body state or sentient field is idiosyncratic. Thus, certain creators habitually rely on a particular sensory modality or combination of modalities reacting variously to other contextual aspects of the moment or period of inspiration, such as mood, unconscious goals, ongoing psychological concerns, body tensions, and so forth. These latter elements probably guide the deployment of the metaphor more than the selection of the metaphorand. On the other hand, if there are several similarly structured metaphorands preconsciously at hand, the contextual elements of the period of inspiration may be decisive in the selection of one of them. In the arts this is more apt to be the case than in science and everyday problem solving. Rhetorical metaphors, infinite in variety, serve the artist, whereas in practical matters recourse must be made to the more limited repertoire of explanatory metaphors.

15. Aristotle, *History of Animals* 8.1.588b.4–11, in *Works* (Chicago: Encyclopaedia Britannica, 1952), 1:114–15.

16. Cicero, *De natura deorum* 2.33f., quoted in *Dictionary of the History of Ideas*, s.v. "Hierarchy and Order."

17. *Dictionary of the History of Ideas*, s.v. "Chain of Being."

18. Homer, *Iliad* 8.19–23, trans. Samuel Butler, in *The Iliad of Homer and the Odyssey* (Chicago: Encyclopaedia Britannica, 1952), 51.

19. John Milton, *Paradise Lost* 5.508–12, in *Poetical Works*, ed. H. C. Beeching (London: Oxford University Press, 1928), 284.

20. *Spectator*, no. 519 (25 October 1712), quoted in *Dictionary of the History of Ideas*, s.v. "Chain of Being."

21. James Thomson, *Summer*, lines 284–86, quoted in *Dictionary of the History of Ideas*, s.v. "Chain of Being."

22. Alexander Pope, *An Essay on Man* 1.237–41, quoted in *Dictionary of the History of Ideas*, s.v. "Chain of Being."

23. This is much too complex and technical a question to enter into here. The interested reader may consult the excellent overview by Carl D. Murray, Werner Lauterborn, and Peter M. Koch in *McGraw-Hill Encyclopedia of Physics*, 2d ed., s.v. "Chaos." A more technical presentation is Robert V. Jensen's in *Encyclopedia of Modern Physics*, s.v. "Chaos." Both articles provide bibliographies.

24. Kuo Hsiang, *Commentary on Chuang Tzu*, sec. 22, 7:54b–55b, in *Sources of Chinese Tradition*, ed. William Theodore de Bary, Chan Wingh-tsit, and Burton Watson (New York: Columbia University Press, 1960), 1:242.

25. Chan Wingh-tsit, "Syntheses in Chinese Metaphysics," in *The Chinese Mind: Essentials of Chinese Philosophy and Culture*, ed. Charles A. Moore (Honolulu: University of Hawaii Press, 1967), 143.

26. Lao Tzu, *The Way of Life*, trans. R. B. Blakney (New York, 1955), 85.

27. Ibid., 42, 95. See also the discussion in Fung Yu-lan, *A History of Chinese Philosophy*, trans. Derk Bodde, 2d ed. (Princeton, 1952), 1:178–79.

28. Lao Tzu, *Way of Life*, 4, 56.

29. *Rig Veda* 10.129, in *Sources of Indian Tradition*, ed. William Theodore de Bary, Stephen Hay, Royal Weiler and Andrew Yarrow (New York: Columbia University Press, 1958), 17.

30. *Lalitavistara*, quoted in de Bary et al., *Sources of Indian Tradition*, 177.

31. *Huai-nan Tzu* 3.1a, in de Bary et al., *Sources of Chinese Tradition*, 1:192.

32. Heinrich Zimmer, *Philosophies of India*, ed. Joseph Campbell (New York: Meridian Books, 1956), 517.

33. Ibid., 518.

34. Hajime Nakamura, *Ways of Thinking of Eastern Peoples: India-China-Tibet-Japan*, (Honolulu: University of Hawaii Press, 1964), 136.

35. Ibid., 573.

36. D. T. Suzuki, "Reason and Intuition in Buddhist Philosophy," in *The Japanese Mind: Essentials of Japanese Philosophy and Culture*, ed. Charles A. Moore (Honolulu: University of Hawaii Press, 1967), 94.

37. Junjiro Takakusu, "Buddhism as a Philosophy of 'Thusness,'" in *The Indian Mind*, ed. Charles A. Moore (Honolulu: University of Hawaii Press, 1967), 99.

38. Leon Festinger, *A Theory of Cognitive Dissonance* (Stanford, Calif.: Stanford University Press, 1957), 24. Original italics.

CHAPTER 3. ACTION SCHEMES AND TOPOLOGICAL TRANSFORMATIONS

1. Bruno Snell, *The Discovery of the Mind: The Greek Origins of European Thought* (Cambridge: Harvard University Press, 1953).

2. David McNeill, *Hand and Mind: What Gesture Reveals About Thought* (Chicago: University of Chicago Press, 1992), 35.

3. Ibid., 263.

4. Ibid., 220.

5. Ibid., 221. Original italicized.

6. Ibid., 29.

7. Stanley Rosner and Lawrence E. Abt, eds., *The Creative Experience* (New York: Grossman, 1970); Brewster Ghiselin, ed., *The Creative Process* (New York: New American Library, 1955); Arthur Koestler, *The Act of Creation* (New York: Macmillan, 1964); Edward S. Tauber and Maurice R. Green, *Prelogical Experience: An Inquiry into Dreams and Other Creative Processes* (New York: Basic Books, 1959); Albert Rothenberg, *The Emerging Goddess: The Creative Process in Art, Science, and Other Fields* (Chicago: University of Chicago Press, 1979).

8. This line of explanation may be used to clarify the dynamics of the creative process. During the creative process, there is usually a sense of urgency, as if some future state were already imagined, probably with the same general characteristics as the initial germ. Particularly in the case of problem solving—and hence in much scientific creative thought—a solution state and the topological and possibly even imagistic scheme of it are known. This will be true, too, for any creative act dictated by preconceived ends, as in much commissioned and occasional work. Sometimes, say, in the writing of fiction or the design of a building, the end may also emerge as a determinative factor. Much of the dynamism of the creativity is then subjugated to working out a series of transformations that will bring the germinal scheme into the end scheme. At this stage, the dancer may move about aimlessly, trying out gestures and movements; the poet may scribble words or even metric patterns; the fiction writer may describe part of an incompletely conceived scene; the scientist may make doodles or quick sketches, notate relationships, or resort to a simple visual image. The underlying schemes are being translated into communicable forms.

Translation of schemes to forms is extremely complex, for at this stage, the whole personal and cultural background of the creator is engaged. At the personal level, there is the background of experiences from which any number of items may be drawn, elicited by various types of association from the matrical schemes of the creative process. Any one of these elicited items may, upon being introduced, significantly alter the ongoing processes. The same is true of the constraints of the given discipline: vocabulary or palette, practice conventions, nature of the communicative medium, body of existing works familiar to the creator, and idiosyncrasies of style, for instance, help to determine the final outcome. Obviously this is a chaotic and therefore unpredictable process. It is not my intent to delve much further into the dynamics involved, as there is not much more that can be said, except in the individual case, where a *post facto* analysis can be made, as exemplified by Lowes's close account of Coleridge's composition of "Ancient Mariner" and "Kubla Khan." I wish to make only one more brief but, I think, critical postulation.

There needs to be a bridge between the germinal schemes, especially the topological skeleton, and the emergent form to which the act of creation ultimately gives rise. Backing up to the moment just before the egg hatches, so to speak, how does the topological schema all of a sudden burst into something articulate? How does it link into a narrative, a painting, a dance—in short, into what I would call in general a discursive form? I suggest that the topological schema is retranslated into an isomorphic body state, which is then experienced as a readiness to act. That is, if the body unconsciously feels back into the schema—rather the reverse of forming a schema originally by abstraction from action routines—it is then in a particular state appropriate to a spectrum of actions. Consider a baseball pitcher in the middle of a pitch. He could continue on and throw the ball, but he could also run, fall backward, drop the ball, fall over sideways, move forward and fall to his knees, spit, yell, etc. What he chooses to do is contextual. Likewise with the creator who has assimilated a scheme into a body state: she has within her a gamut of possible actions for which she is ready, and the actual course of action she pursues from that state of readiness will depend upon all the contextual factors already discussed. She is like a wound spring, ready to drive whatever appropriate mechanism the interface may consist of.

This is, at any rate, a more detailed explanation of the creative process than usually given in the literature. In other accounts, the process is always traced back to a black box in which something mysterious and inexplicable happens. I have tried to clarify every step of the procedure, and in much of the remainder of this chapter I will attempt to show exactly how action schemes work in thought processes

9. Mark Johnson, *The Body in the Mind: The Bodily Basis of Meaning, Imagination, and Reason* (Chicago: University of Chicago Press, 1987), 38–40.

10. Jerome Bruner; Jacqueline J. Goodnow, and George A. Austin, *A Study of Thinking* (New York: John Wiley, 1956), esp. 156–81.

11. A case study may bring all this more clearly into perspective. First, note that the primitive substructure of the geometry of action and perception is carried in most languages by prepositions or their equivalents. As you will see, these are vital keys to the geometric structure of thought. Meanwhile, consider the interesting history of the English preposition, *by*. Originally, the word designated nearness or proximity, as in "They stood by (i.e., near or next to) him." Early on, it was used in swearing and oath taking. "To swear by God," meant to take an oath in the presence of God. This is an extension of geometry, as can be seen in such an expression as "by the beard of Beowulf," an old expletive. Then, proceed to the usage, "to do something by oneself," in one's own presence, in other words with no one else near to assist. Another early usage was in comparisons: to compare one thing *by* another, which again implies juxtaposition. Analogously, "north by west," is stated as meaning north-west, north but with west nearby. Then, in "by land or by sea," the geometry gets more obscure. Returning to the implied juxtaposition of comparison, the word can be extended to the result of comparison: "Six dollars is the amount by which he exceeded the account." Time, being an abstraction remote from any particular concrete circumstance, is commonly spatialized, yielding expressions like "by night" or "by this time tomorrow." And the list reaches further outward:

call her by name
sell by the pound
arrange them by age
by what is said
by guess and by gosh
by hook or by crook

In many idioms, *by* becomes a preposition of instrumentality, specifying the manner in which an action is achieved. This usage accounts for most of the idioms listed immediately above. Some of these expression arise without due process of judgment, by imitation of well-founded usage, so that the original meaning of the word may be completely perverted. Thus, the OED records J. Williamson as saying, "These persons by particular are said to be by the statutes rogues." Still, in deciphering such usages, it is necessary to have recourse to the underlying primitive geometric meaning of the word and the context of the given instance in conjunction with what might be known of analogous forms and usages. In general, *of* and *for*, two of the vaguest prepositions, may be analyzed by equating to *by* and then puzzling out the implications of proximity or connection either by knowledge of usage alone or in conjunction with the context. *Of* and *from* are, so to speak, composite prepositions that do the duty of signifying a whole gamut of relationships that can be construed only from a given context. This is because they were used to translate many Latin and French prepositions having no corresponding usage in English.

Prepositions designate spatial relationships in their etymologically most fundamental sense. But they quickly diversified to cover all kinds of abstract relationships that had to be spatialized to be conceived. Conception is founded on assimilation to terms of action, posture, and feeling of which the human organism is capable. Notions cannot be matched to what falls outside human experience. Prepositions are the syntactic glue that holds together ideas that must be coordinated in abstract relationships. In essence, the exact nature of the specified relationship usually remains ambiguous. As with time, other abstractions tend to become conceptualized by being spatialized, that is, puzzled out in spatial terms. That is why prepositions, or their case equivalents (endings or suffixes added to nouns and their modifiers to indicate their syntactic function in a sentence), all have primitively spatial meanings.

In summation, humans conceive abstractions by imposing spatial schemata, either geometric relationships or patterns of action, on complexes of experience. The elements of these experiences are subsequently contemplated by moving them mentally within the schema or according to the spatial restrictions of the schema. An example would be the complex in which persons enter into various agreements to pay debts, perform promised services, discharge social obligations, etc. These become conceived in terms of the contract—*con*, with or together, + pp. of *trahere*, to draw, that which is drawn together. Geometrically, a contract is a joining together, the connection being via the contract as instrumental abstraction. The contract is said to be *binding*. When one party fails to perform part or all of the contractually agreed action, the contract is said to be "broken," and so on.

12. Johnson, *Body in the Mind*, 29. Original italics.

13. Ibid., 156.

14. *The Encyclopedia of Philosophy*, s.v. "Kant."

15. Johnson, *The Body in the Mind*, 156–57.

16. Ibid., 142.

17. Frederic C. Bartlett, *Remembering: A Study in Experimental and Social Psychology* (London: Cambridge University Press, 1932).

18. M. Head, *Aphasia and Kindred Disorders of Speech* (New York: Macmillan, 1926), 488.

19. John H. Flavell, *The Developmental Psychology of Jean Piaget* (Princeton, N.J.: Van Nostrand, 1963), 52–53.

20. Ibid., 55.

21. David Marr, *Vision: A Computational Investigation into the Human Representation and Processing of Visual Information* (San Francisco: W. H. Freeman, 1992), esp. chap. 2.

22. Roger N. Shepard and Lynn A. Cooper, *Mental Images and Their Transformations* (Cambridge: MIT Press, 1986), 185.

23. Israel Rosenfield, *The Strange, Familiar, and Forgotten: An Anatomy of Consciousness* (New York: Alfred A. Knopf, 1992), 100–101.

24. Ibid., 54–55.

25. Ibid. 84.

26. Ibid., 32. Original parentheses.

27. W. W. Bartley III, "Alienation Alienated: The Economics of Knowledge versus the Psychology and Sociology of Knowledge," in *Evolutionary Epistemology, Rationality, and the Sociology of Knowledge*, ed. Gerard Radnitzky and W. W. Bartley III (La Salle, Ill.: Open Court, 1987), 438.

28.   The central axis is the upright body, which might be in repose or act as a support for some burden directly overhead. Support—etymologically, to hold up from below—has the following verbal synonyms, each with slightly different connotations:

> endure
> suffer
> go through
> put up with
> stand
> submit to
> tolerate
> bear

The first two conceptualize from feeling: *endure* is to harden, and *suffer* is to experience pain. All the others spatialize. *Stand* simply names the posture. *Bear* adds the idea of a weight or burden supported. *Submit to* is likewise to place under with the *to* emphasizing the burden assumed. *Put up with* is a curious prepositional hybrid suggesting the maintenance of the support (put up) in the presence or under the burden of (with) something or someone else. *Tolerate* also derives from a Greek-Latin root meaning "to hold up." *Go through* makes experience a space through which it is necessary to go. These words describe the inner experience of the standing posture.

Words of being and existence, in the Romance, German, and Slavic languages, describe an emergence, a coming into sight. Exist is from *ex*, out, + *sistere*, a duplicative of *stare*, to stand, meaning to emerge. Existence, then, suggests that which can be seen to emerge, presumably from prior obscurity, like a figure on a dark stage slowly revealed by light. It is seeing the upright figure from the outside, from the third-person perspective.

The standing figure can move four ways: to the right, to the left, backward, and forward. Each has connotations that have become deeply ingrained in language. *Right* signifies not only a direction but a measure of correctness and approbation, whereas *left*, sinistrous, early pointed to that which is harmful or injurious. These distinctions undoubtedly rest upon the statistical preponderance of righthandedness over lefthandedness. Conversely, to move forward is positive, because human posture and equilibrium mandate forward motion while engaging in most primary ongoing actions. Backward movement signals withdrawal, suggesting failure or uncertainty. Progress is almost always conceived as moving either from left to right or from the back forward. Expanded to cover a wider variety of primary actions, this gives the following list of connotative values:

> Right-Forward: progress, correctness, forthrightness, honesty, openness, propriety.
> Left-Backward: failure, wrongness, deception, secretiveness, improbity.

Next come the movements of lying down or rising up. Again, they must be deciphered in terms of primary human actions. This is a rather more complex polar couple. First is the simple motion of lying down to sleep and rising up in the morning. In ancient times the night brought darkness, which meant danger, whereas the morning gave light and a greater sense of security. Thus, lying down and rising up are inextricably bound to the dual metaphor of light-dark, embodying clarity and obscurity, knowledge and the unknowable, ultimately life versus death—to live is to be upright and moving, to die is to lie still in the darkness of the earth. It turns out then that *up* or *above* (super-, hyper-, over-) has positive connotations, whereas *down* or *below* (sub-, hypo-, under-) has negative. This carries over to motion in either direction.

There are further dimensions to this duality of rising up or lying down. Rising up marks the beginning of an action; lying or sitting down completes or at least ends it. In discursive thought or the construction of an argument, the process may begin from the static base of a premise, actually rise, rather than advance and finally settle to a conclusion: "The Lord is the ultimate power. There is no power above him. We may reach toward the divine, but we shall never attain it. Therefore, lowly creatures that we are, we must be content with our station in life here on the terrestrial sphere, far below heaven. That is our fate and we must humbly submit to it."

Aside from moving right or left, backward or forward, up or down, there is rotation. The same caveats of right and left apply as in lateral movements. Additionally, rotation can carry the body back to its original position, associating such motion with the spatialized seasonal cycles of time. Rotation also exposes a body to the most complete exterior view— hence such an expression as "turn something around in the mind."

Perhaps most interesting is the connection between rotation and folding in. For example, this is achieved if a something like a cord is attached to the rotating body so that it is wound in around the body. *Involve* catches this very idea, for it means to turn inward. Similarly, *implicate* or *imply* is a folding in. Conversely, to *evolve* is to turn outward, as *explicate* is to fold out or unfold. A further angle on this notion is contained in the word, *insinuate,* which in Latin originally meant to introduce by curving or winding in, as when a troupe of military insinuate themselves into the enemy line. Pole dances with ribbons likewise literally involve all the dancers in a common action.

A body can turn upside down. *Inversion* often describes this, though etymologically it means to turn inside out. Turning inside out, of course, can bring about a reversal of top and bottom, as with a paper bag. In human terms, standing or being stood on one's head usually causes a sense of disorientation because of the radical change in perspective; so, inversion is introduced into discursive thinking often as a sign of at least temporary confusion.

> turn the town on its ear
> turn one's world upside down
> have inverted values
> look at everything upside down

It may also, of course, signify a literal inversion or reversal of order without any emotional connotations.

Separating or joining represents a final possibility of human action. Separating refers to taking something apart or breaking away from a group of other people. Joining means bringing things together or entering into a group. Joining or connecting is so fundamental an action that it is ubiquitous in thought as the favored mode of linking ideas causally, logically and in other more tangential ways. Furthermore, combining is a way to intensify a quality shared by the things joined.

> command and commend = *com*, with (intensive) + *manus,*
> hand + *dare,* to give
> contort = *con* (intensive) + *tortus,* twisted (from *torquere,* to twist)

29. Nowhere is the conflict between transcendentalists and empiricists more clearly drawn than in the battle within mathematics between the formalists and the intuitionists. Looking at human intellectual history in terms of metaphor deployment and at reason as topological manipulation, we can well imagine that somewhere down the line, purely abstract mathematical structures may turn out to have an unsuspected interest over and above the intrinsic fascination they have for those who create them or study them for their own sake. Even contradiction, the structure of paradox, may prove to have topological properties leading to surprising new domains of thought. Indeed, we predict that this will be the case.

30. Aristotle, *Physics* 1.184a.10–25, trans. R. P. Hardie and R. K. Gaye, in *Works* (Chicago: Encyclopaedia Britannica, 1952), 259.

31. Sir Isaac Newton, *Mathematical Principles of Natural Philosophy* 1.1, lemma 1, trans. Andrew Motte, rev. Florian Cajori (Chicago: Encyclopaedia Britannica, 1952), 25.

32. David Hume, *Concerning Human Understanding* 2.11 (Chicago: Encyclopaedia Britannica, 1952), 455.

33. Sigmund Freud, *General Introduction to Psycho-Analysis*, trans. Joan Riviere, in *Major Works* (Chicago: Encyclopaedia Britannica, 1952), 515.

34. Piaget argued for an innateness of basic reflexes and a rather fixed sequence of developmental stages. By comparison, I would say that the body and what it can physically do provide a stable basis for mentation through action schemes and embodied metaphors, but that the deployment of these is encultured. My position is not nature versus nurture but nature and nurture.

35. For examples, see: Gene Weltfish, *Origins of Art* (Indianapolis, Ind.: Bobbs-Merrill, 1953), pl. 27–49.

36. Heinrich Schenker, *Free Composition*, trans. Ernst Oster (London: Longman, 1979); Allen Forte and Steven Gilbert, *Introduction to Schenkerian Analysis* (New York: W. W. Norton, 1982); Nicholas Cook, *A Guide to Musical Analysis* (New York: George Braziller, 1987), 27–66.

37. Rudolph Rieti, *The Thematic Process in Music* (London: Faber & Faber, 1961); Cook, *Guide to Musical Analysis*, 89–115.

CHAPTER 4. THE ANCIENT WORLD

1. For examples, see: N. K. Sandars, *Prehistoric Art in Europe* (Baltimore: Penguin, 1968), pl. 85–86.

2. In myths, abstract qualities are personified. Later speculation depersonalizes the gods by jettisoning anthropomorphism, leaving behind the qualities as agents. The Roman goddess Justitia thus becomes justice as a blindfolded agent. A blindfolded agent in this context would be impartial, and so on. Of course, it could be argued that a sense of the necessity for impartiality in legal procedures was what led to the symbolism of the blindfold in the first place, but the point is that historically that sense passes through the stage of myth before reaching abstract speculation.

3. Tylor, Edward B., "Dream Lore and Superstitions of Primitive Peoples," in *The World of Dreams*, ed. Ralph L. Woods (New York, 1947), 8.

4. Ibid., 9. The reference to "lower races" is an unfortunate and discredited anthropological archaism.

5. Ibid., 10.

6. Rattray, R. S., "Dream Beliefs of the African Ashantis," in Woods, *World of Dreams*, 20–21.

7. Landtman, Gunnar, "The Dream Life of the Kiwai Papuans of British New Guinea," in Woods, *World of Dreams*, 31–32.

8. For a general survey of scientific attempts to explain dreaming, see J. Allan Hobson, *The Dreaming Brain* (New York: Basic Books, 1988). For a brief account of the ideas to which I refer, see *Encyclopedia of Neuroscience*, s.v. "Dreaming."

9. Hans Vaihinger, *The Philosophy of "As If,"* trans. C. K. Ogden, 2d ed. (London: Routledge and Kegan Paul, 1935), 56–57.

10. G. S. Kirk, *Myth: Its Meaning and Functions in Ancient and Other Cultures* (Berkeley and Los Angeles: University of California Press, 1970), 254–61

11. This is a form of externalization of private reality. It follows the brilliant exposition of Philip Rawson:

Perhaps the most important key to the meaning of individual drawings is this. In so far as any drawing amounts to a positive, affirmative statement, it both implies and illustrates the artist's conception of reality. The terms of the drawing are the terms which the artist has found for asserting the validity, or the 'actual presence,' of his statement. However much an affirmative statement may be hedged about with conditions, it comes down in the end to saying: "Such and such IS the case." Drawing methods are a major part of the artist's means for stipulating the 'IS' attributing an affirmative quality to his topic; without them he can make no affirmation. And we may as well take the last jump and realize that, since this is so, implicit in every drawing style is a visual ontology, i.e. a definition of the real in visual terms.

He later develops this visual ontology in terms of graphic types:

Types in my sense represent the assemblage of basic forms which, because of their analogy with other forms of experience on a similar scale, will evoke chains of associated memories and responses. So that, like the lesser forms, they will synthesize emotional meanings which are beyond the reach of words. Because of the general scale and structure of our visual world, some of these provisional unities will tend to equate themselves with what we recognize as objects in the world. . . . For example, Rubens may seem to be designating with his types that kind of woman which we call "Rubensian." In reality, however, he is actually assembling graphic forms and subtypes relating to our experience of flesh (plus fur and fabric), into structured units. These units can be types which may seem to describe everyday categories of the real. But the truth is that they are graphic constructs, which summarize and condense the psychological meaning of the graphic forms of which they are composed. Once we know an artist's work well, and his graphic types have become part of our medial apparatus, we begin to "see" his types in the world. We "see" Rubens' women. We 'see' Samuel Palmer or Rembrandt landscapes. But this is because we are projecting an already formulated type to give the world meaning. (Philip Rawson, *Drawing* [London and New York: Oxford University Press, 1969], 19, 247–48)

The graphic type is therefore a perceptual schema for the social construction of reality. It should be an invaluable tool for relating the visual arts to the overall cultural complex of action schemes and metaphors.

12. Marija Gimbutas, especially in *The Goddesses and Gods of Old Europe* (Berkeley and

Los Angeles: University of California Press, 1982), has outlined much of the prehistoric iconography.

See also Joseph Campbell, *The Mythic Image*, Bollingen series (Princeton: Princeton University Press, 1974); André Leroi-Gourhan, *Treasures of Prehistoric Art* (New York: Harry N. Abrams, n.d.); N. K. Sandars, *Prehistoric Art in Europe*

13. *The New Grove Dictionary of Music and Musicians*, s.v. "Dance."

14. See note 10, above.

15. As an example of what might be done, consider the possibility that Greek logic, including the formalism of Euclid, might throw light on Greek musical theory and practice. Yet I have never seen the two topics yoked in any study of ancient music.

16. W. G. de Burgh, *The Legacy of the Ancient World* (London, 1947), 90.

17. Plato, *Republic* 591, in *The Dialogues* (Chicago: Encyclopaedia Britannica, 1952).

18. E. T. Bell, *The Development of Mathematics* (New York: McGraw-Hill, 1945), 4.

19. Carl B. Boyer, *A History of Mathematics*, rev. Uta C. Merzbach, 2d ed. (New York: John Wiley and Sons, 1989), 41.

20. Morris Kline, *Mathematical Thought from Ancient to Modern Times* (New York: Oxford University Press, 1972), 22.

21. Thomas L. Heath, *Greek Mathematics* (1931; reprint, New York: Dover Publications, 1963), 2.

22. Aristotle, *Metaphysics* 14.1090a.28–29, in *Works*, 1:622–23.

23. Carl B. Boyer, *History of the Calculus and Its Conceptual Development* (reprint, New York: Dover Publications, 1959), 25.

24. Euclid, *Elements* 7, def. 2, in *The Thirteen Books of Euclid's Elements*, trans. Thomas L. Heath, vol. 11 of Great Books of the Western World, ed. Robert Maynard Hutchins (Chicago: Encyclopaedia Britannica, 1952), 127.

25. Quoted in Boyer, *History of the Calculus*, 41.

26. Aristotle, *Metaphysics* 1075b.29–30, in *Works*, 1:606.

27. Boyer, *History of the Calculus*, 25.

28. Ibid., 43.

29. Aristotle, *Physics* 8.5.258a, trans. R. P. Hardie and R. K. Gaye, in *Works*, 343.

30. *Dictionary of the History of Ideas*, s.v. "Macrocosm and Microcosm." My discussion draws heavily on Boas's essay.

31. Plato, *Philebus* 64E, in *The Dialogues*, 637.

32. Aristotle, *Poetics* 8.1451a.30, trans. Ingram Bywater, in *Works*, 385–86.

33. *Encyclopedia of World Art*, s.v. "Proportion."

34. Ibid.

35. Fritz Baumgart, *A History of Architectural Styles* (New York: Frederick Praeger, 1969), 23–24.

36. Spiro Kostof, *A History of Architecture: Settings and Rituals* (New York: Oxford University Press, 1985), 124–25.

37. Rhys Carpenter, *The Aesthetic Basis of Greek Art* (Bloomington: Indiana University Press, 1959), 121–22.

38. Ibid., 123.

39. Ibid., 124–25.

40. Kostof, *History of Architecture*, 125.

41. Quoted in ibid., 126.

42. L. D. Caskey, *The Geometry of Greek Vases* (Boston: Museum of Fine Arts, 1922).

43. *New Grove Dictionary of Music and Musicians*, s.v. "Music of the Spheres."

44. See Lynn Thorndike, *A History of Magic and Experimental Science* (New York: Columbia University Press, 1923) for a comprehensive treatment.

45. "Throughout the second half of the 16th century, there were noteworthy and continuing efforts to apply Plato's counsels, real or supposed, to the actual process of composition. His philosophy, associated with the ideals of beauty and harmonious proportion, was consciously symbolized in the splendid masques presented during the late 1580's by Galilei's friend Giovani de' Bardi." *New Grove Dictionary of Music and Musicians*, s.v. "Plato."

46. Aristotle, *Metaphysics* 1.983a.27–33, trans. W. D. Ross, in *Works*, 1:501.

47. Quoted in Mortimer J. Adler and William Gorman, eds., *The Great Ideas: A Syntopicon of the Great Books of the Western World* (Chicago: Encyclopaedia Britannica, 1952), 897.

48. Plato, *Timaeus* 37, in *Dialogues,*, 450.

49. The image of a thing first seen remains the defining impression from which the thing drifts through time, by aging or otherwise altering. Therefore, the mnemonic image establishes the ur-state, often equated with the essence of the thing.

50. De Bary et al., *Sources of Indian Tradition*, 8.

51. Lao Tzu, *Way of Life*, 66.

52. Quoted in Fung Yu-lan, *History of Chinese Philosophy*, 226.

53. Plato, *Timaeus* 28, in *Works*, 447.

54. Richard Rorty, *Philosophy and the Mirror of Nature* (Princeton: Princeton University Press, 1979).

55. The ancient concept of the good, too, is dyadic. It involves on the one hand a correspondence between a thing or act and the established order (which itself is assumed always to correspond with the natural order) and, on the other, between a contractual agreement and acts that will or will not satisfy that agreement. A word or two may be in order about the related ethical concept of duty. It is not uniquely Greek in origin. As Barker observed long ago, "[T]he notion of duty is essentially implied in every system of morality and every ethical theory." In all Indo-European languages, the words used to express duty derived from expressions for owing. That the Greeks—at least the free citizens—had a highly developed sense of duty toward the poleis is too well known to need rehearsal here. Behind the concept of owing is obviously the metaphor of Debt/Payment, as John Stuart Mills recognized when he wrote: "Duty is a thing which may be exacted from a person, as one exacts a debt. Unless we think that it may be exacted from him, we do not call it his duty." A debt is anything that one person is under obligation to pay to another, the obligation being a written, oral, or tacit contract between the parties involved. Hence, both the Debt/Payment and the Contract metaphors are involved in the concept of duty, something that naturally carries into jurisprudence, where most jurists hold that every law creates a duty (viz., to obey the law).

Ethical good predicated on honoring the dictates of custom and law was generally equated with virtue, although even here most philosophers wanted to elevate virtue above mundane concerns. Marcus Aurelius came closest to the practical, believing justice to be the foundation of all virtues.

The Greek philosophers, however, did not base their arguments for the good on the notions implicit within the ethical fabric of society. Evidently the duties of citizenship in following the law and living up to one's word were too much taken for granted to be the object of speculation. Philosophers were after something that transcends practical ethics. Plato placed the issues of ultimate knowledge in the realm of the ideal. Many subsequent thinkers picked up on Plato's discussions in *Philebus* and *Phaedo*, equating the good with either pleasure (Epicurus opposing Plato) or disengagement of the emotions (the Stoics siding with Plato). Aristotle saw it as the fulfillment of inner potential (entelechy).

56. The same *spirit* or force that permeates nature and determines health infuses the human psyche in the creation of the arts. Indian aesthetics hinges on the concept of *rasa*, literally *taste*, and Chinese, on *ch'i* or *spirit* in the sense of the agency of the Tao that invests everything with dynamism or growth. Aesthetic theorizing along these lines belongs to the medieval period, but the roots plainly go back to the sense of organic order implicit in the Brahman and the Tao. For the Far Easterners, the impulse of aesthetic intuition is unquantifiable; for the Greeks, integers ruled the realm.

57. Mark Duke, *Acupuncture* (New York: Pyramid House, 1972), 55.

58. All this is traced in Rorty, *Philosophy and the Mirror of Nature.*

59. Plato, *The Republic* 10.598, in *Dialogues,* 429.

60. Ibid., 10:597, in *Dialogues,* 428.

61. Aristotle, *Poetics* 1448b.

62. For further discussion, see Katherine Everrett Gilbert and Helmut Kuhn, *A History of Esthetics,* rev. ed. (Bloomington: Indiana University Press, 1953), 59–86.

63. *Hamlet* 3.2.24.

64. W. C. Dampier, *A History of Science,* 4th ed. (Cambridge: Cambridge University Press, 1948), 43.

65. J. D. Bernal, *Science in History,* 3d ed. (New York: Hawthorne House, 1965), 159. Original italics.

66. Ibid.

67. Aristotle, *On the Heavens* 269a.1–8, trans. J. L. Stocks, in *Works,* 1:360.

68. Ibid.

69. Ibid., 270a.14–15, in *Works,* 361.

70. Ibid.

71. Ibid.

72. Jules R. Bemporad and Henry Pinsker, "Schizophrenia: The Manifest Symptomatology," in *Adult Clinical Psychiatry,* ed. Silvano Arieti and Eugene B. Brody, vol. 3 of *American Handbook of Psychiatry,* 2d ed. (New York: Basic Books, 1974), 532.

CHAPTER 5. THE MEDIEVAL PERIOD

1. Plotinus, *Fifth Ennead* 2.1, in *The Six Enneads,* trans. Stephen MacKenna and B. S. Page, vol. 17 of Great Books of the Western World, ed. Robert Maynard Hutchins (Chicago: Encyclopaedia Britannica, 1952), 214.

2. Ibid.

3. Plotinus, *Sixth Ennead* 6.10, in *The Six Enneads,* 314.

4. Roscelin is credited as the founder of medieval nominalism, though nominalism is almost an automatic consequence of the kinds of debate that fostered sectarian splits in medieval Christianity. People cannot debate long on fine distinctions without some of them realizing after a while that words, and therefore universals, can be defined arbitrarily and at will.

5. Harry Elmer Barnes, *An Intellectual and Cultural History of the Western World* (New York: Random House, 1937), 654.

6. Ibid., 481.

7. Ibid., 483.

8. Ibid.

9. Quoted in Arthur Hyman and James J. Walsh, *Philosophy in the Middle Ages: The Christian, Islamic, and Jewish Traditions* (Indianapolis, Ind.: Hackett 1973), 666.

10. Egidius Romanus, *On Ecclesiastical Power* 1.5, in Hyman and Walsh, *Philosophy in the Middle Ages,* 670.

11. John of Paris, *On Papal and Royal Power,* chap. 5, in Hyman and Walsh, *Philosophy in the Middle Ages,* 670.

12. Marsilius of Padua, *The Defender of Peace,* discourse 2, chap. 4, sec. 3, quoted in Hyman and Walsh, *Philosophy in the Middle Ages,* 684.

13. It might be interesting to comment on the role of the sacred text in ideological change. Some may see it as a factor weighted heavily in favor of social stasis, perpetuation of the religious institution, but we suggest just the opposite thesis. In an effort to cover all bases, so to speak, in the control of human behavior, religionists put together an extensive text written over a long period of time (or drawing upon ancient sources) and therefore containing contradictions and areas of textual conflict. What is more, to meet the largest possible number of circumstances, the fiats of the text are couched in suitably ambiguous terms. All these factors will work toward stasis only as long as that is what is desired by the portion of the population holding the means to power. When the balance of power changes or circumstances otherwise alter what is desired, the sacred text is sufficiently encompassing and ambiguous to prove a contrary view.

Keith Thomas, in *Man and the Natural World,* has supplied a splendid narrative of contrary interpretations of the Bible as it relates to man vis-à-vis animals and nature. We shall cite from his work several salient examples. In the late medieval period, the building of human dwellings and the cultivation of the land in difficult rural areas made wild nature seem an enemy to man. Antagonism perceived in nature was explained as the consequence of the Fall. Not an age of pets, though pets were never unknown, the Middle Ages spawned the position that all creatures and all of nature had been created subordinate to man to serve his needs. Man has dominion over nature and can do with it what he pleases. Accordingly, it was claimed that animals have no soul, and finally, with Descartes, that they are like machines, making cruelty toward them a matter of indifference. By the time that the sciences dethroned man from the center of the universe, an inverse counterpoint to the earlier tune had been composed. It revolved around the theme of dominion, which was simply reinterpreted as stewardship. Under stewardship, man had a divine injunction to look after and be kind to all God's creatures. The imperfections of nature were no longer attributed to the Fall but to man's imperfect understanding of the divine plan. As we shall see in retrospect, all this was facilitated by metaphoric shifts during the Renaissance and subsequently. What we must not forget is that Scripture was quoted for each reinterpretation in this changing confrontation between man and nature.

14. Friedrich Heer, *The Intellectual History of Europe,* trans. Jonathan Steinberg (Cleveland and New York: World Publishing Co., 1953), 164.

15. His logic was imperfectly known through Boethius's translation of the *Categories* and the *De interpretationis.* The other three parts of the *Organon* appeared between 1128 and 1159; the *Physics* and *Metaphysics,* around 1200. The *Poetics* remained largely unknown until the sixteenth century.

16. Barnes, *Intellectual and Cultural History of the Western World,* 427.

17. Ibid., 428.

18. Ibid., 432–33.

19. E. von Domarus, "The Specific Laws of Logic in Schizophrenia," in *Language and Thought in Schizophrenia*, ed. J. S. Kasanin (New York: W. W. Norton, 1964), quoted in Jules R. Bemporad and Henry Pinsker, "Schizophrenia: The Manifest Symptomatology," in *Adult Clinical Psychiatry*, ed. Silvano Arieti and Eugene B. Brody, vol. 3 of *American Handbook of Psychiatry*, ed. Silvano Arieti, 2d ed. (New York: Basic Books, 1974), 532.

20. Jules R. Bemporad and Henry Pinsker, "Schizophrenia: The Manifest Symptomatology," in Arieti and Brody, *Adult Clinical Psychiatry*, 532.

21. *Psychiatric Dictionary*, 5th ed., s.v. "Process, Primary Psychic."

22. W. T. H. Jackson, *The Literature of the Middle Ages* (New York: Columbia University Press, 1960), 5.

23. H. de Lubac, "Typologie et Allégorisme," *Recherches de Science Religieuse* (Paris) (1947) 45:180–226.

24. J. W. H. Atkins, *English Literary Criticism: The Medieval Phase* (New York: Peter Smith, 1952), 21

25. Ibid., 22.

26. Jackson, *Literature of the Middle Ages*, 21.

27. "Les symboles sont toujours pluridimensionels. . . . synthèse des contraires, le symbole a une face diurne et une face nocturne. De plus, beaucoup de ces couples ont des analogies entre eux, qui s'expriment aussi en symboles." Jean Chevalier and Alain Gheerbrant, introduction to *Dictionnaire des Symboles* (Paris: Editions Robert Laffont, 1969), xvii.

28. "[L]a première fonction du symbole est d'ordre exploratoire." "Il permet en effet de saisir d'une certaine manière une relation que la raison ne peut définir, parce qu'un terme en est connu et l'autre inconnu." Ibid., xviii.

29. "[I]mage vectorielle ou un schème eidolo-moteur." Ibid., xix.

CHAPTER 6. THE RENAISSANCE

1. It may be advantageous to conceive the Renaissance as a tendency rather than a period. Scholars have made cases for a Carolingian Renaissance, a renaissance of the twelfth century, and so on. It must be admitted that the case for the twelfth century made quite a few years ago by Charles Homer Haskins was notable in bringing to attention a vast literature showing classical learning that remains largely unexamined and untranslated from the obscure mixtures of Latin and vernacular in which they were written. Certainly, too, Haskins demonstrated convincing foundations for the traditional Renaissance of the fourteenth century. Since it is all a matter of historical construction, quarrels over the dating of the period seem barrenly academic.
See Charles Homer Haskins, *The Renaissance of the Twelfth Century* (Cambridge: Harvard University Press, 1927).

2. Philip K. Hitti, *History of the Arabs: From the Earliest Times to the Present* (London: Macmillan, 1951), 378 n. 4. Qinnasrin was an ancient city just south of Aleppo in northern Syria.

3. For a fuller discussion of all aspects of the problem, see A. W. Moore, *The Infinite* (London and New York: Routledge, 1990).

4. For a discussion of negation in Indian philosophy, see: F. Th. Stcherbatsky, *Buddhist Logic* (1930[?]; reprint, New York: Dover Publications, 1962), 1:363–99.

5. Aristotle, *Physics* 4.8.215b, trans. R. P. Hardie and R. K. Gaye, in *Works*, vol. 1 of

Great Books of the Western World, ed. Robert Maynard Hutchins (Chicago: Encyclopaedia Britannica, 1952), 295.

6. Max Jammer, *Concepts of Force: A Study in the Foundations of Dynamics* (Cambridge: Harvard University Press, 1957), 39–40.

7. Thomas Bradwardine, *Tractatus de Proportionibus*, trans. H. L. Crosby Jr. (Madison: University of Wisconsin Press, 1955), 112, quoted in Jammer, *Concepts of Force*, 66–67.

8. Quoted in Jammer, *Concepts of Force*, 90. Julius Caesar Scaliger (1484–1558) was an Italian-born French scholar who, among other things, wrote a book on Aristotle.

9. Galileo Galilei, *Dialogue on the Great World Systems*, trans. Salusbury, ed. Giorgio de Santillana (Chicago, 1953), 250, quoted in Jammer, *Concepts of Force*, 102. Original italics and parentheses.

10. Quoted in Jammer, *Concepts of Force*, 124–25.

11. George Berkeley, *De Motu*, sec. 17, quoted in Jammer, *Concepts of Force*, 204.

12. "[U]n mot qui ne sert qu'à cacher notre ignorance." Quoted in Jammer, *Concepts of Force*, 209.

13. Ibid.

14. Thomas Reid, *Works*, edited by William Hamilton (Edinburgh, 1846), 604, quoted in Jammer, *Concepts of Force*, 230.

15. I do not wish to become embroiled here in a discourse on understanding, nor do I want to imply that no understanding can occur without prior experience. I require only the weak case that all things are understood through the imaginative use of previous experience. That takes care of Santa Claus and unicorns, while leaving unquestioned that there is a sense in which a blind person does not understand color nor a deaf person, sound, in the same way as their respective sensory-unimpaired counterparts. Little more than this simple assumption is required for present purposes.

Exactly how various forms of understanding work must, to my mind, be left for empirical investigation. If certain aspects of my account of things need to be modified by subsequent empirical findings in cognitive science, I am unperturbed by that. The issues with which I am dealing here are broad enough and my claims sufficiently based upon documented cases that I trust to the fact that they may convey something of value even after being adjusted for empirical findings I cannot reasonably foresee.

16. Jammer, *Concepts of Force*, 248.

17. For further details, see J. T. Fraser, *Of Time, Passion, and Knowledge* (New York: George Braziller, 1975), 1–42; J. T. Fraser, ed., *The Voices of Time* (New York: George Braziller, 1966), 1–160.

18. Quoted in Gerald Holton, *Thematic Origins of Scientific Thought* (Cambridge: Harvard University Press, 1973), 72.

19. Ibid., 86.

20. See Eric Werener, "The Last Pythagorean Musician: Johannes Kepler," in *Aspects of Medieval and Renaissance Music*, ed. Jan LaRue (New York: W. W. Norton, 1966), 867–82

21. Letter to H. von Hohenburg, 14 September 1599. Quoted in Werner, "The Last Pythagorean: Johannes Kepler," 874.

22. Thorkild Jacobsen, "Enuma Elish—'The Babylonian Genesis'," in *Theories of the Universe: From Babylonian Myth to Modern Science*, ed. Milton K. Munitz (New York: Free Press, 1957), 8–20.

23. See Harry Elmer Barnes, *Intellectual and Cultural History of the Western World* (New York: Random House, 1937), 582–91, for a full discussion.

24. Ibid., 588.

25. Erich Kahler, *The Tower and the Abyss: An Inquiry into the Transformation of the Individual* (New York: George Braziller, 1957).

26. Howard M. Brown, *Music in the Renaissance* (Englewood Cliffs, N.J.: Prentice-Hall, 1976), 257.

27. Gustave Reese, *Music in the Renaissance* (New York: W. W. Norton, 1954), 519–71, typifies this classic approach.

28. Dom Anselm Hughes and Gerald Abraham, *Ars Nova and the Renaissance, 1300–1540* (London: Oxford University Press, 1960), 426.

29. Paul Henry Lang, *Music in Western Civilization* (New York: W. W. Norton, 1941), 244.

30. For further details, see *New Grove Dictionary of Music and Musicians*, s.v. "Organ."

31. Thomas Morley, *A Plaine and Easie Introduction to Practicall Musicke* (London, 1597), quoted in *New Grove Dictionary of Music and Musicians*, s.v. "Fantasia, I."

32. Victor Rangel-Ribeiro, *Baroque Music: A Practical Guide for the Performer* (New York: Schirmer Books, 1981), 14.

33. Herbert Read, *Icon and Idea: The Function of Art in the Development of Consciousness* (Cambridge: Harvard University Press, 1965).

34. Jose Ortega y Gasset, *The Dehumanization of Art and Other Essays on Art, Culture, and Literature*, trans. Helene Weyl, 2d ed. (Princeton: Princeton University Press, 1968).

35. Erich Auerbach, *Mimesis: The Representation of Reality in Western Literature* (Princeton: Princeton University Press, 1953).

36. Erich Kahler, *The Inward Turn of Narrative*, trans. Richard Winston and Clara Winston (Princeton: Princeton University Press, 1973).

37. Kenneth Clark, *The Nude: A Study in Ideal Form* (New York: Pantheon, 1956).

38. Ursula Hatje, ed., *The Styles of European Art* (New York: Harry N. Abrams, 1965). See also Margaret Finch, *Style in Art History: An Introduction to Theories of Style and Sequence* (Metuchen, N.J.: Scarecrow Press, 1974). This work contains a short but useful bibliography.

CHAPTER 7. THE ENLIGHTENMENT TO 1900

1. William Powell Jones, *The Rhetoric of Science: A Study of Scientific Ideas and Imagery in Eighteenth-Century English Poetry* (London: Routledge and Kegan Paul, 1966), 1.

2. Matthew Prior, *Solomon on the Vanity of the World, a Poem in Three Books*, in *The Literary Works of Matthew Prior*, ed. H. B. Wright and M. K. Spears (Oxford: Clarendon Press, 1959), 1:306–85, quoted in Jones, *Rhetoric of Science*, 57.

3. Moses Browne, *Essay on the Universe*, quoted in Jones, *Rhetoric of Science*, 62.

4. Samuel Bowden, "Poem Sacred to the Memory of Sir Isaac Newton," in *Poetical Essays on Several Occasions* (London, vol. 1, 1733; vol. 2, 1735), quoted in Jones, *Rhetoric of Science*, 126.

5. Quoted in Jones, *Rhetoric of Science*, 64.

6. See Jones, *Rhetoric of Science*, 99–101.

7. Quoted in E. T. Bell, *The Development of Mathematics* (New York: McGraw-Hill, 1945), 211.

8. Ibid., 212.

9. "Rococo ornament . . . assumes that a successful building is a hierarchical order that assigns to each part its proper place, and it assumes that society is such an order. Ornament contributes to the articulation of that order. . . . In this sense ornament can be said to

possess an ethical, not merely an aesthetic significance; ethical in the sense of helping to establish the ethos of a society, which assigns to persons and things their proper places." Karsten Harries, *The Bavarian Rococo Church: Between Faith and Aestheticism* (New Haven: Yale University Press, 1983), 246.

10. It might be argued that the concern for symmetry is the manifestation of a perceptual schema. At this state of our knowledge, it seems to me that is a moot question. If, however, that interpretation is embraced, that perceptual schema would nevertheless conform nicely with the Pattern metaphor as the organizing determinant. In other words, it would be consonant in a culture in which the cosmos was conceived as dominated by order or pattern.

11. Harry Elmer Barnes, *An Intellectual and Cultural History of the Western World* (New York: Random House, 1937), 967–68.

12. *Encyclopedia of Physics*, 2d ed., s.v. "Conservation Laws." Original italics.

13. Ibid.

14. *Encyclopedia of Modern Physics*, s.v. "Elementary Particle Physics." Original parenthesis.

15. Bell, *Development of Mathematics*, 212.

16. Manfred F. Bukofzer, *Music in the Baroque Era* (New York: W. W. Norton, 1947), 388.

17. *New Groves Dictionary of Music and Musicians*, s.v. "Rhetoric and Music."

18. Julien Offray de La Mettrie, *Man a Machine*, trans. Gertrude C. Bussey and M. W. Calkins, French-English ed. (Lasalle, Ill.: Open Court, 1912), 70, 140.

19. Marquis de Sade, *Histoire de Juliette, ou les Prospérités du Vice*, in *Oeuvres Complètes* (Paris: Cercle du Livre Précieux, 1973), 9:26. My translation. Original italics.

20. Ibid., 83. Original italics. My translation.

21. Ibid., 8:399. My translation.

22. Pierre-Simon Laplace, "Recherches, 1. sur l'intégration des équations différentielles aux différences finies, et sur leur usage dans la théorie des hasards. 2. sur le principe de la gravitation universelle, et sur les inégalités séculaires des planètes qui en dépendent." Quoted in *Dictionary of Scientific Biography*, s.v. "Laplace, Pierre-Simon." Laplace repeated this later in his *Essai Philosophique sur les Probabilités*.

23. I forgo a detailed examination of such saving arguments as that of Leibniz based on the notion of preestablished harmony, because in essence that merely extends the mechanism to the whole universe, which is equally inimical to *intent* and *meaning*. And it seems silly to me to resign oneself to a meaningless way of life simply because the deployment of certain metaphors leads to it.

24. Immanuel Kant, *Critique of Pure Reason*, translated by Norman Kemp Smith (London: St. Martin's Press, 1929), 42.

25. Immanuel Kant, *Prolegomena to Any Future Metaphysics*, ed. Lewis White Beck (Indianapolis, Ind.: Bobbs-Merrill, 1950), 83. The editor notes that the translation is based on the Mahafy translation (London, 1872) as revised by Carus (Chicago, 1902).

26. Immanuel Kant, *Critique of Pure Reason*, sect. 21, translated by J. M. D. Meiklejohn, *Great Books of the Western World*, volume 42 (Chicago, 1952), 56.

27. Arthur Schopenhauer, *The World as Will and Idea*, sect. 26, in *The Philosophy of Schopenhauer* (New York, 1928), 94.

28. Friedrich Nietzsche, *Beyond Good and Evil*, S. 19, in *The Philosophy of Nietzsche*, trans. Helen Zimmern (New York: Random House, n.d.), 19–20. Original italics.

29. Ibid., sec. 259, in *Philosophy of Nietzsche*, 200. Original italics.

30. Arthur Berndtson, "Vitalism," in *A History of Philosophical Systems*, ed. Vergilius Ferm (New York: Philosophical Library, 1950), 378.

31. Henri Bergson, *Creative Evolution*, trans. Arthur Mitchell (New York: Henry Holt, 1911), 223–24. Original italics.

32. A. Babloyantz, *Molecules, Dynamics, and Life: An Introduction to Self-Organization of Matter* (New York: John Wiley & Sons, 1986).
Leon Glass and Michael C. Mackey, *From Clocks to Chaos: The Rhythms of Life* (Princeton: Princeton University Press, 1988).

33. It has been suggested that the near-death experience is somehow the result of residual brain cell activity. Internally generated hallucination could plausibly be explained in these terms, but not objective sensory observation, which requires functioning neural pathways from sense organs to brain. Further, there exist in Dr. Moody's dossiers cases where second parties have validated observations made by the temporarily brain-dead patients concerning localities far removed from where they were when clinically expired.

The only solid reason for discounting these findings, which have been verified by the usual scientific methodologies, is that they fly in the face of established scientific belief. History is replete with such instances of denial later to be vindicated (e.g., Semmelweiss's principle of antisepsis, the existence of the vacuum, the idea that the stars and planets are not merely ideal celestial bodies made from the fifth element, etc.), so there seems to me no justification for relegating these findings to the dustbin of quackery merely because they contradict what most present-day scientists want to believe. That is bad science. The same may be said for reincarnation research, most of which *is* inconclusive, but due consideration must be given to the work of Ian Stevenson, professor of psychiatry at the University of Virginia Medical Center, whose methodology is straightforwardly scientific.

The following references should be consulted: Raymond A. Moody Jr., *Life After Life* (New York: Mockingbird Books, 1975; reprint, New York: Bantam Books, 1976); idem, *The Light Beyond: New Explorations* (New York: Bantam Books, 1988); idem, *Reflections on Life After Life* (New York: Bantam Books, 1977); Ian Stevenson, "Reincarnation: Field Studies and Theoretical Issues," in *Handbook of Parapsychology*, ed. Benjamin B. Wolman (New York: Van Nostrand Reinhold, 1977), 631–63; Ian Stevenson, *Ten Cases in India*, vol. 1 of *Cases of Reincarnation Type* (Charlottesville: University Press of Virginia, 1975); idem, *Ten Cases in Sri Lanka*, vol. 2 of *Cases of Reincarnation Type* (Charlottesville: University Press of Virginia, 1977); idem, *Fifteen Cases in Thailand, Lebanon, and Turkey*, vol. 3 of *Cases of Reincarnation Type* (Charlottesville: University Press of Virginia, 1978); idem, *Twenty Cases Suggestive of Reincarnation*, 2d ed. (Charlottesville: University Press of Virginia, 1974).

34. The operation of a so-called simple machine is described mathematically in linear equations. A chaotic system requires nonlinear equations.

35. Barnes, *Intellectual and Cultural History of the Western World*, 959–60.

36. Exactly the same argument for Darwin applies to Freud. All of the ideas he assimilated into his theories were current long before he adopted them and they were in essentially the same form in which they appeared later in his work. All this is given in great detail with massive documentation in Henri F. Ellenberger, *The Discovery of the Unconscious: The History of Dynamic Psychiatry* (New York: Basic Books, 1970).

37. W. P. D. Wightman, *The Growth of Scientific Ideas* (New Haven: Yale University Press, 1953), 395.

38. Charles Singer, *A Short History of Scientific Ideas to 1900* (Oxford: Clarendon Press, 1959), 507. For further details, see Maurice Mandelbaum, "Scientific Background of Evolutionary Theory in Biology," in *Roots of Scientific Thought: A Cultural Perspective*, ed. Philip P. Wiener and Aaron Nolan (New York: Basic Books, 1957), 517–36.

"Darwin did not profess to have invented any of [his main] ideas, and he was particularly cognizant of his debt to Thomas Malthus and Lyell." *Dictionary of the History of Ideas*, s.v. "Evolutionism."

39. Erich Kahler, *The Tower and the Abyss: An Inquiry into the Transformation of the Individual* (New York: George Braziller, 1957), 139.

40. Ibid., 140–41. Kahler's translation of Deffand.

41. Quoted in ibid., 137. My translation.

42. Quoted in William K. Wimsatt Jr., and Cleanth Brooks, *Literary Criticism: A Short History* (New York: Alfred A. Knopf, 1957), 386. Original italics.

43. Samuel Taylor Coleridge, *Biographia Literaria* , edited by John Shawcross (Oxford: Oxford University Press, 1907), 1:202, quoted in Wimsatt and Brooks, *Literary Criticism*, 389.

44. See Mario Praz, *Romantic Agony*, trans. Angus Davidson, 2d ed. (Oxford: Oxford University Press, 1951).

45. John G. Howells, ed., *World History of Psychiatry* (New York: Bruner/Maazel, 1975), 57.

46. *Biblico-Theological Lexicon of New Testament Greek*, 4th ed., s.v. "Diatheke"; *The Anchor Bible Dictionary*, s.v. "Covenant."

Certainly the biblical concept of the covenant between the Jews and their God was sufficiently endemic to the Judaeo-Christian world to supply inspiration for the use of the idea of contract to conceptualize the origins of social order. After all, St. Augustine was one of the earliest to forge the critical moral link between consent and will, without which contractarian theory would not have been possible. Even though he looked to the *bona voluntas* of Cicero and Seneca for precedents, he would have been even more mindful of the biblical parallel.

47. Bertrand Russell, *A History of Western Philosophy* (New York: Simon & Schuster, 1945), 659.

48. See Erich Kahler, *The Inward Turn of Narrative*, trans. Richard Winston and Clara Winston (Princeton: Princeton University Press, 1973).

49. Erich Auerbach, *Mimesis: The Representation of Reality in Western Literature* (Princeton: Princeton University Press, 1953), 408. Original italics.

50. Ibid., 421.

51. John Stuart Mill, *Autobiography and Literary Essays*, in *Collected Works*, ed. John M. Robson and Jack Stillinger (Toronto: University of Toronto Press, 1980), 1:223.

CHAPTER 8. THE TWENTIETH CENTURY

1. Lewis S. Feuer, *Einstein and the Generations of Science*, 2d ed. (New York: Basic Books, 1982).

2. Ibid., 137.

3. Ernst Mach, *Popular Scientific Lectures*, 4th ed. (Chicago, 1910), 104, quoted in Feuer, *Einstein and the Generations of Science*, 32.

4. There is a rather complex etymological history associated with this word, the Latin form of which is *substantia*. Aristotle used the term *ousia* (which we have already examined), to designate the ground of being. In early Greek, *ousia* meant *property* in the legal sense of that which one owns. Remnants of that usage are found in the expression, "a man of substance." From that sense, pre-Socratic philosophers used *ousia* as a synonym for *physis*, a term meaning variously the origin of a thing, that of which it is made, its structure, or a kind or species. Hence, the Aristotelian usage marked no abrupt change. Aristotle did, however, reject

hypokeimenon, standing under, as a proper term for ground of being, preferring the more abstract participial stem of *einai, to be,* apparently because of the similar usage by his predecessors. So much of Greek writing has been destroyed that it is hazardous to extract too much from these early usages. That Aristotle may have been falling back on the First Position metaphor is indicated by the fact that he prominently employed *ousia prote, first being,* to refer to the individual existing thing that could stand as the subject of a proposition. That is, it was that of which some property could be predicated. Any term that could be substituted for such an *ousia prote* in a proposition he called *ousia deutera, second being.* In so doing, he seems to have in mind especially terms naming species and genera, thus harking back to the earlier synonym, *physis.* He regards species, then, as more *substantial* than genera.

5. Albert Einstein, "Reply to Criticisms," in *Albert Einstein: Philosopher-Scientist,* ed. Paul Arthur Schilpp (Evanston, Ill.: Library of Living Philosophers, 1949), 684. Original italics.

6. This is a set of laws that relates the frequency and energy distribution of blackbody radiation to certain variables. The first law states that the wavelength of the spectral distribution is inversely proportional to the absolute temperature of the black body. The second law states that the emissive power of the black body in the wavelength interval of maximum intensity is proportional to the fifth power of the absolute temperature. The third law attempts through a rather complicated formula to express the spectral energy distribution of the radiation at a given temperature. The first and second laws are correct; the third gives good results for short wavelengths but fails at long wavelengths.

7. Max Jammer, *The Conceptual Development of Quantum Mechanics* (New York: McGraw-Hill, 1966), 26–27. Abraham Pais, *Inward Bound: Of Matter and Forces in the Physical World* (Oxford and New York, 1986), 133–36.

8. For a discussion of this, see Max Jammer, *Philosophy of Quantum Mechanics,* 265–96.

9. The whole equation is too technical to be written out and discussed here. But the variable expression usually written b**a** is a three-component element that may be interpreted as designating three constituents of the electron or positron, which is supposedly elementary.

10. In quantum mechanics, there is a distribution of probabilities throughout a given volume. These define the chance of finding, say, a certain particle at various points in the volume. The exact position cannot be known, because to find out where the particle is, you have to shoot other particles at it (like photons of light). When these exploratory particles hit their target, they naturally knock it out of place, like one billiard ball hitting another. Therefore, there is always a degree of uncertainty is such measurements with subatomic particles. This is the essence of the Heisenberg Uncertainty Principle. The uncertainty also arises from more formal mathematical considerations.

11. Planck's constant, approximately 6.626×10^{-27} erg second, gives the dimensional limit of smallness at which energy quanta can exist. It is the ratio of the frequency to the energy of a quantum of radiation.

12. Schwarzchild found these solutions in 1916. They described the space-time field around a symmetrical object like the sun. However, they did not include rotation. The Kerr solutions for rotating stars had to wait until 1963. These solutions to the relativistic field equations are basic to the physics of black holes. They show, for example, at what crucial mass a star will collapse in upon itself to form a black hole.

13. "Kinesthetic image schemas are structured in such a way that they have a basic logic, and it is that structure that is used in reasoning and that gives rise to mathematics." George Lakoff, *Women, Fire, and Dangerous Things: What Categories Reveal about the Mind* (Chicago: University of Chicago Press, 1987), 355.

Although my interpretation of mathematics was formulated prior to my reading Lakoff on the subject, our approaches are much the same.

14. Hilary Putnam, *Reason, Truth, and History* (Cambridge: Harvard University Press, 1981). See also Lakoff, *Women, Fire, and Dangerous Things*, 236–41.

15. R. W. Hamming "The Unreasonable Effectiveness of Mathematics," in *Mathematical Analysis of Physical Systems*, ed. Ronald E. Mickens (New York: Van Nostrand Reinhold, 1985), 15–29.

16. Ashok Vohra, *Wittgenstein's Philosophy of Mind* (La Salle, Ill.: Open Court, 1986).

17. For a discussion, see: Henri F. Ellenberger, *The Discovery of the Unconscious: The History and Evolution of Dynamic Psychiatry* (New York: Basic Books, 1970), 209–10. Franz G. Alexander and Sheldon T. Selesnick, *The History of Psychiatry* (New York: Harper & Row, 1966), 169–70.

18. Thus, in speaking of the mechanism of repression, Freud wrote that the primary system, or the unconscious, "aims at the free outflow of the quantities of excitation," and "we are led to the hypothesis that cathexis through the second system [the preconscious] is at the same time an inhibition of the discharge of excitation." Sigmund Freud, *The Psychology of the Dream-Processes*, in *The Basic Writings of Sigmund Freud*, trans. and ed. A. A. Brill (New York: Random House, 1938), 534–35). The metaphor could also be read as electrodynamic.

19. A. Venkoba Rao, "India," in *World History of Psychiatry*, ed. John G. Howells (New York: Bruner/Maazel, 1975), 628.

20. Ibid.

21. Donald J. Munro, *The Concept of Man in Early China* (Stanford, Calif.: Stanford University Press, 1969), 46–47.

22. J. Sinha, *Indian Psychology*, 2 vols. (Calcutta, 1958, 1961), quoted in A. Venkoba Rao, "India," 628.

23. Kalidas Battacharya, "The Status of the Individual in Indian Metaphysics," in *The Indian Mind: Essentials of Indian Philosophy and Culture*, ed. Charles A. Moore (Honolulu: University of Hawaii Press, 1967), 611. Original italics.

24. Hajime Nakamura, *Ways of Thinking of Eastern Peoples: India-China-Tibet-Japan* (Honolulu: University of Hawaii Press, 1964), 101.

25. Likewise the Hindu concept of *maya* (illusion). All things are *maya*, illusory manifestations of the *Brahman*. *Brahman* is from the root, *brh*, meaning to grow. Thus, the *Brahman* evolves by manifesting *maya*. Its evolving nature is rather like that of Bergson's *élan vital*, imbued with an activating agent.

26. Quoted in Fung Yu-lan, *A History of Chinese Philosophy*, trans. Derk Bodde (Princeton: Princeton University Press, 1952), 2:300.

27. Quoted in D. T. Suzuki, *Zen Buddhism: Selected Writings of D. T. Suzuki*, ed. William Barrett (Garden City, N.Y.: Doubleday Anchor, 1956), 88.

28. Quoted in ibid., 173.

29. Quoted in T'ang Chün-i, "The Individual and the World in Chinese Methodology," in *The Chinese Mind: Essentials of Chinese Philosophy and Culture*, ed. Charles A. Moore (Honolulu: University of Hawaii Press, 1967), 269.

30. Quoted in Suzuki, *Zen Buddhism*, 181.

31. Ibid., 190–91.

32. Quoted in Heinrich Dumoulin, *Zen Buddhism: A History*, vol. 1, *India and China*, trans. James W. Heisig and Paul Knitter (New York: Simon & Schuster, 1988), 194.

33. Hans Vaihinger, *The Philosophy of "As If,"* trans. C. K. Ogden, 2d ed. (London: Routledge and Kegan Paul, 1935), 228, 232.

34. For conceptualizing the mind metaphorically, the problem would seem to be that there is nothing so far common to human experience that is sufficiently like the mind to serve as a satisfactory metaphorand in terms of which to build an understanding of the mind.

It is still possible in theory to resolve the problem by coming at it topologically, as has been done in this century to solve problems in many disciplines. I say this because any group of finite order is isomorphic to some group of permutations. This means that no matter how complex the structure (represented by a group), it can be resolved into some other structure (permutation group) that can, by suitable transformations, be brought into perfect congruence with it. This, of course, assumes that the mind is epiphenomenal, a question on which I remain unconvinced either way.

For a survey and critique of artificial-intelligence theories of the mind, see Daniel Crevier, *AI: The Tumultuous History of the Search for Artificial Intelligence* (New York: Basic Books, 1993).

35. Suzuki, *Zen Buddhism*, 84.

36. Ibid., 96.

37. Quoted in ibid., 169.

38. Quoted in R. H. Blyth, *Haiku* (Tokyo: Hokuseido Press, n.d.), 1:240.

39. *Ch'uan Teng Lu* 22, quoted in Alan W. Watts, *The Way of Zen* (New York: Pantheon, 1957), 126.

40. Sokei-an Sasaki, "The Trancendental World," *Zen Notes* (New York) 1, no. 5 (1954), quoted in Watts, *Way of Zen*, 121.

41. Donald R. Griffin, *The Question of Animal Awareness: Evolutionary Continuity of Mental Experience*, rev. ed. (New York: Rockefeller University Press, 1981); idem, *Animal Minds* (Chicago: University of Chicago Press, 1992); Michael Bright, *Animal Language* (Ithaca: Cornell University Press, 1984).

42. Lancelot I. Whyte, *The Unconscious Before Freud* (New York: St. Martin's Press, 1962); Ellenberger, *Discovery of the Unconscious;* D. Cheng, *Philosophical Aspects of the Mind-Body Problem* (Honolulu: University of Hawaii Press, 1975); Gardner Murphy, *Historical Introduction to Modern Psychology* (New York: Harcourt, Brace and Co., 1949).

43. Franz Alexander and Sheldon T. Selesnick, *The History of Psychiatry* (New York: Harper & Row, 1966), 109.

44. For a general review, see Eugene T. Gendlin, "The Newer Therapies," in *Treatment*, ed. Daniel X. Freedman and Jaryl E. Dyrud, vol. 5 of *American Handbook of Psychiatry*, ed. Silvano Arieti (New York: Basic Books, 1975), 269–89.

45. Richard Rorty, *Philosophy and the Mirror of Nature* (Princeton: Princeton University Press); idem, *Consequences of Pragmatism: Essays, 1972–1980* (Minneapolis: University of Minnesota Press, 1982).

46. Irving Babbit, quoted in *American Composers: A Biographical Dictionary*, s.v. "Babbit, Irving."

47. Brian Gaines, "Foundations of Fuzzy Reasoning." *International Journal of Man-Machine Studies* 8 (1976): 623–68; Arnold Kaufmann, *Introduction to the Theory of Fuzzy Subsets* (New York: Academic Press, 1975); Daniel McNeil and Paul Freiberger, *Fuzzy Logic* (New York: Simon & Schuster, 1993); Lotfi Zadeh, "Fuzzy Sets," *Information and Control* 8, no. 3 (June 1965): 338–53.

48. Caroline Ware, K. M. Panikkar, and J. M. Romein, *The Twentieth Century* (New York: Harper & Row, 1966), 666.

"[I]f Reality itself is the historical development of Reason (which is Hegel's idealist view), then in the fourteenth century Ptolemaic astronomy was *true* (since it was then the highest expression of Reason), whereas now it is false. Thus truth changes with theory-change; and all theories are true (in their own time)." Larry Briskman, "Rationality, Science and History," in *Companion to the History of Modern Science*, ed. R. C. Olby, G. N. Cantor, J. R. R. Christie, and M. J. S. Hodge (London and New York: Routledge, 1990), 175.

49. Gaston Bachelard, *The New Scientific Spirit*, trans. Arthur Goldhammer (Paris: Presses Universitaires de France, 1934; reprint, Boston: Beacon Press, 1984), 6.

50. Patrick A. Heelan, foreword to *The New Scientific Spirit*, by Gaston Bachelard (Paris: Presses Universitaires de France, 1934; reprint, Boston: Beacon Press, 1984), x.

51. Art Berman, *From the New Criticism to Deconstruction* (Urbana and Chicago: University of Illinois Press, 1988), 244.

52. Benjamin Evans Mitchell, *The Theory of Categories* (New York: Academic Press, 1965); Ion Bucur and Aristide Deleanu, *Introduction to the Theory of Categories and Functors* (New York: Wiley-Interscience, 1968).

53. Ware, Panikkar, and Romein, *Twentieth Century*, 151.

54. Ibid.

55. Marvin L. Minsky, *Society of Mind* (New York: Simon & Schuster, 1986).

56. Detractors will be impelled to cavil over my qualification, *somewhat consonant*, pointing out that it is too vague or arbitrary. I will anticipate this objection by indicating that, under my hypothesis, the degree of consonance will necessarily vary chaotically (i.e., in a nonlinear way) and so cannot be precisely quantified generically.

57. Peter Berger and T. Luckman, *The Social Construction of Reality* (New York: Doubleday, 1967).

58. Consider that the domain of random numbers, if infinitely extended, by definition must contain every ordered sequence. Further, chaos, as defined in mathematics, is deterministic. Therefore, looking for order here may not be as foolish as it seems.

59. See, for example, Roger Lewin, *Complexity: Life at the Edge of Chaos* (New York: Macmillan, 1992).

60. William P. Reinhardt, "Classical Chaos, Phase Space, and Semiclassical Quantization," in Mickens, *Mathematical Analysis of Physical Systems*, 169–245.

61. Interestingly, nonlinear dynamics addresses a fuller reality than has hitherto been the case in analytical dynamics. By this I mean that in reality bodies are not, as they are usually treated in analytical dynamics, isolated but are interactive with other bodies. In the famous three-body problem of classical physics—there is a quantum mechanical analogue—it is required to establish the motion of three bodies of similar mass under mutual gravitational attraction and initial conditions of location and directed motion. Three differential equations are presented, forming a nonintegratable system. It can be solved only by methods of approximation. Translation of the problem into phase space restricts the solution and establishes forbidden regions (i.e., motions that will not occur) but does not lead to specific solutions.

Beyond three bodies, the problem becomes hopeless in terms of direct solutions. So-called perturbation methods and, with large enough numbers of bodies, statistical procedures come into play. These are approximation methods. They can yield good results and are not to be scorned, but they do not rely on a causal scaffold. Thus, mathematics here deals not with the structure of reality but rather with Platonic ideals. Restrictions of dynamics, such as these, are wonderful illustrations of Hamming's contentions that in mathematics "we see what we look for" and "science in fact answers comparatively few problems."

Differential equations, then, do not unqualifiedly express the way in which nature works. Especially in relativistic quantum field theory, this is becoming painfully clear. We rely on good statistical guesses that work because the sample is large. But it may just be that the language of mathematics itself needs to be revamped, so that it can be less "ideal" and more "realistic." In view of their enormous success, we would not expect mathematicians to accept such a suggestion with other than derision, but that lies more in the province of psychology than logic.

GLOSSARY OF METAPHORS AND SCHEMES

1. Maximilian Rudwin, *The Devil in Legend and Literature* (La Salle, Ill.: Open Court, 1931), 37–38.

2. Rudolf Arnheim, *Visual Thinking* (Berkeley: University of California Press, 1969).

Bibliography

Alexander, Franz G., and Sheldon T. Selesnick. *The History of Psychiatry.* New York: Harper & Row, 1966.

Allers, Rudolf von. "Vom Nutzen und den Gefahren de Metapher in der Psychologie." *Jahrbuch für Psychologie und Psychotherapie* 3 (1955): 3–15.

Anderson, C. C. "The Latest Metaphor in Psychology." *Dalhousie Review* 38 (summer 1958): 176–87.

Anderson, Timothy. "A Hard Nut to Crack: Evolving English Metaphors for Insanity in Social-Historical Context." *American Imago* 50, no. 1 (spring 1993): 111–30.

Arieti, Silvano, and Eugene B. Brody, eds. *Adult Clinical Psychiatry.* Vol. 3 of *American Handbook of Psychiatry,* edited by Silvano Arieti, 2d ed. New York: Basic Books, 1974.

Aristotle. *Works.* Vols. 8 and 9 of *Great Books of the Western World,* edited by Robert Maynard Hutchins. Chicago: Encyclopaedia Britannica, 1952.

Armstrong, A. H., ed. *The Cambridge History of Later Greek and Early Medieval Philosophy.* Cambridge: Cambridge University Press, 1967.

Arnheim, Rudolf. *Visual Thinking.* Berkeley: University of California Press, 1969.

Atkins, J. W. H. *English Literary Criticism: The Medieval Phase.* New York: Peter Smith, 1952.

Auerbach, Erich. *Mimesis: The Representation of Reality in Western Literature.* Princeton: Princeton University Press, 1953.

Augustine. *The Confessions – The City of God – On Christian Doctrine.* Vol. 18 of *Great Books of the Western World,* edited by Robert Maynard Hutchins. Chicago: Encyclopaedia Britannica, 1952.

Babloyantz, A. *Molecules, Dynamics and Life: An Introduction to Self-Organization of Matter.* New York: John Wiley & Sons, 1986.

Bachelard, Gaston. *The New Scientific Spirit.* Translated by Arthur Goldhammer. Paris: Presses Universitaires de France, 1934. Reprint, Boston: Beacon Press, 1984.

Baker, G. L., and J. P. Gollub. *Chaotic Dynamics: An Introduction.* Cambridge: Cambridge University Press, 1990.

Ballard, Edward G. "Metaphysics and Metaphor." *Journal of Philosophy* 45 (8 April 1948): 208–14.

Baltrusaitis, Jurgis. *Le Moyen Age Fantastique: Antiquités et Exotismes dans l'Art Gothique.* Paris: Flammarion, 1981.

————. *Réveils et Prodiges: Le Gothique Fantastique.* Paris: Armand Colin, 1959.

Barfield, Owen. "The Meaning of the Word 'Literal'." In *Metaphor and Symbol,* edited by L. C. Knights and Basil Cottle. London: Butterworths Scientific Publications, 1960.

Barker, Philip. *Using Metaphors in Psychotherapy.* New York: Brunner/Mazel, 1985.

Barnes, Harry Elmer. *An Intellectual and Cultural History of the Western World.* New York: Random House, 1937.

Bartel, Roland. *Metaphors and Symbols: Forays into Language.* Urbana, Ill.: National Council of Teachers of English, 1983.

Bartlett, Phyllis. *Poems in Process.* New York: Oxford University Press, 1951.

Bartlett, Frederic C. *Remembering: A Study in Experimental and Social Psychology.* London and New York: Cambridge University Press, 1932.

Bartley, W. W., III. "Alienation Alienated: The Economics of Knowledge versus the Psychology and Sociology of Knowledge." In *Evolutionary Epistemology, Rationality, and the Sociology of Knowledge,* edited by Gerard Radnitzky and W. W. Bartley III. La Salle, Ill.: Open Court, 1987.

Battacharya, Kalidas. "The Status of the Individual in Indian Metaphysics." In *The Indian Mind: Essentials of Indian Philosophy and Culture,* edited by Charles A. Moore. Honolulu: University of Hawaii Press, 1967.

Baumgart, Fritz. *History of Architectural Styles.* New York: Frederick Praeger, 1969.

Beardsley, Monroe. "The Metaphorical Twist." *Philosophy and Phenomenological Research* 22, no. 2 (1962): 293–307.

Bell, E. T. *The Development of Mathematics.* New York: McGraw-Hill, 1945.

Bernal, J. D. *Science in History.* 3d ed. New York: Hawthorn Books, 1965.

Berger, Peter I. *The Social Construction of Reality: A Treatise in the Sociology of Knowledge.* New York: Doubleday, 1966.

Bergson, Henri. *Creative Evolution.* Translated by Arthur Mitchell. New York: Henry Holt, 1911.

Berman, Art. *From the New Criticism to Deconstruction.* Urbana and Chicago: University of Illinois Press, 1988.

Bernard, Theos. *Hindu Philosophy.* New York: Philosophical Library, n.d.

Bickerman, E. J. *Chronology of the Ancient World.* London: Thames and Hudson, 1968.

Black, Max. *Perplexities: Rational Choice, the Prisoner's Dilemma, Metaphor, Poetic Ambiguity, and Other Puzzles.* Ithaca: Cornell University Press, 1990.

Blasko, Dawn G., and Cynthia M. Connine. "Effects of Familiarity and Aptness on Metaphor Processing." *Journal of Experimental Psychology: Learning, Memory, and Cognition* 19, no. 2 (March 1993): 295–308.

Bloch, Oscar, and W. von Wartburg. *Dictionnaire Étymologique de la Langue Française.* Paris: Presses Universitaires de France, 1960.

Blumenberg, Hans. "Paradigmen zu einer Metaphorology." *Archiv für Begriffsgeschichte. Bausteine zu einem historischen Wörterbuch der Philosophie* 6 (1960): 5–142, 301–5.

Blyth, R. H. *Haiku.* Vol. 1, *Eastern Culture.* Tokyo: Hokuseido Press, n.d.

Bochner, Salomon. *The Role of Mathematics in the Rise of Science.* Princeton: Princeton University Press, 1966.

Bohm, David, and F. David Peat. *Science, Order, and Creativity.* New York: Bantam Books, 1987.

Bosmajian, Haig A. *Metaphor and Reason in Judicial Opinions*. Carbondale: Southern Illinois University Press, 1992.

Bowden, Samuel. "Poem Sacred to the Memory of Sir Isaac Newton." In *Poetical Essays on Several Occasions*. London: vol. 1, 1733; vol. 2, 1735. Quoted in William Powell Jones, *The Rhetoric of Science: A Study of Scientific Ideas and Imagery in Eighteenth-Century English Poetry* (London: Routledge and Kegan Paul, 1966).

Boyer, Carl B. *A History of Mathematics*. Revised by Uta C. Merzbach. 2d ed. New York: John Wiley & Sons, 1989.

———. *The History of the Calculus and Its Conceptual Development*. 1949. Reprint, New York: Dover Publications, 1959.

Bradwardine, Thomas. *Tractatus de Proportionibus*, 112. Translated by H. L. Crosby Jr. Madison: University of Wisconsin Press, 1955. Quoted in Max Jammer, *Concepts of Force: A Study in the Foundations of Dynamics* (Cambridge: Harvard University Press, 1957).

Bremmer, Jan, and Herman Roodenburg, eds. *A Cultural History of Gesture*. Ithaca: Cornell University Press, 1991.

Bright, Michael. *Animal Language*. Ithaca: Cornell University Press, 1984.

Bronowski, Jacob, and Bruce Mazlish. *The Western Intellectual Tradition: From Leonardo to Hegel*. New York: Harper & Bros., 1960.

Brown, Geoffrey, and Charles Desforges. *Piaget's Theory: A Psychological Critique*. London and Boston: Routledge & Kegan Paul, 1979.

Brown, Howard Mayer. *Music in the Renaissance*. Englewood Cliffs, N.J.: Prentice-Hall, 1976.

Bruner, Jerome; Jacqueline J. Goodnow, and George A. Austin. *A Study of Thinking*. New York: John Wiley, 1956.

Bucur, Ion, and Aristide Deleanu. *Introduction to the Theory of Categories and Functors*. New York: Wiley-Interscience, 1968.

Bukofzer, Manfred F. *Music in the Baroque Era*. New York: W. W. Norton, 1947.

Campbell, Joseph. *The Mythic Image*. Bollingen Series. Princeton: Princeton University Press, 1974.

Carey, J. E., and A. E. Goss. "The Role of Mediating Verbal Responses in the Conceptual Sorting Behavior of Children." *Journal of Genetic Psychology* 90 (1957): 69–74.

Carpenter, Rhys. *The Esthetic Basis of Greek Art*. Bloomington: Indiana University Press, 1959.

Carroll, J. B. "Words, Meanings, and Concepts." *Harvard Educational Review* 34 (1964): 178–202.

Caskey, L. D. *The Geometry of Greek Vases*. Boston: Museum of Fine Arts, 1922.

Cassirer, Ernst. *An Essay on Man*. New Haven: Yale University Press, 1944.

Cassirer, Ernst. *Language and Myth*. Translated by Susanne K. Langer. 1946. Reprint, New York: Dover Publications, 1946.

Cassirer, Ernst. *Philosophie der Symbolischen Formen*. Buch 3, *Phänomenologie der Erkenntnis*. Berlin: Bruno Cassirer, 1929.

———. *Philosophy of Symbolic Forms*. 3 vols. Translated by Ralph Manheim. New Haven: Yale University Press, 1953–57.

Casti, John L. *Alternate Realities: Mathematical Models of Nature and Man*. New York: John Wiley & Sons, 1989.

Cater, H. E., ed. *Henry Adams and His Friends*. Boston: Houghton Mifflin, 1947.

Chan Wingh-tsit. "Syntheses in Chinese Metaphysics." In *The Chinese Mind: Essentials of Chinese Philosophy and Culture.* Honolulu: University of Hawaii Press, 1967.

Charbonneaux, Jean; Roland Martin, and François Villard. *Hellenistic Art.* New York: George Braziller, 1973.

Cheng, D. *Philosophical Aspects of the Mind-Body Problem.* Honolulu: University of Hawaii Press, 1975.

Chevalier, Jean, and Alain Gheerbrant. Introduction to *Dictionnaire des Symboles.* Rev. ed. Paris: Editions Robert Laffont, 1982.

Clagett, Marshall. *Greek Science in Antiquity.* Plainview, N.Y.: Books for Libraries Press, 1955.

Clark, Kenneth. *The Nude: A Study in Ideal Form.* Bollingen Series 35. New York: Pantheon, 1956.

Cohen, I. Bernard. *The Birth of a New Physics.* Rev. ed. New York: W. W. Norton, 1985.

Coleridge, Samuel Taylor. *Biographia Literaria,* 1:202. Edited by John Shawcross. Oxford: Oxford University Press, 1907. Quoted in William K. Wimsatt and Cleanth Brooks, *Literary Criticism: A Short History* (New York: Alfred A. Knopf, 1957).

———. *Selected Poetry and Prose.* Edited by Donald Stauffer. New York: Random House, 1951.

Cometa, M. S., and M. E. Eson. "Logical Operations and Metaphor Interpretation: A Piagetian Model." *Child Development* 49, no. 3 (1976): 649–59.

Cook, Nicholas. *A Guide to Musical Analysis.* New York: George Braziller, 1987.

Coolidge, Julian Lowell. *A History of Geometrical Methods.* Oxford: Oxford University Press, 1940. Reprint, New York: Dover Publications, 1963.

Crease, Robert P., and Charles C. Mann. *The Second Creation: Makers of the Revolution in Twentieth-Century Physics.* New York: Macmillan, 1986.

Crevier, Daniel. *AI: The Tumultuous History of the Search for Artificial Intelligence.* New York: Basic Books, 1993.

d'Abro, A. *The Evolution of Scientific Thought: From Newton to Einstein.* 2d ed. New York: Boni & Liveright, 1927. Reprint. Revised 2d ed. New York: Dover Publications, 1950.

———. *The Rise of the New Physics.* 2d ed. New York: Van Nostrand, 1939. Reprint, rev. 2d ed., New York: Dover Publications, 1951.

Dampier, W. C. *A History of Science.* 4th ed. Cambridge: Cambridge University Press, 1965.

Davidson, Donald. "What Metaphors Mean." *Critical Inquiry* 5, no. 1 (1979): 31–47.

Day, J. C., and F. S. Belleza. "The Relation between Visual Image Mediators and Recall." *Mem. Cognition* 11 (May 1983): 256–57.

de Bary, William Theodore, Stephen Hay, Royal Weiler, and Andrew Yarrow, eds. *Sources of Indian Tradition.* New York: Columbia University Press, 1958.

de Bary, William Theodore, Chan Wingh-tsit, and Burton Watson. *Sources of Chinese Tradition.* 2 vols. New York: Columbia University Press, 1960.

Debidour, V.-H. *Le Bestiaire Sculpté en France.* Paris: B. Arthaud, 1961.

de Burgh, W. G. *The Legacy of the Ancient World.* London: Macdonald & Evans, 1947

Devoto, Giacomo. *Avviamento alla Etimologia Italiana: Dizionario Etimologico.* Firenze: Felice Le Monnier, 1968.

Dietze, D. A. "The Facilitating Effect of Words on Discrimination and Generalization." *Journal of Experimental Psychology* 50 (1955): 255–60.

Dinsmoor, William Bell. *The Architecture of Ancient Greece: An Account of Its Historical Development.* 3d ed. London: B. T. Batsford, 1950.

Duke, Mark. *Acupuncture.* New York: Pyramid House, 1972.

Dumoulin, Heinrich. *Zen Buddhism: A History.* Vol. 1: *India and China.* Translated by James W. Heisig and Paul Knitter. New York: Macmillan and Simon & Schuster, 1988.

Ehrmann, Jacques, ed. *Game, Play, Literature.* New Haven: Yale University Press, 1968. Reprint, Boston: Beacon Press, 1971.

Einstein, Albert. "Autobiographical Notes." In *Albert Einstein: Philosopher-Scientist,* edited by Paul Arthur Schilpp. Evanston, Ill.: Library of Living Philosophers, 1949.

Ellenberger, Henri F. *The Discovery of the Unconscious: The History and Evolution of Dynamic Psychiatry.* New York: Basic Books, 1970.

Euclid. *The Thirteen Books of Euclid's "Elements."* Translated by Thomas L. Heath. Vol. 17 of Great Books of the Western World, ed. Robert Maynard Hutchins. Chicago: Encyclopedia Britannica, 1952.

Féré, Charles. "La Physiologie dans les Métaphores." *Revue Philosophique* 40 (1895): 352–59.

Ferm, Vergilius, ed. *A History of Philosophical Systems.* New York: Philosophical Library, 1950.

Festinger, Leon. *A Theory of Cognitive Dissonance.* Stanford, Calif.: Stanford University Press, 1957.

Feuer, Lewis S. *Einstein and the Generations of Science.* New York: Basic Books, 1982.

Finch, Margaret. *Style in Art History: An Introduction to Theories of Style and Sequence.* Metuchen, N.J.: Scarecrow Press, 1974.

Flavell, John H. *The Developmental Psychology of Jean Piaget.* Princeton: Van Nostrand, 1963.

Flint, Valerie I. J. *The Rise of Magic in Early Medieval Europe.* Princeton: Princeton University Press, 1991.

Forte, Allen, and Steven Gilbert. *Introduction to Schenckerian Analysis.* New York: W. W. Norton, 1982.

Fox-Genovese, Elizabeth. *Feminism without Illusions: A Critique of Individualism.* Chapel Hill: University of North Carolina Press, 1991.

Fraser, J. T. *Of Time, Passion, and Knowledge.* New York: George Braziller, 1975.

———, ed. *The Voices of Time.* New York: George Braziller, 1966

Freedman, Alfred M., Harold I. Kaplaan, and Benjamin J. Sadock, eds. *Comprehensive Textbook of Psychiatry.* 2d ed. 2 vols. Baltimore: Williams and Williams, 1975.

Freedman, Daniel X., and Jarl E. Dyrud, eds. *Treatment.* Vol. 5 of *American Handbook of Psychiatry,* edited by Silvano Arieti, 2d ed. New York: Basic Books, 1975.

Freud, Sigmund. *Basic Writings.* Translated and edited by A. A. Brill. New York: Random House, 1938.

Freud, Sigmund. *Major Works.* Vol. 52 of *Great Books of the Western World,* edited by Robert Maynard Hutchins. Chicago: Encyclopaedia Britannica, 1952.

Friedman, John Block. *The Monstrous Races in Medieval Art and Thought.* Cambridge: Harvard University Press, 1981.

Fung Yu-lan. *A History of Chinese Philosophy.* Translated by Derk Bodde. 2d ed. 2 vols. Princeton: Princeton University Press, 1952.

Gaines, Brian. "Foundations of Fuzzy Reasoning." *International Journal of Man-Machine Studies* 8 (1976): 623–68.

Galileo Galilei. *Dialogue on the Great World Systems*, 250. Translated by Salusbury. Edited by Giorgio de Santillana. Chicago, 1953. Quoted in Max Jammer, *Concepts of Force: A Study in the Foundations of Dynamics* (Cambridge: Harvard University Press, 1957).

Gardner, H., and E. Winner. "The Child is Father to the Metaphor." *Psychology Today* 12, no. 12 (1979): 81.

Gazzaniga, Michael S., and Bruce T. Volpe. "Split-Brain Studies: Implications for Psychiatry." In *Advances and New Directions*, edited by Silvano Arieti and H. Keith H. Brodie, vol. 7 in *American Handbook of Psychiatry*, edited by Silvano Arieti, 2d ed. New York: Basic Books, 1981.

Gazzaniga, Michael S., ed. *The Cognitive Neurosciences*. Cambridge: MIT Press, 1995.

Gendlin, Eugene T. "The Newer Therapies." In *Treatment*, edited by Daniel X. Freedman and Jaryl E. Dyrud, vol. 5 of *American Handbook of Psychiatry*, edited by Silvano Arieti, 2d ed. New York: Basic Books, 1975.

Gerhart, Mary. *Metaphoric Process: The Creation of Scientific and Religious Understanding*. Fort Worth: Texas Christian University Press, 1984.

Ghiselin, Brewster, ed. *The Creative Process*. New York: New American Library, 1955.

Gilbert, Katherine Everett, and Helmut Kuhn. *A History of Esthetics*. Rev. ed. Bloomington: Indiana University Press, 1953.

Gimbutas, Martija. *The Civilization of the Goddess: The World of Old Europe*. Edited by Joan Marler. San Francisco: Harper, 1991.

———. *The Goddesses and Gods of Old Europe: Myths and Cult Images*. Rev. ed. Berkeley and Los Angeles: University of California Press, 1982.

Glass, Leon, and Michael C. Mackey. *From Clocks to Chaos: The Rhythms of Life*. Princeton: Princeton University Press, 1988.

Goss, A. E., and M. C. Moylan. "Conceptual Block-Sorting as a Function of Type and Degree of Mastery of Discriminatory Verbal Responses." *Journal of Genetic Psychology* 93 (1958): 191–98.

Gottschalk, Louis, L. C. MacKinney, and E. H. Pritchard. *The Foundations of the Modern World, 1300–1775*. History of Mankind: Cultural and Scientific Developments, vol. 4. New York: Harper & Row, 1969.

Gozzi, Raymond, Jr. "From 'the road' to 'the fast track'—American Metaphors of Life." *Et Cetera* 50, no. 1 (spring 1993): 73–76.

Gray, Jeremy. *Ideas of Space: Euclidean, Non-Euclidean, and Relativistic*. 2d ed. Oxford: Clarendon Press, 1989.

Griffin, Donald R. *Animal Minds*. Chicago: University of Chicago Press, 1992.

———. *The Question of Animal Awareness: Evolutionary Continuity of Mental Experience*. Rev. ed. New York: Rockefeller University Press, 1981.

Gumpel, Liselotte. *Metaphor Reexamined: A Non-Aristotelian Perspective*. Bloomington: Indiana University Press, 1984.

Hadamard, Jacques. *The Psychology of Invention in the Mathematical Field*. Princeton: Princeton University Press, 1944. Reprint, New York, Dover Publications, 1954.

Hamming, R. W. "The Unreasonable Effectiveness of Mathematics." In *Mathematical Analysis of Physical Systems*, edited by Ronald E. Mickens. New York: Van Nostrand Reinhold, 1985.

Harding, Rosamond E. M. *An Anatomy of Inspiration*. 3d ed. Cambridge: W. Heffer & Son, 1948.

Harries, Karsten. *The Bavarian Rococo Church: Between Faith and Aestheticism*. New Haven: Yale University Press, 1983.

Haskins, Charles Homer. *The Renaissance of the Twelfth Century*. Cambridge: Harvard University Press, 1927.

Hatje, Ursula, ed. *The Styles of European Art*. New York: Harry N. Abrams, 1965.

Hausman, Carl R. *Metaphor and Art: Interactionism and Reference in the Verbal and Nonverbal Arts*. Cambridge and New York: Cambridge University Press, 1989.

Hawkes, Jaquetta, and Leonard Woolley. *Prehistory and the Beginnings of Civilization*. History of Mankind: Cultural and Scientific Developments, vol. 1. New York: Harper & Row, 1963.

Hawkes, Terence. *Metaphor. The Critical Idiom Series*. Edited by John D. Jump. London: Methuen, 1972.

Hayter, Alethea. *Opium and the Romantic Imagination*. Berkeley and Los Angeles: University of California Press, 1968.

Head, M. *Aphasia and Kindred Disorders of Speach*. New York: Macmillan, 1926).

Heath, Thomas L. *Greek Mathematics*. Oxford: Oxford University Press, 1931. Reprint, New York, Dover Publications, 1963.

Heer, Friedrich. *The Intellectual History of Europe*. Translated by Jonathan Steinberg. Cleveland and New York: World Publishing Co., 1953.

Hesse, Mary B. *Forces and Fields*. Westport, Conn.: Greenwood Press, 1962.

———. *Models and Analogies in Science*. Notre Dame, Ind.: University of Notre Dame Press, 1966.

———. *Revolutions and Reconstructions in the Philosophy of Science*. Bloomington: Indiana University Press, 1980.

———. *Science and the Human Imagination*. London: SMC Press, 1954.

Highet, Gilbert. *The Classical Tradition*. New York: Oxford University Press, 1949.

Hitti, Philip K. *History of the Arabs*. 5th ed. London: Macmillan, 1951.

Hitti, Philip K. *The Near East in History: A 5000-Year Story*. New York: Van Nostrand, 1961.

Hobson, J. Allan. *The Dreaming Brain*. New York: Basic Books, 1988.

Holland, Dorothy, and Naomi Quinn, eds. *Cultural Models in Language and Thought*. Cambridge: Cambridge University Press, 1987.

Holton, Gerald. *Thematic Origins of Scientific Thought*. Cambridge: Harvard University Press, 1973.

Homer. *The Iliad of Homer and the Odyssey*. Translated by Samuel Butler.. Vol. 3 of Great Books of the Western World, ed. Robert Maynard Hutchins Chicago: Encyclopedia Britannica, 1952.

Horowitz, Mardi J. *Image Formation and Cognition*. New York: Appleton-Century-Crofts, 1970.

Howells, John G., ed. *World History of Psychiatry*. New York: Bruner/Maazel, 1975.

Hughes, Dom Anselm, and Gerald Abraham. *Ars Nova and the Renaissance, 1300–1540*. The New Oxford History of Music, vol. 3. London: Oxford University Press, 1960.

Huizinga, Johan. *Homo Ludens: A Study of the Play Element in Culture*. London: Routledge and Kegan Paul, 1950.

Hume, David. *An Enquiry Concerning Human Understanding.* Vol. 35 of *Great Books of the Western World,* edited by Robert Maynard Hutchins. Chicago: Encyclopaedia Britannica, 1952.

Hutten, E. H. "The Role of Models in Physics." *British Journal for the Philosophy of Science* 4 (1964): 284–301.

Hyman, Arthur, and James J. Walsh, eds. *Philosophy in the Middle Ages: The Christian, Islamic, and Jewish Traditions.* Indianapolis, Ind.: Hackett Publishing Co., 1973.

Jackson, E. Atlee. *Perspectives of Nonlinear Dynamics.* Cambridge: Cambridge University Press, 1989.

Jackson, W. T. H. *The Literature of the Middle Ages.* New York: Columbia University Press, 1960.

Jammer, Max. *Concepts of Force: A Study in the Foundations of Dynamics.* Cambridge: Harvard University Press, 1957.

———. *Concepts of Space: The History of Theories of Space in Physics.* Cambridge: Harvard University Press, 1954.

———. *The Conceptual Development of Quantum Mechanics.* New York: McGraw-Hill, 1966.

———. *The Philosophy of Quantum Mechanics: The Interpretation of Quantum Mechanics in Historical Perspective.* New York: John Wiley & Sons, 1974.

Johnson, Mark. *The Body in the Mind: The Bodily Basis of Meaning, Imagination, and Reason.* Chicago: University of Chicago Press, 1987.

———. "Metaphor in the Philosophical Tradition." In *Philosophical Perspectives on Metaphor,* edited by Mark Johnson. Minneapolis: University of Minnesota Press, 1981.

———. *Moral Imagination: Implications of Cognitive Science for Ethics.* Chicago: University of Chicago Press, 1993.

———, ed. *Philosophical Perspectives on Metaphor.* Minneapolis: University of Minnesota Press, 1981.

Jones, Roger S. *Physics as Metaphor.* Minneapolis: University of Minnesota Press, 1982.

Jones, William Powell. *The Rhetoric of Science: A Study of Scientific Ideas and Imagery in Eighteenth-Century English Poetry.* London: Routledge & Kegan Paul, 1966.

Kahler, Erich. *The Inward Turn of Narrative.* Translated by Richard and Clara Winston. Bollingen Series. Princeton: Princeton University Press, 1973.

———. *Man the Measure: A New Approach to History.* New York: George Braziller, 1956.

Kahler, Erich. *The Tower and the Abyss: An Inquiry into thee Transformation of the Individual.* New York: George Braziller, 1957.

Kant, Immanuel. *Critique of Pure Reason.* Translated by J. M. D. Meikeljohn. Vol. 42 of *Great Books of the Western World,* edited by Robert Maynard Hutchins. Chicago: Encyclopaedia Britannica, 1952.

———. *Critique of Pure Reason.* Translated by Norman Kemp Smith. London: St. Martin's Press, 1929.

———. *Prolegomena to Any Future Metaphysics.* Edited by Lewis White Beck. Translated by Lewis White Beck from the Carus revision (Chicago, 1902) of the Mahaffy translation (London, 1872). Indianapolis, Ind.: Bobbs-Merrill, 1950.

Katzenellenbogen, Adolf. *Allegories of the Virtues and Vices in Medieval Art: From Early Christian Times to the Thirteenth Century.* Toronto: University of Toronto Press in association with the Medieval Academy of America, 1989.

Kaufmann, Arnold. *Introduction to the Theory of Fuzzy Subsets.* New York: Academic Press, 1975.

Kearns, Michael S. *Metaphors of Mind in Fiction and Psychology.* Lexington: University Press of Kentucky, 1987.

Kellert, Stephen H. *In the Wake of Chaos: Unpredictable Order in Dynamical Systems.* Chicago: University of Chicago Press, 1993.

Kintsch, Walter. "Notes on the Structure of Semantic Memory." In *The Organization of Memory,* edited by Endel Tulving and Wayne Donaldson. New York: Academic Press, 1972.

Kirk, G. S. *Myth: Its Meaning and Function in Ancient and Other Cultures.* Cambridge: Cambridge University Press; Berkeley and Los Angeles: The University of California Press, 1970.

Kittay, Eva Feder. *Metaphor: Its Cognitive Force and Linguistic Structure.* Oxford: Clarendon Press, 1987.

Kline, Morris. *Mathematical Thought from Ancient to Modern Times.* New York: Oxford University Press, 1972.

Kline, Morris. *Mathematics: The Loss of Certainty.* New York: Oxford University Press, 1980).

Knights, L. C., and Basil Cottle, eds. *Metaphor and Symbol.* Proceedings of the Twelfth Symposium of the Colston Researech Society, held in the University of Bristol, 28 March–31 March 1960. London: Butterworths Scientific Publicaations, 1960.

Koestler, Arthur. *The Act of Creation.* New York: Macmillan, 1964.

Kosslyn, Stephen M., and Amy L. Sussman. "Roles of Imagery in Perceptiuon: Or, There Is No Such Thing as Immaculate Perception." In *The Cognitive Neurosciences,* edited by Michael S. Gazzaniga. Cambridge: MIT Press, 1995.

Kostof, Spiro. *A History of Architecture: Settings and Rituals.* New York: Oxford University Press, 1985.

Kranzberg, Melvin, and Carroll W. Pursell Jr., eds. *Technology in Western Civilization: The Emergence of Modern Industrial Society Earliest Times to 1900.* New York: Oxford University Press, 1967.

Kuhn, Thomas. *The Structure of Scientific Revolutions.* 2d ed. Berkeley and Los Angeles: University of California Press, 1970.

Lakoff, George. *More than Cool Reason: A Field Guide to Poetic Metaphor.* Chicago: University of Chicago Press, 1989.

———. *Women, Fire, and Dangerous Things: What Categories Reveal about the Mind.* Chicago: University of Chicago Press, 1987.

Lakoff, George, and Mark Johnson. *Metaphors We Live By.* Chicago: University of Chicago Press, 1980.

La Mettrie, Julien Offray de. *Man a Machine.* French and English texts. Translated by Gertrude C. Bussey and M. W. Calkins. La Salle, Ill.: Open Court, 1912.

Landes, David S. *Revolution in Time: Clocks and the Making of the Modern World.* Cambridge: Belknap Press of Harvard University Press, 1983.

Landtman, Gunnar. "The Dream Life of the Kiwai Papuans of British New Guinea." In *World of Dreams,* edited by Ralph L. Woods. New York: Random House, 1947.

Lang, Paul Henry. *Music in Western Civilization.* New York: W. W. Norton, 1941.

Lao Tzu. *The Way of Life.* Translated by R. B. Blakney. New York: New American Library, 1955.

LaRue, Jan, ed. *Aspects of Medieval and Renaissance Music: A Birthday Offering to Gustave Reese.* New York: W. W. Norton, 1966.

Leroi-Gourhan, André. *Treasures of Prehistoric Art.* Translated by Norbert Guterman. New York: Harry N. Abrams, n.d.

Levin, Samuel R. *Metaphoric Worlds: Conceptions of a Romantic Nature.* New Haven: Yale University Press, 1988.

Lewin, Roger. *Complexity: Life at the Edge of Chaos.* New York: Macmillan, 1992.

Lindley, David. *The End of Physics: The Myth of a Unified Theory.* New York: Basic Books, 1993.

Lowenberg, Ina. "Creativity and Correspondence in Fiction and Metaphor." *Journal of Aesthetics and Art Criticism* 36, no. 3 (1978): 341–50.

Lowes, John Livingston. *The Road to Xanadu: A Study in the Ways of the Imagination.* Boston: Houghton Mifflin, 1927.

Lubac, H. de. "Typologie et Allégorisme." *Recherches de Science Religieuse* (Paris) (1947) 45:180–226.

Mac Cormac, Earl R. *A Cognitive Theory of Metaphor.* Cambridge: MIT Press, 1985.

———. *Metaphor and Myth in Science and Religion.*

Durham, N.C.: Duke University Press, 1976.

Mach, Ernst. *Popular Scientific Lectures.* 4th ed. Chicago, 1910. Quoted in Lewis S. Feuer, *Einstein and the Generations of Science* (New York: Basic Books, 1984).

———. *The Science of Mechanics: A Critical and Historical Account of Its Development.* Translated by Thomas J. MacCormack. 6th American ed. La Salle, Ill.: Open Court, 1960.

Mandelbaum, Maurice. "Scientific Background of Evolutionary Theory in Biology." In *Roots of Scientific Thought: A Cultural Perspective,* edited by Philip P. Winer and Aaron Nolan. New York: Basic Books, 1957.

Marr, David. *Vision: A Computational Investigation into the Human Representation and Processing of Visual Information.* San Francisco: W. H. Freeman, 1982.

Maurer, Armand A. *Medieval Philosophy.* New York: Random House, 1962.

McEvedy, Colin, and Richard Jones. *Atlas of World Population History.* New York: Penguin Books, 1978.

McMullin, Ernan, ed. *The Concept of Matter in Greek and Medieval Philosophy.* Notre Dame, Ind.: University of Notre Dame Press, 1963.

McNeil, Daniel, and Paul Freiberger. *Fuzzy Logic.* New York: Simon & Schuster, 1993.

McNeil, David. *Hand and Mind: What Gesture Reveals About Thought.* Chicago: University of Chicago Press, 1992.

Merrill, M. D., and R. D. Tennyson. "Conceptual Classification and Classification Errors as a Function of the Relationship between Examples and Nonexamples." *Improving Human Performance: A Research Quarterly* 7 (1978): 351–64.

Meyer-Lübke, W. *Romanisches Etymologisches Wörterbuch.* 3d ed. Heidelberg: Carl Winters Universitätsbuchhandlung, 1935.

Mickens, Ronald E., ed. *Mathematical Analysis of Physical Systems.* New York: Van Nostrand Reinhold, 1985.

Mill, John Stuart. *Autobiography and Literary Essays.* In *Collected Works,* edited by John M. Robson and Jack Stillinger. Toronto: University of Toronto Press, 1980.

Milton, John. *Poetical Works.* Edited by H. C. Beeching. London: Oxford University Press, 1928.

Minsky, Marvin L. *Society of Mind.* New York: Simon & Schuster, 1986.

Mitchell, Benjamin Evans. *The Theory of Categories.* New York: Academic Press, 1965.

Moody, Raymond A., Jr. *Life After Life.* New York: Mockingbird Books, 1975. Reprint, New York: Bantam Books, 1976.

———. *The Light Beyond: New Explorations.* New York: Bantam Books, 1988.

———. *Reflections on Life After Life.* New York: Bantam Books, 1977.

Moore, A. W. *The Infinite.* The Problems of Philosophy: Their Past and Present, edited by Ted Honderich. London and New York: Routledge, 1990.

Moore, Charles A., ed. *The Chinese Mind: Essentials of Chinese Philosophy and Culture.* Honolulu: University of Hawaii Press, 1967.

———. *The Indian Mind: Essentials of Indian Philosophy and Culture.* Honolulu: University of Hawaii Press, 1967.

———. *The Japanese Mind: Essentials of Japanese Philosophy and Culture.* Honolulu: University of Hawaii Press, 1967.

Morley, Thomas. *A Plaine and Easie Introduction to Practicall Musicke.* London, 1597. Quoted in *New Grove Dictionary of Music and Musicians,* s.v. "Fantasia, I."

Müller, Friedrich Max. *Lectures on the Science of Language.* 2 vols. New York: Charles Scribner, 1871

Munitz, Milton K., ed. *Theories of the Universe: From Babylonian Myth to Modern Science.* New York: Free Press, 1957.

Munro, Donald J. *The Concept of Man in Early China.* Stanford, Calif.: Stanford University Press, 1969.

Murphy, Gardner. *Historical Introduction to Modern Psychology.* New York: Harcourt, Brace and Co., 1949.

Nakamura, Hajime, ed. *Ways of Thinking of Eastern Peoples: India-China-Tibet-Japan.* Honolulu: University of Hawaii Press, 1964.

Newton, Sir Isaac. *Mathematical Principles of Natural Philosophy - Optics.* Vol. 34 of *Great Books of the Western World,* edited by Robert Maynard Hutchins. Chicago: Encyclopaedia Britannica, 1952.

Nietzsche, Frederick. *The Complete Works of Frederick Nietzsche.* Edited by Oscar Levy. Translated by Maximilian A. Magge. New York: Gordon Press, 1974.

———. *The Philosophy of Nietzsche.* New York: Random House, n.d.

Noppen, J. P. van, S. de Knop, and R. Jongen, eds. *Metaphor: A Bibliography of Post-1970 Publications.* Amsterdam and Philadelphia: John Benjamins, 1985.

Nordenskiöld, Erik. *The History of Biology.* Translated by Leonard Bucknell Eyre. New York: Tudor Publishing Co., 1928.

Ogden, C. K., and I. A. Richards. *Bentham's Theory of Fictions.* Totowa, N.J.: Littlefield, Adams, 1959.

Olby, R. C., G. N. Cantor, J. R. R. Christie, and M. J. S. Hodge, eds. *Companion to the History of Modern Science.* London and New York: Routledge, 1990.

Ortega y Gasset, José. *The Dehumanization of Art and Other Essays on Art, Culture, and Literature.* Translated by Helene Weyl. 2d ed. Princeton: Princeton University Press, 1968.

Pais, Abraham. *Inward Bound: Of Matter and Forces in the Physical World.* Oxford: Clarendon Press; New York: Oxford University Press, 1986.

Panofsky, Erwin. *Idea: A Concept in Art Theory.* Translated by Joseph S. Peake. Columbia: University of South Carolina Press, 1968.

Papin, Liliane. "This Is not a Universe: Metaphor, Language, and Representation." *PMLA* 107, no. 5 (October 1992): 1253–65.

Paretti, Luigi; Paolo Brezzi, and Luciano Petech. *The Ancient World, 1200 B.C. to A.D. 500.* Translated by Guy E. F. Chilver and Sylvia Chilver. History of Mankind: Cultural and Scientific Development, vol. 2. New York: Harper & Row, 1965.

Passmore, John. *Recent Philosophers.* La Salle, Ill.: Open Court, 1985.

Pepper, Stephen C. *World Hypotheses: A Study in Evidence.* Berkeley and Los Angeles: University of California Press, 1942.

Phillips, John L., Jr. *The Origins of Intellect: Piaget's Theory.* San Francisco: W. H. Freeman, 1969.

Piaget, Jean. *The Child's Conception of the World.* Translated by Joan Tomlinson and Andrew Tomlinson. New York: Harcourt, Brace & World, 1930.

———. *The Construction of Reality in the Child.* Translated by Margaret Cook. New York: Basic Books, 1954.

———. *Judgment and Reasoning in the Child.* Translated by Marjorie Worden. New York: Harcourt, Brace & World, 1928.

———. *The Language and Thought of the Child.* Translated by Marjorie Worden. New York: Harcourt, Brace & World, 1926.

———. *The Origins of Intelligence in Children.* Translated by Margaret Cook. New York: International Universities Press, 1952.

Piaget, Jean, and Bärbel Inhelder. *Child's Conception of Space.* London: Routledge and Kegan Paul, 1956.

Pickering, Andrew. *Constructing Quarks: A Sociological History of Particle Physics.* Chicago: University of Chicago Press, 1984.

Plato. *The Dialogues.* Translated by Benjamin Jowett. Vol. 7 of *Great Books of the Western World,* edited by Robert Maynard Hutchins. Chicago: Encyclopaedia Britannica, 1952.

Plotinus. *The Six Enneads.* Translated by Stephen MacKenna and B. S. Page. Vol. 17 of *Great Books of the Western World,* edited by Robert Maynard Hutchins. Chicago: Encyclopaedia Britannica, 1952.

Porteous, J. Douglas. *Landscapes of the Mind: Worlds of Sense and Mtaphor.* Toronto: University of Toronto Press, 1990.

Posner, Michael I., ed. *Foundations of Cognitive Science.* Cambridge: MIT Press, 1989.

Praz, Mario. *The Romantic Agony.* Translated by Angus Davidson. 2d ed. Oxford: Oxford University Press, 1951.

Prigogine, Ilya, and Isabelle Stengers. *Order Out of Chaos: Man's New Dialogue with Nature.* New York: Bantam Books, 1984.

Prior, Matthew. *Solomon on the Vanity of the World, a Poem in Three Books.* In *The Literary Works of Matthew Prior,* edited by H. B. Wright and M. K. Spears, 1:306–85. Oxford: Clarendon Press, 1959. Quoted in William Powell Jones, *The Rhetoric of Science: A Study of Scientific Ideas and Imagery in Eighteenth-Century English Poetry* (London: Routledge and Kegan Paul, 1966).

Ptolemy. *The Almagest.* Translated by R. Catesby Taliaferro. Vol. 16 of *Great Books of the Western World,* edited by Robert Maynard Hutchins. Chicago: Encyclopaedia Britannica, 1952.

Putnam, Hilary. *Reason, Truth, and History.* Cambridge: Harvard University Press, 1981.

Radnitzky, Gerard, and W. W. Bartley III, eds. *Evolutionary Epistemology, Rationality, and the Sociology of Knowledge.* LaSalle, Ill.: Open Court, 1987.

Rangel-Ribeiro, Victor. *Baroque Music: A Practical Guide for the Performer.* New York: Schirmer Books, 1981.

Rao, A. Venkoba. "India." In *World History of Psychiatry,* edited by John G. Howells, 628. New York: Bruner/Maazel, 1975.

Rattray, R. S. "Dream Beliefs of the African Ashantis." In *World of Dreams,* edited by Ralph L. Woods, 2–21. New York: Random House, 1947.

Rawson, Philip. *Drawing.* London and New York: Oxford University Press, 1969.

Read, Herbert. *Icon and Idea: The Function of Art in the Development of Consciousness.* Cambridge: Harvard University Press, 1965.

Reese, Gustave. *Music in the Middle Ages.* New York: W. W. Norton, 1940.

———. *Music in the Renaissance.* New York: W. W. Norton, 1954.

Reichenbach, Hans. *The Rise of Scientific Philosophy.* Berkeley and Los Angeles: University of California Press, 1951.

Reid, Thomas. *Works,* 604. Edited by William Hamilton. Edinburgh, 1846. Quoted in Max Jammer, *Concepts of Force: A Study in the Foundations of Dynamics* (Cambridge: Harvard University Press, 1957).

Reinhardt, William P. "Classical Chaos, Phase Space, and Semiclassical Quantization." In *Mathematical Analysis of Physical Systems,* edited by Ronald E. Mickens, 169–245. New York: Van Nostrand Reinhold, 1985.

Reisser, Morton F., ed. *Organic Disorders and Psychosomatic Medicine.* Vol. 4 of *American Handbook of Psychiatry,* edited by Silvano Arieti. 2d ed. New York: Basic Books, 1975.

Ricoeur, Paul. *The Rule of Metaphor: Multi-Disciplinary Studies of the Creation of Meaning in Language.* Toronto and Buffalo: University of Toronto Press, 1977.

Rieti, Rudolph. *The Thematic Process in Music.* London: Faber & Faber, 1961.

Rips, L. J. "Inductive Judgements about Natural Categories." *Journal of Verbal Learning and Verbal Behavior* 14 (1975): 665–81.

Robinson, Enders A. *Einstein's Relativity in Metaphor and Mathematics.* Englewood Cliffs, N.J.: Prentice-Hall, 1990.

Rorty, Richard. *Consequences of Pragmatism: Essays, 1972–1980.* Minneapolis: University of Minnesota Press, 1982.

———. *Philosophy and the Mirror of Nature.* Princeton: Princeton University Press, 1979.

Rosch, Eleanor. "Human Categorization." In *Studies in Cross-Cultural Psychology,* edited by Neil Warren. London: Academic Press, 1977.

———. "Natural Categories." *Cognitive Psychology* 4 (1973): 328–50.

Rosch, Eleanor, and B. B. Lloyd, eds. *Cognition and Categorization.* Hillsdale, N.J.: Lawrence Erlbaum, 1978.

Rosenfield, Israel. *The Strange, Familiar, and Forgotten: An Anatomy of Consciousness.* New York: Alfred A. Knopf, 1992.

Rosner, Stanley, and Lawrence E. Abt, eds. *The Creative Experience.* New York: Grossman, 1970.

Rothenberg, Albert. *The Emerging Goddess: The Creative Process in Art, Science, and Other Fields.* Chicago: University of Chicago Press, 1979.

Rucker, Rudy. *The Fourth Dimension: Toward a Geometry of Higher Reality.* Boston: Houghton Mifflin, 1984.

Rudwin, Maximilian. *The Devil in Legend and Literature.* La Salle, Ill.: Open Court, 1931.

Rumelhart, David E. "Some Problems with the Notion of Literal Meanings." In *Metaphor and Thought,* edited by Andrew Ortony, 71–82. 2d ed. Cambridge: Cambridge University Press, 1993.

Russell, Bertrand. *A History of Western Philosophy.* New York: Simon and Schuster, 1945.

Ryle, Gilbert. *The Concept of Mind.* New York: Barnes and Noble, 1949.

Sacks, Sheldon, ed. *On Metaphor.* Chicago: University of Chicago Press, 1978.

Sade, Marquis de. *Histoire de Juliette, ou les Prospérités du Vice.* Vols. 7–8 in *Œuvres Complètes.* Paris: Cercle du Livre Précieux, 1963.

———. *Oeuvres Complètes.* 15 vols. Paris: Cercle du Livre Précieux, 1962–64.

Sandars, N. K. *Prehistoric Art in Europe.* Baltimore: Penguin Books, 1968.

Sarbin, Theodore. "Anxiety: Reification of a Metaphor." *Archives of General Psychiatry* 10 (1964): 630–38.

Sarton, George. *A History of Science: Ancient Science through the Golden Age of Greece.* Cambridge: Harvard University Press, 1952.

———. *A History of Science: Hellenistic Science and Culture in the Last Three Centuries B.C.* Cambridge: Harvard University Press, 1959.

Sasaki, Sokei-an. "The Transcendental World." *Zen Notes* (New York) 1, no. 5 (1954). Quoted in Alan Watts, *The Way of Zen* (New York: Pantheon, 1957), 121.

Schade, Herbert. *Dämonen und Monstren.* Regensburg: Verlag Friedrich Pustet, 1962.

Schechter, B. A. "Animism and the Development of Metaphoric Thinking in Children." Ph.D. diss, Columbia University, 1980.

Schencker, Heinrich. *Free Composition.* Translated by Ernst Oster. London: Longman, 1979.

Schlanger, Judith. "Metaphor and Invention." Translated by Yvonne Burne. *Diogenes* 69 (spring 1970): 12–27.

Schilpp, Paul Arthur, ed. *Albert Einstein: Philosopher-Scientist.* Evanston, Ill.: Library of Living Philosophers, 1949.

———. *Philosophy of Ernst Cassirer.* Evanston, Ill.: Library of Living Philosophers, 1949.

Schopenhauer, Arthur. *The Philosophy of Schopenhauer.* New York: Modern Library, 1928. Reprint, New York: Carlton House, n.d.

Searle, John R. *Expression and Meaning.* Cambridge: Cambridge University Press, 1979.

Sharma, Chandradhar. *Indian Philosophy: A Critical Survey.* New York: Barnes and Noble, 1960.

Shepard, Roger N., and Lynn A. Cooper. *Mental Images and Their Transformations.* Cambridge: MIT Press, 1986.

Shibles, Warren A. *Metaphor: An Annotated Bibliography and History.* Whitewater, Wisc.: The Language Press, 1971.

Shulz, Bruno. "The Mythologizing of Reality." In *Letters and Drawings of Bruno Shulz,* edited by Jerzy Ficowski. New York: Harper & Row, 1988.

Singer, Charles. *A Short History of Scientific Ideas to 1900.* Oxford: Clarendon Press, 1959.

Singer, Charles; E. J. Holmyard and A. R. Hall, eds. *A History of Technology: From Early times to Fall of Ancient Empires.* New York and London: Oxford University Press, 1954.

Singer, Charles, E. J. Holmyard, A. R. Hall, and Trevor I. Williams, eds. *A History of Technology: The Mediterranean Civilizations and the Middle Ages.* New York: Oxford University Press, 1956.

Sinha, J. *Indian Psychology.* Calcutta, 1958, 1961. Quoted in A. Venkoba Rao, "India," in *World History of Psychiatry,* edited by John G. Howells (New York: Bruner/Maazel, 1975), 628.

Smith, Edward E. "Concepts and Induction." In *Foundations of Cognitive Science,* edited by Michael I. Posner, 501–26. Cambridge: MIT Press, 1989.

Smith, J. W. "Children's Comprehension of Metaphor: A Piagetian Interpretation." *Language and Speech* 19, no. 3 (1976): 236–43.

Snell, Bruno. *The Discovery of the Mind: The Greek Origins of European Thought.* Cambridge: Harvard University Press, 1953.

Spariosu, Mihai I. *Dionysus Reborn: Play and the Aesthetic Dimension in Modern Philosophical and Scientific Discourse.* Ithaca: Cornell University Press, 1989.

Stcherbatsky, F. Th. *Buddhist Logic.* 2 vols. Leningrad: Academy of Sciences, c. 1930. Reprint, New York: Dover Publications, 1962.

Stehle, Philip. *Order, Chaos, Order: The Transition from Classical to Quantum Physics.* New York: Oxford University Press, 1994.

Sternberg, Robert J. *Metaphors of Mind: Conceptions of the Nature of Intelligence.* Cambridge and New York: Cambridge University Press, 1990.

Stevenson, Ian. *Ten Cases in India.* Vol. 1 of *Cases of Reincarnation Type.* Charlottesville: University Press of Virginia, 1975.

———. *Ten Cases in Sri Lanka.* Vol. 2 of *Cases of Reincarnation Type.* Charlottesville: University Press of Virginia, 1977.

———. *Fifteen Cases in Thailand, Lebanon, and Turkey.* Vol. 3 of *Cases of Reincarnation Type.* Charlottesville: University Press of Virginia, 1978.

———. *Twenty Cases Suggestive of Reincarnation.* 2d ed. Charlottesville: University Press of Virginia, 1974.

Stewart, Ian. *The Problems of Mathematics.* 2d ed. Oxford and New York: Oxford University Press, 1992.

Strutterheim, Cornelius F. P. *Het Begrip Metaphoor.* Amsterdam: H. J. Paris, 1941.

Suppe, Frederick, ed. *The Structure of Scientific Theories.* 2d ed. Urbana and Chicago: University of Illinois Press, 1977.

Suzuki, D. T. "Reason and Intuition in Buddhist Philosophy." In *The Japanese Mind: Essentials of Japanese Philosophy and Culture,* edited by Charles A. Moore. Honolulu: University of Hawaii Press, 1967.

———. *Zen Buddhism: Selected Writings of D. T. Suzuki.* Edited by William Barrett. Garden City, N.Y.: Doubleday Anchor, 1956.

Takakusu, Junjiro. "Buddhism as a Philosophy of 'Thusness.'" In *The Indian Mind: Essentials of Indian Philosophy and Culture.* Honolulu: University of Hawaii Press, 1967.

T'ang, Chün-i. "The Individual and the World in Chinese Mythology." In *The Chinese Mind: Essentials of Chinese Philosophy and Culture.* Honolulu: University of Hawaii Press, 1967.

Tart, Charles T., ed. *Altered States of Consciousness: A Book of Readings*. New York: John Wiley and Sons, 1969.

Tauber, Edward S., and Maurice R. Green. *Prelogical Experience: An Inquiry into Dreams and Other Creative Processes*. New York: Basic Books, 1959.

Thomas, Keith. *Man and the Natural World: A History of the Modern Sensibility*. New York: Pantheon Books, 1983.

Thomas, Owen. *Metaphor and Related Subjects*. New York: Random House, 1969.

Thorndike, Lynn. *A History of Magic and Experimental Science*. 8 vols. New York: Columbia University Press, 1923.

Toulmin, Stephen, and June Goodfield. *The Discovery of Time*. Chicago: University of Chicago Press, 1965.

Tulving, Endel, and Wayne Donaldson, eds. *Organization of Memory*. New York: Academic Press, 1972.

Turbayne, Colin. *The Myth of Metaphor*. New Haven: Yale University Press, 1962.

Turner, Mark. *Death is the Mother of Beauty: Mind, Metaphor, Criticism*. Chicago: University of Chicago Press, 1987.

Tyler, Edward B. "Dream Lore and Superstitions of Primitive Peoples." In *The World of Dreams*, edited by Ralph L. Woods. New York: Random House, 1947.

Tymoczko, Thomas, ed. *New Directions in the Philosophy of Mathematics*. Boston: Birkhäuser, 1986.

Vaihinger, Hans. *The Philosophy of "As If."* Translated by C. K. Ogden. 2d ed. London: Routledge & Kegan Paul, 1935.

van Fraassen, Bas C. *Laws and Symmetry*. Oxford: Clarendon Press, 1989.

Vohra, Ashok. *Wittgenstein's Philosophy of Mind*. La Salle, Ill.: Open Court, 1986.

Vonnessen, Franz. "Die Ontologische Struktur der Metapher." *Zeitschrift für Philosophische Forschung* 13 (1959): 397–419.

Vosniadou, Stella. *Context and the Development of Metaphor Comprehension*. Champaign: University of Illinois at Urbana-Champaign , [1988].

Vosniadou, Stella, and A. Ortony, eds. *Similarity and Analogical Reasoning*. Cambridge: Cambridge University Press, 1989.

————. *The Emergence of the Literal-Metaphorical-Anomalous Distinction in Young Children*. Champaign: University of Illinois at Urbana-Champaign; Cambridge, Mass.: Bolt Beranek and Newman, 1982.

Ware, Caroline, K. M. Panikkar, and J. M. Romein. *The Twentieth Century*. History of Mankind: Cultural and Scientific Developments, vol. 6. New York: Harper & Row, 1966.

Watts, Alan W. *The Way of Zen*. New York: Pantheon, 1957.

Weiler, Gershon. *Mauthner's Critique of Language*. Cambridge: Cambridge University Press, 1970.

Wellek, René, and Austin Warren. *Theory of Literature*. New York: Harcourt, Brace & World, 1949.

Weltfish, Gene. *The Origins of Art*. New York: Bobbs-Merrill, 1956.

Wheelwright, Philip. *Metaphor and Reality*. Bloomington: Indiana University Press, 1962.

Whitrow, G. J. *Time in History: Views of Time from Prehistory to the Present Day*. Oxford and New York: Oxford University Press, 1988.

Whyte, Lancelot I. *The Unconscious Before Freud*. New York: St. Martin's Press, 1962.

Wiener, Philip, and Aaron Noland, eds. *Roots of Scientific Thought: A Cultural Perspective*. New York: Basic Books, 1957.

Wiet, Gaston, Vadime Elisséeff, Philippe Wolff, and Jean Naudou. *The Great Medieval Civilizations*. History of Mankind: Cultural and Scientific Developments, vol. 3. New York: Harper & Row, 1975.

Wightman, W. P. D. *The Growth of Scientific Ideas*. New Haven: Yale University Press, 1953.

Wimsatt, William K., and Cleanth Brooks. *Literary Criticism: A Short History*. New York: Alfred Knopf, 1957.

Wittkower, Rudolf. *Allegory and the Migration of Symbols*. London: Thames and Hudson, 1977.

Wolman, Benjamin B., ed. *Handbook of Parapsychology*. New York: Van Nostrand Reinhold, 1977

Woods, Ralph L., ed. *The World of Dreams*. New York: Random House, 1947.

Wyss, Dieter. *Depth Psychology: A Critical History*. Translated by Gerald Onn. New York: W. W. Norton, 1966.

Yoos, George. "A Phenomenological Look at Metaphor." *Philosophy and Phenomenological Research* 32, no. 1 (1971): 78–88.

Zadeh, Lotfi. "Fuzzy Sets." *Information and Control* 8, no. 3 (June 1965), 338–53.

Zimmer, Heinrich. *Philosophies of India*. Edited by Joseph Campbell. New York: Meridian Books, 1956.

Index

action scheme: early concepts of, 72;
Johnson on, 71; Piaget on, 72
action schemes: and discourse, 67, 70–72;
and the nature of mathematics,
195–97
Adams, Henry: quoted, 35
algebra: introduction from Islam, 134
Anaxagoras: on cosmos, 55
Anaximander: on cosmos, 55
Aristotle: on causality, 103; on the ether,
112–14; on force, 140; and medieval
science, 127; on number, 97; *Physics*,
76–77; on time, 104
art: Renaissance, 152–53; topological
schematizing in, 82–85

Babbit, Irving: quoted, 208
Balzac, Honoré de: use of Organism
metaphor, 178
Barnes, Harry Elmer: quoted, 123, 129
beauty: classical idea of, 99–102
Bergson, Henri: élan vital, 168
Berkeley, Bishop: on force, 141
Bible: and Great Chain of Being, 57;
quoted, 124
bind scheme: and causality, 176; and social
contract, 149
body image, 73–74; action schemes and
meaning, 242n. 28
Bowden, Samuel: quoted, 155
Bradwardine, Thomas: on force, 140
brahman, 60
breath metaphor, 33; and alchemy, 128;
and élan vital; and essence, 112–14;

and heat, 147; and ideal forms, 120;
and spirit, 33, 114–15

Cantor, Georg: and set theory, 192
Cassirer, Ernst: quoted, 23
category theory, 210–11
causality: and cosmic order, 103; and
Parent metaphor, 139
change: and cosmic order, 104
chemistry: Renaissance, 136–38
Chuang Tzu: on change, 105
coding, coarse, 12–13
cognitive dissonance: Festinger on, 63; and
metaphor stability, 62
commodity metaphor: and disease, 48
conservation laws, 157–59
container metaphor, 21; Lakoff and
Johnson on, 32; and solipsism, 176;
and the void, 75
cosmic order: and causality, 103; and
change, 104–5; and disease, 108; and
mathematics, 102–3; and time, 103–4
cosmos: in Buddhism, 60–61; in Confu-
cianism, 61; in Greek thought, 53; in
Hinduism, 59–60; in Taoism, 58–59
creative process, 235n. 14; and action
schemes, 239n. 8
cut/join scheme: and social contract, 149

Darwin, Charles: and evolution, 171–72;
and Great Chain of Being, 58
debt/payment metaphor: and human
rights, 175; and social contract, 149
deconstructionism, 23

278

Democritus: atomism, 50
depersonalization: and metaphorization, 98
divine plan, 37–38
dreams: and metaphorization, 88–89
dynamics, nonlinear, 259n. 61

Einstein, Albert: on creative process, 235 n. 14; on functions of the scientist, 186
élan vital: and Breath metaphor, 168
Euclid: on number, 97
evolution: and Organism metaphor, 171

family metaphor: and hierarchy, 156
first position metaphor: and chemistry, 137–38; and hierarchy, 63–64
floor/ground metaphor: and concept of substance, 186
force, 27–29; history of concept, 139–43
free will: and Mechanism metaphor, 166–67
Freud, Sigmund: *General Introduction to Psychoanalysis*, 78; metaphors used by, 31

Galileo: on divine plan, 38; on force, 27, 140–41
Gelasius I: quoted, 124
geometry, analytic, 135
geometry, non-Euclidean, 160
gesture: and topological transformations, 65–66
good: concept of, 247n. 55
graphic types, 245n. 11
Great Chain of Being, 53; and evolution, 171; history of, 54
group theory, 157–60

Heisenberg, Werner; and electron, 51
hemispheric specialization, 46–48
Heraclitus: on cosmos, 55
Huizinga, John: quoted, 35
Hume, David, 176; *Enquiry Concerning Human Understanding*, 77–78

icons, 91
ideal forms, 105–7
indwelling agencies: and force, 139–43; as

heuristic devices, 110–11; and will, 168
infinity, 135–36
insanity: changing concepts of, 173–74

John of Paris: quoted, 124
Johnson, Mark, 11, 12, 30; on action schemes, 71; quoted, 36, 37

Kahler, Erich: theory of history, 197
Kant, Immanuel: on causality, 167
Kepler, Johann: and Mechanism metaphor, 144; and Platonic forms, 53
knowledge, relational, 45–46; and hemispheric specialization, 46
Kuhn, Thomas, 13

Lakoff, George, 11, 30; quoted, 36, 37
La Mettrie, Julien: on human beings as machines, 163
Lao Tzu: on cosmos, 59; on the Tao, 105
light metaphor: and understanding, 44
Locke, John, 14
logic: formal; and metaphorization, 69–70
lot/share scheme: and human rights, 175

Mach, Ernst, 14; on physical concepts, 183
macrocosm/microcosm, 99; and theory of humors, 112
Marr, David: primitives and action schemes, 72
Marsilius of Padua: use of Parent metaphor, 125–27
mathematics: and cosmic order, 102–3; during the Enlightenment, 155–60; Greek, 96–98; medieval, 129; modern, 191–97; Renaissance, 134–35; topological schematizing in, 80–82
Mauthner, Fritz: quoted, 14
McNeil, David: on gesture, 65–66
mechanism metaphor: in the arts; and atom, 51; and baroque ornamentation, 156; in biological sciences, 145–46; decline of, 175–79; in economic sphere, 174–75; and concept of human being, 162–66; limitations of, applied to human beings, 169–70; contrasted

mechanism metaphor *(continued):*
  with Organism metaphor, 144–45; in
  physics, 143–45
metaphor: Aristotle on, 21; Ballard on, 25;
  Barfield on, 26–27; Beardley on, 24;
  Bentham on, 21; Black on, 24; Cicero
  on, 21; Coleridge on, 22; Davidson on,
  24; defined, 35, 43–44; discursive, 31;
  formation in children, 27; Geoffrey of
  Vinsaufon on, 21; Group Mu on, 24;
  Herder on, 21; Muller on, 38;
  Nietzsche on, 22; paraphrasing, 24;
  rhetorical, 31; Richards on, 24; Searle
  on, 24; Shelley on, 21; Strutterheim
  on, 25
metaphorand: defined, 51
metaphor deployment, 48–50
metaphorization: as a mode of thought,
  24
metaphors: as a code, 229n. 10; decline of,
  in modern times, 209–13; and
  etymology, 33–34
metaphors, root, 38–40; determining,
  31–35; families of, 39–40
Milton, John: and Great Chain of Being,
  57
mind: Eastern concepts of, 200–204;
  modern concepts of, 197–99; Ryle on,
  49
mirror metaphor, 31; and axiomatics, 160;
  and doctrines of correspondence, 102;
  and dualism, 109; and ideal forms,
  106; and universals, 120
music: and action schemes, 91–93;
  Renaissance, 150–52; and topological
  schemes, 83, 150–52
myth, 90–91

near-death experience, 254n. 33
negation, 74–75
Newton, Sir Isaac: on divine plan, 38;
  Principles, 77, 79
Nietzsche, Friedrich: on will to power,
  167–68
numbers: Arabic notation, 134; continuity
  of value, 135
nyat (ground of being), 201

one/many metaphor: and atom, 50; and
  Eastern concept of cosmos, 60, 62; and
  Eastern epistemology, 107; and
  concept of number, 144; and the self in
  Eastern thought, 200
order. *See* cosmic order; cosmos
organism metaphor: and disease, 48; and
  evolution, 170–72; contrasted with
  mechanism metaphor, 144–45

parent metaphor: and force, 98; and ideal
  forms, 119–20; in medieval thought,
  118–19, 122–23; and the state, 122–25
pattern metaphor, 32–33; and Aristotelian
  natural motion, 52; and atom, 50; and
  causality, 139; and classical worldview,
  53; and cosmic order, 109–10; and
  destiny, 177; and hierarchy, 63; and
  qualities, 139; and science, 103
Pepper, Stephen C., 17; on root metaphors, 230n. 18
physics: classical, 52–54; Renaissance,
  143–45
Piaget, Jean: on assimilation, 50
Planck level, 232n. 38
Plato: on cosmos, 56; on ideal forms, 105
Platonic ideas. *See* ideal forms
Plotinus: and Great Chain of Being, 56;
  quoted, 119–20
Pope, Alexander: and Great Chain of
  Being, 57
prepositions: action schemes and meaning,
  240n. 11; and topological relations,
  68–69
Prior, Matthew: quoted, 154–55
proportion: in classical art, 100–101
prototype theory, 36–38
psychopathology: metaphors used in, 206
Putnam, Hilary: on set theory, 195

quantum theory, 187–91

rationalism: reaction against, 172–73
rationalization: and metaphor stability, 62–
  63
reality: social construction of, 29–30
relativity, theory of, 183–87

rhetorical figures: and metaphorization, 93–94
Rosenfield, Israel: on body image, 73–74
Russell, Bertrand: on Hume, 176

sacred texts: and social change, 249 n. 13
Sade, Marquis de: on human beings as machines, 163–65
Sasaki, Sokei-an; on satori, 204
satori, 202–3
Schopenhauer, Arthur: on cosmic will, 167
Schulz, Bruno: quoted, 35
semantic fields, 86–87
set theory, 192
space, 202
Stendhal (Henri Beyle): on human motivation, 177–78
sunyata, 60, 62
Suzuki, D. T.: on emptiness as ground of being, 201; on satori, 203
symmetry: and classical idea of beauty, 99–102; in Greek thought, 106–7

tathata, 62
tertium comparationis, 90
Thomas Aquinas, Saint: argument for the existence of God, 235n. 13
Thompson, James: and Great Chain of Being, 57
time: and cosmic order, 103–4
topological schematization: in the arts, 82–85; in mathematics, 80–82; in music, 83, 150–52
topological transformations: defined, 14; and discourse, 75–80
topology, 192–95
trinity, 121

up/down scheme, 68

vacuum: modern concept of, 232n. 39
Vaihinger, Hans: on concept of space, 202
vis viva, 27

will to power, 167–68
word/speech metaphor: and disease, 48